RECENT DEBATES IN SIKH STUDIES

RECENT DEBATES IN SIKH STUDIES

An Assessment

J.S. GREWAL

MANOHAR
2011

First published 2011

ISBN 978-81-7304-883-8

Published by
Ajay Kumar Jain *for*
Manohar Publishers & Distributors
4753/23 Ansari Road, Daryaganj
New Delhi 110 002

Typeset by
Ajay Arts
New Delhi 110002

Printed by
Salasar Imaging Systems
Delhi 110 035

To all those scholars
who aspire to become
liberal historians
of the Sikh Tradition

Contents

Part Five
METHODOLOGY FOR RELIGIOUS STUDIES

Preface

As a National Fellow of the Indian Council of Historical Research in 1994-7 I studied the contemporary controversies in Sikh Studies and wrote two books: *Historical Perspectives on Sikh Identity*, published by Punjabi University in 1997, and *Contesting Interpretations of the Sikh Tradition*, published by Manohar in 1998.

The reviews of the *Contesting Interpretations* underscored three points: one, that the book unfairly defended W.H. McLeod; two, that there was no real debate; and three, that the book was useful in clarifying the issues but the author had not expressed his own views on the issues.

When the publishers of the *Contesting Interpretations* thought of a new edition, I thought of excluding the part related earlier to historical writing on the Sikhs and including the debate on Sikh identity and bring it up to date. All the earlier chapters have been revised; a few have been amplified, and a new chapter on martyrdom has been added. Only the issues debated are now in focus. My own views generally figure at the end of a chapter or a section.

All the twelve chapters fall into five parts. The first four chapters relate broadly to foundation of Sikhism and the Sikh community. Three other chapters relate essentially to Sikh identity. Two relate to the sacred texts. Two others relate to the Singh Sabha Movement and the interpretation of Sikh identity and martyrdom. One chapter relates to the historical method. The introductory chapter suggests the need for a dialogue in the light of the emergence and the course of recent controversies. The concluding chapter is a general reflection on the nature of the debate.

In the past decade, I was able to study the Sikh scripture and other Sikh literature in greater depth, resulting in a somewhat altered perspective on various issues related to Sikh history. This understanding is reflected, directly or indirectly, in the present treatment and summing up of the debate. The positions taken by different scholars on each of the basic issues are clearly stated.

I have tried to retain the Punjabi spellings of the words common with other languages. A Glossary of non-English words and terms has been added for the convenience of readers, but this book is meant equally for those who are familiar with the outline of Sikh history.

I am grateful to Professor Indu Banga for going through the typescript very thoroughly and giving a number of useful suggestions. I am thankful to Dr Sheena Pall for preparing the Glossary, to Dr Karamjit K. Malhotra for help in preparing the book for publication, and to Ms Parneet Minhas for preparing the typescript with care. As always, the Manohar Publishers have been very considerate. I may only add that a separate volume on historical writing on the Sikhs is ready for publishing.

Chandigarh
4 October 2009

J.S. GREWAL

Introductory: The Need for a Dialogue

Since the past four decades more than a score of historians, among other scholars, have debated on issues of Sikh history. A fresh controversy which started before 1970 grew to become intense and bitter with the deepening of political crisis in the Punjab and the growing interest in Sikh Studies in North America. The attitude of the contestants began to harden into grooves which adversely affected the growth of Sikh Studies. Eleven chapters in this book are devoted to the themes debated in the last three decades of the past century while one chapter deals with a new theme that has emerged more recently – the tradition of martyrdom.

BEGINNING OF THE CONTROVERSY

When W.H. McLeod's *Guru Nanak and the Sikh Religion* first appeared in 1968, it was criticized rather harshly by some Sikh scholars on account of his treatment of the *Janamsakhis* or the life of Guru Nanak. It was the veteran Sikh historian Ganda Singh who wrote in his defence, upholding the historian's right to seek rational explanation. He defended McLeod against the charge of 'malafide' intentions too. However, Ganda Singh did not accept all the conclusions drawn by McLeod with regard to the events of Guru Nanak's life. By contrast, McLeod's exposition of the 'teachings' of Guru Nanak appeared to be lucid and convincing.[1] Another Sikh scholar looked upon McLeod's exposition of Guru Nanak's teachings as 'the most systematic, the most cogent and the most sympathetic'.[2]

On the publication of McLeod's *Evolution of the Sikh Community* in 1975, he was seriously criticized by a professional historian, Fauja Singh, who pointed out that McLeod gave no importance to the ideology of Guru Nanak in his exposition of 'the growth of the Sikh community'. McLeod acknowledged Guru Nanak as the founder of the Sikh Panth but not of the Sikh faith, and attributed Sikh militancy to the Jat culture. This was, however, open to question. His view that the institutions of corporate and scriptural Guru appeared gradually in response to contemporary circumstances and cultural patterns of the Jats was considered contrary to historical facts'. His theory of gradual evolution of the Sikh code of discipline during the eighteenth century was based on the assumption that the *Rahitnamas* were of later origin. Also, his opinion that the different ingredients of the Khalsa code owed their origin to the cultural patterns of the Jats was untenable so far as 'the basic code' was concerned.[3]

Fauja Singh appreciated McLeod's essay on the *Janamsakhis* as 'probably the best of the whole lot'. It explained their nature, purpose and function and their importance as historical evidence. In the essay on Sikh scriptures, McLeod took cognizance of 'the controversy regarding the three versions of *Adi Granth*, but left the problem unsolved. In his short treatment of the *Dasam Granth*, he raised the issue of the impact of the hill culture on the evolution of the Sikh Panth during the eighteenth century but did not state how. McLeod's view that the Sikh Gurus abolished the caste system in the religious sphere completely and in social matters partially was closer to historical realities than the extreme view that the Sikh Gurus abolished the caste system completely and established full equality, or that they abolished caste distinctions only in the religious field. However, McLeod took 'a static' view of caste. On the whole, Fauja Singh came to the conclusion that McLeod's formulations were mostly conjectural and demanded scholarly investigation. There was substantial ground to regard them as ill-founded.[4]

The Evolution of the Sikh Community was criticized more severely by Daljeet Singh. In his view, McLeod's treatment of five major themes in a little over a hundred pages tended to become speculative rather than academic. Nearly the whole structure of his book was based on the premise that Sikhism offered 'no new religious thesis'. Its equation with 'the Sant tradition' failed to explain 'the prophetic mission of Guru Nanak'. McLeod attributed the socio-political and military activities of the Sikhs to 'the influence of Jat elements amongst Sikh ranks' without empirical evidence in support of this hypothesis. His hypothesis about the impact of the Shakti cult ignored the glaring fact that 'the age old acceptance of the same cult by the hill people never inspired them to throw off the Muslim yoke'. In his hypothesis about the 5Ks he 'neither shows that these Ks were Jat symbols in the region before their adoption by the Sikhs nor explains why those disappeared from among all the Jats of the neighbouring regions of Haryana, Rajasthan and Pakistan'. McLeod made 'the simplistic assumption' that Guru Nanak's mission was the same as that of the *bhaktas.* He invoked entities like the Jat culture and the Shakti cult to explain 'the organization and the socio-political objective and struggle' of the Sikh Gurus. But the growth of the Sikh Panth cannot be explained without reference to the ideology of the Gurus which served as 'a cementing and directive force' in Sikh history.[5]

BEGINNING OF INTEREST IN SIKH STUDIES IN NORTH AMERICA

By this time, South Asian area programmes had been launched in North America, and a few graduate students became 'Punjab specialists'.[6] The *Sources of Punjab History*, edited by Gustafson and Jones, was published by Manohar in 1975 while the *Arya Dharm* of Kenneth Jones was published by the University of California in 1976. Among the 'Punjab specialists' were at least two scholars who took interest in the Sikhs: N. Gerald Barrier, whose *The Sikhs and Their Literature* had been published by Manohar in 1970, and Tom G. Kessinger, whose *Vilayatpur* had been published by the University of California in 1974.

The first conference on Sikh Studies in the United States was held at Berkeley in 1976. The papers presented to the conference were published in 1979 as *Sikh Studies: Comparative Perspectives on a Changing Tradition.* The presence of Sikhs in the United States had become relevant for Sikh Studies. The major concern of the conference was how to develop Sikh Studies in North America. Mark Juergensmeyer emphasized that Sikhism formed an important subject of study as a rich religious tradition in itself. Its study could lead to 'a more complex interpretation of the whole of India's cultural history'. It was relevant for comparative studies in the areas of textual criticism, mythology, social studies and political thought.[7]

John C.B. Webster detailed the remarkable expansion of Sikh Studies in the Punjab. Books, monographs and articles were published by a large number of scholars associated with many new academic institutions. A number of periodicals and the *Encyclopaedia of Sikhism* were started. However, there were some handicaps. Religion and theology had not been taught as scholarly disciplines in Indian universities. Even in historical scholarship the methodology in relation to the Sikh religious tradition was not strong. Consequently, the expansion was of the traditional type, and in conformity with the currently accepted orthodoxy. The scholars in the West should be prepared for the charge that they were foreign scholars who either did not understand or simply attacked the Sikhs and Sikhism, using methods which did not apply to Indian religious traditions.[8] The last observation took notice of the criticism of McLeod's work on the Sikhs. N. Gerald Barrier emphasized the importance of developments within Sikhism between 1870 and 1920 for studying division and unity in Sikhism, the nature and function of Sikh institutions, the social and political mobilization of Sikhs under British rule, and the evolution of theological and historiographical trends among Sikh intellectuals.[9]

Eugene F. Irschick suggested that Sikhism should neither be regarded as unique nor as less significant than any of the other religious traditions of the world. If the goal of Guru Nanak was to eliminate caste and social differentiation 'we must look at the way in which it was achieved or fell short of its original goals'.[10] Ainslee T. Embree observed that the history of Sikhism appeared to provide material for a very important contribution to all the great themes: 'religion and the rise of capitalism, the relationship between social dislocation and social dynamism, the creative role of minorities, even that grandest of all, the differences between Western and Indian culture'. There were clear indications that Sikh Studies could provide material for exploring new frontiers that would deepen our knowledge of how societies functioned.[11]

The American scholars participating in the conference tended to assume that the views of the Western scholars on the Sikh tradition were valid.[12] Kenneth E. Bryant was aware of the opposite views expressed by scholars on whether or not Sikhism was a sect of

Hinduism. He made a clear distinction between Vaishnava and *sant* poetry. However, like McLeod, he bracketed Guru Nanak with Kabir in the process.[13] Karine Schomer pointed out that the historians of Indian religion had tended to oversimplify the medieval religious situation by classifying all important figures, movements and literatures as representative of either *saguna bhakti* or *nirguna bhakti.* The label *nirguna bhakti* failed to distinguish between the individual *sants* and the organized sects or *panths* developed by their followers. A comparison of the *Guru Granth* tradition with the Dadu-panthi tradition of Kabir appeared to bring out 'the unique features of Sikhism as an organized religion'. This did not mean, however, that Schomer was making a distinction between Guru Nanak and Kabir.[14]

W.H. McLeod underlined the need for textual analysis of the *Adi Granth.* In his view, Bhai Jodh Singh's *Sri Kartarpuri Bir de Darshan*, which was meant to establish the authenticity of the *Granth* compiled by Guru Arjan, had left the problem unsolved. The verses incorporated in *Banno Bir* were not deleted but left incomplete in *Kartarpuri Bir.* It was conceivable, therefore, that the Kartarpur text was in fact a later recension and its scribe, appreciating the problem raised by the hymns in question, simply omitted the remainder in each case. To establish 'a sure and certain text', it was necessary to launch a sustained campaign of textual analysis.[15] C.H. Loehlin reproduced the notes taken by him and J.C. Archer on the *Kartarpuri Bir* in 1946, together with a note by Bhai Jodh Singh who had examined the manuscript and made a complete record of its contents in 1945. The authenticity of *Kartarpuri Bir* appeared to be established but many scholars claimed originality for *Banno Bir* because it contained three passages missing from the Kartarpur manuscript. Furthermore, the claim of a Sikh scholar that the *Guru Granth Sahib* was the only authentic scripture of the world required that the issue was put beyond all doubt. For both McLeod and Loehlin, thus, the authenticity of *Kartarpuri Bir* was not yet established.[16]

In Canada, the first conference on Sikh Studies was held in February 1987. The presence of a large 'diaspora' of Canadian Sikhs in the province of Ontario, especially in Toronto, and their keenness to encourage the study of Sikh history and religion provided the general context for this conference. To serve as a kind of 'catalyst' for the conference was the presence of W.H. McLeod at the

University of Toronto as a Commonwealth Fellow. Working on two different projects, he was conducting an undergraduate course on the Sikh Religious Tradition. His presence induced Milton Israel and Joseph T. O'Connell to organize a conference on Sikh Studies. Unfortunately, McLeod suffered a serious stroke in New York where he was to give lectures at the Columbia University. He could not participate in the conference at Toronto but his paper was included in the proceedings titled, *Sikh History and Religion in the Twentieth Century*, published in 1988. McLeod's paper outlined the concepts which needed to be studied for evolving a systematic Sikh theology. In his view, an integrated and comprehensive account of Sikh theology had yet to be written.[17]

Harjot Oberoi argued that Hindus and Sikhs had shared positions within a single social structure, and the religious categories 'Hindu' and 'Sikh' were ambiguous, fluid and fragile. He argued further that distinctively Sikh lifestyle rituals were absent among the Sikhs before the influence of the Singh Sabhas became pervasive. Therefore, the Sikhs in their earlier history were encompassed in 'Hindu' society. Bhai Kahn Singh Nabha 'brought almost four centuries of Sikh tradition to an end' in 1897 when he published his *Ham Hindu Nahin* (We are not Hindus). Oberoi noticed, however, that in many ways the *Rahitnama* literature of the pre-colonial period had foreshadowed the homogeneous Sikh identity and religious boundaries of the late nineteenth century.[18]

A CRITICAL RESPONSE FROM THE PUNJAB

The growing conviction that McLeod's formulations were seriously flawed was reflected clearly in the *Perspectives on the Sikh Tradition* published in 1986. It was edited by Gurdev Singh, a former judge of the Punjab and Haryana High Court. His professed purpose was to present a thorough refutation of McLeod's propositions. Khushwant Singh's 'foreword' to this book reinforced the impression that McLeod was finally refuted. In his *Guru Nanak and the Sikh Religion*, McLeod had come to the conclusion that the life-story of Guru Nanak was based on fiction, and that Guru Nanak had merely stated the religious beliefs current during his time and should not therefore be regarded as 'the founder of a new faith'.

In his *Evolution of the Sikh Community,* McLeod expressed the view that large-scale intrusion of Jats into the Khalsa Panth, rather than something planned out by Guru Hargobind and Guru Gobind Singh, was the main cause of the metamorphosis of the pacifist Nanak-Panthis into the militant fraternity of the Khalsa. Furthermore, McLeod questioned 'the authenticity of the baptismal ceremony of the Baisakhi of 1699' and discounted the *Rahitnamas* as 'subsequent compilations'. McLeod was 'on weak ground' and some of his conclusions were 'erroneous'. The record had to be set right in order to establish that the Sikh religious tradition was not 'an edifice built on hot air or make believe'. This was what the *Perspectives on the Sikh Tradition* was supposed to have done.[19]

Justice Gurdev Singh attributed eight propositions to McLeod: one, that he places Guru Nanak within the Sant tradition; two, that his successors did not preach one set of doctrines, giving up at one stage his teachings in favour of militancy; three, that the Panth got armed not because of any decision of Guru Hargobind but because of the Jat influx; four, that the traditional account of the founding of the Khalsa cannot be accepted; five, that the Sikh code of discipline and Sikh symbols were evolved during the eighteenth century and not promulgated by Guru Gobind Singh on the Baisakhi of 1699; six, that the Gurus denounced the caste system but they were not sincere or serious in removing caste differences; seven, that the succession of *Granth Sahib* as the Guru after Guru Gobind Singh was a subsequent adoption and not due to his injunction; eight, that the authenticity of the current version of *Guru Granth Sahib* is open to question.[20]

For Justice Gurdev Singh, all these propositions stand refuted in the *Perspectives on the Sikh Tradition.* Noel Q. King's essay underlines the basic fault in McLeod's methodology in dealing with the *Janamsakhis* for the life of Guru Nanak. Daljeet Singh's essays establish the originality and the uniqueness of the Sikh faith. Hari Ram Gupta establishes the authencity of baptismal ceremony on the Baisakhi of 1699. Ganda Singh and Harbans Singh prove that Guru Gobind Singh abolished the system of personal Guruship by vesting Guruship in the *Granth Sahib.* Jagjit Singh demonstrates that caste distinctions were abolished by the Gurus in both theory and practice, and that 'militarization' of the Sikh movement was a logical outcome of Sikh ideology and deliberate decisions of the Gurus and not of the influx of Jats, or any economic crisis or impact of the Shakti cult.[21]

Justice Gurdev Singh initially dwelt on the motives of McLeod as much as his 'misrepresentation' of the Sikh tradition. Even a hurried glance through McLeod's works would reveal his propensity to propagate that Sikhism did not deserve much consideration because it was only 'a rehash of an effete Hindu creed'. As a Christian missionary in the Indian Punjab, McLeod is said to have realized that missionary work had no future unless the faith of the new generations in the Sikh tradition was undermined. For this purpose he adopted an unusually critical approach towards Guru Nanak and the Sikh faith. His aim was to shake the faith of the younger generation of the Sikhs in their religion, their Gurus, their scriptures, their institutions, 'and all that they inherit'.[22] Many of McLeod's critics would invoke his missionary motive to explain his lack of empathy with the Sikh tradition or lack of its understanding.

Two years later, a conference of Sikh Studies was organized by the Sikh community of North America at the California State University, Long Beach. Apart from contributors to the *Perspectives on the Sikh Tradition,* some scholars from the Panjab, Punjabi and Guru Nanak Dev universities made their contribution to this conference. The other participants were from North America and the U.K. In the volume of proceedings published later as *Advanced Studies in Sikhism,* it was stated that the recent Western writings in the field of Sikh Studies had generally been 'quite peripheral in their scope and inadequate in their approach'.[23]

Daljeet Singh criticized W.H. McLeod and Harjot Oberoi from the viewpoint of methodology. He argued that the methodology and tools of social sciences were inadequate for the study of religion because they related to its empirical aspects and left out its spiritual base. Thanks to their methodology, the observations made by McLeod and Oberoi displayed a singular lack of understanding of the essentials of Sikhism and its difference from Vedanta, Vaishnavism and Nathism.[24]

Among the other critics of McLeod was Surinder Singh Kohli who denounced him for his treatment of the evolution of the Sikh Panth and its militarization. Kohli emphasized that the discipline of created to live and fight for the cause of Dharma.[25] Madanjit Kaur asserts that there is a strong tradition in support of the 5 Ks but does not produce any contemporary evidence.[26] She supports the tradition of the vesting of the authority of Guruship in *Guru Granth Sahib* against McLeod's view of the evolutionary character of the Khalsa *rahit* and doctrines.[27] Gobind Singh Mansukhani cited a *hukamnama* of Guru Gobind Singh, dated 23 May 1699, in support of the 5 Ks, which refers to *kes, kachh, kirpan* and *kara.* There is no reference to *kangha.*[28]

With reference to some 'oblique but incorrect' observations made by McLeod to throw doubt on the authenticity of the *Kartarpuri Bir* even after the publication of Bhai Jodh Singh's *Kartarpuri Bir de Darshan,* Daljeet Singh himself made a detailed study of the manuscript at Kartarpur, coming to the conclusion that 'the Kartarpuri Bir is incontrovertibly the authentic Adi Granth prepared by the Fifth Guru'.[29] The objections raised by McLeod and others were without any 'factual or rational' basis. McLeod's bias was understandable: he had a long association with a Christian Missionary Centre in the Punjab.[30]

Gurdarshan Singh Dhillon criticized Harjot Oberoi for selecting some features of the late nineteenth-century Sikhism and projecting them back as an integral part of the earlier or original Sikhism as 'Sanatan Sikhism'. There was no credible evidence that the worship of Sakhi Sarvar, Gugga Pir, Sitala Devi and village ancestors was spread widely among the Sikhs or that it was universally tolerated. The norms against such practices were not created by the Singh Sabhas. They are enshrined in the Sikh scripture.[31]

A whole section of the *Advanced Studies* contains 'a critique of some writings on Sikhism'. James R. Lewis gave a new version of his papers published in 1985 and 1987, relating to mispresentations of Sikh tradition in world religions textbooks in terms of factual errors, the notion of syncretism, and contrast between the supposed pacifism of Guru Nanak and the militancy of Guru Gobind Singh.[32] The other scholars who offered criticism were Jagjit Singh with regard to caste, and S.S. Kohli and Surjit Singh with regard to the *Janamsakhis.*[33]

Between the *Perspectives* and the *Advanced Studies,* on the whole, there is a basic continuity in terms of old contributors, old themes, and old works, with much substantive repetition and only some supplementary material. The issue of textual analysis was brought to the fore. Notice was taken of an article by Harjot Oberoi, adding the Singh Sabha Movement to the themes for debate.

Towards the end of 1990, seven 'international' conferences were held in England and North America at London, Toronto, Vancouver, Berkeley, Chicago, Washington and New York, sponsored by a number of Sikh organizations. Nearly half of the participants were those whose papers had been included in the *Perspectives on the Sikh Tradition* and the *Advanced Studies in Sikhism*. They contributed a score of papers while an equal number was contributed by new scholars. At least three of the new scholars were associated with universities and study of the Sikh tradition. Others were independent scholars with or without any connection with academic institutions. Apart from the old themes, some new themes were taken up for discussion. Some old and new works were criticized but, on the whole, a number of expositions were marked by positive projection. The papers were published in two volumes in 1992 as *Fundamental Issues in Sikh Studies* and *Recent Researches in Sikhism.*

In the *Fundamental Issues*, Kharak Singh and Daljeet Singh wrote on the Punjab problem to correct the views of Oberoi and McLeod.[34] Gurtej Singh questioned the views of D.P. Ashta and Rattan Singh Jaggi on the authenticity of the *Dasam Granth* (which had been given great importance by McLeod in connection with the influence of the hill culture on the Sikh Tradition).[35] McLeod is criticized rather incidentally by Madanjit Kaur in relation to the episode of the goddess, by Harnam Singh Shan in a paper on the originality of Sikhism, by Daljeet Singh in a paper on Sikh identity, and by G.S. Mansukhani in a paper on the origin and development of Sikh Studies.[36]

Kharak Singh made a frontal attack on McLeod and Oberoi in his advocacy for a World Institute of Sikhism. He refers to 'a former missionary in India' who had produced eight books relating to Sikhism. His thesis revolved around eight points (which had been listed in the *Perspectives*). This 'missionary' managed to enlist a few associates from India as well as abroad, with whose assistance he had been holding conferences and delivering lectures to propagate his theses. For want of an organized resistance to his claim to being an authority on Sikhism he had been taken quite seriously in some quarters in the West. Chairs established in Canadian universities for Sikh Studies with collections from Sikhs are manned by this group. These Chairs had added a new dimension to the problem of misrepresentation of Sikhism. They were spoiling the image of Sikhs and damaging Sikhism. The *Perspectives on the Sikh Tradition* and the *Advanced Studies in Sikhism* are claimed to present a meaningful response to the growing misrepresentation of Sikhism and the Sikhs. Daljeet Singh and Jagjit Singh had produced commendable works. Nonetheless, the situation demanded further concerted and coordinated efforts. 'Fundamental research needs to be conducted into the doctrines of Sikhism. An authentic interpretation of the Gurbani is required. The basic literature of Sikhism has to be studied in depth. There are some real and substantial controversies which need to be resolved.' For all this a centre of Sikh Studies was needed, 'a full-fledged World Institute of Sikhism'.[37]

In *Recent Researches,* Kharak Singh brings out the 'misrepresentation' of Sikhism in the encyclopaedias published in the West from 1917 to 1977, containing a large number of errors of fact and understanding. James R. Lewis talks of some unexamined assumptions in Western studies of Sikhism. It had become commonplace among the Western students of the Sikh religion to refer to the supposedly baneful effects of orthodoxy on Sikh scholars studying their own tradition. This carried the implication that while the Western academics were free to produce truly objective scholarship, their interests and commitments could introduce the value-judgements embedded in them, like syncretism, neo-Sikhism, and the early pacifism *versus* later militancy. The Western scholars were said to be giving a 'differential treatment' to the Sikh religion.[38]

Gobind Singh Mansukhani presents his own methodology for the appraisal of sources for Sikh Studies as an alternative to the historical method.[39] Gurdarshan Singh Dhillon presents his own understanding of the relations between the British rulers and their Sikh subjects to correct the views expressed by McLeod, Barrier and Richard Fox.[40]

Dhillon refutes the views expressed by Harjot S. Oberoi in his 'From Ritual to Counter-Ritual: Rethinking the Hindu-Sikh Question, 1884-1915'. For his emphatic assertion that the Sikhs had shown little collective interest in distinguishing themselves from the

Hindus before the late nineteenth century, Oberoi does not define Sikhism and looks upon the groups like the Udasis and the Sakhi Sarvarias, among several others, as 'living within the framework of the Sikh faith'. He takes a narrow view of religion when he says that it was meant for the individual salvation of man.[41] Another scholar, Gurbakhsh Singh, finds Oberoi's paper to be 'totally propagandist'. His idea that Sikhism can be equated with the practices of those who called themselves Sikh without any reference to the norms of the Sikh faith, was found to be absurd.[42]

Some of the papers in *Recent Researches* were meant to demonstrate the role of Sikh ideology in Sikh history; like the paper by Gurtej Singh on the 'political ideas' of Guru Nanak, the papers by Daljeet Singh and Jagjit Singh and on the ideal of *miri-piri*, and by G.S. Dhillon on the policies and attitudes of Maharaja Ranjit Singh.[43]

EXTENSION OF THE DEBATE

The issue of textual criticism in relation to the Sikh scripture and the issue of Sikh identity were debated more furiously in the early 1990s than ever before. Piar Singh's *Gatha Sri Adi Granth* appeared in 1992 as a scholarly search for the genuine contents of the *Granth* prepared by Guru Arjan. The Kartarpur manuscript in his view was not the *Granth* prepared by Guru Arjan. Within a month, the sale of the book was suspended by Guru Nanak Dev University as its publisher. Two weeks later the Shiromani Gurdwara Prabandhak Committee (SGPC) imposed ban on research on the *Guru Granth*. Piar Singh was summoned to appear at the Akal Takht on 31 March 1993 and ordered to do penance for forty days. On 13 May he requested the Acting Jathedar of the Akal Takht to apprise him of the objectionable passages in his book. He received no reply. In defence of his *Gatha* he wrote another book which was published in 1996 as the *Gatha Sri Adi Granth and the Controversy*. In this work, Piar Singh stoutly maintains that the *Kartarpuri Bir* was 'a fake copy and not the original *Adi Granth* prepared by Bhai Gurdas'.[44]

Another scholar summoned to the Akal Takht was Pashaura Singh whose doctoral thesis, 'The Text and Meaning of the Adi Granth', was supervised by W.H. McLeod and submitted to the University of Toronto in 1991. A book published in 1994 as *Planned*

Attack on Aad Sri Guru Granth Sahib: Academics or Blasphemy was meant to denounce Pashaura Singh and his research as reinforcing McLeod's efforts to cast doubt on the authenticity of the *Kartarpuri Bir* and, therefore, on the *Guru Granth.*[45] A revised version of Pashaura Singh's thesis has been published as *The Guru Granth Sahib: Canon, Meaning and Authority,* exploring the concept of scripture from the Sikh perspective and seeking to understand the processes of canon formation and the vesting of Guruship in the *Adi Granth.* He has underscored the role of the *Adi Granth* in the personal piety of individual Sikhs and the corporate identity of the Sikh community.[46]

Both Pashaura Singh and Piar Singh were criticized by Trilochan Singh who looked upon Pashaura Singh as 'a willing victim' of McLeod's propaganda machinery and Piar Singh as an accomplice. Trilochan Singh was emphatic that an article attributed to C.H. Loehlin was concocted by McLeod's 'clique', after the putative author's death, to serve their purpose. This article was actually an appendix to Loehlin's *The Granth of Guru Gobind Singh and the Khalsa Brotherhood,* published in 1971. According to Trilochan Singh, Piar Singh was a fan of McLeod and persuaded Guru Nanak Dev University to purchase *MS 1245* to be made available to Pashaura Singh for his doctoral research. McLeod suggested this type of research to Piar Singh, and his work follows Pashaura Singh's thesis without mentioning it.[47] Evidently, this is fantasy rather than research.

Trilochan Singh's real target in his book was McLeod. He appreciates Trumpp amidst all his faults, but there is no redeeming feature of McLeod's work. Trilochan Singh refers to his 'art of subterfuge and evasion', his 'nefarious designs', his 'naked antagonism, and open malicious hostility'. McLeod is 'neither honest nor rational, nor reasonable and logical in his analysis of historical events, nor does he anywhere, in any of his books follow the minimum rules of academic ethics'. Trilochan Singh's critique of McLeod is generally misplaced but it may be seen as a measure of the gulf between their understanding of Sikh history, religion and culture.[48]

Gurinder Singh Mann published *The Goindval Pothis: The Earliest Extant Source of the Sikh Canon* in 1996, arguing in favour of the authenticity of the extant *Goindval Pothis* and their use by Guru Arjan for preparing the *Kartarpuri Bir.*[49] He has published a revised version of his doctoral thesis as *The Making of Sikh Scripture,* presenting a cogent and comprehensive picture based primarily on a large number of manuscripts.[50] Several scholars have questioned the authenticity of the earlier manuscripts like the *Goindval Pothis* and the *MS 1245.* Balwant Singh Dhillon has argued against Gurinder Singh Mann and Pashaura Singh, and provided a detailed analysis of the *Guru Harsahai Pothi,* the *Goindval Pothis,* and the *MS 1245* in his *Early Sikh Scriptural Tradition: Myth and Reality.*[51] Textual criticism and textual studies on the whole have come a long way.

Concern for Sikh identity explains the response to Harjot Oberoi's *The Construction of Religious Boundaries: Culture, Identity and Diversity in the Sikh Tradition,* published as a revised version of his doctoral thesis in 1994. Oberoi has put forth the hypothesis that the Sikhs were not unduly concerned with establishing distinct religious boundaries before the advent of colonial rule in the Punjab. Even the growing hegemony of the Khalsa did not put an end to religious fluidity within the Sikh tradition which was marked by immense diversity. Oberoi asserts that the new social and cultural forces of the period of colonial rule helped the Singh Sabhas to recast Sikh tradition in a monolithic mould and to marginalize other identities. A new world-view replaced the old and transformed the earlier Sikh tradition into modern Sikhism.[52]

The *Invasion of Religious Boundaries,* 'a critique of Harjot Oberoi's work', published in 1995 contains 32 articles and reviews and 8 appendices questioning the legitimacy and justification of appointing Harjot Oberoi to the Chair of Punjabi and Sikh Studies at the University of British Columbia. Some of the articles included in the *Invasion of Religious Boundaries* had been published earlier, like those of Daljeet Singh, G.S. Dhillon, Noel Q. King and Kharak Singh. These are meant to provide the basic information on some of the issues raised in the book. Many titles of reviews indicate the drift of their argument: 'journey into obscurity'; 'academics or imagination'; 'a stranger to Sikhism'; 'an attempt at destruction'; 'scholar or saboteur'; 'an unpardonable excess'; 'mischievous propaganda is not research'. Oberoi's work appeared to undermine a distinct Sikh identity. Indeed, his exposition of 'Sanatan Sikhism' was extremely misleading. Contemporary evidence refuted his assumption and argument, that there was no dominant Sikh identity before the advent of the Singh Sabhas.[53]

DEFENCE OF WESTERN SIKH STUDIES

The critics of McLeod, Oberoi, Pashaura Singh and others feel convinced that they have successfully exposed misrepresentations of Sikh history and Sikhism, and produced considerable literature as an alternative reading. A large number of Sikh scholars appear to agree with them. But this is not the view of those who have been criticized or those who appreciate their work.

A conference held at Columbia University in 1989 resulted in the publication of *Studying the Sikhs: Issues for North America* in 1993. The editors, John Stratton Hawley and Gurinder Singh Mann, noticed the 'marked tensions between academics and believers' that had affected the field of Sikh Studies in recent years and created a concern that surfaced in 'almost every chapter of the book'.[54]

Mark Juergensmeyer observed that Sikh Studies in the West had to be a part of some existing academic field and, therefore, subject to that field's interests, limitations, and academic fads. The subject matter of religious studies had changed dramatically in the 1960s and 1970s, to make the field less pious and 'religious' in its orientation and more objective and 'intellectually respectable'. The rallying cry of this new trend was 'methodology'. The tendency of the scholars of religious studies to align their field with the Enlightenment ethos of the secular university had serious implications for Sikh Studies. The guardians of standards within the field look for scholarship that is objective in approach, sophisticated in method, cross-cultural in significance, and contextual in historical analysis. In Sikh scholarship in the Punjab, the main thrust was to show the distinctiveness of the faith rather than its connections and similarities to other traditions. Another main emphasis was to demonstrate solidarity with the community in projecting an integral, unified, and autonomous culture. This set the stage for an unhappy confrontation between the 'two views' of scholarship.[55]

According to Juergensmeyer, though McLeod's *Guru Nanak and the Sikh Religion* proved to be one of the most controversial works, his approach seemed to be common place to most Western scholars: separating hagiography from historical facts and placing the historical figure in his contemporary cultural and political context. McLeod's work was not much different from Albert Schweitzer's *The Quest for the Historical Jesus* which was written almost a hundred years earlier. The fact that McLeod was a non-Sikh examining a problem in Sikh history for an audience consisting primarily of Western academics made the issue more sensitive. Whereas in the West he came to be regarded as the premier scholar of Sikhism, in India, and elsewhere in Sikh communities, he was often seen as being hostile to the Sikh faith. This raised the issue of approach to scholarship: 'is a tradition's own understanding of its history to be explicated and affirmed or are the historical data of a tradition available for cross-cultural analysis?' Juergensmeyer's preference surely is for the modern modes of analysis.[56] On this basis, criticism of McLeod's work becomes misplaced. The possibility of differences between academic interpretations is left out. Juergensmeyer's statement becomes an unqualified defence of McLeod's position. Indeed, Juergensmeyer supports McLeod's view of the Sikh tradition as derived from the *sants* and brackets Guru Nanak himself with the *sants*.[57]

N. Gerald Barrier postulates two approaches to Sikh historiography, the one more familiar in the Punjab and the other more at home in Western universities. The former, with certain shared preconceptions and commitments, tended to reinforce a respect for the Gurus, a sense of historical continuity, a clear differentiation between Sikhism and Hinduism from the time of the first Guru, and a hagiographic treatment of Sikh historical figures. They who follow this approach tend to discount the writings of those who hold different views as ill-informed research by 'outside' scholars lacking sympathy for Sikhism or, worse, as a carefully orchestrated attempt to undermine an accurate view of Sikhism. The scholars trained in the Western universities questioned traditional sources and applied rigorous textual analysis in treating documents that related to other historical and religious traditions. They tended to regard Sikhism as an evolving religious and cultural tradition, one that mirrors and in turn affects the environment in which it was evolved.[58] McLeod's critical research had aroused strong debate among the Sikhs. The issues raised by this debate had to be carefully considered (in the light of Barrier's observations). Harjot Singh Oberoi's work was criticized by Sikh historians who claimed a single line of authoritative practice from Guru Gobind Singh up to the present.[59] The way in which Barrier presents the debate indicates that he does not see much point in the criticism of McLeod or Oberoi.

With reference to his persistent doubts about the authenticity of *Kartarpuri Bir*, McLeod says that he had merely raised questions with the intention of promoting academic discussion. Even now, though Gurinder Singh Mann had confirmed the authentic status of the Kartarpuri manuscript, 'several questions still await answer'.[60] However, if the authenticity of the Kartarpur manuscript is accepted, the other questions are of little historical consequence.

Joseph T. O'Connell observes that there was a network of vocal Sikhs who were evidently troubled by 'the thrust of rigorous critical scholarship' with a bearing upon the religious history of the Sikhs. The main voices were from Delhi and the Punjab but they had like-minded associates in the United States with influence in Sikh associations and access to community publications. O'Connell goes on to refer to the Long Beach conference and its negative side. What seemed to unite the various papers was not so much a vision of what constructive work an independent Sikh centre for learning and research might do, 'but the negative bond of being united against contemporary academic research on Sikh history and religion'. Some of the writers failed to distinguish between criticizing views and imputing motives or otherwise attacking the personal integrity of those with whom they disagreed or whom they just did not fathom. There was always some degree of tension between those committed to scholarly inquiry and those committed to preserving and fostering a religious way of life.[61] Thus, for O'Connell too, the criticism by Sikh scholars was of no consequence.

In 1999, the Oxford University Press in New Delhi brought out an omnibus volume of McLeod's four books (published earlier by the Clarendon Press) as *Sikhs and Sikhism*. In 2000, his major articles were published as *Exploring Sikhism: Aspects of Sikh Identity, Culture and Thought*. His work on the *Rahitnamas*, entitled

Sikhs of the Khalsa, was published in 2003, his translation of the *Prem Sumarag* in 2006 as *The Testimony of a Sanatan Sikh,* and his *Essays in Sikh History, Tradition, and Society* in 2007. Among the recent publications of McLeod is also his *Discovering the Sikhs: Autobiography of a Historian,* published by Permanent Black in 2004.

In his *Autobiography,* McLeod says that he regards himself as a historian of religion who follows the established methods of historical research. Trained in the Western methods of historical research, he adheres to Western notions of historiography. His primary objective has been to communicate 'an understanding of the Sikh people and their religion to educated *Western* readers'. Western understanding underlines all that he has written 'and no apology is offered for it'.[62] This candid statement is interesting in view of the charge of Eurocentrism that his critics have levelled against McLeod.

The Western historical method in McLeod's view confronts tradition, sometimes accepting it, sometimes doubting it, and all too frequently rejecting it. This view of the historical method presents its function in negative terms and constricts its scope. McLeod postulates a simple dichotomy between the 'Western historian' and the 'traditionalist historian'. The attitude of the Western historian is firmly rooted in the Enlightenment, which dictates that all conclusions should be rational and based on sound sources. 'This is light years away from the attitude that takes its stand firmly on revelation and accepts as true that which is divinely revealed.' The two world-views stand in complete opposition to each other.[63] However, what is relevant for debate is the bearing of a world-view on historical writing, and not the world-view itself.

The comments of his critics do not make much sense for McLeod. Mentioned among them are Fauja Singh, Gurdev Singh, Khushwant Singh, Daljeet Singh, Kharak Singh, Gurtej Singh, Gurdarshan Singh Dhillon and Trilochan Singh. McLeod recognizes, however, that research on the origins of the Sikh scripture has left him far behind.[64] He admits that Sainapat's evidence has a good claim to be accepted that 'Guru Gobind Singh named the Khalsa as his heir'.[65] On all other issues, McLeod merely explains or defends his position. He tells the reader to choose between him and his critics: 'My works stand as I have written them, and readers will need to decide whether they are acceptable or whether the comments of my critics make better sense.'[66]

McLeod thinks that the campaign against him began to decline in 1996. Gurdev Singh, Daljeet Singh and Jagjit Singh were no longer alive, and the later publications of the critics like Darshan Singh and H.S. Dilgeer showed that 'criticisms were running into sands'. The attacks from 'academic sources' appeared to have lost much of their frequency and fervour. McLeod expected his *Sikhs of the Khalsa* to produce at least a brief outburst when published, and not a lengthy struggle, but no notice has been taken of this work by his critics. McLeod thinks that Sikh interests have largely shifted away from 'foreign academics and their alleged allies'.[67] He does not entertain the possibility that his critics have come to believe that they have demolished all his hypotheses and produced a wide range of alternative reading for those who may be interested in studying the Sikhs and Sikhism.

MY OWN AWARENESS

I completed my doctoral research a year before McLeod started research at the School of Oriental and African Studies in London in 1963. I was teaching at the Panjab University, Chandigarh, when McLeod returned to the Punjab in 1965 to teach at Batala. My book on Guru Gobind Singh (written jointly with S.S. Bal) was published a year before McLeod's *Guru Nanak and the Sikh Religion* came out in 1968. It is a happy coincidence that I have remained associated with McLeod and his work since that time, and with the development of Sikh Studies in India and abroad.

In 1976 I participated in a conference on 'Religious Change and Cultural Domination' held at Mexico City and contributed a short paper on 'The Sikh Panth: 1500-1850'.[68] For the Berkeley conference in 1976, I presented 'A Perspective on Early Sikh History'.[69] Differences with McLeod were implicit in both these papers but I was not much aware of those differences. I was invited to the Toronto conference in 1987 to speak on the 'legacies of the Sikh past for the twentieth century'. McLeod's *Evolution of the Sikh Community* was relevant for the theme. I appreciated his work by saying that it was possible to adapt it for my purpose 'with only a mild disagreement here and a minor modification there'. McLeod had not posed the problem directly and I could outline the significant developments of the pre-colonial period of Sikh history in 'slightly different terms'. These were related to the *Guru Granth*, the doctrine of Guru Panth, *raj karega Khalsa*, and social and ideological differentiation within the Sikh Panth. My address was different from McLeod's work in scope and thrust.[70]

For *Studying the Sikhs* I was invited to update an earlier lecture on the state of Sikh Studies. It was published as 'A Brief History of Sikh Studies in English', outlining the developments from J.D. Cunningham's *History of the Sikhs* (1849) to W.H. McLeod's *Who is a Sikh?* (1989). This outline ended with a brief comment on the controversy which had raised some important issues. This controversy, I suggested, could be fruitful if it made the critical scholars more aware of 'the implications of their apparently innocuous findings for believers' and if it helped their critics to become 'more clearly aware of the real implications of "methodological atheism" that characterizes all rational-empirical research in the world today'.[71] I had a vague inkling that there was no dialogue between the 'Western historian' and the 'traditionalist historian' of McLeod's formulation. This was the background to my serious and sustained interest in the controversy.

NOTES

1. *The Panjab Past and Present*, vol. IV, pt. 2 (October 1970), p. vii.
2. Ibid., vol. VI, pt. 1 (April 1972), pp. 234, 237.
3. Ibid., vol. XI, pt. 1 (April 1977), pp. 178-82.
4. Ibid., pp. 182-5.
5. *Journal of Sikh Studies*, vol. IV, no. 1 (February 1977), pp. 166-9.
6. N. Gerald Barrier, 'The Evolution of Punjab Studies in North America', *The Panjab Past and Present*, vol. XVI, pt. 2 (October 1982), pp. 398-406.
7. Mark Juergensmeyer, 'The Forgotten Tradition: Sikhism in the Study of World Religions', in *Sikh Studies: Comparative Perspectives on a Changing Tradition*, ed. Mark Juergensmeyer and N. Gerald Barrier, Berkeley: Berkeley Religious Studies Series, 1979, pp. 13-23.
8. John C.B. Webster, 'Sikh Studies in the Punjab', in ibid., pp. 26-32.

9. N. Gerald Barrier, 'The Role of Ideology and Insitution-Building in Modern Sikhism', in ibid., pp. 41-51.
10. Eugene F. Irschick, 'Sikhism as a Category of Study', in ibid., pp. 53-4.
11. Ainslie T. Embree, 'Locating Sikhism in Time and Place: A Problem for Historical Surveys', in ibid., pp. 55-62.
12. See, for example, *Sikh Studies: Comparative Perspectives on a Changing Tradition*, pp. 21, 59, 61.
13. Kenneth E. Bryant, '*Sant* and *Vaishnava* Poetry: Some Observations on Method', in ibid., pp. 65-74.
14. Karine Schomer, 'Kabir in the *Guru Granth Sahib:* An Exploratory Essay', in ibid., pp. 75-89.
15. W.H. McLeod, 'The Sikh Scriptures: Some Issues', in ibid., pp. 97-111.
16. C.H. Loehlin, 'Textual Criticism of the Kartarpur Granth', in ibid., pp. 113-18.
17. W.H. McLeod, 'A Sikh Theology for Modern Times', *Sikh History and Religion in the Twentieth Century*, ed. Joseph T. O'Connell et al., New Delhi: Manohar, 1990, pp. 32-43.
18. Harjot S. Oberoi, 'From Ritual to Counter-Ritual: Rethinking the Hindu-Sikh Question, 1884-1915', in ibid., pp. 136-58.
19. Khushwant Singh, 'Foreword', in *Perspectives on the Sikh Tradition*, ed. Gurdev Singh, Patiala: Siddharth Publications (for Academy of Sikh Religion and Culture), 1986, pp. ix-x.
20. 'Introduction', in ibid., pp. 8-10.
21. Ibid., pp. 14-36.
22. Ibid., pp. 4-5.
23. *Advanced Studies in Sikhism*, ed. Jasbir Singh Mann and Harbans Singh Saraon, Irvine, CA: Sikh Community of North America, 1989, Preface, pp. vii-viii.
24. Daljeet Singh, 'Issues of Sikh Studies', and 'Sikhism, Vaishnavism, Vedanta and Nathism: A Comparison', in ibid., pp. 16-29 and 33-55, respectively.
25. Surinder Singh Kohli, 'Constant Unity of Sikh Thought', in ibid., pp. 98-108.
26. Madanjit Kaur, 'The Creation of the Khalsa and Prescribing of the Sikh Symbols', in ibid., pp. 195-213.
27. Madanjit Kaur, 'The Guruship and Succession of Guru Granth Sahib', in ibid., pp. 121-37.
28. Gobind Singh Mansukhani, 'Sikh-Rahat-Maryada and Sikh Symbols', in *Advanced Studies in Sikhism*, pp. 174-91.
29. Daljeet Singh, 'Authenticity of the Kartarpuri Bir', in ibid., pp. 138-60.

30. Daljeet Singh, *Essays on the Authenticity of Kartarpuri Bir and the Integrated Logic and Unity of Sikhism*, Patiala: Punjabi University, 1987, pp. 1-87.
31. Gurdarshan Singh Dhillon, 'Singh Sabha Movement: A Revival', in *Advanced Studies in Sikhism*, pp. 234-62.
32. James R. Lewis, 'Misrepresentations of the Sikh Tradition in World Religions Textbooks', in ibid., pp. 265-77.
33. Surinder Singh Kohli, 'Janamsakhis: Their Value and Importance', in ibid., pp. 301-16. Surjit Singh, 'A Study of W. Hew McLeod's Methodology as Employed in his Work "The Evolution of Sikh Community" : The Janamsakhis' [*sic*], in ibid., pp. 317-25.
34. Kharak Singh, 'Sikh Ideology, Fundamentalism and Punjab Problem', in *Fundamental Issues in Sikh Studies*, ed. Kharak Singh, Gobind Singh Mansukhani and Jasbir Singh Mann, Chandigarh: Institute of Sikh Studies, 1992, pp. 136-59. Daljeet Singh, 'Punjab River-Waters Dispute', in ibid., pp. 198-228.
35. Gurtej Singh, 'Two Views of Dasam Granth', in ibid., pp. 179-86.
36. Madanjit Kaur, 'Devi Worship Story: A Critique', in ibid., pp. 170-8. Harnam Singh Shan, 'Sikhism: An Original Distinct Revealed and Complete Religion', in ibid., pp. 41-2, 52. Daljeet Singh, 'The Sikh Identity', in ibid., pp. 106-15.
37. Kharak Singh, 'Need for World Institute of Sikhism', in ibid., pp. 238-54.
38. James R. Lewis, 'Some Unexamined Assumptions in Western Studies of Sikhism', in *Recent Researches in Sikhism*, ed. Jasbir Singh Mann and Kharak Singh, Patiala: Punjabi University, 1992, pp. 286-98.
39. Gobind Singh Mansukhani, 'An Integrated Methodology for Appraisal of Sources for Sikh Studies', in ibid., pp. 109-21.
40. Gurdarshan Singh Dhillon, 'The Sikh Rule and Ranjit Singh', in ibid., pp. 347-72.
41. Gurdarshan Singh Dhillon, 'Sikh Identity: A Continuing Feature', in ibid., pp. 226-46.
42. Gurbakhsh Singh, 'From Ritual to Counter Ritual: A Critical Analysis', in ibid., pp. 273-85.
43. Gurtej Singh, 'Political Ideas of Guru Nanak: The Originator of the Sikh Faith', in ibid., pp. 61-71. Daljeet Singh, 'Sikhism: A Miri Piri System', in ibid., pp. 42-60. Jagjit Singh, 'The Doctrine of "Meeri-Peeri" ', in ibid., pp. 136-49. Gurdarshan Singh Dhillon, 'The Sikhs, and the British, 1849-1920', in ibid., pp. 173-225.
44. Piar Singh, *Gatha Sri Adi Granth and the Controversy*, Michigan: Anant Education and Rural Development Foundation, 1996, p. 114. For Piar Singh's earlier analysis of the *Kartarpuri Bir*, see his *Gatha Sri Adi*

Granth (Pbi), Amritsar: Guru Nanak Dev University, 1992, pp. 174-209.

45. *Planned Attack on Aad Sri Guru Granth Sahib: Academics or Blasphemy*, ed. Bachittar Singh Giani, Chandigarh: International Centre of Sikh Studies, 1994.
46. Pashaura Singh, *The Guru Granth Sahib: Canon, Meaning and Authority*, New Delhi: Oxford University Press, 2000.
47. Trilochan Singh, *Ernest Trumpp and W.H. McLeod As Scholars of Sikh History Religion and Culture*, Chandigarh: International Centre of Sikh Studies, 1994, pp. 343-76.
48. Ibid., pp. 60, 87, 294, 299.
49. Gurinder Singh Mann, *The Goindval Pothis: The Earliest Extant Source of the Sikh Canon*, Cambridge (Massachusetts): Harvard University Press, 1996.
50. Gurinder Singh Mann, *The Making of Sikh Scripture*, New Delhi: Oxford University Press, 2001.
51. Balwant Singh Dhillon, *Early Sikh Scriptural Tradition: Myth and Reality*, Amritsar: Singh Brothers, 1999.
52. Harjot Oberoi, *The Construction of Religious Boundaries: Culture, Identity and Diversity in the Sikh Tradition*, New Delhi: Oxford University Press, 1994.
53. *Invasion of Religious Boundaries*, ed. Jasbir Singh Mann, Surinder Singh Sodhi and Gurbakhsh Singh Shergill, Vancouver: Canadian Sikh Study and Teaching Society, 1995.
54. *Studying the Sikhs: Issues for North America*, ed. John Stratton Hawley and Gurinder Singh Mann, Albany: State University of New York Press, 1993, p. 4.
55. Mark Juergensmeyer, 'Sikhism and Religious Studies', in ibid., pp. 9-14.
56. Ibid., pp. 14-16.
57. Ibid., p. 20.
58. N. Gerald Barrier, 'Sikh Studies and the Study of History', in ibid., pp. 25-33.
59. Ibid., pp. 33-45.
60. W.H. McLeod, 'The Study of Sikh Literature', in ibid., pp. 55-9.
61. Joseph T. O'Connell, 'Sikh Studies in North America: A Field Guide', in ibid., pp. 123-7.
62. Hew [W.H.] McLeod, *Discovering the Sikhs: Autobiography of a Historian*, Delhi: Permanent Black, 2004, pp. 125, 127-30.
63. Ibid., pp. 130-1.
64. Ibid., p. 163.
65. Ibid., p. 148.
66. Ibid., p. 135.

67. Ibid., pp. 188-91.
68. J.S. Grewal, 'The Sikh Panth: 1500-1850', in *Religious Change and Cultural Domination*, ed. David N. Lorenzen, Mexico City: El Colegio de Mexico, 1981, pp. 193-8.
69. J.S. Grewal, 'A Perspective on Early Sikh History', in *Sikh Studies: Comparative Perspective on a Changing Tradition*, pp. 33-9.
70. J.S. Grewal, 'Legacies of the Sikh Past for the Twentieth Century', in *Sikh History and Religion in the Twentieth Century*, pp. 18-31.
71. J.S. Grewal, 'A Brief History of Sikh Studies in English', in *Studying the Sikhs: Issues for North America*, pp. 161-73.

PART ONE

FOUNDATION OF SIKHISM AND THE SIKH COMMUNITY

CHAPTER 1

The Life of Guru Nanak

The early European writers were interested in the life of Guru Nanak but they had no substantial evidence to go by. The 'discovery' of *Janamsakhis* appeared to be of great importance. However, the sceptical attitude of the European writers towards the supranatural and mythical elements predisposed them to give a short shrift to the *Janamsakhis.* Ernest Trumpp provided the first notable example. In the early twentieth century, Sikh writers too were critical of the *Janamsakhis.* J.C. Archer was the first scholar to suggest that the *Janamsakhis* presented the 'formless' and the 'factual' Nanak rolled into one. He expected some Sikh scholar to search for the historical Nanak. This, however, was undertaken by W.H. McLeod.

CRITICAL ANALYSIS OF THE *SAKHIS*

With the professed intention of applying rigorous historical methodology to the sources of Guru Nanak's life, McLeod turned to the *Adi Granth* and the first *Var* of Bhai Gurdas, the four Janamsakhi traditions and the two versions of the eighteenth-century *Mahima Prakash.* The *Janamsakhis* appeared to provide the most promising source. On this assumption he takes up 124 *sakhis* mostly from the *Puratan* and *Miharban* versions, and the *Var* of Bhai Gurdas, for critical analysis. This list in his view is comprehensive enough to include all important incidents of Guru Nanak's life mentioned in all the known sources of his life.

McLeod mentions a number of considerations for classifying these *sakhis* as 'the established, the probable, the possible, the improbable, and the impossible'. His first consideration is 'the incidence of the miraculous or plainly fantastic'. A *sakhi* that is far removed from the realities as they are known today becomes immediately suspect. McLeod points out, however, that the inclusion of a miracle 'does not necessarily mean that the whole *sakhi* must be rejected. In most cases this may be required, but in others the possibility of a substratum of truth must be borne in mind.'[1] He does find a few instances in which the kernel appears to be acceptable despite the shell of miracle. His second consideration is the testimony of external sources, as in the case of Daulat Khan Lodi, Babur, and an inscription in Baghdad. The evidence of Guru Nanak's own compositions is the third consideration. The fourth is the measure of agreement or disagreement in the various *Janamsakhis* themselves. The relative reliability of the different *Janamsakhis* is the fifth consideration. Genealogical references are treated as more reliable than others. Finally, there is the consideration of geography: a greater degree of confidence is placed in detail relating to Guru Nanak's life in the Punjab than what concerns his life outside the Punjab.

On these criteria, 39 *sakhis* out of 124 are discarded as impossible. Among these are *sakhis* which involve a strong element of the supranatural or infringement of known historical chronology: the field restored, the stationary shadow of a tree, food from God's court, the *bhagats* revealed in stars, a girl turned into a boy, meeting with Kaliyuga, meeting with Khwajah Khizr, stopping of the rock at Panja Sahib, the cannibal's cauldron, meetings with Shaikh Farid and Shaikh Bahauddin Zakariya, discourse with figures like Namdev, Kabir, Ravidas and Beni, or with Shaikh Sharaf of Panipat. There are 18 other *sakhis* which according to McLeod are improbable. These include *sakhis* like *khara sauda,* discourse with Abdul Rahman of Iran, or with Raja Harinath, Raja Mitr Sain and Raja Jagannath, the food of Lalo and Bhago, and a visit to Nanakmata. Thirty of the *sakhis* belong to the category of possible, like 'the watering of the fields' at Hardwar, discourse with the *pandits* at Benares, visit to Rameshwaram, or Hinglaj, or to Mathura and Kurukshetra. Of the remaining thirty-seven *sakhis,* some are assigned to the probable category, and others are discussed individually for classification.

McLeod's method can be illustrated with reference to some concrete points. The Janamsakhis agree about the year of Guru Nanak's birth but not about the month. Between Kattak (Kartik) and Baisakh, McLeod is inclined to accept the latter as more probable because of the 'weight of evidence and scholarly opinion' in its favour. Similarly, about the place of Guru Nanak's birth, McLeod is inclined to prefer Chahal, his mother's village near Baraki in Lahore district, over Rai Bhoi di Talvandi (the present Nankana Sahib) where his father lived, because of the weight of the evidence of the *Miharban Janamsakhi* and the significance of the name Nanak. Of the three conflicting dates for the death of Guru Nanak, McLeod looks upon 7 September 1539 as the most likely on the basis of the entries made in the Kartarpur manuscript of the *Granth Sahib.* Since all Janamsakhis agree that Kalu, a Bedi Khatri of Rai Bhoi di Talvandi, was Guru Nanak's father, this is accepted by McLeod without reservation. In the same manner, Tripta is accepted as his mother. His sister was probably named Nanaki whose husband, Jai Ram, was employed as the steward (*modi*) of Daulat Khan Lodi. The evidence on the other close relations of Guru Nanak also appears to be acceptable, like the one on his close companion, Mardana. That oral evidence on these matters can be regarded as rather strong finds support in the *Janamsakhis.*

The evidence on the Sultanpur interlude, shorn of its supranatural details, may point to an authentic tradition, including the name of the administrator of Sultanpur, Daulat Khan. A personal meeting with Babur at Saidpur, on the other hand, is most unlikely though not impossible. McLeod argues in fact that the *Babur-vani* verses were composed with a general reference to the battles between the Mughals and the Afghans rather than with reference to any specific incident. This suggestion is based on the character and contents of these verses. There is strong proof for the foundation of Kartarpur by Guru Nanak, though we are not sure about the exact year of its foundation. Guru Nanak's visits to Pakpattan and Multan are very probable, but not so his visit to Mecca and Medina, or even Baghdad for which independent evidence is also considered and rejected. The discourse with the Siddhas on Mount Sumeru is also improbable. 'This is not to say that Guru Nanak never visited the Himalayas, nor indeed can we maintain with assurance that he did not penetrate as far as Mount Kailash and Lake Manasa.'[2] But there is no 'acceptable evidence' for such a visit in the *Var* of Bhai Gurdas and the Janamsakhis. Similarly, Guru Nanak's visit to Assam, Dacca, or Sri Lanka and his meeting with Sajjan, the swindler, remain within the realm of possibility but without any credible proof.

McLeod comes to the general conclusion that the *Janamsakhis* provide us only an outline for the concrete events of Guru Nanak's life, leaving lengthy periods covered by no more than a general comment, or a single detail. The *Janamsakhis* do remain the most important source, but they cannot be taken at their face value. What we find in the *Janamsakhis* is 'the Guru Nanak of legend and of faith, the image of the Guru seen through the eyes of popular piety seventy-five or hundred years after his death'.[3] It is an important image. But it is not the image of the actual life of Guru Nanak, the Nanak of history.

In his *Evolution of the Sikh Community,* McLeod reiterates that the Janamsakhis can serve a useful purpose with regard to our knowledge of the historical Nanak if they are subjected to rigorous scrutiny. Unlike the prisoner in a court of law, the *Janamsakhis* must be 'held guilty until proved innocent'.[4] However, McLeod regards these as indispensable for understanding how the 'myth' of Guru Nanak was evolved and transmitted. The term myth is used in 'a strictly technical sense' and not as a synonym for 'legend'. The development, purpose and function of the *Janamsakhis* are also discussed in the *Evolution of the Sikh Community.* McLeod illustrates the usefulness of this literature for the seventeenth-century Sikh Panth and the historian of the seventeenth-century Punjab. His essay, thus, is not merely an elaboration of what he had done in *Guru Nanak and the Sikh Religion.* The *Janamsakhis* themselves become a subject of study. McLeod's critics are interested only in his treatment of the *Janamsakhis* for the life of Guru Nanak.

CRITICISM OF 'NEGATIVE APPROACH'

Justice Gurdev Singh is of the opinion that Professor W.H. McLeod in his *Guru Nanak and the Sikh Religion* made 'an assiduous effort to destroy or distort the prevailing image of this great prophet asserting that the incidents of his life narrated in his numerous biographies have no historical basis but are the brainchild of his devotees who sought to glorify him by attributing supernatural power to him'.[5] Gurdev Singh goes on to state that even the *Adi Granth* which treasures the hymns of Guru Nanak and his successors is ignored by McLeod, despite specific references in some of the hymns to contemporary events like the invasion of Babur. The *Janamsakhis* narrating the events of Guru Nanak's life are discarded as 'hagiographic accounts with a very substantial portion of legend and of very little historical value'. McLeod summarily rejects all that smacks of miracle in his examination of the various incidents in the *Janamsakhis.*[6] Summing up his conclusions McLeod says:

> The Janam-sakhis have served as the vehicle of a powerful myth, one which still commands acceptance within the society which developed it. The myth which they express may be briefly stated as follows. Baba Nanak was the divinely commissioned giver of salvation. To all who would seek salvation the way lies open. The means of salvation consists in loyalty to the person of Baba Nanak and acceptance of his teachings. This is the myth. The form which was developed to give it expression was the narrative anecdote which, in relating some incidents concerning the life of Nanak, sought to authenticate the claims made on his behalf. These anecdotes collected into anthologies or structured biographies, constitute the Janam-sakhis.[7]

This view does not surprise Gurdev Singh because McLeod starts with the assumption that *Janamsakhis*, like the Gospels, are mainly collections of 'myths' developed during the first two centuries of Sikh history by the imagination of the followers of Guru Nanak. This treatment is wholly untenable in the eyes of Justice Gurdev Singh, especially in view of the authentic hymns of Guru Nanak treasured in the *Adi Granth* and other contemporary and almost contemporary evidence.

Justice Gurdev Singh believes that the following passage in *The Evolution of the Sikh Community* indicates McLeod's 'negative attitude':

> The basic point which needs to be made as far as the authentic Nanak material is concerned is that the Janam-sakhi tradition can provide no more than pointers to possibilities. Each of these possibilities must be subjected to rigorous scrutiny and only when it is actually established can it be accepted. Unlike the person in a court of law Janam-sakhis must be held guilty unless proved innocent. Given the hagiographic nature of the Janamsakhis and their general lack of reliability as far as the historical Nanak is concerned material which cannot be positively established should only rarely be given the benefit of doubt.[8]

With this attitude, asks Gurdev Singh, is it any wonder that McLeod finds next to nothing as positive evidence of historical Nanak in the various *Janamsakhis* and other source material, including the *Adi Granth* and the *Vars* of Bhai Gurdas?

Finally, Justice Gurdev Singh quotes a passage from James A. Veitch to stress the importance of the works like the *Janamsakhis* in dealing with the lives of great religious teachers:

> Of course it is difficult to distinguish between what happened in the life of the historical person Nanak, and how later traditions interpreted the impact he made upon the contemporary religious scene. Later generations, in recapturing the founding vision of Guru Nanak tend to fill out the record with stories which are more interpretative. This should not surprise the European reader: thinking and writing in historical terms is a phenomenon which has had a relatively short history in the West. Stories which are part and parcel of all religious traditions provide the media through which truths are expressed. The question to be asked of stories illustrating difficult incidents in the life of founders of the great religious traditions (such as Guru Nanak, Gotama, Muhammad, and Jesus) is not did it really happen in the way described? but what religious truth is being expressed in this story?[9]

In the light of this passage quoted by Justice Gurdev Singh with appreciation, his criticism of McLeod appears to consist of two essential points. First, McLeod is not justified in rejecting the factual authenticity of all his evidence. Secondly, he has missed the basic thrust of the *Janamsakhis*: projection of religious truths.

IMPLICATIONS FOR A POSITIVE APPROACH

On the first point, McLeod says that there was 'a brief flurry of activity intended to probe its findings and to test them rigorously'. Scholars were dispatched to places which figure prominently in the traditional records and which have received special attention in his analysis: Assam, Sri Lanka and Baghdad. The effort to refute him lost its drive when the information collected from Sri Lanka in support of Guru Nanak's visit was shown by McLeod to be 'wholly inaccurate'. However, despite his critical assessment of the value of the *Janamsakhis* for the life of Guru Nanak, most publications from within the Panth continue to treat the *Janamsakhis* as acceptable sources for the life of Guru Nanak. McLeod sees a rationalizing process at work by which 'the grosser elements' are eliminated. The *Puratan* rather than the *Bala* tradition has come to occupy the more prominent position as the source for the life of Guru Nanak.[10]

All the scholars are not convinced that McLeod has said the last word even on the factuality of the *Janamsakhi* evidence. However, they have not noticed a twist in McLeod's approach. He starts with the idea of writing on the life of Guru Nanak and ends up with answering the question 'what do the Janam-sakhis tell us about the concrete incidents of Guru Nanak's life'? In the process, he comes to attach all importance to 'certainties' and very little to 'probabilities'. Consequently, he leaves out a host of relevant questions and possible approaches to the life of Guru Nanak.[11]

Even in terms of certainties we know more about Guru Nanak than about any other religious figure of the medieval period. He lived for seventy years: for about twenty years in a village of the Rachna Doab, for about ten years in the town of Sultanpur in the Jalandhar Doab, for about a quarter of a century on visits to places of pilgrimage at least in the Indian subcontinent, and for about fifteen years leading a more or less settled life at Kartarpur in the upper Rachna Doab. He preached a message that became acceptable to a considerable number of persons, and thereby founded the nucleus of a new community of his followers. Obviously, his was not an ordinary life. He wrote a large volume of powerful poetry of great beauty in which he comments on all important aspects of the contemporary social order, polity and religion. Undoubtedly, he kept his eyes and ears open when, as he says in his own poetic expression, he visited numerous towns and cities in all the nine regions of the earth.

The *Janamsakhis* by their very nature leave much out of the crowded life of Guru Nanak. To capture something of his life we need a three-pronged approach which combines the evidence of the *Janamsakhis* and the compositions of Guru Nanak with information not directly related to his life. For example, we know that Sultanpur was the seat of an influential *shiqdar*, Daulat Khan Lodi, who was later to become the governor of Lahore. It was a flourishing town on the route from Delhi to Lahore. Its populace consisted of Hindus and Muslims, following diverse professions. It is difficult to imagine that there was no one in Sultanpur to expound or to administer Islamic law, or that there was no Sufi to represent Islamic mysticism. It is safe to assume that there were Khatri shopkeepers and traders, Brahman priests and astrologers. There were many who served Daulat Khan in the administration of the territory under his jurisdiction. There were *qanungos* to assist the administrator in the assessment of land revenue. There were others to assist him in its collection. Indeed, there was an official storehouse (*modikhana*) for the revenues collected in kind. This information, combined with the evidence of the Janamsakhis, may convince us that Jai Ram, an Uppal Khatri, who was married to Guru Nanak's sister, was an employee of Daulat Khan. On his request and surety, Guru Nanak was given employment in the *modikhana* of Daulat Khan. For about a decade Guru Nanak performed his duties well, living as a householder in Sultanpur. His two sons, Sri Chand and Lakhmi Chand, were born there. But neither his service to Daulat Khan Lodi nor his attention to his family was the most notable aspect of his life at Sultanpur. He was in search of something more important, the purpose of human life. Possibly, he had met wandering ascetics (*sadhs*) in or near Rai Bhoi di Talvandi. In Sultanpur he could meet the representatives of both 'Hinduism' and Islam. Religious discussions between Hindus and Muslims were not uncommon in the fifteenth-century Punjab. Guru Nanak meditated on the mysteries of life and reflected on views expressed by others on some of the fundamental questions of life. His search for truth ended in a sense of divine calling. This marked the end of his stay in Sultanpur around 1500.

Now, in the compositions of Guru Nanak, we have proof of his intimate knowledge of both orthodox Islam and the Sufis. Where did it come from? His stay at Sultanpur opens up a great probability. In the absence of a better explanation, this probability would amount nearly to certainty. This is one situation in which the evidence of the *Janamsakhis* and the *Adi Granth*, seen in conjunction with secular evidence, makes a lot of sense. Evidently, the broad outline of Guru Nanak's life delineated by McLeod himself can be meaningfully filled up with reasonable certainty or high probability.

What is far more important than all these points is the fact that Guru Nanak was the founder of a faith and much of his life would relate to his mission. The personal and secular aspects of his life would surely be interesting but not so significant or important as his mission. And this brings in the question of 'religious truths' enunciated and propagated by Guru Nanak. What McLeod calls the 'myth' of Guru Nanak is the most important aspect of the *Janamsakhis*. Each *sakhi* is an interpretation of Guru Nanak's status, doctrine or ethics. With this awareness, we may turn to McLeod's *Early Sikh Tradition* which in his own eyes is his most scholarly work.

DETAILED STUDY OF THE *JANAMSAKHIS* AND ITS LIMITATIONS

McLeod's *Early Sikh Tradition* was meant to examine the *Janamsakhis* 'as examples of hagiographic growth-processes, as sources of Punjab history for the post-Nanak period within which they developed, as a cohesive factor in subsequent Sikh history, and as the earliest works of Panjabi prose'.[12] As hagiographic accounts of Guru Nanak's life, the *Janamsakhis* provide an interpretation of his life, a myth. McLeod underlines that myth is not synonymous with legend. In fact, the distinction between legend and myth is of 'much greater importance than the difference between legend and the authenticated historical event'. The myth uses both history and legend for its own purpose. It is 'a construct of human imagination, developing out of an actual situation and seeking to give meaning to that situation'. It is an interpretation of a given array of circumstances, evolved in response to particular needs to fulfil its distinctive function for the society within which it takes shape. When a myth ceases to fulfil its function, 'it must either change or make way for a more effective substitute'.[13] It is in this sense that the *Janamsakhis* are said to have served as 'the vehicle of a powerful myth': the myth that Guru Nanak was 'the divinely commissioned giver of salvation. To all who would seek salvation the way lies open. The means of salvation consists in loyalty to the person of Baba Nanak and acceptance of his teaching.'[14]

McLeod takes notice of the manuscripts and printed versions of the principal *Janamsakhis*: the *Bala*, the *Puratan*, the *Miharban*, the *Gyan-Ratnavali*, the *Mahima Prakash* and the *Janamsakhis* known as *LDP 194* and *B40*, besides miscellaneous works closely related to *Janamsakhis.* They were written in Gurmukhi script, and in varying blends of Punjabi dialects, with the exception of the *Miharban Janamsakhi* which is mostly in Sadhukkari containing elements of Punjabi and Braj. Having introduced the reader to the entire range of *Janamsakhi* literature, McLeod takes up its analysis in the second section of the *Early Sikh Tradition* which constitutes about two-thirds of the book.

A broad outline of the *Early Sikh Tradition* would make it absolutely clear that McLeod is no longer concerned primarily with the question how much the *Janamsakhis* do or do not tell us about the actual events of Guru Nanak's life. He wants to understand their nature and character in terms of their genesis and growth with reference to their constituents and forms, and the sources which their compilers used. Furthermore, he wants to know their purpose, function and value, which are taken up in the third section of the book.

The objective of the *Janamsakhi* compilers was avowedly religious. 'Salvation is the issue which concerns them and the promulgation of a particular way of salvation constitutes their conscious intention.' He who accepts Guru Nanak as his guide will attain to salvation. He must heed the words enshrined in the Guru's sacred utterances; he must listen to the exemplary narratives of the Master's life; and he must join the community of the Master's followers. The compilers of the *Janamsakhis* equate the sacred utterances of Guru Nanak with *shabad* which in his compositions is 'the inner voice of God'. Remembrance of 'the Name' was to be practised individually as well as in congregation (*satsang*). 'The singing of *kirtan* within the regular *satsang* was accepted as normative by the *Janam-sakhi* narrators and one of their purposes was to encourage the practice.' Faith was due not to a theory but to a particular person who had propounded the doctrine of salvation 'with a unique clarity and beauty'. The status thus attributed to Guru Nanak is depicted to be 'the result of a divine commission received direct from God'. To have the Guru's *darshan* in person should be the first preference of a follower. Short of that, he should listen to the Guru's words and to what he did in his lifetime. The *Janamsakhis,* thus, were meant to provide a 'satisfactory substitute'.

They were meant to set forth 'a soteriological interpretation of the life of Nanak'. This interpretation, or 'myth', was conveyed through anecdote, discourse and an occasional declaration of faith. Besides the primary purpose of confirming and strengthening the Sikhs in their faith, the intention of the narrators was also 'the conversion of others to the same interpretation'. The popularity of the *Janamsakhis* was closely bound up with their purpose. They would continue to serve a viable function 'as long as religious interests retain a primacy within the Panth'.

The function of the *Janamsakhis* is quite distinct from their avowed purpose: it concerns the role which they have played in the history of the Panth. 'The primary function which they served from the late sixteenth century to the early eighteenth century must be construed in terms of Panthic cohesion, a role which the narrators and compilers would never have suspected'. The personality of the first Guru was projected not merely through the line of successors but also through the *Janamsakhis*. In McLeod's view, loyalty to a person is far more effective in maintaining cohesion in a community than loyalty to a doctrine. The replacement of the historical Nanak by the Nanak of myth made him all the more prominent. Amidst all the changes which the Sikh community has experienced and witnessed in the course of its history, loyally to the person of Guru Nanak has remained the *sine qua non* of faith. Without faith in Guru Nanak, a person cannot be a Sikh.[15]

The *Janamsakhis* bear witness to the faith of the followers of Guru Nanak primarily in the seventeenth century. Above all else, Baba Nanak is 'the giver of salvation'. Through the multitude of the Janamsakhi anecdotes emerges 'the uniqueness of the figure' of Guru Nanak. The surviving memories of his authentic personality get blended with traditional symbols, which in a particular tradition may produce the image of a great ascetic. But this is not the dominant image of most *Janamsakhi* traditions. As time passes, Baba Nanak becomes Guru Nanak, the transition symbolizing his status as the Supreme Teacher. He was much more than a *bhala faqir* or a *bada bhagat*; he was a *mahapurakh*, an *avtar* of Raja Janak and, in fact, God (*paramesar*). 'Whatever he does is true and whatever he says is true. The Guru is God not a man.' In the *Janamsakhi* image of Guru Nanak there are two other allied themes: Nanak the unifier, the one to whom both Hindus and Muslims must owe allegiance, and the theme of 'triumph over Islam' in which the faith promulgated by Guru Nanak transcends all other dispensations, including Islam. The third theme, which is close to Guru Nanak's own attitude, is that of encounters with the Naths resulting in their discomfiture.[16]

According to McLeod, the settings provided by the *Janamsakhi* narrators for the incidents of Guru Nanak's life were derived in form and in detail from 'their own contemporary experience', and hence their value for the historian. A lengthy account of Guru Nanak's wedding, for instance, may be taken as a description of seventeenth-century wedding. This would be true also of the Janamsakhi descriptions of Guru Nanak's funeral. The general background against which the *Janamsakhis* set their tales is that of the rural Punjab. McLeod argues in fact that 'the Sikh Panth of this period must have been almost exclusively a rural community'. Within this general context, three social groups appear to constitute the seventeenth-century Sikh community: Khatris, Jats, and artisans, in that order of standing. An awareness of a distinct identity is emerging in the Janamsakhis: the followers of Guru Nanak (Nanak-Panthis) have a distinct form of salutation, distinct place and modes of worship, and the distinctive ideas of *nam-simran*, *ashnan* and *seva*.[17]

The historical evidence of the *Janamsakhis* is not confined to the Sikh community. The rural Punjab speaks through them 'with an authentic voice'. The existence of substantial wealth among some Khatris and its use by them is one example. The existence of landless labourers is another. It is generally in a circumstantial manner that the *Janamsakhis* yield their significant information concerning the wider life of the seventeenth-century rural Punjab. There is virtually nothing in these on dates, chronologies and mighty events but there is enough on 'the unspectacular life of the people' to make the *Janamsakhis* a unique source of historical information on the Punjab.[18] The locale and specific ideas of the compilers are reflected in the *Janamsakhis*. Thus, the *Janamsakhis* can yield information on the sub-regions of the Punjab as well as on the sectarian interests within the Sikh community.

The *Janamsakhis* are the first examples of sustained Punjabi prose. In fact, they have continued to exercise perceptible influence upon the style and imagery of later generations of Punjabi writers.

Together with the *Adi Granth,* the works of the Sufis, and eventually the Western models, they rank as a major influence in the development of Punjabi literature. McLeod does not hesitate to prophesy that when Punjabi eventually receives the attention it deserves the *Janamsakhis* would receive a significant share of this recognition.

McLeod goes into the 'constituents' of the *Janamsakhis* rather systematically. Their first constituent in terms of temporal priority, but not quantity, is authentic memory and actual observation. The major constituents are the works of Guru Nanak and the received tradition, especially the ascetic ideal. The received tradition consisted of an amalgam of Puranic lore, tales from the *Ramayana,* the *Mahabharata,* the *Yoga-Vasishtha,* Nath legends, Sufi hagiography and, occasionally, the Buddhist *Jatakas.* Though it is possible to identify the dominant elements as Puranic, Epic, Nath or Sufi, a single tradition could incorporate all of them. This hypothesis is illustrated with reference to the Epics, the Puranas, and the Nath and Sufi traditions.

For the use of the compositions of Guru Nanak, the standard procedure is outlined by McLeod with the caution that it is by no means invariable. Guru Nanak's own words in a *shabad* or a *shalok* give answers to an interlocutor's question and serve as a nucleus for the discourse. The interlocutor's question or comment is followed by a *shalok* or by the first stanza of a *shabad.* Another question or comment is followed by the second stanza or another *shalok,* and so the discourse proceeds until the *shabad* has been completed or the supply of suitable *shaloks* is exhausted. A setting is provided in order to introduce the discourse and in a brief conclusion the interlocutor submits to the Guru. This point is illustrated with a few examples. McLeod points out that this procedure was not a conscious attempt to construct historical situations. Therefore, the question of deliberate fabrication does not arise. All the quotations used are not from the compositions of Guru Nanak, and they are not necessarily authentic. Here, again, it cannot be maintained that there was an attempt at deceit. The number of Guru Nanak's compositions which served the purpose of 'generating' *sakhis* was not very large.[19]

The ascetic ideal can be regarded as a part of the received tradition, but it has a peculiar significance in being opposed to Guru

Nanak's own emphatically stated beliefs against renunciation. 'It is a measure of the power exercised by the ascetic tradition that it could so effectively reassert itself against Nanak's explicit opposition.' This emphasis on an old ideal, according to McLeod, seems to have been the work of an ascetically inclined group within the Sikh community. This group was influential because of the appeal of the deeply rooted ideals of asceticism in the Indian tradition. In any case, there are several *sakhis* which represent Guru Nanak as the performer of austerities, and a person who sought complete withdrawal from the world.[20]

McLeod thinks that most *sakhis* were products of a blending of all the four constituents, and a single constituent is rarely found in complete isolation. The Sikh tradition can be seen as drawing much of the material from earlier traditions. Nevertheless, it possesses 'a freshness and novelty of its own'. This was because of its new focus and also 'a result of the function it served in giving expression to the distinctive needs of the new community'.[21]

The purpose of the *Janamsakhis* dictated appropriate forms. The patterns familiar to the audiences could be adapted to serve the specific needs of the new community. Perhaps the most engaging form used by the narrators of the *sakhis* was that of the 'narrative anecdote'. These anecdotes are divided by McLeod into four categories: moralistic anecdotes, chimeric fairy-tales, devotional legends, and aetiological legends. Each in its distinctive way served to express the same myth. McLeod gives examples of *sakhis* falling within each category before moving on to the next form, the narrative discourse. Based on the *shabads* and *shaloks* of Guru Nanak, the narrative discourse turned into 'didactic discourse' when a lengthy exegetical supplement was added. This form is a characteristic of the *Miharban Janamsakhi.* When it appears in some other tradition, it may be treated as a borrowing from the *Miharban.* The didactic discourse offered a convenient vehicle for the ascetic ideal. Apart from this rather 'unorthodox' intrusion, there were some deviant traditions which in tone and content ranged from mild heterodoxy to virulent polemic. McLeod gives examples of such 'heterodox discourses'. Lastly, there are *sakhis* which embody the norms of Sikh conduct. These, in McLeod's view, can be seen as the seeds from which the later Rahitnamas were to grow.[22]

The *sakhi* tradition in diverse forms expanded with speed because of the great role that oral tradition played in their growth, evolution and transmission. Written collections began to be made within a hundred years of Guru Nanak's death, embodying the various phases of development. The oral tradition remained supreme, without any restraint other than the requirements of the myth which they were intended to express. The narrator who addressed the local congregations (*sangats*) possessed considerable freedom to bring his points home to the audience. At the second stage of written recording, much greater concern was shown for chronology and an effort was made to order the assortment of *sakhis* into a coherent sequence. Expository material was also added to the narrative anecdotes and discourses, accounting for a notional third stage in the development of the written collections.[23]

The fourth phase, according to McLeod, began only with the introduction of the printing press. The first lithographed edition of a *Janamsakhi* appeared in 1871. It was a *Bala Janamsakhi.* More elaborate editions appeared subsequently. McLeod believes that the Bala tradition had become more popular than the others already in the eighteenth century. Macauliffe brought the *Puratan* tradition to the fore in his *Sikh Religion*, and a few years later, Karam Singh, 'the historian', sealed the fate of the *Bala* tradition with his *Katik kih Visakh*, but only for the scholars. The *Bala* tradition has not yet lost popularity in the Punjab.[24]

The evolution of individual *sakhis* is discussed by McLeod with a number of examples: Guru Nanak's visit to Multan, Mula the Khatri, Sajjan the robber, the rich man's pennants, Guru Nanak's return to Talvandi, his discourse with Shaikh Brahm, his visit to Mecca, discourses with Naths, Raja Shivnabh, Guru Angad, and Mardana and Bala. These are 'representative' *sakhis*, according to McLeod, and each represents a certain characteristic.[25] Last of all, he takes up the question of 'sources' used by the compilers of the *Janamsakhis* with particular attention to the *B40 Janamsakhi* and the *Adi Sakhis.* The pattern that emerges is not simple. The intricacy of the pattern reflects the complexity of the process.[26]

McLeod expected his *Early Sikh Tradition* to have created some discussion as a detailed examination of the constituents, forms, assembly and transmission, sources, and purpose. However, 'not a leaf stirred'. The book was not reviewed and it 'sank like a stone'. This was a considerable disappointment for McLeod because this book was in his opinion the best that he had ever written.[27]

McLeod does not tell us why he regarded this book as his best. It is clear, however, that it is a very scholarly work. But it is not read even by scholars. I have suggested that his scholarship in this book appears to run in neutral gear. He is certainly aware that there are several 'traditions' of the *Janamsakhis*, reflecting the lines of divisions among the Sikhs. The relationship between the two, that is, a sectarian group and its Janamsakhi tradition, can be very interesting and meaningful. But McLeod says virtually nothing about it. Another aspect of the *Janamsakhis* which McLeod has underlined is the 'myth' of Guru Nanak which they embody. This aspect of the *Janamsakhis* is by far the most important, particularly if seen in relation to the different traditions. But McLeod has only a few paragraphs of a general nature on the 'myth' of Guru Nanak whereas the 'myths' of Guru Nanak in different *Janamsakhi* traditions are as many interpretations of his doctrines, ethics, attitudes and status. By ignoring the two most important aspects of the *Janamsakhis*, which are closely interlinked, McLeod has produced a work of scholarship that suggests that a rigorous methodology by itself does not make any work interesting or important.[28]

NOTES

1. W.H. McLeod, *Guru Nanak and the Sikh Religion*, Oxford: The Clarendon Press, 1968, p. 68.
2. Ibid., pp. 121-2.
3. Ibid., p. 147.
4. W.H. McLeod, *The Evolution of the Sikh Community*, New Delhi: Oxford University Press, 1975, p. 26.
5. Gurdev Singh (ed.), *Perspectives on the Sikh Tradition*, Patiala: Siddharth Publications, 1986, 'Introduction', p. 6.
6. Loc. cit.
7. Ibid., pp. 6-7.
8. Ibid., p. 7.
9. Ibid., p. 8.
10. W.H. McLeod, *Early Sikh Tradition*, Oxford: The Clarendon Press, 1980, p. 7.
11. Ibid., p. 9. Before writing *Guru Nanak in History* in 1969, I had men-

tioned to McLeod my intention of writing a book on Guru Nanak. Without any hesitation he said that there was no possibility of writing a historical biography of Guru Nanak. When I mentioned the basic approach for my book, he agreed that such a study could be meaningful. My *Guru Nanak in History* is not a biographical study but it is a serious study of Guru Nanak nonetheless.

12. McLeod, *Early Sikh Tradition*, p. 7.
13. Ibid., p. 9.
14. Ibid., p. 10.
15. Ibid., pp. 244-6.
16. Ibid., pp. 248-56.
17. Ibid., pp. 266-7.
18. Ibid., pp. 268-9.
19. Ibid., pp. 64-73.
20. Ibid., p. 74.
21. Ibid., p. 79.
22. Ibid., p. 81.
23. Ibid., pp. 82-105.
24. Ibid., pp. 117-73.
25. Ibid., pp. 174-234.
26. W.H. McLeod, *The Sikhs: History, Religion and Society*, New York: Columbia University Press, 1989, pp. 19-20.
27. Hew [W.H.] McLeod, *Discovering the Sikhs: Autobiography of a Historian*, Delhi: Permanent Black, 2004, pp. 150-1.
28. For the 'myths' of Guru Nanak in the *B40 Janamsakhi*, see J.S. Grewal, 'The *B40 Janamsakhi*', *Lectures on History, Society and Culture of the Punjab*, Patiala: Punjabi University, 2007, pp. 167-217. See also, J.S. Grewal, 'The *Janamsakhi* Traditions', in ibid., pp. 141-66.

CHAPTER 2

The Faith of Guru Nanak

The faith of Guru Nanak is one of the oldest themes in Sikh Studies. Interest in his ideas and practices involved the issue of their relationship with the contemporary systems, both Hindu and Muslim. The question of the status of the faith, message, teachings or ideology of Guru Nanak was raised at the very beginning of Sikh Studies. Different answers were given to this question. One simply was that the Sikhs represented a Hindu 'sect'. Another was that Sikhism represented a syncretism, a mixture, of Hindu and Islamic beliefs, especially of Bhakti and Sufism, carrying the implication that there was little original in it. Yet another view was that Sikhism represented a new faith, a new religion. This view was presented by a number of Western writers before it came to be expounded and projected by Sikh scholars as a divine dispensation. The recent controversy regarding the faith of Guru Nanak can be appreciated in the context of this background.

According to Justice Gurdev Singh, W.H. McLeod propagates that Sikhism has nothing new to offer. Guru Nanak did not originate a new set of teachings or a new school of thought. All that he offers is a clear expression of the *nirguna sampradaya.* The following which gathered around Guru Nanak was certainly the original nucleus of the Sikh Panth, but that does not make Guru Nanak the founder of Sikhism.[1] McLeod holds the view that Guru Nanak stands firmly within 'the so called Sant Tradition of Northern India'.[2] Justice Gurdev Singh feels concerned about McLeod's view of the origins of Sikhism, and not with his exposition of the teachings of Guru Nanak.

SANT SYNTHESIS MADE COHERENT

McLeod discusses the teachings of Guru Nanak in terms of (a) the nature of God, (b) the nature of the unregenerate man, (c) the divine self-expression, and (d) the discipline. We may sum up his ideas on each of these aspects for a proper understanding of his position.

The figure '1' at the very beginning of the *mulmantar* declares the unity of God. In his primal aspect God is *nirgun* – absolute, unconditioned, devoid of all attributes. He is formless (*nirankar*). He is boundless and infinite; he is ineffable; he is eternal, without beginning, beyond time, unborn, non-incarnated; he is unknowable, completely beyond the range of human comprehension. However, of his own volition, he became *sagun* in order that man might know him. He is the creator of the universe and a participant in the life of the universe, watching, directing and upholding it as its sustainer. As the sovereign Lord, the wielder of absolute authority, God is immanent in the universe. He is everywhere and in everything. He is the bestower of liberation. He unites the worshipper with himself through his grace.[3]

The unregenerate man has a *man* (heart, mind, soul) that is erratic and leads him into worldly attachments. It is controlled by *haumai*, the source of pride and the epitome of self-centredness. The outward expressions of a man dominated by *haumai* are evil passions which mark the *manmukh*. Because of these evil passions the unregenerate man remains sunk in *maya*, seeking fulfilment in attachment to worldly things. For Guru Nanak the world is real but impermanent, or 'false'. *Maya* is basically untruth as opposed to Truth. So long as man remains entangled in *maya* it is impossible for him to appreciate Truth. He remains chained to the wheel of death and rebirth, in perpetual separation from God.[4]

When we proceed to inquire 'precisely *how* God communicates with man', we encounter the specific contribution of Guru Nanak's theology, 'a contribution which offers the most significant example of his positive originality': the concept of divine self-expression in the compositions of Guru Nanak. The first key term is the Word (*shabad*). It is the vehicle of revelation. The Word embraces all that is Truth, all that expresses the nature of God and the means of attaining him. It may be perceived in the divine laws governing the universe as well as in the ineffable mystical experience. If the Word distinctly is the medium of communication, the Name (*nam*) is the object of communication. The communicator of divine Truth is the Divine Preceptor (*guru*), equated with God, the voice of God within man, and with the Word. In the thought of Guru Nanak, Divine Order (*hukam*) signifies the divinely instituted and maintained principle governing the existence and movement of the universe, and expressed in the moral world. It is an all-embracing principle, 'the sum total of all divinely instituted laws; and it is a revelation of the nature of God'. The fifth key idea is Truth (*sachch*). Its appropriation lends to liberation which, in the last analysis depends on God's grace (*nadar*). There is nothing man can do to 'earn' grace.[5]

To move towards salvation offered by the Guru in the Word, the individual has to cleanse himself of all evil. Inward devotion paves the way. True religion is to be found not in external practices but in the inward disciplines of love, faith, mercy, and humility, expressed in righteous and compassionate deeds and in the upholding of all that is true. Loving devotion to God is to be expressed through *nam simran* and fear of God. Meditation on the nature and qualities of God is the core of Guru Nanak's religious discipline; it must overflow in words and deeds. This meditation has a corporate as well as individual application. From this meditation results the experience of *vismad* which, in turn, becomes a stimulus to more exalted meditation. This experience involves wonder and ecstasy. With the ever-widening *vismad* develops an increasing sense of joy and peace. The accent is strongly upon ascent to higher and yet higher levels of understanding and experience. This ascent is particularly evident in Guru Nanak's famous figure of the five *khands*. The fifth and the final state is Sachch Khand, the realm of Truth, the goal and the ultimate end of human existence, the final consummation of man's ascent to God. The blending of light within human beings with the divine light brings about a condition of peace, consummate joy and perfect tranquillity, a condition transcending all human telling. This state is the goal of human life.[6]

McLeod goes on to state that all religious systems have antecedents which defy ultimate scrutiny. Guru Nanak too received an inheritance, but to regard him as the mere mediator of other men's ideas would be 'altogether mistaken'. The inheritance was transformed in his hands. Moreover, the pattern which was produced by this transformation has endured. There have been subsequent developments of considerable significance, but this same pattern has remained the core and essence of the continuing Sikh faith. McLeod equates Kabir and Guru Nanak because they both offer synthesis. However, in each case, 'the nature of the synthesis reflects the personality of its author'. In imparting endurance to Sikhism, the clarity and coherence of Guru Nanak's thought and the designation of a successor 'have been factors of fundamental significance'. Nevertheless, his thought is said to be closely related to that of the Sant tradition of northern India.[7]

In the traditional religions of India, according to McLeod, external authority and conventional ceremony constituted the essence, except in three dissenting movements: Bhakti in Vaishnavism, the Naths in Shaivism, and the Sufis in Islam. 'The Sant tradition was essentially a synthesis of the three principal dissenting movements, a compound of elements drawn mainly from Vaishnava Bhakti and the Hathyoga of the Nath Yogis, with a marginal contribution from Sufism.' The Sants expressed their beliefs in a language that was closely related to that of the common people, as in the case of Namdev, Ravidas and Kabir, who all came from low caste groups. This tradition was by far the most important element which Guru Nanak inherited from the past or absorbed from contemporary patterns. However, he reinterpreted this tradition in the light of his own experience and in accordance with his own personality.[8] McLeod argues in some detail that Islamic influence on Guru Nanak was not of fundamental significance. Indeed, it was mediated to him through the Sant synthesis. Conventional Hindu beliefs and Islam were 'not regarded as fundamentally right but as fundamentally wrong'.[9]

It is accordingly incorrect to interpret the religion of Guru Nanak as a synthesis of Hindu beliefs and Islam. It is a synthesis in which Islamic elements are relatively unimportant. The pattern evolved by Guru Nanak, according to McLeod, is a reworking of the Sant synthesis, one which does not depart far from its Sant source in its fundamental components. The categories employed by Guru Nanak are the categories of the Sants, the terminology he uses is their terminology, and the doctrines he affirms are their doctrines. Guru Nanak's thought was a precise copy of what earlier Sants had developed because he did not transmit his inheritance unchanged. He received a synthesis and he passed it on in a form which was in some measure amplified and in considerable measure clarified and integrated. This applies in particular to his understanding of the manner of divine communication with man. Guru Nanak's concepts of *Sabad*, *Nam*, *Guru*, and *Hukam* carry us beyond anything that the works of earlier Sants offer in any explicit form. It is Sant thought which we find in his works, but it is Sant thought expanded and reinterpreted. The result is a new synthesis, a synthesis which is cast within the pattern of Sant beliefs but which nevertheless possesses a significant originality and, in contrast with its Sant background, a unique clarity. It possesses, moreover, the quality of survival, for it remains today the substance of a living faith.[10]

McLeod restates his position on the issue of 'origins' in *The Evolution of the Sikh Community*. He admits that in a certain sense Guru Nanak can be regarded as a founder. The following which gathered around him was certainly the original nucleus of the Sikh Panth and if we are to follow organizational lines on our movement back through history we shall be able to proceed no further than this nucleus. In another sense, however, the term 'founder' can be misleading. It does suggest that Guru Nanak originated not merely a group of followers but also 'a school of thought, or set of teachings'. This can be accepted in a highly qualified sense. 'If we place Guru Nanak within his own historical context, if we compare his teachings with those of other contemporary or earlier religious figures, we shall at once see that he stands firmly within a well-defined tradition. What Guru Nanak offers us is the clearest and most highly articulated expression of the *nirguna sampradaya*, the so-called Sant tradition of Northern India.'[11]

In a recent publication McLeod reiterates his view that Guru Nanak can be regarded as the founder of the Sikh Panth, and 'in a certain sense the Panth can be construed as coterminus with the Sikh faith'. But this does not imply that Guru Nanak cannot be placed within the Sant tradition. Must we conclude that Guru Nanak was a Sant? According to McLeod, if it is a strictly neutral question of antecedent and influence the answer must be in the affirmative.

If, however, the question implies a lack of originality on the part of Nanak the answer must be an emphatic negative. Plainly there is much that is profoundly original in the hymns which we find recorded under his distinctive symbol in the *Adi Granth*. There is in them an integrated and coherent system which no other Sant has produced; there is a clarity which no other Sant has equalled; and there is a beauty which no other Sant has matched. There is, moreover, the question of permanence. The fact that Nanak appointed a successor to follow him is scarcely unique, but nothing in the Sant experience can compare to the Panth which was eventually to emerge from that decision.[12]

McLeod seems to clarify but not to change his position. The Sikh Panth originated with Guru Nanak but not the important ideas woven into his religious thought.

McLeod's analysis does not end there. He seeks a synthesis between the glimpses provided by the *sakhis* and the personality of the Guru that emerges from his works. He infers that Guru Nanak gave 'practical expression to his own ideals' during the last three decades of his life. These were the years when he was surrounded by disciples who received instruction from him. This was also the period of his definitive utterances which presumably were recorded by his disciples. He combined a life of disciplined devotion with worldly activities set in the context of normal family life and a regular *satsang*. *Kirtan* was presumably held in the early morning after individual meditation and in the evening after the day's work. The instruction delivered in the regular gathering of disciples would have the same emphasis upon the greatness of God, His gracious self-revelation, the perils of human condition, and the paramount necessity of meditation on the divine Name as we find in his compositions. Those who placed their confidence in status conferred by caste, or by wealth, would be sternly admonished. Nath Yogis would be the natural opponents, both because of the manner in which their theories and practices conflicted with those of Guru Nanak and the considerable influence which they still exercised over the popular mind of the Punjab. Like his disciples, the Guru probably performed daily labours. He maintained an essentially practical participation in the everyday affairs of his community and of the world beyond.[13]

The combination of piety and practical activity which Guru Nanak manifested in his own life was bequeathed to his followers. At its best it is a piety devoid of superstition and a practical activity compounded with determination and an immense generosity. It explains much that has happened in the Punjab during the last four centuries.[14]

A NEW DISPENSATION

Justice Gurdev Singh refers to the revelatory status of Guru Nanak's utterances and emphasizes the universality of his doctrine, the originality of his thought, and the social orientation of his egalitarian ideas, citing the views of scholars like Muhammad Mujeeb, Harbans Singh and Attar Singh, and quoting the well-known passage of J.D. Cunningham in which he underlines the uniqueness of Guru Nanak in laying the foundations of 'a new nationality'. Sikhism stands by itself as a faith. It rejects idol-worship and the caste system. A Sikh accepts the householder's life and responsibilities 'to carry out the Attributive Will of God' and to solve the problems of man through 'a continuous virtuous endeavour'; he works not only for his own emancipation but also for 'the good of the society'.[15] This summing up reflects the views expressed by Daljeet Singh in his 'comparative study' of Nathism, Vaishnavism and Sikhism in the *Perspectives.*

According to Daljeet Singh, the two most popular religious systems in northern India in the time of Guru Nanak were Nathism and Vaishnavism. Therefore, the relevant question to ask was whether or not these systems contributed anything to the fundamentals of Sikhism. For a proper answer to this question it was necessary to identify the essentials of each of the three systems and then to compare them in terms of similarities and dissimilarities. The basic questions to ask of each system relate to its metaphysical view, its view of the world as real or illusory, its spiritual goal, the discipline or methods to be followed to achieve the goal, the role of the person who has achieved the goal, and the overall world-view of the system. Ideology is important because it is intimately linked to both perception and activity. For a proper study of religion it is necessary to adhere to the principle of the unity of experience, ideology and activity, and never to ignore the activities of the author of a religious system. 'Deeds alone are the true index of the ideology of the author'. This emphasis is needed because scholars trained in 'a behaviouristic, or mechanical methodology' have the tendency to trace one religious development from a preceding one. Such a chain becomes 'a virtual denial of the validity, the very novelty, and the free character of the religious experience'. A revelatory religion is 'by its very nature new'.[16]

However, neither Nathism nor Vaishnavism was authored by

a single person. The origins of these systems were so remote that nothing directly and certainly was known of the views and actions of those persons who may be looked upon as their protagonists. The final goal of Nathism was 'complete dissociation' from the world, involving a 'wholly passive and blissful union' with Shiva. The primary object of Nathism was 'to gain powers' and liberation from 'the oppression of the world'. Being ascetical, the Nath system was monastic. There were twelve sects, each founded by a disciple of Gorakh Nath. A person entering any of these sects was to remain celibate; he was not to engage himself in any gainful activity, sustaining himself by begging for his food; and he was to observe *ahimsa.* His appearance was marked, among other things, by rings in his split ears, ashes on his almost naked body, and a necklace of *rudraksha* beads. The Shudras were not admitted to a Gorakh Nathi order. Women generally were not initiated, but exception could be made for widows. The prominent elements of discipline in Nathism were Yogic practices, and the raising of *kundalani* with a view to union with Lord Shiva. Both before and after liberation, the Yogi had no social responsibilities. In its approach to the world, its ethics, and its discipline, Nathism embodied a world-view of 'life-negation'.[17]

Four streams of thought joined in the Vaishnava system of the pre-Christian centuries. The mystic system of love was not there even in the *Gita*, not even as an idea or a base for future development. The Bhakti movement started with Ramanuja. Daljeet Singh gives a brief account of Madhava, Ramananda, Tulsidas, Vallabha and Chaitanya as well. The chief features of Vaishnava Bhakti were a pantheistic or dualistic world-view, belief in the Vedas and their ritualistic mysticism, adherence to caste system and its social prohibitions, the other-worldly attitude (though the world was deemed to be real), and merger of the human soul in Brahman as the goal. There was no involvement in the world of man, no stress on the moral life except for personal purity and aid to meditation, and no social role for the *jivan-mukta.* The Vaishnavas believed in Avtarhood and practised idol-worship. The basic scriptures of the Vaishnava system were the Vedas and the Upanishads, to which the *Gita* was added later. The caste system was wholly accepted. The theory of Avtarhood absorbed all kinds of divergent and heterodox systems. The ritualism of the Vedic religion remained a part of Vaishnavism. Any transformation of the love of God into the service of man was obviated by all these features. Daljeet Singh thus concludes that, 'moral life, at best, meant only a sense of ritualistic or formal piety without the least reaction to any social evil, injustice or cruelty much less to any political oppression or tyranny'.[18]

Daljeet Singh then points out that the Sikh Gurus were uncompromising monotheists. Their conception of God enables us to understand the origin and course of the Sikh tradition, and the significance of Sikh institutions and practices. God is both transcendent and immanent, not in two parts, stages or phases. The transcendent God is everywhere, in each heart, place and particle. God is the creator and the 'ocean of attributes, values and virtues'. He is inextricably linked with the universe through his attributive or immanent aspect. God's virtues and attributes indicate his perpetual interest in man and the universe. They give validity and spiritual sanctity to moral life 'which in many other systems is deemed to be an entanglement'. Everything is governed by God's will but it is not deterministic because God is creative and 'all movement in life is towards a creative freedom'. God never takes birth or form. The God of will is also a God of grace. His activity is incomprehensible except in terms of His grace or freedom. Sikhism is often described as the way of Nam (*nam marga*) because Nam is the Reality supporting and directing the created world. Nam may be called 'the creative and dynamic' immanence of God which directs the manifest world of force and form.[19]

Furthermore, the world is real. It is the place for righteous activity. Creative work and virtuous deeds are of fundamental importance. Living in this world is not a bondage but a rare opportunity. Man's struggle provides an opportunity for his progress. Man in his normal state is dominated by self-will and animal propensities. His main limitations and problems arise from his *haumai*, the self-centred human individuality created by God for man's survival and progress. *Haumai* is opposed to Nam: 'the two cannot be at the same place'. This means that egoism, not the worldly life as such, is opposed to the spiritual life. 'The way to God is through life, not through its renunciation.' Self-centredness must be substituted by God-centredness. The way to higher achievement lies in being altruistic or moral instead of being self-centred. God-centredness and inactivity are a contradiction in terms. Because of the presence of God in man it is possible for man to become conscious of God and to develop a new state of consciousness. Ultimately, it is God's grace that unites man with Nam. For that, however, it is necessary to turn to God and to carry out his will. The mission of the Sikh Gurus was to turn every self-centred individual (*manmukh*) into a God-centred person (*gurmukh*).[20]

The Sikh Gurus made a radical departure from the Indian tradition in their conception of the goal of human life. The dictum that states this goal is well known: 'Everything is lower than Truth, but higher still is truthful living.' Not only to know the truth but also to live the active life of truth is the ideal. To carry out God's will through creative activity in the universe as God's instrument is the ideal of life. Blissful union is not an end in itself, but 'union with a view both to knowing His Will and carrying it out'. The spiritual and moral life are virtually synonymous and coextensive; creative and moral life is the goal in Sikhism. The Sikh of the Guru is described as Gurmukh. He has no *haumai*, he is godly and virtuous, he carries out God's will, taking part in all fields of life, and his aim in life is to make all others God-centred. In Daljeet Singh's view, moral life or service of man and the company of God-centred persons constitute two of the principal modes of discipline in Sikhism.[21]

The third mode of discipline is prayer and remembering God. There is a considerable emphasis on contemplation in the *Adi Granth.* This contemplation does not mean yogic practices or any mechanical means of worship. Meditation involves the awe of God while embarking on any activity or making any decision. Prayer in Sikhism expresses the humility of the devotee, reminds him of the need of continuous search for God, represents perpetual seeking for God's grace, and is a humble attempt at communion with him so as to draw upon his light and energy in the fight against evil and for the positive expression of love. 'The very fact that the Gurus started no monastic system shows conclusively that they never advocated prayer as an independent mode of spiritual training.' One is emancipated 'while laughing and playing in life'; the God-centred lives truth 'while a householder'.[22]

Daljeet Singh underlines the great importance of ethical life in

Sikhism. The ethical principles in Sikhism are inter-connected and represent different facets of a single concept. The basis of human equality and brotherhood flows from the conception of God as the creator of all. The goal of a truly moral or spiritual living is closely linked with the idea that the world is real. The movement from comparative imperfection to comparative perfection, from comparative necessity to freedom is an outcome of the idea that God is 'the ocean of attributes and values'. God-consciousness is the greatest social virtue since it directs every activity towards the good of all and not towards self-interest alone. Denunciation of caste prejudices, oppression of the rulers, tyranny of the invaders, and corruption of the officials springs from Sikh ethics. Creation of alternative moral institutions was the obverse of this criticism of evil institutions. So long as the end was moral and spiritual the use of force was also justified. Equally radical was the Gurus' attitude towards women. They were never considered to be evil. No human life was possible without them. They were to be equal partners with men. The social, moral and religious implications of this change were enormous. Economic inequality too was criticized by the Gurus. They commended honest work and the production of goods as the moral and spiritual duty of man. To react against social and political wrongs, to face and reshape life boldly, was a corollary of the Sikh ethical ideals.[23]

It is not surprising that the Gurus denounced the ways and the ideals of the Naths and rejected their methods, and their other-worldly approach. The two systems present opposite world-views. Nathism rejects the world and life as misery, but Sikhism accepts them as spiritually meaningful. Nathism was characterized by withdrawal from the world, asceticism, *ahimsa*, celibacy, the downgrading of women, solitude and yogic practices. But in Sikhism, virtuous participation in the world, the householder's life and responsibilities, the consequent raising of the status of women, and the love and service of man in all spheres of his life become logically necessary because God in Sikhism is attributive. Sikhism and Nathism take the world to be real, but the two systems have entirely different methodologies, goals and world-views. There is hardly a meeting ground between the two systems.[24]

Vaishnavism was a part and parcel of the Brahmanical complex.

Its scriptures were the Vedas and the Upanishads. Bhakti in Vaishnavism was basically formal and ritualistic, and marked by devotional idol-worship in temples. It did not lead to virtuous deeds in the social field. Sikhism denies the authority of the Vedas and the Upanishads, discards belief in *avtars*, and rejects the Vedic conception of caste. Once the fundamentals of Vaishnavism are rejected, the question of any similarity between the two systems does not arise. While Sikhism is strictly theistic, Vaishnavism is broadly pantheistic. Unlike the Vaishnava saints, the Sikh Gurus insist on virtuous deeds to seek the grace of God. Vaishnavism accepts 'the sensual path' as an alternative spiritual approach, but Sikhism rejects it. The 'non-participation' of the Vaishnava saints was an inevitable consequence of their ideology and objectives. By contrast, the Sikh Gurus always espoused causes in defence and aid of righteousness. On the whole, whereas Nathism and Vaishnavism are 'quietist', Sikhism is 'activist'. The contrast between the two is 'too glaring to be glossed over'. Daljeet Singh comes to the conclusion that far from being connected, Nathism and Vaishnavism on the one hand, and Sikhism on the other, were 'completely contrasted in their fundamentals, ideologies, goals, methodologies and world-views'. An 'activist amalgam' had never emerged in the history of Nathism and Vaishnavism for two thousand years when they existed side by side. There was little possibility of a Nath-Vaishnava synthesis emerging in the medieval centuries. There was thus no possibility of such a synthesis resulting in the 'activist' Sikh faith.[25]

For Daljeet Singh, McLeod's views about Sikhism, Nathism and Vaishnavism are 'not only without any basis but also betray an ignorance of the history and the essentials of the three systems'. McLeod places Guru Nanak within the Sant tradition, a synthesis of elements from Vaishnava Bhakti, Hathyoga and Sufism, which carries the implication that Guru Nanak did not originate a school of thought, or a set of teachings, and he cannot be regarded as the 'founder' of Sikhism. Simply because Guru Nanak used Nath terminology in his works, McLeod talks of 'influence'. Furthermore, he ignores the role of Sikh ideology in Sikh history and looks for other 'influences' on later Sikhism. All these views stand implicitly refuted by Daljeet Singh's own exposition of the Sikh movement.[26]

BASIC DIFFERENCES

The basic differences between McLeod and Daljeet Singh relate to (a) interpretation of Guru Nanak's ideology and (b) his status as the originator of the Sikh movement. The differences on the first arise essentially out of the degree of importance they give to the socio-political implications of Guru Nanak's ideas. McLeod does not ignore the importance of Guru Nanak's ideas for 'practical activity'. In his view, Guru Nanak discarded the idea of renunciation in favour of the life of a householder, and he disapproved of status based on caste or wealth. However, McLeod is silent about the implication of the idea of equality for the position of women, and he does not see any political implications of the verses known as *Babur-vani.* Clearly, thus, McLeod does not look upon 'practical activity' as central to his interpretation of Guru Nanak's ideology. In fact, he lays much greater emphasis on 'interiority' and the ideal of emancipation. Daljeet Singh interprets Guru Nanak's 'ideology' essentially in terms of practical activity, underlining all its socio-political dimensions. For him, *jivan-mukti* is a prelude to altruistic social action on a higher plane of consciousness. He has little to say about loving devotion (*bhakti*). The differences between McLeod and Daljeet Singh on the issue of ideology are basic and important.

On the issue of the status of Guru Nanak as the founder of Sikhism, Daljeet Singh looks upon his utterances as 'revelation', with the implication that he founded a totally new system which had nothing to do with the religious systems prevalent in India. McLeod refers to Guru Nanak's spiritual experience resulting in his conviction of a divine call to lead men to emancipation, but he does not attach much importance to the verses which are generally quoted in support of the revelatory status of his utterances. Daljeet Singh underlines the uniqueness of Guru Nanak's ideology; McLeod attaches importance to antecedents for his ideas in the context of his times. The *nirguna sampradaya* of McLeod's conception differentiates Guru Nanak from all his contemporaries except those who belonged to this *sampradaya.* What was common to all the Sant figures was, for instance, rejection of the idea of incarnation, belief in a God who is neither Rama nor Allah (but both), and the concepts of Nam, Shabad and Guru.

Not in the *Perspectives* but elsewhere Daljeet Singh has addressed himself to the question of relationship between Sikhism and the 'radical bhagats' like Kabir and Ravidas. They represented a distinct school of Bhakti. Kabir, for instance, rejected Vaishnavism as well as the Vedas. Daljeet Singh does not deny that the concepts of the Guru and the Shabad are common to Kabir and Guru Nanak. Both of them denounced the caste system too. However, the differences between them were more important. The goal of life for Kabir is a blissful union with God in which human personality is dissolved. Kabir believes in self-surrender, recommends ceaseless singing of God's praises, and virtually suggests withdrawal from the world. He is a firm advocate of *ahimsa.* With his ascetical bias, Kabir does not think well of women. In fact, he tends to bracket woman with *maya.* Consequently, the world for him becomes a snare. Above all, Kabir 'never took any interest in the social or temporal affairs of his times'. Thus, though theism was common to both Sikhism and the Bhagats and both rejected the fundamentals of Hinduism and denounced the caste ideology, the views of the Bhagats about the reality of the world-views of the two systems contrasted in terms of goals, methodologies and the social role of the liberated-in-life. On the whole, therefore, McLeod's 'Sant tradition' is closer to Vaishnavism and Shaivism than to Sikhism.[27]

In sum, McLeod gives primacy to what Guru Nanak shares with 'the Sants'. Daljeet Singh gives primacy to what he does not share. McLeod looks upon ideas as important in themselves. Daljeet Singh looks for their bearing on social action. McLeod seeks an understanding of Guru Nanak primarily in his environment and secondarily in his personality. Daljeet Singh sees his whole system as underpinned by his spiritual experience and moral vision. Daljeet Singh's interpretation is more comprehensive than McLeod's. It takes into account not only the words of Guru Nanak but also his acts.

A FRESH ASSESSMENT

Guru Nanak's comment on the contemporary social order, polity and systems of religious beliefs and practices is extraordinarily comprehensive. He talks of the whole society and a number of social practices; he comments on the government and administration and political events. He talks of the Vaishnavas, Shaivas and Shaktas.

He talks about the ascetics of various categories, including the Jain monks. He is equally concerned with Islam in both its orthodox and Sufi forms. It is significant to note that he looked upon contemporary religion in terms of three traditions: the Brahmanical, the ascetical and the Islamic. All the three stand bracketed in the *Japuji*, revealing Guru Nanak's basic attitude towards all the three: none of them was authoritative for him.[28] I have argued recently that, among other things, Kabir's ideology was less comprehensive than Guru Nanak's and it remained unrelated to institutionalization which, by contrast, was the fundamental concern of Guru Nanak.[29]

The egalitarian ideology of Guru Nanak, clothed in new institutuions, became the basis of a new kind of social organization. Institutionalization was reinforced and elaborated by his successors and the increasing number of Sikhs made them increasingly aware of their entity and importance. Their self-image in the *Guru Granth Sahib* reflects their growing sense of distinction. Guru Arjan's *halemi raj* represents the entire dispensation of Guru Nanak and his successors as the result of the new ideology of Guru Nanak. The essential constituents of this dispensation were the Gurus and the Sikhs, their institutions, their scripture and their sacred space, their organization and their human and material resources. This dispensation is an expression of God's grace for the redemption of humankind in the Kaliyuga. There is no question of its comparison with any other.[30]

The expression of this self-awareness can be discerned in the compositions of Guru Nanak. A new socio-religious fraternity has come into existence, consisting of his Sikhs who meet in congregation for worship led by the Guru. In his dialogue with Siddhs, Guru Nanak refers to his path as 'Gurmukh panth', with praises of God as 'our captial' and the all-pervading light of God as 'our support'; he who drinks the nectar of the Guru's instruction becomes acceptable in the divine court, attaining the state of liberation. Without the True Guru one does not find the Name and there can be no liberation without the Name. The right door and the right home is found through the Guru. There is only one door and only one path; the Guru is the ladder for the divine court.

The Guru and the Sikhs, together, represent a new kind of

association. This association is called *sangat, Gur-sangat, Gursant-sabha, sant sabha, Sikh sabha*, or *sadh sabha.* There is no doubt whatever that Guru Nanak is talking of the Sikh congregation. In the *sant-sabha* one finds the Guru and receives the gift of liberation. The One Name is recited in the *sat-sangat* and the True Guru gives the understanding that the Name alone is ordained by God. The praises of God in the *sant-sabha* become the best of acts in accordance with *Gurmat.* By turning to the Guru in the *sangat* of *sants* one acquires the merit of pilgrimage to sixty-eight places by the Guru's sight (*dars*). The *sevaks* of the Guru reflect on his *shabad* in *sat-sangat,* realize the divine presence within, and become the means of liberation for others. Rare are such persons in the world who reflect on the Guru's *shabad,* remain detached, swim (across the ocean of death and re-birth) and enable others to swim across. Misery and suffering end with joining the *gursant-sabha*; one is united with God. The Guru is like a sacred river: the dirt of sins is removed by bathing in this river (through the *sant-sabha* and by acting in accordance with the Guru's guidance). In the *gur-sangat* one recognizes God by recognizing his presence within.

The way in which Guru Nanak refers to the Sikhs, the Guru, and the *sangat* enables us to appreciate some of the other verses which have a close bearing on the new dispensation. He who receives the gift of God's praises (*sifat-salah*) is the king of kings. All the sixty-eight places of pilgrimage are at the feet of the Guru. The ones who praise the One Lord are good; they are imbued with the love of the *shabad*; their *sangat* is the source of bliss; they are honoured with the order of truth and the banner of the True Name; they recognize *hukam* and live in accordance with it. The *girhi* (*grihi*) *sevak* who is attached to *gurmat* is a Sikh who practises *bhagti* through *nam, dan,* and *isnan* as a householder.

The Sikh of the Guru rises above the considerations of caste (*jat-baran*) and family (*kul*) by reflecting on the *shabad* in accordance with the Guru's instruction. The persons who have discarded the distinctions of caste are actually the Sikhs of the Guru. In the Guru's presence, as in the court of God, there is no consideration for caste or birth. There is a kind of reversal. They who are alien to the Name have no honour. They who forget God are of low caste. The followers of Guru Nanak have lodged the True One in their hearts and they are never forgetful of the Name. They sing God's praises in congregation in the Guru's presence. Referred to as Sikhs, *sevaks* and *bhagats*, they have found the Guru's door; they are dedicated to *bhagti* through *nam*, *dan*, and *isnan*. They are householders, detached-in-attachment.

Guru Nanak's comment on certain customs suggests their replacement by new practices. The traditional songs for marriage should be replaced by hymns of joy (*sohila*) on the union with God. The singing of Guru Nanak's *Alahanian* was meant to replace the traditional modes of lamentation. Equally futile was the performance of *kirya* by the Brahmans for the dead man's sojourn in the next world which involves the feeding of Brahmans and the floating of lamps. There was no room for these traditional rites and rituals in the ideology of Guru Nanak. His comment carries the implication that singing of Guru Nanak's hymns relating to these rites and rituals are the alternative for his followers. This process was carried forward by his successors.

There is a divine sanction behind Guru Nanak's dispensation. He was called by God to his court and given the robe of true adoration with the nectar of the True Name. They who taste it through the Guru's instruction attain to peace. The ministrel spreads the message of the *shabad*. He utters the divine *bani* as he receives it from the Lord. 'I have spoken what you have made me speak'. They who follow the Guru's path reap the profit of liberation through the *bani* and the *shabad* of the Guru. 'Regard the *bani* of the true Guru as nothing but true; he is one with God.'

Guru Nanak himself looked upon the new dispensation as distinct from the known religious traditions. Compared with the *gian* of Guru Nanak's conception, the Vedas are found wanting. They talk of virtue (*pun*) and vice (*pap*) and of heaven and hell. The *gian* of Guru Nanak involves adoration of the greatness of the True One and the True Name. Truth is reaped by sowing truth and the devotee finds a place in the divine court. The Vedas talk of trade. *Gian* is the capital received through God's grace. Without this capital no trader can carry any merchandise with him. People talk of the four cosmic ages, each with its own way laid down in the Veda. For Kaliyuga, the Veda prescribed was the *Atharvana*. For Guru Nanak, however, the way to liberation in Kaliyuga is the one advocated by him:

appropriation of the Name, recognition of *hukam*, and living in accordance with the divine will.[31]

These unexplored dimensions of Guru Nanak's compositions suggest a clear sense of distinction based on ideology and praxis. Its counterpart is totally missing in the compositions of Kabir, Namdev and Ravidas who are regarded as the most important figures in the Sant Tradition.

NOTES

1. Gurdev Singh (ed.), *Perspectives on the Sikh Tradition*, Patiala: Siddharth Publications, 1986, 'Introduction', p. 5.
2. Ibid., p. 9.
3. W.H. McLeod, *Guru Nanak and the Sikh Religion*, Oxford: The Clarendon Press, 1968, pp. 163-77.
4. Ibid., pp. 177-89.
5. Ibid., pp. 189-207.
6. Ibid., pp. 207-26.
7. Ibid., pp. 149-51.
8. Ibid., pp. 151-7.
9. Ibid., pp. 158-61.
10. Ibid., p. 161.
11. W.H. McLeod, *The Evolution of the Sikh Community*, New Delhi: Oxford University Press, 1975, p. 5.
12. W.H. McLeod, *The Sikhs: History, Religion and Society*, New York: Columbia University Press, 1989, pp. 18-19; also pp. 22-31.
13. McLeod, *Guru Nanak and the Sikh Religion*, pp. 227-30.
14. Ibid., pp. 231-2.
15. Gurdev Singh (ed.), *Perspectives on the Sikh Tradition*, 'Introduction', pp. 15-21.
16. Daljeet Singh, 'Origin of the Sikh Faith', in ibid., pp. 55-8.
17. Daljeet Singh, 'Nathism', in ibid., pp. 59-75.
18. Daljeet Singh, 'Vaishnavism', in ibid., pp. 76-99.
19. Daljeet Singh, 'Sikhism', in ibid., pp. 100-7.
20. Ibid., pp. 107-15.
21. Ibid., pp. 116-24.
22. Ibid., pp. 125-30.
23. Daljeet Singh, 'Comparison of Nathism, Vaishnavism and Sikhism', in ibid., pp. 131-9.
24. Ibid., pp. 131-5.
25. Ibid., pp. 135-6.

26. Ibid., pp. 139-40.
27. Daljeet Singh, *The Sikh Ideology*, Amritsar: Singh Brothers, 1990, pp. 112-13.
28. J.S. Grewal, 'The Bani of Guru Nanak', *Lectures on History, Society and Culture of the Punjab*, Patiala: Punjabi University, 2007, pp. 101-29.
29. J.S. Grewal, 'Guru Nanak and his Panth', *The Sikhs: Ideology, Institutions and Identity*, New Delhi: Oxford University Press, 2009, pp. 3-21.
30. J.S. Grewal, *A Study of Guru Granth Sahib: Doctrine, Social Content, History, Structure and Status*, Amritsar: Singh Brothers, 2009, p. 156.
31. Ibid., pp. 134-7.

CHAPTER 3

Evolution and Transformation of the Sikh Panth

To account for change is considered by some historians as the primary concern of historical writing. Interest in the development of the Sikh Panth involved the issue of causation from the very beginning of Sikh Studies. The early European writers tried to account for the change in 'Sikhism' (equating the term with the Sikh Panth) in terms of external environment in the form of repression and persecution by the Mughal state. J.D. Cunningham introduced the factor of ideology with great emphasis on the relevance of the faith of Guru Nanak for the development of the Sikh Panth. He also extended the scope of social environment by adding 'ethnicity' to the political factor which was generally invoked by his predecessors. That the historians of the Sikhs have been conscious of the role of ideas and the role of environment in history of the Sikh Panth is evident from the key terms they have used. Gokul Chand Narang talks of the transformation of 'Sikhism', carrying the implication that Sikh ideology did not remain the same. Banerjee talks of the evolution of 'the Khalsa', taking into account the ideas of Guru Nanak and his successors but emphasizing the crucial role of social environment, including ethnicity. Teja Singh and Ganda Singh talk of 'transfiguration' deliberately to hammer the point that developments in Sikh history were inspired by one and the same ideology expounded by Guru Nanak and his successors. W.H. McLeod, does not deny the role of ideas in theory, but concentrates on the social environment in his exposition of 'institutionalization' and 'militarization'.

INSTITUTIONALIZATION DICTATED BY CHANGE IN ENVIRONMENT

One of the salient propositions which, according to Justice Gurdev Singh, have been put forth by McLeod to 'belittle the Sikh faith in the eyes of the English speaking people' and to 'shake the faith of the younger generation of the Sikhs in their religion' is that the ten Gurus never preached 'one set of religious doctrines or system'. Guru Amar Das created new institutions 'on the old Hindu lines'; this was precisely what Guru Nanak 'had spurned'. Then, from the time of the sixth Guru onwards, 'the teachings of Guru Nanak were completely given up in favour of a militant pose in response to socio-political situation'. The arming of the Panth was not the result of any decision by Guru Hargobind; it was due to the Jat influx in the Panth. The growth of militancy was due primarily to 'the impact of Jat cultural patterns and to economic problems which prompted a militant response'.[1]

For McLeod, Sikh history offers 'an unusually coherent example of how a cultural group develops in direct response to the pressure of historical circumstances'.[2] The historians like Harbans Singh, Khushwant Singh and Gokul Chand Narang think of the development of Sikh community as marked by 'three major stages'. The first of these was the work of Guru Nanak who founded Sikhism and the Sikh Panth. The second stage came in the time of Guru Arjan who incurred the displeasure of the Mughal authorities and suffered the death of a martyr. Guru Hargobind responded to the manifest intention of the state to put down the developing Panth by arming his followers and inculcating martial instincts. The religious teachings of Guru Nanak were retained but those who practised them were now prepared to defend their right to do so by 'military means'. The third stage began when Guru Gobind Singh fused the military aspect with the religious by promulgating the Order of the Khalsa on the Baisakhi of 1699 in view of the growing hostility of the hill *rajas* and the Mughal authorities and the weakness of his followers. In McLeod's view, the importance of these three stages cannot be disputed, but in this interpretation, the process starts too late and ends too soon. It oversimplifies the events and over-emphasizes their importance and significance. What is needed is 'a more radical concept of development' so that it can take into consideration 'a much wider range of historical and sociological phenomena' and it can express 'a much more intricate synthesis'.[3]

McLeod's essay on the evolution of the Sikh community tends to become a critique of 'the generally accepted understanding' of the subject rather than an exposition of the subject. He does not know whether or not any important development took place in the time of Guru Nanak's first successor, Guru Angad, from the viewpoint of evolution. In the time of Guru Amar Das, however, a large well with eighty-four steps was dug at Goindval and, according to the Sikh tradition, it was meant to serve as a *tirath*, or centre of pilgrimage for the Sikhs. This should not be interpreted as a doctrinal change because the compositions of Guru Amar Das are 'in accord with those of the first Guru'. However, Guru Amar Das may be seen as forging bonds 'other than those based upon religious belief'. The second generation of Sikhs was coming up, needing new bonds. Besides the pilgrimage centre, Guru Amar Das provided 'distinctive festival-days, distinctive rituals, and a collection of sacred writings'. McLeod thinks that Guru Nanak had 'rejected all of those'. His successor was compelled to return to them 'in different and more difficult circumstances'. His 'innovations' must be seen as 'concessions to social needs, not as a conscious shift in doctrine'. In fact, they were no innovations because Guru Amar Das did little more than 'reintroduce traditional Hindu customs'. McLeod qualifies this statement by pointing out that the 'pilgrimage-centre is in Goindval. It is not at Hardwar, nor at Kurukshetra, nor at any of the other places which his followers might have visited'. Furthermore, the Sikh Panth was developing a consciousness of 'its own separate nature'. Its links with Hindu tradition are very clear but so too is the intention 'to draw lines which will imply distinction'.[4]

Another development which appears to have started in the time of Guru Amar Das was an increase in the number of Jats in greater proportion than before. McLeod is prepared to 'allow a measure of doubt' on this point. He feels sure, however, that this development was taking place by the time of Guru Arjan (1581-1606). This inference is drawn from the founding of Tarn Taran, Sri Hargobindpur and Kartarpur, all of them in Jat territory. It is reinforced with reference to Jat influence in the Sikh Panth during the time of Guru Hargobind on the basis of the *Dabistan-i Mazahib*. Since the Sikh Gurus rejected the theory of caste and raised Jats to positions of high authority in the new Panth, the Jats felt attracted to it. They had improved their economic position by abandoning pastoralism in favour of agriculture and they could improve their social position by joining the Sikh Panth. Their egalitarian background also attracted them to a *panth* that was more egalitarian than the society around. Their entry was presumably facilitated by the fact that Khatris commonly served as teachers of the Jats. It is significant that Mughal hostility was developing during this period. It should not be attributed solely to Jahangir's orthodoxy, or to the prompting of his Naqshbandi courtiers. 'The increasing influence of the Jats within the Sikh Panth suggests that Jahangir and his subordinates may well have had good reason for their fears, and that these would not have related exclusively, nor even primarily, to the religious influence of the Guru.'[5]

The Jats constituted the elite of the Punjab villages as peasants and landlords because of their considerable energy.[6] They did not enter the Panth empty-handed. They would have been bearing arms many years before the death of Guru Arjan. Their mere presence would impart to the Panth a militant appearance. In any case, maintains McLeod, 'the arming of the Panth would not have been the result of any decision by Guru Hargobind'. However, the death of Guru Arjan may have persuaded his son and successor of 'the need for tighter organization'. The influence which the Jats enjoyed in the time of Guru Hargobind increased with the passage of time. Therefore, the growth of militancy within the Panth 'must be traced primarily to the impact of Jat cultural patterns'.[7] To this cause were added others later. A militant response could be due to 'economic problems'. McLeod does not elaborate this point. Another factor mentioned is the Shakti cult of the hill culture. It penetrated the Jat culture of the plains and 'produced yet another stage in the evolution of the Panth'. For Guru Gobind Singh the characteristic name of God was All-Steel (*sarabloh*), and he used a two-edged sword for stirring baptismal water. In his writings and in those which were produced at his court there are constant references to the mighty exploits of the Mother Goddess, one of the most notable being his own *Chandi di Var.* It is in the works of Guru Gobind Singh and 'in the developments which followed his death' that McLeod sees the influence of the hill culture most plainly.[8]

In a recent work McLeod talks of the various attitudes and theories in relation to the issue of transformation in Sikh history. The theory which has long dominated Sikh historiography on this point was first put forth by J.D. Cunningham in a rather stirring statement:

> It was reserved for Nanak to perceive the true principles of reform, and to lay those broad foundations which enabled his successor Gobind to fire the minds of his countrymen with a new nationality, and to give practical effect to the doctrine that the lowest is equal with the highest in race as in creed, in political rights as in religious hopes.[9]

As a recent example McLeod quotes Jagjit Singh:

> The Sikh movement was an organic growth of the Sikh religion or the Sikh view of life. The founding of the Sikh Panth outside the caste society in order to use it as the base for combating the hierarchical setup of the caste order, and the creation of the Khalsa for capturing state power in the interests of the poor and the suppressed, were only a projection, on the military and political plane, of the egalitarian approach of the Sikh religious thesis.[10]

For McLeod, this view of the Sikh movement implies that the Gurus envisaged a particular pattern for the Panth and the actual form which it assumed corresponded to their intentions. It gives too much credence to conscious intention and to the role of ideas in history to leave any scope for the operation of other factors. McLeod's own view is that the progressive development of the Panth 'must be explained not merely in terms of purposeful intention but also (and in significant measure) by the influence of social, economic and historical environment'.[11]

INSTITUTIONALIZATION AS IDEOLOGY IN OPERATION

Jagjit Singh's essay on the militarization of the Sikh movement begins with 'some specific points raised by McLeod'. The proposition that 'the arming of the Panth could not have been the result of any decision of Guru Hargobind' and that 'the growth of militancy within the Panth must be traced primarily to the impact of Jat cultural patterns and to economic problems which prompted a militant response', raises three issues: the question of leadership and initiative, the impact of Jat cultural patterns, and the relevance of economic problems which prompted a militant response.[12]

To underline that the Sikh Gurus were the real leaders of the community, Jagjit Singh makes the general proposition that there were three turning points in Sikh history during the times of the Gurus: a break with the ascetic tradition, rejection of the caste structure, and militarization of the Panth. All the three changes represented departures from the prevailing tradition. 'Only a purposeful and determined leadership could have brought about the said departure.'[13] If Jahangir felt concerned about the growing Jat following of Guru Arjan, why does he say in his *Memoirs* that he ordered the Guru's execution because of his blessing to the rebel Prince Khusrau? If the mere entry of Jat elements into the Sikh ranks could arouse the fear of the authorities, a similar action should have been taken against the Minas and the Handalis whose following also included Jats. But this was not done, because they did not challenge the political authorities of the day: they did not have the socio-political concerns which the Sikh Gurus had. Moreover, there is no basis for McLeod's assumption that the Jats were armed and the Khatris were not. Among the Cherished-Five, who were willing to lay down their lives for the tenth Guru, there was only one Jat. When the Khalsa were divided into five fighting units in the early eighteenth century, two of them were headed by Khatris (and one by a Ranghreta). This does not suggest Jat dominance. In any case, Jagjit Singh feels convinced that 'the initiative and determination for carrying on the armed struggle against the established state was invariably that of the Guru and not that of his followers'.[14]

Jagjit Singh does not accept the proposition that the Jats who came to pay homage to the Guru came armed. When the Sikhs complained to Guru Gobind Singh that they were harassed on their way to Anandpur, they were advised to come armed. The bearing of arms could not have been a Jat peculiarity; no exception could be made in their case if the policy of the state was to keep the populace disarmed. Jagjit Singh argues further that the Jats started joining the Sikh movement in large numbers only after the decision of Guru Hargobind and Guru Gobind Singh to militarize the Panth. Therefore it was a case of Sikh ideology influencing the Jats and not of the Jat character moulding the Sikh movement. The inspiration from Sikh ideology turned even the castes lower than the Jats into a fighting class. Evidently, 'the Sikh movement needed no goading from the Jats for its militarization'.[15]

About the impact of economic conditions on militarization, Jagjit Singh states that the responses of the Jat peasantry and the lower castes to economic problems were not uniform. Nor did they produce the same or similar results. The Sikh political struggle lasted for three generations and it was waged by the lower castes as much as by the Jat peasantry. What sustained their struggle was a distinct ideology with clear-cut revolutionary aims. 'It is, therefore, idle to trace the source of a revolutionary movement, divorced from its ideology and leadership, to sheer economic causes.'[16] Equally pointless in Jagjit Singh's view is the conjecture that the synthesis of the Devi cult with the Jat culture had much to do with the evolution of militancy in the Sikh Panth. The cult of the Goddess was not dominant in the countryside inhabited by the Sikhs. If the Devi cult inspired the Jats who visited Anandpur, why did that inspiration disappear afterwards?[17]

In the second part of his essay, Jagjit Singh takes up the question of militarization in a wider context. He can see no signs of any shared motivation in the Jat organization 'which could urge the Jats for sustained action, much less for a political adventure'. The Jats of the Sikh tract 'lacked even the *gotra* solidarity beyond the village level'.[18] There was a spirit of equality among the Jats, and it was reinforced by the *bhaichara* system of land tenure. However, this egalitarianism was confined to their clans. They conformed to 'the hierarchical pattern of the caste system', having no qualms about submitting to the higher castes or dominating the lower ones. Jagjit Singh maintains that like the peasantry in general, the Jats lacked political aspiration and initiative.[19]

By contrast, what bound the Sikhs together in the Sikh Panth was 'the primacy of the Sikh ideals rather than any caste, clan or regional interests and sentiments'. The creation of the Khalsa provided the 'real organizational base'. Recruitment to this order was strictly on an individual and voluntary basis. 'No caste or clan loyalties were involved, because no one could become a member of the Khalsa brotherhood without being baptized, and no one could be baptized without taking the five vows.' The *misls* were not formed 'on the basis of caste or clan affiliation'. The spirit of equality among the Sikhs was altogether different from that of the Jats. A product of Sikh ideology, the Sikh egalitarian approach was not marked by dichotomy towards the higher or lower castes. The Sikh movement was an egalitarian revolution in social as well as political terms. If its objectives were not fully realized, its actual achievement was so considerable that it can be looked upon as more significant than the French Revolution. It enabled the individuals belonging to the lowest castes in the traditional Indian society to come into political power which gave them a new social status. The genesis of the Sikh revolutionary spirit thus lay essentially in the religion of the Sikhs which stands for social and political equality.[20]

Jagjit Singh concludes that McLeod's hypothesis about the militarization of the Sikh movement is untenable on more than one count. There is no reason to infer that Jats were the predominant element in the Sikh Panth when Guru Hargobind decided to militarize the movement; they were not predominant in the battles of Guru Gobind Singh, or those of Banda Bahadur. There is nothing to suggest that the Jats used to come armed when they came to pay homage to the Gurus. The keeping of sword was not a speciality of Jat culture and, therefore, the Sikh movement could not have borrowed it from the Jats. Nor did the Sikh movement need the inspiration of the Devi cult for its militancy. The Sikh militancy must by viewed in relation to the Sikh egalitarian revolution: it was geared to achieve the essential purpose of capturing political power.[21]

CONTEMPORARY EVIDENCE

A major difference between Jagjit Singh and McLeod is about the number and proportion of Jats in the Sikh Panth. Jat predominance in the Panth is firmly established in the census of 1881. This census did not record the non-Singhs or the so-called Sahajdharis. The general statements on the composition of the Sikh Panth during the late eighteenth century indicate Jat preponderance. Among the Sikh chiefs of this period, there was one from a family of carpenters and another from a family of distillers of liquor; all the other important

Sikh chiefs were Jat and they numbered over a score. The presence of Sikhs with low caste background in the Panth during the early eighteenth century is beyond any doubt, but their proportion in the Sikh population could not be very large. Jat representation among the Masands is mentioned by the author of the *Dabitan-i Mazahib* in the mid-seventeenth century, and Jats are mentioned by Bhai Gurdas among the eminent Sikhs of the Gurus. Coming after an overwhelming presence of Khatris among the prominent Sikhs, this evidence can be taken as an indication of the increasing number of Jats. What exactly was their proportion in the Sikh Panth in the late sixteenth or the early seventeenth century cannot be estimated from the evidence available at present. It leaves much scope for hunches and conjectures. It is interesting to note that whereas McLeod attaches importance to their presence in the Sikh Panth before the martyrdom of Guru Arjan, Jagjit Singh looks upon the measures of Guru Hargobind as a factor responsible for their increased number in the Panth. Significantly, the eminent Sikhs of Guru Arjan in the *Vars* of Bhai Gurdas are predominantly Khatri. The *Dabistan* was written a few decades later.

McLeod says in a footnote that he owes the hypothesis of the Shakti cult to Niharranjan Ray but Ray talks only of the prevalence of the cult. McLeod's view that the Shakti cult of the hills blended with the Jat culture of the plains to produce one more synthesis to accentuate militancy is based essentially on the evidence of the *Dasam Granth*, consisting of a few works attributed to Guru Gobind Singh and the largest bulk to others. The Goddess figures less prominently in the *Dasam Granth* than Krishna and Rama. They symbolize legitimacy of the use of physical force in the cause of righteousness. In this respect, the *Dasam Granth* elaborates and reinforces the idea present in the *Guru Granth Sahib* that God protects his saints and destroys the wicked. Sikh literature of the late eighteenth and the early nineteenth century suggests considerable importance of the Goddess as well as Rama and Krishna. But the evidence is merely suggestive. McLeod does not elaborate or substantiate his point. The nature and extent of the influence of the *Dasam Granth* on the Sikhs during the eighteenth century has not yet been studied.

The condition of the peasantry in the early seventeenth century was by no means depressed. If anything, the Sikh *zamindars* were as affluent as the Sikh traders. Finally, the historian who has underlined the importance of the agrarian crisis for the Sikh revolt against the Mughals has also emphasized that religious ideology provided the source of cohesion for the oppressed Sikh peasantry.[22]

Jagjit Singh makes no comment on McLeod's view of evolution or institutionalization before we come upon what they call 'militarization'. McLeod ignores the time of Guru Angad which in his view was merely a continuation of the position in the time of Guru Nanak. Even so, it would mean consolidation. McLeod appears to assume that Guru Nanak had established no institution whereas there is clear evidence of congregational worship in the *bani* of Guru Angad and of *langar* in the *savayyas* of the Bhatts. Furthermore, Guru Angad used the epithet 'Nanak' for himself, carrying the declaration that he was holding his office in continuity with Guru Nanak. Guru Angad equated the Guru with Guru Nanak and his *bani* with *shabad* or divine self-revelation. He popularized the Gurmukhi script. All these measures were of great relevance and importance for the evolution of the Sikh Panth.

For the time of Guru Amar Das, McLeod notices the *baoli* and invokes the Sikh tradition to argue that a place of pilgrimage was being created. There is no contemporary or near contemporary evidence that the *baoli* was regarded as sacred. The Sikhs of Guru Amar Das would come to Goindval for his *darshan* which was regarded as a pilgrimage: 'there is no *tirath* like the Guru'. 'The Guru is the pool of nectar (*amritsar*).' McLeod goes on to call it a 'Hindu' practice as if only 'Hindus' had places of pilgrimage. In fact, he assumes that Guru Nanak, like the Sants of McLeod, was opposed to institutionalization. It needs to be emphasized, however, that Guru Nanak's idea was to replace what he saw as effete institutions with new ones. The institutions of Gurdwara and the Granth as well as the institution of Guruship can be traced to Guru Nanak. McLeod talks of distinctive festival days as if the Sikhs were continuing with the celebration of Baisakhi and Diwali in the traditional way. Distinctive 'rituals' are indicated by Guru Nanak in his *Alahaniam* and *Sohila*. The fact that he collected his own *bani* and the Sikhs used it for worship would show that Guru Amar Das's 'collection of sacred writing' was a logical step forward. These were no 'innovations' because institutionalization was a primary concern of Guru Nanak, and not becaue Guru Amar Das was reintroducing only traditional Hindu customs as contended by McLeod.[23]

McLeod concedes that the Sikh Panth was developing a consciousness of 'its own separate nature' but adds that links with Hindu tradition are equally clear. The historians of the Sikh faith and the Sikhs in the sixteenth century have seldom studied the compositions of Guru Nanak's successors for evidence. Rejection of the Brahmanical, ascetical and Islamic traditions is as emphatic in the compositions of Guru Amar Das as in the compositions of Guru Nanak, and Guru Amar Das declares that the path of Guru Nanak is the only valid and efficacious path to liberation in the Kaliyuga.[24]

Historians of the Sikhs refer to the Sikh Panth as having become 'a state within the state' by the early seventeenth century. The institution of Guruship, the compilation of the Granth by Guru Arjan as the Sikh scripture, the organization of the Sikhs through the *masand* system, their financial resources and independence, the towns founded by the Gurus, especially Ramdaspur, the Harmandar and the tank called *amritsar*—all these features of the development of the Sikh Panth appear to be relevant for describing it as 'a state within the state'. It is generally not known or appreciated that Ramdaspur was an autonomous town with which the Mughal administrators had nothing to do. Guru Arjan refers to the divine rule (Ram-raj) established in Ramdaspur. Another term that he uses is *halemi raj*, not for Ramdaspur but for the entire dispensation of Guru Nanak and his successors in which there is no oppression and no coercion. This dispensation is the means of redemption of humankind. It is, thus, not 'a state' 'within the state' but a parallel dispensation with no territorial limits.[25]

On the whole, McLeod's attempt at explaining the development of the Sikh Panth and its politicization without any reference to Sikh ideology has resulted in a dubious hypothesis. In any case, his explanation tends to be mono-causal, which is always an inadequate explanation of a complex historical development.

NOTES

1. Gurdev Singh (ed.), *Perspective on the Sikh Tradition*, Patiala: Siddharth Publications, 1986, 'Introduction', p. 9.

2. W.H. McLeod, *The Evolution of the Sikh Community*, New Delhi: Oxford University Press, 1975, p. 2.
3. Ibid., pp. 3-5.
4. Ibid., pp. 7-9.
5. Ibid., pp. 9-10, 12.
6. Ibid., pp. 10-11.
7. Ibid., pp. 12-13.
8. Ibid., p. 13.
9. W.H. McLeod, *The Sikhs: History Religion and Society*, New York: Columbia University Press, pp. 35-8.
10. Ibid., pp. 39-40.
11. Ibid., p. 40.
12. Jagjit Singh, 'The Militarization of Sikh Movement', in *Perspectives on the Sikh Tradition*, pp. 325-6.
13. Ibid., p. 327.
14. Ibid., pp. 328-31.
15. Ibid., pp. 331-9.
16. Ibid., pp. 339-41.
17. Ibid., pp. 341-2.
18. Ibid., pp. 342-7.
19. Ibid., pp. 347-54.
20. Ibid., pp. 378-9.
21. Ibid., p. 380.
22. Irfan Habib, *The Agrarian System of Mughal India 1556-1707*, New Delhi: Oxford University Press, 2002 (paperback, rpt.), pp. 393-4. In the case of the Sikh revolt 'religion almost entirely replaced caste as the cementing bond among rebel ranks'.
23. J.S. Grewal, 'Guru Nanak and his Panth', *The Sikhs: Ideology, Institutions and Identity*, New Delhi: Oxford University Press, 2009, pp. 3-21.
24. J.S. Grewal, *A Study of Guru Granth Sahib: Doctrine, Social Content, History, Structure and Status*, Amritsar: Singh Brothers, 2009, pp. 140-5; 54-6, 73-4, 83-4, 89-90, 95-6, 108-11, 115, 119-20, 123.
25. Ibid., pp. 149-56.

CHAPTER 4

The Khalsa *Rahit* and Doctrines

An important proposition attributed to W.H. McLeod by Justice Gurdev Singh relates to the Khalsa *rahit.* McLeod does not accept the traditional account of the founding of the Khalsa on the Baisakhi day of 1699. He has 'compulsive reasons for skepticism'. He goes to the length of saying that 'the traditions relating to the period of Guru Gobind Singh must be, in some considerable measure, set aside. The slate must be wiped clean and must not be re-inscribed until we have ascertained just what did take place during the eighteenth century'. According to McLeod, the Sikh code of discipline (*rahit maryada*) and symbols were evolved during the eighteenth century 'as a result of gradual growth' and not of any pronouncement by Guru Gobind Singh on the Baisakhi day of 1699.[1]

Justice Gurdev Singh does not say anything about the doctrine of Guru Panth in McLeod's informed conjecture. He objects only to McLeod's treatment of the doctrine of Guru Granth. He thinks it is unfair on McLeod's part to suggest that *Granth Sahib* was installed as Guru to serve as cohesive force for the leaderless community after the execution of Banda Bahadur and not because of an injunction of Guru Gobind Singh. Justice Gurdev Singh believes that there is an unbroken tradition that Guru Gobind Singh vested Guruship in the *Granth Sahib* in perpetuity, deliberately putting an end to the line of personal Gurus. There is another reason for rejecting McLeod's suggestion. The martial Khalsa could have chosen the *Dasam Granth* as a more suitable instrument of cohesion, if cohesion was their concern. They owned and revered the *Granth Sahib* because of the Guru's injunction and 'never entertained the idea of any individual succeeding the Tenth Guru, nor of a successor other than Guru Granth Sahib'.[2]

AN EVOLUTIONALARY HYPOTHESIS

McLeod refers to the year 1699 as the high point of Sikh tradition which presents the institution of the Khalsa on the Baisakhi of that year as the climax of all that had preceded and the fount of all that followed. According to the Sikh tradition, Guru Gobind Singh reflected on the perils of his situation and the weakness of his timid followers, and he devised a plan to infuse a spirit of strength and unity. He summoned his followers from far and wide on that day and they came in thousands. When the Baisakhi fair was in full swing the Guru suddenly appeared before his followers and, with his sword raised aloft, demanded the head of any of his Sikhs. A hush fell upon the concourse and he had to repeat the demand. A loyal Sikh came forward and he was conducted into a tent. The thud of a descending sword was heard outside and the Guru reappeared with his bloodstained weapon to demand a second head. Another Sikh came forward and the process was repeated till the number reached five. Then the Guru drew back the side of the tent, and horror turned into amazement when the gathering observed corpses of five decapitated goats beside the five alive volunteers.[3]

Guru Gobind Singh is believed to have delivered a sermon on this occasion in which he declared the five volunteers to constitute the nucleus of a new brotherhood, the Khalsa. Those who chose to join this brotherhood were to abandon pride of caste, the old scriptures and places of pilgrimage and the worship of minor gods and goddesses, and *avtars.* They were to follow only God and the Guru. A new baptismal ceremony was adopted by mingling sweets with water, stirring it with a two-edged sword in an iron bowl. This *amrit* was administered to the five foundation members. They administered the same baptism to the Guru himself. All others who were willing to join the brotherhood and to accept its discipline were invited to take baptism, and many thousands of all castes came forward to take it. The discipline promulgated at this time included dissociation with five groups of people consisting of all those who had at different times disputed succession to Guruship, together with their successors and followers, and all those who cut their hair. Various other prohibitions were enjoined, notably tobacco, meat from animals slaughtered in the Muslim fashion, and sexual intercourse with Muslim women. Members of the new brotherhood were to wear the 5 Ks as symbols and to add 'Kaur'. Thus was established a powerful brotherhood which in unity, loyalty, and courage was to struggle against overwhelming odds, survive the cruellest of persecution, and rise ultimately to political supremacy in less than a century on the ruins of the Mughal power and Afghan pretensions.[4]

McLeod says that 'we find a clearly defined Khalsa Panth with formulated religious doctrines, a coherent code of discipline, and the strong conviction that it has been born to rule' at the end of the eighteenth century. But was this the position immediately after the creation of the Khalsa, or even in the second decade of the eighteenth century? McLeod is extremely skeptical. He argues that the eighteenth century on the whole was a critical period, marked by warfare, disaster and eventual triumph. The Khalsa responded to its distinctive problems by finding distinctive solutions. In both tribulation and success the expanding Khalsa was ever seeking a self-understanding and a self-definition. Therefore, the traditional explanation must be evaluated in the light of what we find in the period extending from the institution of the Khalsa in 1699 to the capture of Lahore by Ranjit Singh in 1799. Our knowledge of this period is rather limited. 'Traditions abound but so too do compulsive reasons for skepticism. What we do know, however, indicates that the traditions relating to the period of Guru Gobind Singh must be, in some considerable measure, set aside. The slate must be wiped clean and must not be reinscribed until we have ascertained just what did take place during the eighteenth century.' In other words, there are features of the received tradition relating to the Baisakhi of 1699 which were actually incorporated later. It does not mean that the entire tradition stands rejected. 'We may be sure that something certainly did happen on the Baisakhi day of 1699, and that some of the traditions will eventually turn out to be substantially accurate.' The fact that the Khalsa did eventually establish an effectual claim to represent the orthodox form of the Sikh Panth lends considerable support to the traditional hypothesis. However, McLeod maintains that it does not follow that every feature of the tradition has to be literally and uncritically accepted.[5]

In McLeod's view, the whole of Khalsa *rahit* or the code of discipline was not promulgated on the Baisakhi day of 1699 and it did not continue unchanged. If we examine the written codes or the

Rahitnamas of the eighteenth century we find that 'the conventions of the Khalsa were in the process of evolution during this period'. The question of 5 Ks, for instance, was not 'finally settled until well into the eighteenth century'. Furthermore, McLeod sees the influence of Jat cultural patterns in the evolution of the five symbols. The same complex of Jat culture and contemporary circumstances accounts for the explicit prohibitions which find a place in the Khalsa discipline. The prohibitions directed against the consumption of *halal* meat and intercourse with Muslim women do not reflect the 1699 situation. In fact, they accord well with the eighteenth-century struggle against the Mughals and, more particularly, against the Afghans. Presumably, the same situation accounts for the ban on the use of tobacco. More examples could be cited to support the view that the discipline evolved gradually during the course of the eighteenth century in response to inherited patterns and the impact of contemporary events. The *Rahitnamas* invoke the authority of Guru Gobind Singh in order to acquire the sanction needed to enforce the code. Their contents cannot be treated as a record of the actual instructions of Guru Gobind Singh.[6]

Justice Gurdev Singh criticizes McLeod for suggesting that the doctrines of Guru Panth and Guru Granth arose out of the need for cohesion during the eighteenth century, and not because of Guru Gobind Singh's explicit injunction. According to the Sikh tradition, the functions of the Guru after the death of Guru Gobind Singh were vested jointly in the body of the believers (the Khalsa Panth) and the scripture (the *Granth Sahib*). McLeod suggests that this tradition could 'perhaps be a retrospective interpretation, a tradition which owes its origin not to an actual pronouncement of the Guru but to an insistent need for maintaining the Panth's cohesion during a later period'.[7] For McLeod there were several cohesive ideals and institutions at work during the eighteenth century, like Amritsar as a religious centre, a distinctive Sikh historiography, and the conviction that 'the Khalsa shall rule' (*raj karega khalsa*). More important, however, was the Khalsa code of discipline. But the most important was the doctrine of Guruship.

McLeod states that the personality of Guru Nanak was a cohesive factor of continuing importance in two distinct ways. There was a line of successors deemed to be one person in ten manifestations in different bodies, a torch lit from another torch giving the same flame. The function of this doctrine was 'a simple extension of the first Guru's authority' and it continued to serve a cohesive role until the death of Guru Gobind Singh. Another cohesive factor was provided by the *Janamsakhis*. They provided a single focus of common loyalty for all members of the Panth. Distinctive ceremonies for birth, marriage and death tended to reinforce cohesion. This purpose was served also by the appointment of Masands to various *manjis*. The cohesion was weakened by the disputes about succession to Guruship in the seventeenth century. The question of the Panth's cohesion became exceedingly acute after Guru Gobind Singh's death.[8]

In the literature of the early seventeenth century McLeod sees indications of 'a developing doctrine of the Guru Panth, a doctrine which affirms that in the absence of the personal Guru the local sangat, or congregation, within any area possesses the mystical power to make decisions on his behalf'. After the death of Guru Gobind Singh, especially after the failure of the personal leadership of Banda Bahadur, 'a new theory of leadership was needed'. Three things were necessary for a new theory to be effective. It should permit ample freedom to small scattered groups; it should preserve the ideal of a unified authority; and it should possess a powerful sanction. An answer to this need was provided by the doctrine of the corporate and scriptural Guru. During the eighteenth century it was the corporate aspect of the doctrine which possessed the greater importance and which served to impart a measure of cohesion to the community. Later, however, the doctrine of the corporate Guru 'effectively lapsed and an undisputed primacy was given to the scriptural Guru theory, a primacy which continues to this day'.[9]

Dispersion of the Sikhs during the eighteenth century was relevant for the emergence and crystallization of the doctrine of Guru Panth. Like the Sikh *sangats*, or congregations, the Khalsa *jathas* were widely scattered and within both of them the instrument of authority increasingly came to be identified with the group itself. The Guru was present in the *sangat* and the corporate voice was accordingly the voice of the Guru. 'The Guru, though absent in the body, is very much present in spirit wherever his words are devoutly sung'. They who participate in this *kirtan* (communal singing) with genuine devotion manifest the Guru's own presence in their assembly and when they speak as an assembly 'they speak as the Guru'. For any particular purpose, five representatives (*panj piare* or the 'five beloved') could be chosen temporarily to exercise the authority of the *sangat.* However, the military needs and the extension of the Khalsa influence shifted the Panth's primary interest from the *sangat* towards the *jatha,* and later towards the *misl.* This shift carried with it the belief in the presence of the Guru in the *jatha.* 'As military and eventually political issues began to command an increasing attention, the doctrine was extended to cover the quasi-parliamentary sessions of the Sarbat Khalsa.' McLeod goes on to add that the need of cohesion did not end with the local *sangat.* The *misl sardars* also had their problems to solve and the doctrine of Guru Panth proved to be well suited to their needs. This doctrine found explicit expression in the institution of the *gurmata,* rooted in the theory 'that corporate decisions of the Sarbat Khalsa were to be regarded as the word of the Guru with the full force of his authority to back it'. Although essentially a response to military needs, the doctrine expressed in an unusually coherent form the more general religious doctrine of the Guru's continuing presence within any congregation of his disciples.[10]

McLeod further suggests that when Ranjit Singh extinguished 'the *misl* system' and replaced it with a strong and relatively centralized monarchy, the need of the doctrine of Guru Panth was no longer there. The monarchy itself now assumed the cohesive role as the *Sarkar Khalsa,* or the rule of the Khalsa. In this situation the *gurmata* could only be regarded as a positive hindrance. As a result, the theory of the Guru Panth quickly lapsed into disuse, leaving the issue of religious authority to the doctrine of scriptural Guru, the *Guru Granth.* 'All other questions previously determined by reference to the corporate Guru were meanwhile appropriated by Ranjit Singh and later by his British successors.' The way was being prepared for the ascendancy of the doctrine of Guru Granth by the custom of deciding all *gurmatas* in the presence of the scripture during the eighteenth century itself. In fact, it was due to this reason that the *gurmata* held a special sanctity. In the time of Ranjit Singh, the scripture assumed primary religious authority.[11]

LIMITATIONS OF THE HYPOTHESIS

Justice Gurdev Singh invokes the authority of Hari Ram Gupta in the *Perspective on the Sikh Tradition* to refute McLeod.[12] Gupta draws largely upon 'secondary' works. A single secondary work is cited in more than half of the references. Gupta himself is rather modest about his linguistic competence. The major contemporary sources cited by him, having been written before the event, have nothing to say about the 'founding of the Khalsa'.[13]

For the founding of the Khalsa, Hari Ram Gupta relies heavily on Macauliffe, supplemented indiscriminately by the works of M'Gregor, Bhai Vir Singh, Bhagat Lakshman Singh, Kartar Singh, and Indubhusan Banerjee. The authority of Sainapat is invoked but only to make the point that Guru Gobind Singh 'invited the entire audience' at Naina Devi to attend 'the grand function' at Anandpur later.[14] The early nineteenth-century authority of Bhai Santokh Singh is cited by Gupta on the point that 'the tobacco leaf resembles the ear of a cow, and so the Guru prohibited its use'.[15] Bhai Nand Lal's authority is invoked on the point that the Sikhs should not worship tombs, graves and relics of cremation.[16] Thus, the evidence cited by Gupta relates to points which have no bearing on Justice Gurdev Singh's criticism of McLeod.

Gupta gives a fanciful interpretation of 'the meaning of the Khalsa' without citing any evidence whatever. The salutation '*Wah Guru ji ka Khalsa, Wah Guru ji ki Fateh*', according to him, was given by Guru Gobind Singh to the Khalsa with a view to 'giving to the Singhs an optimistic view of life in the midst of trials and tribulations which lay ahead of them'. The Guru was in search of a word that should have 'the sanctity of five and the presence of God'. This word was *Khalsa*. It consists of five letters: *khe, alif, lam, swad* and *alif* or *hae*. The first stands for *khud* or oneself; the second for both Akal Purkh and Allah; the third for *labbaik*; the fourth for Sahib or Master; and the fifth for *azadi* or freedom (if it is taken to be *alif*) and for *huma* (if it is taken to be *hae*), the legendary bird about which it was believed that 'every head it overshadows, in time bears a crown'. Gupta takes his fanciful interpretation to a breaking point when he explains *labbaik*: the Singhs enter into pleasant conversation with the Lord; God himself asks the Singhs 'What do you want from me? Here am I. What would you have?' and the Singhs reply, 'Lord! give us liberty and sovereignty'.[17]

After this, it does not come to us as a surprise that, according to Gupta, Guru Gobind Singh evolved the 'formula of five' for the guidance of the Khalsa: five beliefs, five symbols, five vows, five deliverances, and five rules of conduct. The five beliefs are: belief in Akal Purkh, *Guru Granth*, the greetings *Wah Guru ji ka Khalsa Wah Guru ji ki Fateh*, and Guru Nanak's *Japji*. These 'beliefs' amount only to four. The five symbols are easier to count and remember: *kesh*, *kangha*, *kirpan*, *kara* and *kachh*. It may be pointed out that Gupta cites no evidence on this point. The five vows are: not to cut hair, not to smoke, not to eat *halal* meat, not to wear a cap, and not to worship tombs, graves and relics of cremation. The five deliverances are: *dharam nash*, *karam nash*, *janam nash*, *sharam nash* and *bharam nash*. Only for the first of these, Gupta provides an 'authority': Bhagat Lakshman Singh's biography of Guru Gobind Singh in English. The five rules of conduct are: starting every enterprise after a prayer, helping one another and the Panth, practising riding and using arms, not coveting another's wife. Only for the last of these Gupta cites an authority, that of Macauliffe.[18] Gupta's account of the birth of the Khalsa, thus, is not based on contemporary or near contemporary sources. Justice Gurdev Singh's impression turns out to be entirely wrong.

It does not follow, however, that McLeod's hypothesis is valid. He places the Khalsa conviction to rule in the course of the eighteenth century but by now it is clear that the *raj karega khalsa* couplet has come down from the days of Guru Gobind Singh.[19] McLeod suggests that all the 5 Ks came from the Jat cultural patterns in combination with the developments of the eighteenth century. But the evidence for wearing *kesh* is contemporary and McLeod himself pairs *kangha* with the *kesh*. Similarly, there is contemporary evidence for bearing arms, and we know that Guru Gobind Singh attached great importance to the sword. McLeod pairs *kara* with the sword. There is contemporary evidence for *kachh* (drawers), and also for ban on the use of tobacco. Much of McLeod's interpretation sprang from his view that the *Gursobha* was not written in 1711, a view which he has modified. The Rahitnamas too were placed by McLeod several decades later than the time of Guru Gobind Singh, though he concedes by now that at least one Rahitnama was composed a few years after Guru Gobind Singh's death. In any case, the ban on sexual intercourse with 'Muslim' women could come later, but not much later. The ban suggests not merely a state of armed struggle but also a situation in which the Khalsa could be victorious (because the possibilities of such 'intercourse' were there normally for the victors). This situation definitely emerged for the first time in the time of Banda Bahadur. Furthermore, the ban was an extension of the general injunction against extramarital intercourse. It may be interesting to add in this connection that Qazi Nur Muhammad admires the Singhs specifically for their restraint: they never molest the women of the vanquished. McLeod mentions the ban on *halal* meat not only as a later introduction but also as an anti-Muslim gesture. It must be remembered, however, that *jhatka* was the customary Indian method of decapitating goats for meat. The *halal* meat carried a religious significance which could make it unacceptable to Guru Gobind Singh and the Khalsa. Without denying the evolutionary character of the *rahit*, it is possible to maintain that much of the *rahit* is contemporary or near contemporary with the tenth Guru.

According to Justice Gurdev Singh, Ganda Singh has examined the question of succession to Guru Gobind Singh in all its details, and has 'unreservedly rejected the suggestion that an individual had succeeded the Tenth Master as the Guru of the Sikhs'. Ganda Singh's assertion is 'unequivocal' that before his death Guru Gobind Singh had 'installed Granth Sahib as the perpetual Guru of the Sikhs'. Harbans Singh has examined the issue from another angle as well. The word was to take the place of the Guru sooner or later. When Guru Gobind Singh declared the *Guru Granth Sahib* to be his successor, the 'inevitable' took place. The Guruship could be made lasting 'only through the Word'. These conclusions are believed to be based on ample historical evidence.[20]

Ganda Singh's essay was written primarily to establish that Guru Gobind Singh died on 6-7 October 1708 and he was actually cremated at Nander. This could demolish the myth created by Sewa Das, an Udasi sadhu, in his *Parchian*, written in 1708, that Guru Gobind Singh had bodily gone to heaven. This myth was reinforced by Koer Singh in his *Gurbilas* in 1751. Ganda Singh's second concern was more important: to authenticate beyond doubt that Guru

Gobind Singh did not appoint anyone of his followers to succeed him and commanded his followers to look upon the Word of the great Masters 'embodied in their holy book, the *Granth Sahib*, as their Guru, from then on known as the *Guru Granth Sahib*.[21]

At the end of his essay Ganda Singh refers to a *Bhatt Vahi* quoted by Guninder Kaur in her *Guru Granth Sahib: Its Physics and Metaphysics*, which contains an entry regarding the *Guru Granth Sahib* as the future Guru of the Sikhs. The earliest literary work cited by Ganda Singh himself is the *Sri Gur Sobha*, written by Sainapat in 1711. A day before his death, Guru Gobind Singh responded to a question of his followers by announcing that he had 'bestowed his physical form upon the Khalsa' (*bakhsh dio khalis ko jama*) and that 'the Limitless and the Eternal Word was the True Guru' (*satguru hamara apar apara shabad bichara ajar-jaran*). The Guru's last message and his final commandment in unmistakable terms and clear words was that he did not appoint any particular individual as his successor and that 'the Khalsa under the guidance of the Divine Word – the *gurbani* – was to be the future physical and spiritual representative of the Guru'. That the Sikhs accepted this creed is evident from the *Rahitnama* of Bhai Nand Lal in which it is stated by the Guru himself that his two forms were the *Granth* and the Khalsa. In the *Gurbilas Chhevin Patshahi*, generally believed to have been written in 1718, the author invariably uses the epithet 'Guru Granth'. In another manuscript in Ganda Singh's possession, relating to the death of Guru Gobind Singh, the Sikhs are entrusted to *sri sahib* and the *shabad* 'the great Word, as given in the Granth Sahib'.[22]

From the second half of the eighteenth century comes the evidence of Koer Singh, Kesar Singh Chhibber and Sarup Das Bhalla. The statements quoted from Koer Singh are to the effect that Guru Gobind Singh did not appoint anyone as his successor; the entire Khalsa had been entrusted to the protection of 'the Wielder of the Sword' (*asiketu*); the Khalsa should accept 'the embodiment of the Word' (*shabad ka rup*) as their shield; and they should recognize *Sri Granth* as the ever-present *darshan* of the Guru. Koer Singh also mentions how the *Adi Sat-Guru* was accepted by Guru Gobind Singh as the Guru. The phrase 'Guru Granth' occurs in Koer Singh's work at several places. Kesar Singh Chhibber refers to the last commandment of Guru Gobind Singh: 'The *Granth* is the Guru;

you hold the garment (seek the protection) of the Timeless God' (*bachan kita Granth hai Guru lar pakro Akal*). Sarup Das Bhalla states that '*Sri Guru Granth Sahib* was recognized in place of the Guru'. The eighteenth-century Persian and English writers cited by Ganda Singh refer to the end of personal Guruship after the death of Guru Gobind Singh. Sohan Lal Suri, the author of the *Umdat ut-Tawarikh*, written in the reign of Ranjit Singh, mentions the *Granth Sahib* as the Guru. Ghulam Muhiyuddin refers to the last commandment of Guru Gobind Singh: 'There is no difference between the Guru and the Granth.' This is repeated by Ernest Trumpp in his *Adi Granth* and by Bhai Kahn Singh Nabha towards the end of the nineteenth century. Some other writers mention the Khalsa as well as the *Granth Sahib* as the Guru after the death of Guru Gobind Singh. Among them are Cunningham, Muhammad Latif, Sant Singh (the author of the *Bayan-i Khandan-i Karamat Nishan-i Bedian*), and Macauliffe.[23]

Harbans Singh goes into the process by which the *Granth Sahib* was prepared by Guru Arjan and says that he enjoined the Sikhs to regard the *Granth* as equal with the Guru and to make no distinction between the two. The word enshrined in the Holy Book was always revered by the Gurus and their followers as of divine origin. One day the Word was to take the place of the Guru. The line of personal Gurus could not have continued for ever. 'The inevitable came to pass when Guru Gobind Singh declared the Guru Granth Sahib to be his successor.' Ever since the passing away of Guru Gobind Singh, the understanding and conviction of the Sikh community has been that 'the Guru Granth is Guru Eternal'. Harbans Singh labours this point because, among other things, certain cults among the Sikhs still owning personal *gurus* asked for authentic evidence to the effect that Guru Gobind Singh had named the *Granth Sahib* his successor.[24]

Apart from the evidence of Bhai Nand Lal, Sainapat and Koer Singh, which is cited by Ganda Singh, Harbans Singh cites three sources which are supposed to be contemporary or very close to the time of Guru Gobind Singh. One of these is the *Bhatt Vahi* to which Ganda Singh made only a reference. This evidence is a part of the collection of *vahis* (*bahis* or scrolls) made by Giani Garja Singh, but not yet published. These *vahis* were written in a script called *bhatakshri*, 'a kind of family code like *lande* and *mahajani*'. The only scholar to have worked on these materials was Giani Garja Singh. The entry quoted by Harbans Singh, with translation in English, comes from the *Bhatt Vahi Talauda Pargana Jind.* In this entry, Guru Gobind Singh places five pice and a coconut before the *Granth Sahib,* bows before it, and then tells the *sangat*: 'It is my commandment: Own Sri Granthji in my place. He who so acknowledges it will obtain his reward. The Guru will rescue him. Know this as true'. Another document cited is a letter of Mata Sundari, which is now in the village of Bhai Rupa. In this document the Sikhs are told to believe only in ten Gurus and not in Banda Bahadur and Ajit Singh, to believe only in the Timeless One, and to go only to the ten Gurus 'in search of the Word'. The Guru 'resides in *sabda*'. The third piece of evidence cited is that of a Sanskrit manuscript in which Guru Gobind Singh declares that the *Granth,* 'which itself is the doctrine of the Guru, shall be your teacher. This is what you should see; this is what you should honour; this is what should be the object of your discourse'. Referring to the evidence of Sainapat, Harbans Singh adds that, along with the *Guru Granth Sahib,* 'the Khalsa was now the person visible of the Guru'.[25]

The essential difference between the early evidence used by Ganda Singh and Harbans Singh lies in the latter's use of the *Bhatt Vahi* which makes explicit reference to 'Sri Granthji' in connection with succession to Guru Gobind Singh. They both accept the authenticity of this source. However, the nature and character of *Bhatt Vahis* has not yet been examined critically to evaluate their authenticity. Both Ganda Singh and Harbans Singh place the *Gurbilas Patshahi Chhevin* in the second decade of the eighteenth century. It has been argued by some other scholars that this work belongs to the early nineteenth century. Therefore, the most reliable early evidence used by Ganda Singh and Harbans Singh is the *Sri Gur Sobha* of Sainapat. At the time of its writing, *shabad-bani* was embodied only in the *Adi Granth.* The equation of the *Adi Granth* with the Guru is quite explicit in the *Rahit-Nama* of Chaupa Singh which is placed by McLeod around the mid-eighteenth century, but it appears to be earlier. This *Rahit-Nama* equates the Khalsa with the Guru, and the Guru with the Khalsa. It is clear, therefore, that the enunciation of Guru Gobind Singh crystallized into the doctrines of Guru Granth and Guru Panth in the early eighteenth century.

IN THE FINAL ANALYSIS

Both on the Khalsa *rahit* and the doctrines of Guru Granth and Guru Panth, McLeod's hypothesis is seriously flawed. That the *rahit* could not remain static is rightly underlined by him, but this general statement is not very helpful if we treat all items of the *rahit* as of equal importance. Sikh literature related to *rahit*, including the *Rahitnamas*, lays great stress on the religious life of the Khalsa and this part of the *rahit* establishes a profound continuity with the pre-Khalsa tradition. With regard to the changes introduced by Guru Gobind Singh, by far the most important were the baptism of the double-edged sword, the unshorn hair, the epithet Singh, the bearing of arms, and the duty of fighting for the establishment of Khalsa Raj. On all these points there is contemporary evidence. Of all the negative injunctions, by far the most frequent and emphatic is the one with regard to the use of tobacco. The evidence for this injunction too is contemporary.

About the 5 Ks, the basic items are *kesh*, *kirpan* and *kachh*, for which there is contemporary evidence. The remaining two, that is *kangha* and *kara* even according to McLeod, can go with *kesh* and arms. What is new is the formula of 5 Ks and not the substantive items. McLeod may turn round and say that he was talking of the formula appearing later, but this is not what he is saying in *The Evolution of the Sikh Community*. His suggestion that these symbols came from the Jat culture is equally off the mark. The real point about the *kesh* is not merely 'long hair' but the sanctity attached to the *kesh*. There is no evidence that the Jats attached any sanctity to the *kesh*. The *kachh* can never be associated with them. Despite their supposed fondness for arms, the *kirpan* had no fascination for them and there is no evidence of its use by the Jats.

McLeod's hypothesis about Guruship was actually based on the assumption that the *Sri Gur Sobha* was composed in 1741. He has now come round to the view that it can be placed in 1711. Therefore, on both the Guru Panth and the Guru Granth we have contemporary evidence. The author of the *Sri Gur Sobha* was a court poet of Guru Gobind Singh. Meanwhile, quite a few scholars have accepted McLeod's hypothesis. Therefore, it needs to be underlined that it is not valid. Neither was the doctrine of Guru Granth preceded by the doctrine of Guru Panth nor was the doctrine of Guru Panth completely dropped in the early nineteenth century. McLeod is also mistaken in asserting that the doctrine of Guru Panth found no advocates in the early nineteenth century.

NOTES

1. Gurdev Singh (ed.), *Perspectives on the Sikh Tradition*, Patiala: Siddharth Publications, 1986, 'Introduction', p. 9.
2. Ibid., pp. 9-10, 28-9.
3. W.H. McLeod, *The Evolution of the Sikh Community*, New Delhi: Oxford University Press, 1975, pp. 14-15.
4. Ibid., pp. 15-16.
5. Ibid., pp. 16, 19.
6. Ibid., pp. 50-3.
7. Gurdev Singh (ed.), *Perspectives on the Sikh Tradition*, pp. 10, 29.
8. McLeod, *The Evolution of the Sikh Community*, pp. 39-44.
9. Ibid., pp. 44-5.
10. Ibid., pp. 46-9.
11. Ibid., p. 50.
12. Hari Ram Gupta, 'Guru Gobind Singh's Creation of the Khalsa in 1699', in *Perspective on the Sikh Tradition*, pp. 149-79.
13. Ibid., pp. 149-61.
14. Ibid., p. 161.
15. Ibid., pp. 170, 178 n. 60.
16. Ibid., pp. 170, 178 n. 61.
17. Ibid., pp. 168-9.
18. Ibid., pp. 169-72.
19. Karamjit K. Malhotra, 'The Earliest Manual on the Sikh Way of Life', in *Five Centuries of Sikh Tradition: Ideology, Society, Politics and Culture* (Essays for Indu Banga), ed. Reeta Grewal and Sheena Pall, New Delhi: Manohar, 2005, pp. 55-81.
20. Gurdev Singh (ed.), *Perspectives on the Sikh Tradition*, 'Introduction', p. 30.
21. Ganda Singh, 'Guru Gobind Singh designates Guru Granth Sahib to be the Guru', in ibid., pp. 183, 193-4, 196.
22. Ibid., pp. 186-7, 191-2.
23. Ibid., pp. 194-210.
24. Harbans Singh, 'The Guru Granth Sahib: Guru Eternal for the Sikhs', in ibid., pp. 211-17, 223-4.
25. Ibid., pp. 217-23.

PART TWO

IDENTITY AND SOCIAL ORDER

CHAPTER 5

The Early Sikh Identity

The Panth of Guru Nanak is prophesied in the *Janamsakhis*. It was obviously a post-eventum prophecy. Therefore, it is safe to assume that the existence of this Panth was taken for granted in the early seventeenth century when the *Janamsakhis* were being compiled. Even an outsider like the author of the *Dabistan-i Mazahib* could write on the 'Nanak-Panthis' by the middle of the century. He used an alternative epithet for them: the 'Sikhs-of-the-Guru' (*Gursikhan*). This takes us back to the time of Guru Nanak. The Sikhs of the Guru, literally, had come into existence in the lifetime of Guru Nanak. The outsiders referred to them as Nanak-Panthis not only because they believed in Guru Nanak as the fountainhead of their faith but also because all his successors represented the same light and the same office: they were 'Nanak'.

The *Dabistan-i Mazahib* is one of the earliest Persian works to be translated into English. A fresh translation of the portion dealing with the Nanak-Panthis has been published recently in *Sikh History from Persian Sources*. For the author of this work, the Nanak-Panthis or the Sikhs of the Guru were a distinct entity. Their identity was based on their peculiar doctrines and institutions, and their social attitudes, including their sense of commitment to matters temporal as well as spiritual.

DISTINCT BUT NOT UNIFORM

W.H. McLeod has discussed Sikh identity directly in *Who is a Sikh*? The starting point for his discussion is Guru Nanak's doctrine of the Name (*nam*) in which incarnation, idol worship, temples, pilgrimages and sacred scripture stand rejected. Interior discipline excludes exterior custom. The Name finds its supreme manifestation in the creation and, thus, it is the ever present and all-pervading presence of God. To perceive this presence is to gain access to the means of mystical unity with God, a condition of supreme peace which ends the cycle of transmigration. The practice of *nam simran* involves regular meditation which reveals the presence of God all around and within oneself. The condition of emancipation could be achieved during the present life within one's inner being. The message of *nam simran* was reinforced by the first four successors of Guru Nanak and consequently it was embodied in the *Adi Granth*. It commands the same loyalty within the modern Sikh Panth.[1]

No particular pattern of doctrines or devotional practices could by itself create followers, emphasizes McLeod. The primary basis of the community of followers which gathered around Guru Nanak was his personality, which inspired veneration. The hymns he composed had an attractive quality. To this legacy was added his decision to choose a successor, establishing a lineage and ensuring a succession that was recognized as legitimate till the death of Guru Gobind Singh. This decision gave rudimentary organization to the Panth of Guru Nanak and ensured its continuing existence beyond his lifetime. Guru Amar Das established the *manji* system which later developed into the *masand* system. Through accredited deputies the Gurus ensured contact with congregations of Sikhs which had increased in numbers and were too distant for personal contact. Another 'innovation' traditionally attributed to Guru Amar Das is compulsory commensality (*langar*) for which men and women of all castes sat in rows to eat together in the *dharamsala*. The institution of *langar* 'plainly matched the intention of Guru Nanak'. This convention struck at a major aspect of caste, 'thereby advancing the process of defining a distinctive Sikh identity'.[2]

Another variety of 'innovation' is said to concern external ritual, which might appear to be in conflict with Guru Nanak's intention, like the digging of a sacred well (*baoli*) at Goindwal to serve as a place of pilgrimage for Sikhs. The decision to excavate the sacred pool which marked the founding of Amritsar is also attributed to Guru Amar Das. Two other examples of 'external ritual' introduced by Guru Amar Das relate to festival days and compilation of sacred books (*pothis*) which can be regarded as the prototype of the sacred scripture compiled by Guru Arjan in 1603-4. The martyrdom of Guru Arjan in 1606 marked a significant turning point in the development of the Panth, but the continuities remained important so much so that what can be said about the early Sikh Panth 'applies with equal force to its seventeenth-century successor'. The faith remained essentially the same in terms of its doctrinal content. The permanence of the Panth was ensured by 'ritual and administrative measures introduced by the early Gurus'.[3]

Were the Nanak-Panthis (the followers of Guru Nanak and his successors) conscious of distinctions which the historians can observe in the objective situation of the Panth? What was their self-image? For McLeod, the *Adi Granth* and the works of Bhai Gurdas give 'a normative response', an interpretation of the message of the divine Name. There is another range of understanding in the *Janamsakhis.* 'Baba Nanak' represents piety and spiritual wisdom as the supreme exemplar of the only sure path to deliverance. The title 'Guru' makes its appearance when Guru Nanak's role as the Great Teacher is brought into focus. 'All who acknowledge him as Master and practise the simple discipline which he enjoined will find peace in this present world and liberation in the hereafter'. The *Janamsakhi* understanding of the key-doctrine of the *nam* is much less subtle and the practice of *nam simran* means repeating 'Guru, Guru'. The path of Guru Nanak is summed up in the ideal of *nam-dan-isnan.* The concepts of *sangat* and *kirtan* are emphasized in the *Janamsakhis* 'as a regular feature of the corporate life of the Nanak-panth'. The *dharamsala* conferred 'a distinctive identity on the Nanak-panth'. The Vaishnavas have their temple, the Yogis have their *asan*, the Muslims have their mosque, and the Nanak-Panthis have their *dharamsala.* They also have their unique salutation in addition to the distinctive ideal of *nam-dan-isnan.* The *Janamsakhi* recognition of Guru Angad as the chosen successor and the prominence given to Guru Nanak's disputations with the representatives of other recognized *panths* are said to be two more indicators which strengthen the impression that the emergent Sikh Panth was in the process of 'drawing its own boundaries and defining its own distinctive identity'.[4]

The positive indications of distinctive identity are then qualified by features which imply hesitation. The sense of separateness is diminished by implied comparisons with Vaishnavas, by the suggestion that Guru Nanak might adopt various 'panthic' identities, and the occasional claim that he regarded himself as a Hindu. As refracted through the *Janamsakhis*, the Nanak-Panth was in the process of self-definition but had 'not yet achieved a clear awareness of separate identity'. It was in the process of 'becoming' without a sure awareness of 'having arrived'. McLeod underlines, however, that this was the popular view. In the works of Guru Arjan and Bhai Gurdas there is a strong sense of Panthic identity. The intellectual elite within the Sikh Panth moved more rapidly towards a sense of distinct identity than the general body of the Panth. The 'boundaries' might be indistinct 'but not the centre'. McLeod maintains that this difference between the elite and the bulk of the Panth would persist throughout the history of the Panth, with a difference of degree during the past hundred years or so.[5]

In general terms, Sikh identity in the early Panth was defined 'by a common loyalty, by common association, and by common practice'. Veneration for Guru Nanak and his legitimate successors underwent a progressive change as the image of Nanak changed from 'Baba' to 'Guru' and to 'True King'. All who regarded themselves as Sikhs acknowledged fealty to the spiritual lineage from Guru Nanak to Guru Gobind Singh. The custom of gathering at a *satsang* for regular *kirtan* sessions was also a specific and essential feature of the Nanak-Panthi identity. It was greatly strengthened by the practice of singing 'the Gurus' own compositions', which gave to the Nanak-Panthi gathering 'its own distinctive identity'. The nature of the Sikh *kirtan* encouraged a particular concept of the divine Word. Together with the compilation of the *Granth* by Guru Arjan, it prepared the way for a fundamental doctrine. 'The doctrine which it foreshadowed affirms the eternal presence of the mystical Guru within the sacred scripture and wherever his followers gather as an assembly of the Panth'.[6]

McLeod goes on to add that true to the teachings of the Gurus, Sikh assemblies intended to be open to men and women of all castes. Identities based on caste were not obliterated but caste had nothing to do with access to liberation. The most important constituents of the Panth were Khatris, Jats and Tarkhans. A significant number of outcastes was added much later. The *Janamsakhis* make it perfectly plain that Sikhs were to live as ordinary men and women. 'Deliverance from the cycle of transmigration was to be achieved by remaining in the world, not by withdrawing into ritual or ascetic seclusion'. During the seventeenth century, external influences began to impinge significantly on the Panth and led eventually to a 'radical reshaping'. McLeod's reference here is to the emergence of the Khalsa identity from 1699 onwards.[7]

DISTINCT BUT 'UNFIXED'

Harjot Oberoi gives a summary account of the early Sikh Panth. Guru Nanak's fundamental teaching was that 'those who wished to transcend the constant cycle of birth and death should live in accordance with the will of the Creator, which meant spending life on earth immersed in *nam simran* or remembrance of the Divine Word'. In his 'interior religiosity' there was no place for austerities, penances, pilgrimages or formal worship at established religious places such as mosques and temples. This 'minimalist teaching' was hard to sustain. Significant axes of identity were provided by the successors of Guru Nanak: 'allegiance to the person of Guru Nanak and his nine successors; identification with their teachings (*bani*); the foundation of congregation (*sangat*); the setting up of elaborate pilgrim centres at places like Goindwal and Amritsar; the convention of a communal meal (*langar*) and the compilation by Guru Arjan of an anthology, commonly known as the Adi Granth'. This last development turned the Sikhs eventually into a 'textual community', a group who ordered their everyday life in correspondence with the text.[8]

Oberoi looks upon the compositions of Bhai Gurdas as exceptionally good for 'understanding early Sikh identity'. A Sikh should rise daily before dawn, bathe, and recite the sacred compositions of the Gurus; he should visit a *dharamsala* and participate in the activities of the assembled *sangat*. He should practice the precepts of the Guru to lead a harmonious life. Bhai Gurdas underlines 'the centrality' of belief and abiding faith in the person and utterances of the Sikh Gurus, and the need to visit the *dharamsala*; he lays repeated emphasis on the *sangat* as 'a body of practitioners in faith'. He hammers the point that Muslims miss the correct path, and Hindus are caught in the snare of empty rituals and social inequalities. The solution for him is 'a Sikh way of life, a distinctive third path to human problems'. The ideal man is *gurmukh*, a follower of the Sikh Gurus and their doctrines. There is a suggestion here of a new idiom, a separate community of believers, and 'reworking of the social order'. Though Bhai Gurdas is not 'completely unaware of boundaries', he is said to have made no explicit statement on 'an independent Sikh identity'.[9]

The implicit nature of Sikh identity in the writings of Bhai Gurdas, according to Oberoi, becomes explicit with the emergence and dissemination of the Janamsakhi literature. This genre would not have grown enormously 'had there not been a growing awareness of issue of identity'. In one anecdote in a Janamsakhi Guru Nanak is commissioned by God to launch his own distinct religious community in the world. The members of this community were to be known as Nanak-Panthis. They were to have their distinctive salutation, like the salutation of the Vaishnava Panth, the Sanyasi Panth, the Yogis and the Muslims. As the Vaishnavas had their temples, the Yogis their *asans*, the Muslims their mosques, so the followers of Guru Nanak would have their *dharamsalas*. The ideal of the Nanak-Panthis was to do *nam*, *dan* and *isnan*, and they were to keep themselves unspotted while remaining householders.[10]

Having said all this, Oberoi goes on to state categorically that Sikhs were still in the process of evolution and growth, and the category 'Sikh' was still flexible, problematic and substantially empty. There was still critical space at the centre and periphery of the community which had not been 'appropriated and shaded in the colours of a dominant religious ideology'. The label 'Sikh' had not yet become 'hegemonic'.[11] What Oberoi has in mind is that there was no single way of expressing association with the Sikh movement. The term 'Nanak-Panth' was related to the person of Guru Nanak. He is 'always transforming and wandering'. He delights in mixing up the sartorial styles of Muslim *pirs* and Hindu ascetics, 'chooses companions and disciples whose castes and religion do not match'. In consonance with this 'kaliedoscopic persona', Nanak is called Guru, *bhagat*, *sadh*, *faqir*, *darvesh*, and *pir*. The logic underlying this multiplicity is 'to convey the ever-transforming personality of Nanak'. Oberoi concludes that there was 'no fixed Sikh identity in the early-Guru period', just as there was no fixed image of Guru Nanak in the *Janamsakhis*.[12]

According to Oberoi, the verse of Guru Arjan which ends with the line 'I am neither Hindu nor Muslim' cannot be interpreted to mean that the Sikhs formed a 'distinct religious community'. This verse was written in response to an older verse by Kabir and re-inforces his thought. Both speak of rejecting 'the received Hindu and Muslim orthodoxies, of not taking part in their formal modes of worship and pilgrimage, of finally asserting that the mystery of the Supreme is to be resolved in one's heart'. They were not 'discounting one set of categories to embrace a new set of labels'.[13] Similarly, the collation of the *Adi Granth* cannot be interpreted as a declaration of 'the separation of the Sikh Panth from other religious traditions'. The *Adi Granth* did become a key cultural marker of Sikh ethnicity, but much later than the seventeenth century. Such anthologies of devotional literature were not uncommon in the seventeenth century, and their compilers and readers did not perceive the texts as statements of 'sectarian intent'. Oberoi gives the example of a manuscript compiled in Rajasthan twenty-one years before the *Adi Granth*, known to scholars as the *Fatehpur manuscript*. The bulk of this manuscript is made up of Sur Das's compositions. But it contains the works of thirty-five other poets, including Kabir, Namdev, Ravidas, Parmanand and Kanha. That this manuscript has common features with the *Adi Granth* is clear enough: both these anthologies have diverse contributors and 'heterodox textually'. Oberoi concludes that these features of the *Adi Granth* were 'far more the manifestation of a fluid Sikh identity than a signifier of exclusivity'. For Oberoi, on the whole, thus, the identity of the early Sikh Panth remained 'unfixed'.[14]

DISTINCT WITHOUT QUALIFICATION

Daljeet Singh's approach to Sikh identity is different from that of McLeod and Oberoi. His first concern is to demonstrate the 'sovereignty' and 'independence' of Sikh religion. Guru Nanak's spiritual experience and his conception of God acquire crucial importance in this context. He had experienced God and his dynamic and creative character. God is immanent as well as transcendent; he has a will; he is the ruler and protector of the universe; he is the source of all values and virtues; and he has interest in human life. Sikh ideology springs from this conception of God. The experience of blissfulness is there, but far more important is active participation in social life after that experience. Human deeds become all important: truthful living is higher than truth. The goal of life is not merely *nirvana* but carrying out the altruistic will of God. The *gurmukh* is the person who carries out God's will. He lives God in life. He accepts all challenges of life and supports the cause of the weak and the righteous. Thus, Sikh ideology explains the dynamism and ethical activities of the Gurus and their followers. This gives distinctive identity to Sikhism and the Sikhs.[15]

Unlike Sikhism, the Indian systems are said to be dichotomous, drawing a clear line between spiritual and empirical life; they encourage monasticism, asceticism and withdrawal; they look upon the world as a distraction; they regard celibacy as a virtue; they consider woman as a temptress; they value *ahimsa*; and they support the system of caste, untouchability and pollution. Judaism and Islam are whole life systems (not dichotomous), but they are exclusive in character. Also, at a later stage in their history, monasticism and asceticism appear as an important phenomenon. Christianity accepts involvement in life but prescribes non-resistance to evil. Monasteries and nunneries appear in its history later, and still later secularism and communism which pose a virtual dichotomy between religious and empirical life. Sikhism is a whole life system, like Judaism and Islam; but it is free from exclusiveness, and leaves no room for monasticism and withdrawal. The concept of *miri-piri* and the ideal of *sant-sipahi* are an integral part of Sikhism. Asceticism, celibacy and downgrading of women are rejected in Sikhism together with caste ideology and *ahimsa*. All these features were rejected by Guru Nanak who organized 'a whole-life system of householder' participating in all walks of life and remaining socially responsible. Thus, Sikhism from the very beginning was different from both Indian and Semitic religions, maintains Daljeet Singh.[16]

The Sikh scripture, *Guru Granth Sahib*, is 'the most emphatic pronouncement about the distinct and independent identity of Sikhism'. This separate and authentic compilation was needed because the Gurus had 'a new thesis' to give to mankind. It closed the door to all possible controversies, and embodies a complete and final message.[17] Sikhism, furthermore, was different from the *bhakti* religions (including those of Kabir, Namdev, Ravidas and others): it was meant to be the basis of a new society or Panth. For this purpose Guru Nanak established centres to ensure that practical shape was given to his ideals. He started the institution of *langar* 'which was wholly revolutionary in his times'. Not only Shudras but also Muslims could sit at the same platform. Guru Nanak started the institution of succession so that the social order he had visualized and initiated should develop further. His successors created new centres as part of a widening network. The idea was to knit the Sikhs together as a separate Panth or people. Guru Hargobind raised the institution of the Akal Takht. The Sikh society presented a parallel socio-political organization. Tension with the state grew and led ultimately to open clashes. Guru Gobind Singh organized the institution of *sant-sipahi*, the Khalsa, with the *amrit* ceremony. The wearing of *kirpan*, which was prescribed for the Khalsa, indicated that 'the Sikhs had neithter to abandon or relax in regard to their responsibility of reaction against injustice and oppression, nor had this society to relapse into a group of *sants* unconcerned with the problems of the empirical life and their responsibility to solve them'. Thus, from the very start the Gurus were aiming at the creation of 'a people imbued with the ideal of *sant-sipahi*, based on *miri-piri* or whole-life doctrine of Guru Nanak'. The identity of the Sikhs was recognized by the political rulers of the day. Both in the field of religion and that of social growth this identity was unquestionable. 'The institution of the Panth started by Guru Nanak, the system of succession and the Ten Masters who nurtured and matured the Sikh society, the institution of *langar*, brotherhood and equality, coupled with the institution of work and production, can be explained only on the assumption that Guru Nanak had a separate thesis which was calculatedly sought to be implemented'. Having discussed identity in terms of spiritual experience, the conception of God, ideology, the character of Sikhism, scripture, and the Panth, Daljeet Singh seeks to emphasize that 'Sikh identity is not in any manner artificial, it is the one that was clearly created and proclaimed by the Gurus themselves'.[18]

THE THREE VIEWS COMPARED

We can look back and see that McLeod takes into account the doctrines, institutions, rituals, and the social character of the Sikh Panth as well as the consciousness of a distinctive identity among the Sikhs. The doctrine of *nam* in the hymns of Guru Nanak was much more sophisticated than in the Sant tradition. Logically, the concept of *nam simran* also differed. The goal was emancipation which could be achieved in one's lifetime as a householder. Renunciation and withdrawal were rejected. The path was open to men and women of 'all castes'. McLeod does not mention 'all creeds'. Rejection of caste distinctions was given a tangible shape in the *langar.* McLeod seems to suggest as if this institution was introduced after Guru Nanak, though it was in harmony with his attitude towards caste. The compositions of Guru Nanak and his successors were used for *kirtan.* Here, again, the implication seems to be that the practice was introduced after Guru Nanak. The practice of using the hymns of the Gurus for *kirtan* led to the compilation of sacred hymns, resulting in the subsequent compilation of the *Adi Granth*, which got linked up with the doctrine of Guruship. He sees great significance in Guru Nanak's decision to choose a successor. However, he does not refer to the doctrine of interchange between the position of the Guru and the Sikh, which was based on Guru Nanak's decision and which eventually became the basis of the doctrine of Guru Panth. Among 'external rituals' McLeod mentions centres of pilgrimage but there is no reference to life-cycle rituals in which Guru Amar Das and Guru Ram Das were carrying forward the message of Guru Nanak. McLeod does not refer to the adoption of Gurmukhi as the script for the sacred scripture, which was a prominent mark of distinction. This critique of McLeod's position would show that the case for a distinct Sikh identity is actually far stronger than what he makes out. McLeod refers to Guru Nanak being presented as a 'Hindu' in certain situations. Since the connotation of 'Hindu' in the seventeenth century was not the same as in the twentieth, the Janamsakhi evidence has to be interpreted as his denial that he was a 'Muslim'. McLeod leaves the impression that the consciousness of distinct identity was quite clear among the intellectual elite, or at the centre, but it was not equally clear among the mass of the Sikhs, or at the periphery.

Oberoi's conception of Guru Nanak's 'minimalist teaching' minimizes the significance of what Guru Nanak had said and ignores what he had done. He notices the development of the Sikh Panth as an objective reality and what he regards as markers of distinction, but he does not attach much importance to them. In his view, Bhai Gurdas was not altogether unaware of boundaries but did not make an explicit statement on independent Sikh identity. However, Bhai Gurdas's conception of Sikhism as a distinctive path and the Sikh *sangat* as a peculiarly Sikh institution is nothing short of a declaration of distinct religious identity. The *sangat* of Bhai Gurdas is synonymous with the Panth. Oberoi appears to give some special meaning to 'religious identity' which he does not clarify in this part of his book. Elsewhere, however, he appears to imply that religious identity means the social identity of a religious community. This assumption introduces ambiguity into his own analysis.

Oberoi expects that only one term should have been used for the Panth of Guru Nanak by Bhai Gurdas and not the terms like Gurmukh-Panth, Nirmal-Panth and Gursikh as well as Nanak-Panth. Except Gursikh, these terms do refer to the Panth. The multiplicity of epithets used for the Panth does not change the identity of the Panth itself, just as the multiplicity of epithets used for God does not compromise the unity of Godhead. Similarly, the persona of Guru Nanak presented by Oberoi ignores the essential thrust of the *Janamsakhis* on the uniqueness and universality of Guru Nanak's message. The Panth of Guru Nanak is projected as different not only from the Muslims but also from the Panths of the Vaishnavas, the Sanyasis and the Yogis (which are now regarded as 'Hindu'). The epithets of Guru, *bhagat*, *faqir*, *darvesh* and *pir* are meant to convey the idea of his status to different audiences. This convention does not diffuse the persona of Guru Nanak. The consistency of his ideas brings his personality into sharp relief.

The hymn of Guru Arjan emphasizes the distinction of religious ideas and practices, and is not merely a rejection of 'orthodoxy'. It has to be interpreted in the context of the compositions of Guru Arjan and his predecessors. Oberoi's interpretation is too constrictive to be valid. Despite diverse contributions, the primacy given to the *bani* of the Gurus in the *Adi Granth* is quite unmistakable. Furthermore, the *Adi Granth* contains the 'contributions' of 'Shaikhs' as well as 'Bhagats'. Would Oberoi suggest that the Sikhs regarded themselves as both 'Muslim' and 'Hindu'? If 'heterodox textuality' means something different from diverse authorship and content, Oberoi does not make it clear. If the implication is that there are doctrinal contradictions in the text of the *Adi Granth,* Oberoi does not demonstrate. His insistence on 'unfixed' identity of the Sikh Panth does not appear to be an inference drawn from empirical evidence but an a priori assumption. His interpretation of the evidence used becomes forced and far-fetched. The statement that 'identity' of the early Sikh Panth was fluid and unfixed essentially means that the Sikh Panth was not distinct from the 'Hindu' society. This poses the problem of defining 'Hindu' society in the sixteenth and seventeenth centuries, and of placing 'religious communities' or Panths in that society. But Oberoi does not do this. His conception of the 'Indic' blurs the issue. Consequently, the term 'Nanak-Panth' or 'Sikh Panth' appears to lose all meaning for Oberoi though it carried a lot of significance for the contemporaries, both Sikh and non-Sikh.

Daljeet Singh attaches great importance to what was said and done by Guru Nanak. Sikh identity for him is essentially the identity of Sikhism. He underlines the close connection between the ideas of Guru Nanak and the institutions he founded. He emphasizes the importance of ideology in Sikh history. In his view, the intention of Guru Nanak and his successors was to found and develop a new kind of social order. Thus, the doctrines, the institutions, the rituals and the social attitudes of the Sikhs were all interlinked to give them a distinct identity from the very beginning. The rulers of the time did not take long to recognize the distinctive identity of the Sikhs. The culmination came with the order of the Khalsa which clearly defined Sikh identity once for all.

McLeod makes a good case for distinct identity in the pre-Khalsa Sikh tradition but qualifies it by bringing in the notion of the centre and the periphery, the elite and the masses. Oberoi invokes more or less the same empirical evidence as McLeod, but views Sikh identity as not yet fixed or clearly defined. He minimizes the significance of both the objective socio-cultural realities and the subjective consciousness of distinction inspiring the Sikhs. On the whole, for Daljeet Singh, a distinct Sikh identity was not only fully formed in the time of the Gurus but it was also their creation, resulting from the ideas of Guru Nanak and the ideals, institutions and actions based on them. He is not bothered about 'uniformity' or 'fixity' in his conceptualization of identity.

EXTERNAL EVIDENCE AND THE SIKH SELF-IMAGE

McLeod and Oberoi refer to the evidence of Bhai Gurdas, the *Janamsakhis* and even the Gurbani, but without studying this evidence in detail.[19] They have ignored the *Dabistan-i Máẓahib* altogether.

The dictionary meaning of *dabistan* is 'a school'. It is used as a metaphor for a book. The dictionary meaning of *mazhib* (singular of *mazahib*) is a creed, a sect, a set of doctrines or a set of institutes. People who profess a creed or who belong to a sect, or who subscribe to a set of doctrines or institutes are referred to as *tabqa, ta'ifa, jama'at, guroh, firqa* or *panth.* These terms are used more or less as synonyms, though the meaning can differ in certain contexts. In the eyes of the author of the *Dabistan* each category taken up by him was a distinct entity. We can even say that each category of people had a distinct identity. Whether or not it was an independent identity is a matter for further examination.

The *Dabistan* is divided into a number of *ta'lims,* literally 'lessons' or 'instructions'. We may call them 'parts'. Each part is further divided into *nazars,* literally 'views' or 'visions' or 'sights'. We may refer to them as 'sections'. The second part deals with the fundamentals of the various categories of people in the Indian subcontinent. However, it is entitled *dar baz namudan aqaid-i hinduan.* It is meant to unravel the fundamental ideas, tenets, beliefs and attitudes of 'the Hindus'. At one level the Hindus of the *Dabistan* are the peoples of India (*ahl-i Hind*). At another level, they are equated with the Brahmans (*brahama*) and, by extension, with the people who followed the Brahmanical systems of belief and practice. This context has to be kept in view.

The part dealing with 'the Hindus' is divided into twelve sections. The first three sections relate to the 'orthodox' (*mutasharri*) among the Hindus. They believed in the four Vedas, the four *yugas,* and the four-caste social order. They had their Shastras, Smritis and Puranas. They held the Epics in high esteem. They subscribed to the doctrines of *karma,* transmigration, and incarnation. They worshipped idols in temples. They used the sacred thread and the sacred mark, and they performed *yagya* or *hom.* They upheld the practice of *sati.* The author of the *Dabistan* distinguishes the

Vedantists from the 'orthodox': the former sought liberation through knowledge (*gian*). Their philosophy is expounded in the fourth section. In the fifth section are discussed the ideas of the Sankhians who propounded the doctrine of Purusha and Prakriti. The sixth section deals with Yoga – with the twelve *panths* of the *jogis* and the ten *panths* of the Sanyasis as its most conspicuous representatives. The seventh section relates to the Shaktas who worshipped the Goddess under various names, including Jagdamba and Durga. The Vaishnavas are the subject of the eighth section which takes into account the various orders of the Bairagis. Among them are included Kabir and Namdev. The ninth section deals with the Charvaks as the upholders of materialism. The tenth section relates to *ahl-i tark* who made logic the mainstay of their philosophy. The eleventh section talks of the Jatis (Jain monks). They subscribed to the doctrine of transmigration but not to the doctrine of incarnation. In fact, the Jain monks disapproved of the laws (*shari'at*) of the Brahmans. We can see that these eleven sections cover a vast ground, dealing with religions and philosophies of the peoples of India.

What is implicit in the title of the second part is made explicit in the title of its twelfth section: *dar 'aqaid-i mukhtalifa-i ahl-i Hind.* It deals with the religious principles and practices of the peoples of India other than those treated in the first eleven sections. The first category taken up in the twelfth section is that of the 'Muslim Sufis', with their fourteen orders traced to two of the disciples of Hasan Basri, including the Chishtiya and the Suhrawardiya orders. Peculiarly Indian were other categories of *fuqara* (plural of *faqir*) in India (who were not Muslim). Among them were the followers of Gosain Hari Das, known as Niranjanis; the followers of Dadu, known as Dadu-Panthis; and the followers of Baba Piara, known as Piara-Panthis. Then there were the worshippers of the Sun, the Moon, the Stars, the Fire, the Water, the Wind and the Earth. Significantly, the last category taken up in this section is that of the Nanak-Panthis, also known as *Gursikhs.*

What we have said so far may give the impression that the Nanak-Panthis stand bracketed with rather unimportant categories. But that would be a wrong impression. In the first place, the Sufis are also treated in this section as a category of the men of piety in India. Furthermore, though the Nanak-Panthis form only a part of a section, the space given to them is more than the space given to any whole section in this part of the book. The 'orthodox' Hindus alone get more space than the Nanak-Panthis because three sections are given to them. The traits of the Nanak-Panthis noted by the author of the *Dabistan* distinguish them from all other peoples treated in the book. The Sikhs did not make any distinction between Guru Nanak and his successors, regarding them all as one. Indeed, if anyone of them did not regard Guru Arjan (the fifth *mahal*) exactly as Guru Nanak (the first *mahal*) he was treated as an unbeliever (*kafir*). That explains why every Sikh was regarded as the Sikh of Guru Nanak, and why the Panth was called the Nanak-Panth.

The Sikhs looked upon their Guru as the 'true king' (*sachcha patshah*) in contrast with the temporal king. The Guru's representative (*gumashta*) was called Masand (from the Persian Masnad) to indicate his importance. The Masands used to come to the Guru at the time of Baisakhi, bringing with them offerings collected from the Sikhs, and receiving a turban from the Guru as a mark of honour. A large number of persons became Sikhs of the Guru through their mediacy. There was hardly any city in which there were no Sikhs, and the Masands used to collect offerings from all the cities and towns. To demonstrate that the Sikhs did not care for the distinctions of caste, the author of the *Dabistan* underlines that a Brahman could accept a Khatri as his leader, and a Khatri could accept a Jat as his leader, though the latter belonged to the lowest category of Vaishyas. In fact, many of the important Masands of the Guru were Jats. And Brahmans and Khatris became Sikhs of the Guru through their mediacy. If a Sikh visited another in the name of the Guru, he was to be treated like the Guru himself. The collective prayer of the Sikhs was regarded as more efficacious than the prayer of a single person, even that of the Guru.

Like the principle of inequality, the Sikhs rejected the idea of renunciation (*udas* or *tark-i duniya*). That was why they took either to agriculture, or trade or service (*naukari*). Being productive, they could contribute towards the Guru's treasury. The author of the *Dabistan* observed that Guru Hargobind maintained 700 horses, 300 horsemen, and 60 matchlockmen on a permanent basis at Kiratpur. This was the result of a deliberate policy in which hunting, eating of meat, wearing of arms, and martial activities were encouraged. Being a teacher, Guru Hargobind could think of giving practical lessons to his opponents in the battlefield in effective use of the sword. The Sikhs did not observe any Brahmanical taboos about food and drink. There was nothing of the worship (*'ibadat*) and austerities (*riazat*) stipulated by the law books of the Hindus (*shara'-i Hinduan*) among the Sikhs. The Sikh belief in transmigration distinguished them from Muslims, and the Sikh insistence on the unity of God distinguished them from Hindus. The followers of Guru Nanak had nothing to do with idols in temples. An incident is related in the *Dabistan* to underline that the Sikhs had no respect for goddesses. A Sikh of Guru Hargobind broke the nose of an idol to show how helpless the goddess was and how foolish were they who believed in her power. The Sikhs never recited the Hindu scriptures (*mantarha-i Hunud*). Indeed, the *bani* of Guru Nanak was in the language of the peasants of the Punjab (*zuban-i jattan-i Panjab*); his followers had no concern with Sanskrit which was regarded by the Hindus as the language of gods.[20] This description underscores the distinctive character of Sikh doctrines and practices in relation to the three great religious traditions of the seventeenth-century India: the Islamic, the ascetical and the Brahmanical. Coupled with the evidence of the *Janamsakhis*, Bhai Gurdas, and the *Guru Granth Sahib*, the *Dabistan* clinches the issue of the distinctiveness of early Sikh identity.

It must be pointed out that no scholarly attention has been paid to Sikh self-image in the *Guru Granth Sahib*. How the Gurus themselves looked upon the emergence of the Sikh Panth makes it absolutely clear that they thought of the path of Guru Nanak as totally new and they looked upon the Sikh Panth as the instrument of universal redemption. It is difficult to find a stronger statement of a distinct Sikh identity.[21]

NOTES

1. W.H. McLeod, *Who is a Sikh? The Problem of Sikh Identity*, Oxford: the Clarendon Press, 1989, pp. 7-10.
2. Ibid., pp. 120-31.
3. Ibid., pp. 13-14.
4. Ibid., pp. 15-18.

5. Ibid., p. 18.
6. Ibid., pp. 18-19.
7. Ibid., pp. 20-2.
8. Harjot Oberoi, *The Construction of Religious Boundaries: Culture, Identity and Diversity in the Sikh Tradition*, New Delhi: Oxford University Press, 1994, pp. 47-58. With his primary interest in the late nineteenth and the early twentieth century, Oberoi devotes only one chapter to the pre-colonial period as the background for his study.
9. Ibid., pp. 50-1.
10. Ibid., pp. 51-3.
11. Ibid., p. 53.
12. Ibid., pp. 55-6.
13. Ibid., pp. 56-8.
14. Ibid., pp. 54-8.
15. Daljeet Singh, 'The Sikh Identity', *Essentials of Sikhism*, Amritsar: Singh Brothers, 1994, pp. 255-8.
16. Ibid., pp. 259-61.
17. Ibid., pp. 261-2.
18. Ibid., pp. 262-5.
19. There is no indication that all the *Vars* of Bhai Gurdas were analysed by Oberoi and even McLeod from the viewpoint of identity. Such an exercise, however, leaves no doubt that Bhai Gurdas looked upon the Sikh Panth as distinct from all the peoples of the world, being the only Gurmukh Panth.
20. *Sikh History from Persian Sources*, ed. J.S. Grewal and Irfan Habib, Delhi: Tulika/Indian History Congress, 2001, pp. 59-84. It is important to note that Guru Nanak was concerned with the three religious traditions mentioned here, and he rejected all the three. See J.S. Grewal, 'The Bani of Guru Nanak', *Lectures on History, Society and Culture of the Punjab*, Patiala: Punjabi University, 2007, pp. 101-29.
21. J.S. Grewal, *A Study of Guru Granth Sahib: Doctrine, Social Content, History, Structure and Status*, Amritsar: Singh Brothers, 2009, pp. 134-57.

CHAPTER 6

The Khalsa Identity

Daljeet Singh does not go beyond the institution of the Khalsa in his formal discussion of the Sikh identity, presumably on the assumption that an independent Sikh identity was fully formed in the Khalsa once for all. W.H. McLeod and Harjot Oberoi, on the other hand, continue their discussion of Sikh identity after the institution of the Khalsa. They appreciate the importance of the Khalsa for a distinctive Sikh identity. However, they differ widely on the issue whether or not the Khalsa-Sikh identity remained dominant after the establishment of Sikh rule in the late eighteenth and the early nineteenth century.

DISTINCT AND CONTINUOUS

Two chapters in McLeod's *Who is a Sikh*? relate to the eighteenth century: one on the Khalsa and its *rahit* and the other on 'the Khalsa in the eighteenth century'. If we concentrate on the substance of his argument, ignoring the way in which it is developed, we find that he is aware of the change brought about by the institution of the Khalsa in 1699. The features which clearly emerge from the earliest known evidence are: an initiation ceremony involving use of the sword; instruction to initiates to keep their hair uncut and to wear weapons as a matter of course; to adopt the name 'Singh'; and not to smoke *hukka*. To this core were added other items of the Khalsa *rahit* during the eighteenth century through a gradual process. In the time of Banda Bahadur there was still a dispute regarding the proper form of Khalsa observances.[1]

By the end of the eighteenth century, however, the Khalsa identity is said to have become the predominant Sikh identity, and the Khalsa stood clearly distinguished from 'Hindus'. McLeod tries to isolate some elements of the evolving Khalsa tradition. For one thing, 'Muslims' became the enemy; they represented a threat to *dharma*, and their touch was polluting. Heroic resistance to tyranny, to the point of death if necessary, became an essential element of the Khalsa tradition. Heroic literature became popular as *gurbilas*. A firm belief in their own triumph led the Khalsa to the conviction that they were meant to rule (*raj karega khalsa*). The *Dasam Granth*, according to McLeod, became a part of the canon. The militant spirit it breathed, matched that of the eighteenth-century Khalsa. For the same reason, the cult of the Goddess exercised a strong fascination within the Panth. Due as much to such elements as to the Khalsa *rahit*, the Khalsa were quite distinguished from their contemporaries. They were distinguished relatively from the Nanak-Panthis of the early Sikh tradition whose identity was not so clearly pronounced as that of the Khalsa.[2]

McLeod maintains that the eighteenth-century Sikh tradition was nonetheless intimately linked with the earlier Sikh tradition. The linkages were both doctrinal and institutional. The doctrine of eternal Guru which had emerged in the early Sikh Panth was carried forward into the eighteenth century and beyond. References in the compositions of the Gurus and Bhai Gurdas to the *bani* and the *sangat* point towards a developed doctrine. From *bani* as the Guru to *Granth* as the Guru, and from the *sangat* as the Guru to the entire body of the Khalsa as the Guru, the line of development was logical and clear. 'It accommodated the final version within the established tradition of the Nanak-Panth.' The doctrine of Guru Panth found tangible expression in the *gurmata* and the Dal Khalsa during the eighteenth century. The doctrine of Guru Granth emerged to become more important in the early nineteenth century.[3]

The *dharamsala* of the early Sikh Panth developed into the *gurdwara* of the eighteenth century. Erecting shrines at locations associated with particular events in the lives of the individual Gurus became common, particularly after the establishment of Khalsa rule. The *dharamsalas* continued as the centres for *kirtan*. Eventually, however, the term *gurdwara* came into common currency. This was because the *sangat* which met in the *dharamsala* came to be looked upon as the Guru. Furthermore, the *Granth Sahib*, which too was looked upon as the Guru, came to be placed in at least the important *dharamsalas*, and the place appropriately became the Guru's door (*gurdwara*).[4] McLeod does not say so, but this change in the term used for the sacred space reflected its enhanced importance in the eyes of the Sikhs.

Since all the Sikhs did not become Singhs, the Sikh Panth was larger than the Khalsa. The continuing presence of non-Khalsa Sikhs is indicated by the *B40 Janamsakhi* which was completed in 1733. In the *Chaupa Singh Rahit-Nama*, which was compiled in the mid-eighteenth century, there are references to Sahajdhari Sikhs who, presumably, continued to live as Nanak-Panthi Sikhs, sustaining an identity which was much less precise than that of the baptized Khalsa. However, they too were expected to keep their *kesh* and whiskers uncut. McLeod looks upon the Udasis as 'an obscure group' whose affiliation to the Sikh Panth was uncertain. In terms of visibility and participation in the Panth's evolving tradition, they were rather peripheral. The Sahajdharis were scarcely more prominent. 'Throughout the eighteenth century it is the Khalsa which occupies the stage, consciously dominant in all that passes as Sikh history and easily communicating the impression that all such history is in fact Khalsa history.' For John Malcolm at the beginning of the nineteenth century, the Khalsa stood clearly separated from 'the Hindu', but not so the other Sikhs. Another way of referring to the two main categories of Sikhs was to talk of the Sikhs of Guru Gobind Singh and the Sikhs of Guru Nanak. This situation, according to McLeod, presents the 'problem of defining the Panth'.[5] In other words, a single definition did not cover all Sikhs. Alternatively, a simple definition of the Panth could not take into account the differences between the Khalsa and the non-Khalsa Sikhs. Uniformity is assumed by McLeod to be relevant for identity.

DISTINCT BUT REPLACED BY SANATAN SIKHISM

According to Oberoi, the Sikh movement had begun to move beyond the existing cultural traditions after the execution of Guru Arjan. A continuous Jat influx and a protracted conflict with an increasingly hostile state gave rise to new cultural patterns in the seventeenth century. The institution of the Khalsa ended 'ambiguities of Sikh religiosity'. Following the imperial paradigm, Guru Gobind Singh undertook to establish direct contact with the Sikhs as his Khalsa and removed the debilitating mediacy of the Masands. He instructed the Khalsa to get confirmed through the new initiation rite of *khande ki pahul*, maintain unshorn hair, and bear arms. Every Sikh was expected to become the Guru's Khalsa, but some of his closest disciples did not undergo Khalsa initiation. In seeking to turn the 'fluid world of Indic religious identities upside down' the Khalsa faced great opposition. Sainapat's statement that 'on one side stands the Khalsa and on the other the world' underlines that the Khalsa met opposition even from Sikhs.[6]

Nevertheless, the first three quarters of the eighteenth century were marked by 'production and reproduction' of Khalsa cultural identity. The *Rahitnama* literature dwells not only on *khande ki pahul* for initiation but also on life-cycle rituals to mark birth and death. For marriage, however, the old lineage and caste customs continued to be followed. But the choice of the bridegroom was restricted to Sikhs. These life-cycle rituals gave enduring form to a fluid identity. The boundaries established by these rituals were reinforced by a long inventory of tabooed behaviour. Among the tabooed items was sexual intercourse with a Muslim woman, offering prayers at a tomb, or visiting a mosque or a Hindu temple. Furthermore, the Khalsa established firm control over the central shrine at Amritsar and enunciated duties in relation to the sacred space and its management. In the eighteenth-century situation, the 'Muslim' became a powerful signifier of 'otherness'. There were a dozen other groups, both Sikh and Hindu, with whom the Khalsa were expected to have no contact. A 'distinctive Khalsa normative order had emerged by the second half of the eighteenth century, and Khalsa identity became hegemonic within the Sikh tradition'.[7]

Oberoi does not fail to notice that the Khalsa cultural formation was 'not all new'. Its links with the past were visible in the Khalsa doctrines of Guru Panth and Guru Granth. The Khalsa cultural formation had some limitations too. The dissemination of Khalsa identity was restricted by the given means of communication. Sikh sacred geography, routes of pilgrimage and anniversaries to commemorate events of the Sikh past were still in their infancy. The Sikhs had not yet formulated distinctive marriage and mortuary rituals. The *Adi Granth* had not yet become the exclusive focus of Sikh religiosity. Its status as a sacred text is said to be shared by the *Dasam Granth*. 'Although the Sikh tradition was considerably purged of its fluidity by the new imaginative categories and religious practices of Khalsa Sikhs, there was still ample room within it for ambiguity, inversion and conflicting interpretations.'[8]

Oberoi talks of the paradox of Khalsa and Sahajdhari duality in the late eighteenth century. All Sikhs were not happy with either the dramatic triumph of the Khalsa or the dominance of a Khalsa identity. In support of this view Oberoi refers to the work of Kesar Singh Chhibber. Nevertheless, the Khalsa Sikhs went from one success to another and their identity continued to attract recruits in increasing numbers. Paradoxically, however, as the Khalsa mode attained hegemony within Sikh tradition, it simultaneously came to be accepted that there were alternative ways of being a Sikh. The Sikh Panth was 'not coterminus with the Khalsa'. The Sikhs other than the Khalsa were often referred to as Sahajdharis. Oberoi feels sure that Udasis and Nanak-Panthis were included in the Sahajdhari category. To demonstrate that there was a close correspondence in 'the religious identities' of Sahajdharis, Nanak-Panthis and Udasis, Oberoi cites a document containing instructions for the guidance of the Mahant of an Udasi establishment in Bihar. There is no reference to Nanak-Panthis in this document. The Mahant is told to 'remain celibate', but there is nothing else in the document which may be regarded as exceptionable by a Sahajdhari Sikh. In fact, the instructions professedly related to what a Sahajdhari Sikh should or should not do. Oberoi draws the inference that Udasis were included in the Sahajdhari category.[9]

Talking of 'Sahajdharis', Oberoi actually concentrates on the Udasis who for him are 'perhaps the most conspicuous and widely patronized segment among the Sahajdhari Sikhs'. In many ways 'the Sahajdhari Sikhs' totally inverted Khalsa categories of thought and religious boundaries. They cut their hair; they did not carry arms; they had a radically different line of succession; and they did not accept a text as a *guru*. They began to manage key Sikh shrines, including the Harmandar (for a short time) and they set up their own establishments at pilgrimage centres like Amritsar, Hardwar and Benares. The model of Sikhism they enunciated diverged considerably from that of the Khalsa Sikhs. They differed from the Khalsa in their attitude towards hair, codes of dress and modes of salvation. 'In appearance perhaps no two persons could have looked more different than a Khalsa Sikh and an Udasi of the eighteenth century.' Ironically, having actually described the Udasis, Oberoi looks upon his statement as a description of radical differences between the 'Khalsa and Sahajdhari modes of identity'.[10]

In his explanation of the existence of 'duality in Sikh identity' Oberoi refers to the need of the Khalsa rulers for 'all the allies they could get'. Who could be better than the Sahajdharis who recognized Nanak as a guru, read and recited verses from the *Adi Granth*, served in large number as custodians of important Sikh shrines, and wrote mythical narrative of Sikh Gurus and textual commentaries on Sikh scripture? Here, Oberoi is talking actually of the Udasis. The Khalsa rulers also needed a reliable network of intermediaries 'to impress the new command and collect revenue for the state's coffers'. The *chaudharis* who served as intermediaries belonged both to the central hierarchy of the state and the organization of the *biradari*, or the clan. The recognition given to *chaudharis* meant the absorption of 'local segmentary lineages'. And this implied conservation of the pre-existing framework, with all its rituals and life-cycle ceremonies associated with Brahmanical Hinduism and 'its accompanying social system encapsulated in the varna hierarchy'. Thus, the paradox in the coexistence of Khalsa and Sahajdhari identities was 'part of the complex process of state formation'. Here, Oberoi is not talking of the Udasis. He is talking of the landholding clans in the countryside. In order to suggest that Sikhs were included in this category, Oberoi cites a passage from John Malcolm which refers to Jats and Gujars continuing their old practices, especially in relation to matrimony and commensality, after becoming Sikhs. Actually, however, this passage qualifies the statement: they could practice those civil usages and customs which did not infringe 'the tenets of Nanac, or the institutions of Guru Govind'.[11]

Oberoi comes to the conclusion that the increase in the number of Khalsa Sikhs during the late eighteenth century did not imply a corresponding decrease in the number of Sahajdharis. Records of revenue grants to religious establishments and mythical literature point towards 'a highly vibrant non-Khalsa tradition'. Oberoi goes on to add that an 'extraordinary fusion of Khalsa and non-Khalsa identities' marked out Sikh tradition of the late eighteenth century from 'what was to follow under colonial rule'.[12]

MISCONCEPTIONS

Both McLeod and Oberoi agree that the institution of the Khalsa carried the implication that Singhs were distinct from 'Hindus' as well as the other religious communities of India. Both of them notice the existence of non-Khalsa Sikhs during the eighteenth century, referring to them as Sahajdharis.

Indeed, the *Chaupa Singh Rahit-Nama* is addressed to both the Sahajdhari and the Keshdhari Sikhs. This does show that both were regarded as members of the Panth. But who were these Sahajdharis? Quite clearly they did not include the groups which are denounced and virtually excommunicated in the *Rahit-Nama*, like the followers of Prithi Chand and his successors (called Minas), the followers of Dhir Mal and his successors, or the followers of Ram Rai and his successors, or those who followed any of the former Masands or their descendants. Both McLeod and Oberoi state that many Sikhs of Guru Gobind Singh did not become his Khalsa through the initiation of the double-edged sword. Nevertheless, they believed in the ten Gurus and shared some of the doctrines and practices of the 'Singhs'. McLeod notices the suggestion that these Sikhs could have been treated as Sahajdharis. The use of the terms *sahajdhari* and *keshdhari* for the two categories of Sikhs indicates that the former Khalsa was now looked upon as consisting of *keshdhari* Singhs and *sahajdhari* Sikhs, both regarded as members of the Panth. This is the position in some of the *hukamnamas* of Guru Gobind Singh, issued after 1699, and also in the *hukamnamas* of Mata Sundari and Mata Sahib Devi till 1730.[13] It is not without significance that the compiler of the *Chaupa Singh Rahit-Nama* visualizes individuals entering the Panth as Sahajdharis through an initiation resembling *charan pahul* in which the Guru's place is taken by the *Guru Granth*. In other words, an outsider could join the Khalsa Panth as a Sahajdhari or a Keshdhari.

Oberoi argues that there was no difference in the identities of Sahajdharis, Nanak-Panthis and Udasis. Therefore, we may try to identify the Nanak-Panthis and the Udasis, as we have tried to identify the Sahajdharis. The term 'Nanak-Panthi' was generally used by Persian writers for all the followers of Guru Nanak and his successors. Even during the eighteenth century when they actually talked of 'Singhs' they could use the term 'Nanak-Panthi'. This blanket term served their purpose, because they were not interested in any differences within the Panth. For them the term Nanak-Panthi covered all categories of Sikhs: the Khalsa, the Sahajdhari, and the others. Our concern is to identity these 'others'. Oberoi finds the easy way out by merely equating them with the Sahajdharis. But there were 'Nanak-Panthis' other than the Sahajdharis in the eighteenth century. These were precisely the groups which stand excommunicated in the Rahitnamas. They did not subscribe to the line of succession from Guru Nanak to Guru Gobind Singh; they believed in a living *guru*; and they did not look upon the *Adi Granth* as the Guru. The most notable among them were the Minas, the Dhir Mallias and the Ram Raiyas. Oberoi takes notice of them in the context of the groups with which the Khalsa were not to have any contact, but then he forgets about them. In order to talk of 'fusion' between the Khalsa and the Nanak-Panthis, it is necessary to go into their mutual relationship. They never became a recognized component of the Sikh Panth, except those individuals who became Singhs or Sahajdharis.

We have noted that Oberoi's Sahajdharis are virtually 'Udasis'. We know that they regarded Guru Nanak as a notional founder of their orders. They had altogether different lines of succession, starting actually with Sri Chand. If Oberoi thinks that they became a part of the Sikh Panth in the late eighteenth century, it would be necessary to show how. All that he mentions is their literary activity and the patronage of their establishments by the Sikh rulers. But the Sikh rulers patronized non-Sikh as well as Sikh religious establishments. Thus, neither the 'Nanak-Panthis' nor the Udasis can be regarded as Sahajdharis who were closely aligned with the Singhs.

THE KHALSA IN THE TIME OF SIKH RULE

For McLeod, much of the eighteenth-century Khalsa tradition was carried forward into the nineteenth century. At its opening in 1801, Ranjit Singh is said to have become the Maharaja which must have struck many as fulfilment of the *raj karega khalsa* prophecy. Ranjit Singh's administration was informed by the spirit and attitudes of the eighteenth century. Individual Muslims were employed in state service but hostility towards Muslims was not yet wholly exorcised. The institution of *gurmata* was suppressed but loyal *sardars* were duly rewarded, and substantial largesses were bestowed on prominent Sikh shrines. Conspicuous respect was paid to the traditions of the Khalsa at the court. Coinage bore the image of Guru Nanak. The administration was known as Sarkar Khalsaji, and the royal court was called Darbar Khalsaji. In several ways, thus, the state administered by Ranjit Singh was an authentic extension of eighteenth century Khalsa ideals.[14] Some of the statements made here by McLeod are factually incorrect but even correct statements in their place would not affect his basic argument.

The outward forms of the Khalsa tradition which emerged in the eighteenth century seem to have suffered comparatively little change during the first half of the nineteenth. J.D. Cunningham in the 1840s refers to the merging of castes, the Khalsa rite of initiation, 'devotion to steel', uncut hair, blue clothing, use of the name 'Singh' and a strict ban on smoking. The use of *kachh* distinguished Sikhs from Hindus. The presence of the Guru was recognized in the *Adi Granth*, and in any gathering of five Sikhs. One could frequently hear *Vaheguruji ka Khalsa* and *Vaheguruji ki Fateh.* For Cunningham as much as for Malcolm, the Sikhs were distinct from Hindus. If anything, Cunningham is more emphatic about the predominance of Khalsa identity among the Sikhs. This perception, adds McLeod, is strongly supported by the contemporary Sikh literature.[15]

The *Gurbilas* tradition extended well into the nineteenth century. Even if we leave out Koer Singh's *Gurbilas Patshahi Das* and the anonymous *Gurbilas Chhevin Patshahi*, we have the works of Bhai Santokh Singh and Ratan Singh Bhangu, both of which appeared in the 1840s. Bhangu's *Guru Panth Prakash* vigorously affirmed the distinctive nature of the Khalsa identity and claimed that this was the identity which Guru Gobind Singh had intended his followers to adopt. McLeod is inclined to look upon Gian Singh's *Panth Prakash* and his *Tawarikh Guru Khalsa* as a kind of extension of the genre. In any case, his works can be regarded as examples of 'the sustained predominance of the Khalsa identity', an identity which for McLeod extends from the eighteenth century to the early twentieth and 'onwards to the present day'. Cunningham was familiar with the *Rahitnamas* of Bhai Nand Lal and Bhai Prahlad Singh. Two major works appeared in the early decades of British rule in the Punjab: the *Prem Sumarag* and the *Sau Sakhian*. Both these works were popular among the Namdharis who, as McLeod points out, emphasized the importance of Khalsa identity. Whatever the strength of the Sahajdharis, it was demonstrated for McLeod not by the Udasis but by the Nirankaris and the early Namdharis.[16]

Oberoi's view of Sikh tradition in the early nineteenth century is radically different. He refers to it as 'Sanatan' Sikh tradition and believes that it displaced the eighteenth-century Khalsa tradition. In his view, this new tradition had begun to emerge in the late eighteenth century, and remained dominant in the nineteenth century. For the present, however, we propose to confine our discussion to his treatment of the early nineteenth century. It may be helpful to avoid as much as possible the term 'Sanatan' in this discussion to grasp the substance of Oberoi's hypothesis.[17]

Oberoi starts with the texts. According to him, the *Dasam Granth* was held at par with the *Adi Granth* as a devotional text. The bulk of this text related to the Goddess, twenty-four *avtars* of Vishnu, seven of Brahma and two of Rudra. These materials came from the Puranas, the *Ramayana* and the *Mahabharata*. With its inbuilt appeal for diverse identities, the *Dasam Granth* was 'a wonderful vehicle' to reconcile 'Khalsa/Sahajdhari paradox'. It became a 'great code'. Furthermore, Koer Singh in his *Gurbilas Patshahi Das* recommends that his readers pay the same attention to Puranic literature as they would to the *Adi Granth*. He views Guru Gobind Singh as a reincarnation of Vishnu, and makes the Guru prophesy that there would be ten more manifestations. Another writer, Bhai Santokh Singh, views Guru Nanak as an *avtar* of Vishnu, and maintains that he accepted the Vedas as authoritative. In the *Gurbilas Chhevin Patshahi*, Guru Hargobind is portrayed as the twenty-fourth reincarnation of Vishnu. The implication is clear to Oberoi: all these authors subscribed to the idea of incarnation, recognized texts other than the *Adi Granth*, and looked upon the *Dasam Granth* as equally authoritative. They represented the 'Sanatan' world-view. From belief in *avtars* to the worship of images was only a small step. But Oberoi does not clarify when images were installed in the Sikh shrines.[18]

The impact of the 'great code' on Sikh consciousness is seen by Oberoi in an exposition of the *Japji* by 'an enigmatic figure by the name of Anandghan'. Oberoi quotes his exposition of *sat nam karta purakh* to illustrate his point. Anandghan relies on Puranic literature to back his interpretation. He does not feel the need of turning to the works of the Sikh Gurus for understanding Sikh ideology. Indeed, Gurbani is no longer central to the attainment of liberation. Besides Anandghan, 'tens of thousands' of peoplepicked up this message from the 'geat code'.[19]

Anandghan's religious identity is not known. In Oberoi's terminology, he would be a Sahajdhari. But Anandghan is generally treated as an Udasi. Oberoi also refers to 'the Khalsa framework' acknowledged by 'Sanatan Sikhism'. The Khalsa were expected to follow the *Rahitnamas*, and not 'the Brahmanical codes'. Theoretically, they were obliged to give up the caste system, but in practice they may have found it hard to reconcile their religious injunctions with the social reality.[20] Oberoi says nothing more about the 'Khalsa' in the early nineteenth century. Who were they? and where were they? and how were they different from 'the Singhs' who could be seen everywhere? Is he referring to the Akalis and the Nihangs? Oberoi thinks that he has satisfactorily delineated Sanatan conceptions of 'scripture, myth, doctrine, self definition and social practice'. But the reader may not feel satisfied with this delineation. His exposition of 'Sanatan' is not at all clear.

Oberoi turns to agencies through which Sanatan tradition was transmitted. This task is said to have been performed by three kinds of men: members of Guru lineages, holy men, and traditional intellectuals. Prominent among the descendants of the Gurus were Sodhis and Bedis, the descendants respectively of Guru Ram Das and Guru Nanak. Oberoi refers especially to the Sodhis of Anandpur. The information he provides relates to the late eighteenth or the late nineteenth century, but not to the early nineteenth. The names Nahar Singh, Udai Singh, Khem Singh and Chaur Singh suggest that these individuals had joined the Khalsa some time in the eighteenth century. The information on the Sodhis of Har Sahai and Kartarpur comes from the late nineteenth century. We know, however, that Sodhi Wadbhag Singh of Kartarpur was admitted to the Khalsa order in the late eighteenth century. The Sodhis enjoyed large *jagirs* in the early nineteenth century, but there is no information on what they believed and practised. The Bedis shared eminence with the Sodhis and enjoyed large *jagirs*. The most celebrated Bedi of the period was Sahib Singh. Significantly, he was the first baptized 'Singh' in the family. Like several others, he appears to have joined the Khalsa order in the second half of the eighteenth century. He was greatly respected by Ranjit Singh and received large *jagirs* from him. Sahib Singh's experience was shared by some other Bedis but none of them was equally eminent. However, we know little about the religious role of the Bedis in the Khalsa Panth during the early nineteenth century.[21]

Close in rank to the Guru lineages in 'the sacred hierarchy of the Sikh community' were holy men known as Bhais, Sants or Babas, like Bhai Bir Singh, Bhai Mahraj Singh and Bhai Ram Singh. They were known for their piety and their understanding of the *Adi Granth*. Miracles were attributed to them, but they did not claim such powers. Their blessings were prized. Some other Bhais mentioned by Oberoi are Sant Singh, Ram Singh, Gobind Ram and Gurmukh Singh. All of them were important individuals. But there is no information on their ideas or attitudes. 'Perhaps the most creative and institutionalized among the three groups upholding, interpreting and transmitting Sikh tradition were the traditional intellectuals.' This category included the Udasis and the Nirmalas. While there is some information on the Udasis in the early nineteenth century, there is very little on the Nirmalas. Oberoi's information on the latter comes from the second half of the nineteenth century. 'The other half of the traditional intellectuals included *granthis*, *pujaris*, *dhadis*, *rababis*, *ragis*, *gianis*, and *bhais* – a sort of sacred support staff that performed different functions for the body of the Sikh believers.' The Gianis and Bhais ran educational institutions. Out of their 'collective learning and wisdom' emerged Bhai Santokh Singh who was a distinguished student of Giani Sant Singh.[22] This is all that Oberoi tells us about the transmitters of the Sanatan Sikh tradition. Information about what they transmitted comes again from the late nineteenth century. Oberoi simply assumes that what was true of the late nineteenth century was true also of the early nineteenth.

'Sanatan Sikhism', for Oberoi, 'deeply transformed Sikh thinking and religious practices', but very little information is actually given by him on 'thinking', or 'religious practices'. He goes on to add that the Khalsa and Sahajdhari components now became firmly enshrined within the 'great tradition'. 'Sahajdharis' were not merely tolerated; they controlled Sikh shrines and articulated theology, mythology, and 'in short the entire framework of their tradition'. Who are these Sahajdharis? The only important category known to Oberoi in the early nineteenth century is that of the Udasis. Are these Sahajdharis in fact Udasis? In any case, if the Sahajdharis and the Khalsa formed the two components of the Sikh Panth, who were the Sanatan Sikhs? For Oberoi, Sanatan Sikhism was primarily a 'priestly' religion. A critical distinction was made between religious intermediaries and the lay people. All Sikhs required formal initiation, either through *khande ki pahul* or through *charan amrit*, this came to be given by religious intermediaries. Furthermore, all distinguished religious specialists were regarded as *gurus*. Even Sikh chiefs and rulers are known to have prostrated themselves at their feet to seek blessings. These statements are not supported by evidence adduced by Oberoi. In any case, if Sanatan tradition was primarily 'the religious universe' of the Sikh elites, it could be the outlook of a small minority.[23]

Nevertheless, for Oberoi, the early nineteenth century was marked by the Sanatan 'episteme' which replaced the eighteenth-century Khalsa tradition. As noticed earlier, the impact of the *Dasam Granth* is stated to be reflected in the works of writers like Koer Singh and Bhai Santokh Singh. But their evidence is used by Oberoi rather selectively. Koer Singh, for example, underlines the importance of the line of succession from Guru Nanak to Guru Gobind Singh. He looks upon the institution of the Khalsa as the most momentous development in Sikh history, which ensured the establishment of Sikh rule. He emphasizes the necessity of following the Khalsa *rahit* which was promulgated by Guru Gobind Singh himself. Koer Singh is explicit on the point that Guru Gobind Singh rejected the *Dasam Granth* in favour of the *Adi Granth* for bequeathing Guruship to the scripture. He refers to the *Adi Granth* as Guru Granth. The doctrine of Guru Panth was equally important for Koer Singh.[24] To refer only to what he says about the Puranas or incarnations is to misconstrue his basic position. Since Koer Singh subscribes to the essential doctrines of the Khalsa, his other ideas can be treated actually as secondary or even marginal. In other words, in dealing with writers like Koer Singh and Bhai Santokh Singh it is more appropriate to place them within the Khalsa rather than a new tradition. Oberoi is thus left with the evidence only of the 'enigmatic' Anandghan. Since he was an Udasi, Oberoi remains confined to the Udasis for the early nineteenth century. He does catalogue the transmitters of Sikh tradition during this period and also points out their importance. But they were invariably 'Singh' rather than Udasi, and there is no information on what they transmitted. The earliest known evidence on the composition of the *Sikh Panth* leaves little doubt about the numerical superiority of the 'Singhs' who dominated almost all walks of life among the early nineteenth-century Sikhs. Did they represent Oberoi's Sanatan Sikhism? If so, Oberoi does not tell us how. His whole hypothesis of 'Sanatan Sikhism' in the early nineteenth century appears to be vague and vacuous.

The major works of Sikh literature, the chronicles of the period, and the works of Malcolm and Cunningham, seen in their totality, do not support Oberoi's hypothesis of 'Sanatan Sikhism'. By far the most important identity of the Sikhs was that of the Khalsa Singhs. Even the Sahajdhari movements of the early nineteenth century were anti-Brahmanical, and supportive of a distinct Sikh identity.[25]

NOTES

1. W.H. McLeod, *Who is a Sikh? The Problem of Sikh Identity*, Oxford: The Clarendon Press, 1989, pp. 44, 48.
2. Ibid., pp. 49-51, 57-60.
3. Ibid., pp. 52-6.
4. Ibid., pp. 56-7.
5. Ibid., pp. 44-6, 57, 60.
6. Harjot Oberoi, *The Construction of Religious Boundaries: Culture, Identity and Diversity in the Sikh Tradition*, New Delhi: Oxford University Press, 1994, pp. 58-62.
7. Ibid., pp. 69-71, 90-1.
8. Ibid., pp. 90-1.
9. Ibid., pp. 75-8.
10. Ibid., pp. 76, 78-81.
11. Ibid., pp. 81-9. The passage from Malcolm is quoted on page 88.

12. Ibid., p. 90.
13. *Hukamname: Guru Sahiban, Mata Sahiban, Banda Singh ate Khalsa Ji De* (Pbi), ed. Ganda Singh, Patiala: Punjabi University, 1967, nos. 50, 54-5, 57, 67-8, 73-4, 78, 85.
14. McLeod, *Who is a Sikh*?, pp. 62-3.
15. Ibid., p. 66.
16. Ibid., pp. 65, 67-8.
17. See Oberoi, *The Construction of Religious Boundaries,* pp. 92-3.
18. Ibid., pp. 93-110.
19. Ibid., pp. 100-2.
20. Ibid., p. 108.
21. Ibid., pp. 108-16.
22. Ibid., pp. 116-36.
23. Ibid., pp. 137-8.
24. Koer Singh, *Gurbilas Patshahi 10* (Pbi), ed. Shamsher Singh Ashok, Patiala: Punjabi University, 1968, pp. 19, 57, 129-30, 138, 238.
25. For a brief analysis of contemporary evidence on Sikh beliefs and practices and Sikh attitudes, see J.S. Grewal, 'Sikhism from the Late Eighteenth to the Early Twentieth Century', *Journal of Regional History*, vols. XI-XII (New Series), 2005-6, pp. 9-14.

CHAPTER 7

Equality, Caste and Gender

Comments on the egalitarian character of the Khalsa began to appear in the late eighteenth century in the works of European writers. They refer particularly to the rejection of caste distinctions for initiation into the Sikh Panth. They refer also to Sikh practices in commensality and connubium. The Sikh writers of the twentieth century have laid great emphasis on the norm of equality in relation to caste and gender. However, there were no studies of gender relations and there were only cursory remarks on the prevalence or absence of caste in the Sikh social order. C.H. Loehlin can be seen as a scholar who showed some interest in the question of caste. Like the earlier writers, he saw the character of the Sikh social order as relevant for the issue of Sikh identity. The first writer to give a rather elaborate exposition of caste in the Sikh Panth was Professor Jagjit Singh. He saw in the Sikh Panth an egalitarian social order springing from Sikh ideology. W.H. McLeod's essay on caste in the Sikh Panth was not written with reference to Jagjit Singh's work. Nevertheless, he showed greater concern for empirical realities and gave more importance to social environment. Both of them look at caste in the larger context of the character of the Sikh social order.

One of the propositions attributed by Justice Gurdev Singh to McLeod is that the Gurus denounced the caste system but they did not appear to be 'sincere or serious in removing caste differences'.[1] McLeod has accused them of insincerity by gleefully introducing the 'fib' that the Jats bewail that there was never a single Jat Guru, and the Gurus did not marry outside the Khatri fold. Justice Gurdev Singh believes that there were no such critics. He asserts that Jagjit Singh, 'himself a Jat', has examined the Sikh attitude towards caste in all its aspects and has demonstrated 'how untenable and unfair is McLeod's criticism and charge of insincerity against the Gurus'.[2]

LIMITED ROLE OF THE PRINCIPLE OF EQUALITY

McLeod introduces the issue of caste in the Sikh Panth with reference to the comments of British observers of the Sikh society during the last two decades of the eighteenth century. One such comment is that the Sikhs consisted 'mostly' of the Jat 'tribe'. Another comment is that the acceptance of the Sikh doctrine 'causes an essential deviation' from the Hindu system. The wonderful barriers 'constructed and affixed' for the 'different ranks and professions' among the people were overthrown by the Sikh doctrine. In other words, caste distinctions stood obliterated within the eighteenth-century Sikh Panth.[3] McLeod thinks that the statement on the obliteration of caste within the Sikh Panth has to be substantially qualified. A British writer of the first decade of the nineteenth century observed that the Sikhs allowed 'foreigners of every description' to join their standard, to sit in their company, and to shave their beards but, except in the case of the Jats, they did not consent to intermarriage. Furthermore, they did not eat or drink from the hands of 'an alien' unless he was a Brahman. Indeed, the Sikhs professed 'the highest veneration' for Brahmans. McLeod draws the inference that there were restrictions on intermarriage and commensality within the Sikh Panth. In support of this inference he refers to 'Punjabi sources' of the eighteenth century as well as to nineteenth- and twentieth-century observations, which reveal an insistent regard for marriage alliances along conventional lines, qualified only by a limited measure of freedom in the case of the Jats. Entry into the Panth was open to all, and caste was certainly 'discounted' but by no means 'obliterated'. It survived 'in terms of commensality and marriage patterns'.[4] Thus, besides the caste constituency of the Panth, there arises the question of the survival of caste observances within the Panth. Though separate, the issues of constituency and observances are intimately related, and McLeod decides to treats them 'concurrently'.

Guru Nanak declared his attitude in a famous and oft-repeated couplet: 'Worthless is caste and worthless an exalted name. For all mankind there is but a single refuge.' This is only one of his numerous pronouncements on caste, and many more could be added. McLeod adds two more to the effect that the divine light in a man and not his caste is important 'for there is no caste in the hereafter'. In the hereafter 'name and caste count for nothing'. Caste status provided no help to an individual in his quest for salvation. In fact, it was a positive hindrance because it nurtured a detrimental pride. This message is repeated by Guru Nanak's successors. Guru Amar Das, for instance, emphasizes that your deeds and not your caste determine your fate because when you die 'you do not carry your caste with you'. The message is carried forward by Guru Ram Das when he says that there are four castes but 'he who meditates on God he it is who is supreme'. The message is repeated by Guru Arjan who included in the *Granth Sahib* the works of 'low-caste' poets, two of whom had denounced caste in strong terms.[5]

McLeod thinks than the expression of what may be called egalitarian ideas was accompanied by certain actions which re-inforce the impression that the Sikh Gurus were 'vigorous and practical denunciators of caste'. Guru Amar Das, for instance, introduced the practice of 'compulsory commensality' which was meant to strike at the very heart of an important aspect of caste. A reference in the works of Bhai Gurdas suggests that *karha prasad* deposited in a common dish by the low caste or even the outcaste Sikh as an offering was consumed by high caste Sikhs. This custom was observed by the Khalsa of Guru Gobind Singh who, moreover, drank from a common bowl at the time of initiation. In the first five Sikhs initiated into the Khalsa Order, the Cherished-Five, was witnessed a representative range from the high caste Khatri through middle caste Jat to low caste barber and washer man. If the utterances of the Gurus suggest that salvation was open to all regardless of caste, the institution of *langar*, distribution of *karha prasad* in the *gurdwaras*, and baptism from a common bowl indicate that their denunciation of caste was meant to be 'carried significantly further'.[6] In other words, whereas there is no ambiguity about the ideal of equality, the relevant question to ask is in what ways and to what extent this egalitarian ideal was actualized in the Sikh Panth.

McLeod refers to the fact that all the nominated successors of Guru Nanak were Khatri and that all the Gurus had matrimonial alliances with Khatris to suggest that they were vigorously opposed to 'the *vertical* distinctions of caste' but they were content to accept caste 'in terms of its *horizontal* linkages'. McLeod goes on to elaborate this statement. He sets aside the classical *varna* model commonly understood as a uniform hierarchical system with the Brahman at the top and the Shudra at the bottom. Below the pyramid were the outcastes like the sweepers and leather workers. This model can provide only a misleading starting point. Therefore, McLeod prefers to start with two of its components which were the most important and meaningful to the individuals concerned: the *zat* (*jati*) and the *got*. The former was an endogamous group consisting of several smaller units (*gots*) which were exogamous.[7]

Despite the horizontal *got* and *zat* relationship, Indian society was strongly hierarchical. One could expect to find the society of a particular area ordered within a distinct pattern of rank and status. While the Sikh Gurus continued to accept the beneficial patterns of horizontal connection, they denied the justice of privilege or deprivation based upon notion of status and hierarchy. In other words, they were opposed to the discriminatory aspects of vertical relationship. McLeod looks upon the issues of caste constituency and attitudes within the Sikh Panth in the dual context of horizontal and vertical relationships. He finds it significant in this context that Bhai Gurdas does not conceal the caste affiliation of the important Sikhs of the Gurus in the early seventeenth century. It is also significant that the number of castes represented in Sikh Panth was quite large. Nevertheless, the largest number of his eminent Sikhs came from the Khatri caste, indicating that Khatri leadership within the early Panth extended much beyond the actual line of Gurus.[8]

The evidence of the *Dabistan-i Mazahib* coupled with that of Bhai Gurdas shows that in the early seventeenth century, though the Khatris enjoyed a particular prominence within the diverse following which constituted the Panth, a share in leadership was entrusted to individual Jat members. This presumably reflected the numerical importance of Jats within the Panth. This numerical importance greatly increased during the course of the seventeenth and eighteenth centuries, producing the strong Jat predominance noted by the early European observers towards the end of the eighteenth century. Jat preponderance was matched by an increase in Jat authority. McLeod mentions two processes to account for this situation: the accession of Jats to the Khalsa, and the failure of other castes, notably the Khatris, to join the Khalsa in numbers corresponding to their position within the earlier Nanak-Panth. The continuance of the non-Khalsa Sikhs after the institution of the Khalsa is borne out by the *B40 Janamsakhi* and the early British censuses. Significantly, Khatris are prominent among these Nanak-Panthi Sikhs but the Jats are absent. The egalitarian implications of the Khalsa initiation rite, which would present a serious deterrent to Brahmans as well as Khatris, partly explain this development. Brahman Sikhs in fact became a rare phenomenon after the institution of the Khalsa.[9]

The caste constituency of the Khalsa Sikhs becomes much clearer in the census returns of 1881. The largest constituent, 66 per cent of the total Khalsa Sikh population of over 1,700,000, came from Jats. There was a spectacular drop in the second-largest constituent, the Tarkhans (carpenters), who formed 6.5 per cent. Next came two outcaste groups, the Chamars with 5.6 per cent and the Chuhras with 2.6 per cent. The Khatris, with a mere 2.2 per cent, were a little behind the Aroras with 2.3 per cent. They were followed by twenty other castes but only five of them were more than 1 per cent: the Kambos, Lohars, Jhiwars, Nais and the Rajputs. The Brahmans and Kalals (Ahluwalias) were among those who formed less than 1 per cent of the Khalsa Sikh population. By far the largest bulk of Sikh population consisted of agrarian castes, followed at a great distance by outcastes and artisan castes. They lived mostly in the countryside. The mercantile castes, with less than 5 per cent of the total, lived mostly in towns and cities.[10]

The overall Sikh population increased after 1881, affecting the number and proportion of various castes within the Panth but without any appreciable change in the basic pattern. By 1931 the total number of Sikhs was over 4,000,000. It included the non-Khalsa Sikhs but their number was less than 300,000. A switch from Hindu to Sikh explained the great increment in excess of natural increase. This was observed chiefly among the agrarian, artisan and the outcaste groups, in response to a belief that the change would result in enhanced status. That the Sikh Panth retained its egalitarian appeal is indicated by the caste return of half a century from 1881 to 1931. This process was promoted by the reforming zeal of the Singh Sabha protagonists and the political concerns of the Akali Dal. Insistence on equality was a fundamental aspect of Singh Sabha policy, reinforced by the threat of conversion of Sikh outcastes to Christianity. The Singh Sabha movement was also responsible for an increase in the proportion of Khalsa Sikhs within the Panth.[11]

For further light on the subject, McLeod turns to particular castes in the Sikh Panth. The civil administrators looked upon the Jats as the finest peasantry in India and the military authorities regarded them as one of the finest 'martial races'. However, careers and professions among Jat Sikhs were not confined to agriculture and the army. More significant from the present viewpoint was 'the pronounced rise in status which marks the history of the Sikh Jats over recent centuries'. In terms of status no Jat feels 'inferior or downtrodden'. The experience of Sikh Jats as rulers and their dominance in the countryside have enabled them to rise above the low status traditionally assigned to Jats. The same factors may account for their political skills. Two other features mark the Sikh Jat society. The absence of formalized social stratification within the endogamous *zat* is one: no Sikh Jat *got* is regarded as above another in status. The other is that the Sikh Jats follow the customary rules or propinquity in marriage: a matrimonial alliance within the same *got* is as a rule forbidden. In his own eyes a Sikh Jat remains a Sikh even if he cuts his beard or smokes tobacco. But if a Khatri shaves he is regarded as Hindu by others and soon comes to regard himself as one.[12]

In spite of their small numbers, the Khatris retain their prominence in commerce and industry, government service, higher education and the professions. They claim an elevated position in Punjabi society. However, the difference between them and the Jats has shrunk as the Jats have moved upwards. Unlike the Jats, the Khatris are divided into at least a few endogamous groups, consisting of four, twelve or fifty-two *gots*. A fourth endogamous group has arisen, consisting of the four Khatri *gots* of the Sikh Gurus – Bedi, Trehan, Bhalla and Sodhi. Confessional differences are comparatively less important among the Khatris and marriages between Hindu and Sikh Khatri families have always been very common. Since the Khatris have not looked upon Sikh identity as a means of enhancing social or ritual status, their number and proportion in the Panth have actually declined during the twentieth century. This does not mean that they regard their membership of the Panth with indifference. If anything, they take it more seriously than the Jats. The Khatris have played an important role in the affairs of the Sikh Panth, a role that is out of all proportion to their small numbers. The Aroras appear to have entered the Panth later than the Khatris, but they have caught up with them since the early nineteenth century. However, though their role in the Panth has been somewhat similar to that of the Khatris, it has been a little inferior.[13]

The artisan and outcaste groups regard membership of the Sikh Panth as a means of improving status. The Tarkhans present an unusually interesting case. They must have entered the Panth in imitation of the Jat landowners whom they traditionally served in a client relationship. The most famous of all Tarkhan Sikhs was Jassa Singh Ramgarhia, a *misl* leader who established his own principality. The name Ramgarhia has been taken up by an increasing number of Sikh Tarkhans since the end of the nineteenth century, with the obvious intention of replacing a lowly title with one of acknowledged repute. A few other castes have joined the Ramgarhias to form a new, composite, and distinctively Sikh *zat*. They have taken up new professions in a bid for upward mobility. The Ranghreta or Mazhabi and Ramdasia Sikhs, the erstwhile Chuhras and Chamars, increased their numbers in the Panth during the early twentieth century in a desire to purge the traditional taint of the outcaste status. Their hope of achieving this end through the egalitarian traditions of the Khalsa has been partially fulfilled.[14]

Accordingly to McLeod, two general hierarchies can be discerned in Punjabi society, one urban and the other rural. Within Sikh society the two intersect without losing their essential clarity. The Sikh component of the urban hierarchy is very small and very distinct, with Khatris occupying a superior ranking and with Aroras close behind. At the base are the Mazhabis and Ramdasias. The Ramgarhias are clearly above them, but equally clearly they are below Khatris and Aroras. The position of the erstwhile outcaste and artisan groups in the countryside is similar to their position in towns and cities, but their numbers in the countryside are much larger. Indeed, the rural hierarchy is numerically much larger and the massive Jat constituency commands the heights. In terms of order, the rural hierarchy is less clear than the urban hierarchy. Many of the features commonly regarded as typically Sikh are characteristically the features of the predominant constituent, the Jats.[15]

McLeod has placed a good deal of stress upon 'the caste diversity' in the Sikh Panth, and on the fact that notions of status based on caste are by no means extinct within it. He points out, however, that this should not conceal 'the significant degree to which the Panth has succeeded in eliminating many of the discriminatory aspects of caste'. He goes on to add that the Sikh insistence on equality is far from being a pious myth. 'Freedom within the Panth may not be a total freedom but it represents an impressive achievement nevertheless and an endeavour which is still proceeding. Sikhs are above all else loyal to the Guru. The question of equality within the Panth offers no exception to this inflexible rule.'[16]

CRUCIAL ROLE OF IDEOLOGY

Jagjit Singh has not written with reference to McLeod's essay on the subject. Therefore, there is no criticism of McLeod in Jagjit Singh's essay. His objective is to show how the Sikh Gurus steered away from the shackles of the 'constitutive elements' of 'the caste system' to create a new society.[17] In order to bring their achievement into high relief Jagjit Singh gives an exposition of the Indian caste system. One could find elements of caste in other countries too: antipathies based on the differences of race or colour, taboos regarding human beings and animals or even callings, notions of purity and impurity, restrictions on marriages, differences of status based on heredity, social disabilities or segregation. But in India alone could one find all such elements woven into an organic whole. In the Indian system over 3,000 sub-castes were meticulously arranged in an hierarchical social pyramid in which each sub-caste was fixed irrespective of its political and economic position. Practically all aspects of the social behaviour of each subcaste were regulated by fixed rules and codes. These sub-castes were, by and large, endogamous groups, and they worked sedulously to isolate themselves from each other in other social matters too. Nothing could change this hierarchical pattern. Marginal exceptions were made, but only to preserve the overall structure. There was practically no upward social mobility. The Indian caste system was thus a continuously downgrading process.[18] Restrictions on connubium and commensality were the most outstanding features of caste hierarchy. All the constituents of the caste system were interdependent and interlocked both horizontally and vertically in the social fabric.

Three main factors accounted for this unique social formation in India. First, the 'caste ideology' based on the principle of human inequality by birth gave pre-eminence to caste status. Wealth and power could serve only as the adjuncts of this status. The authority for caste ideology was provided by religious scriptures and it was reinforced by the concept of *varnashrama dharma.* The system was further cemented by custom, ritual and ceremonies, the notion of pollution and purity, and the theory of *karma.*[19] The second factor was the support provided to the system by the Brahmans who served as its ministers and ideologues.[20] The third factor mentioned by Jagjit Singh is the caste society itself as the primary institution based on caste ideology.[21]

Jagjit Singh underlines that the Sikh movement broke away from the caste ideology and the caste society from the very beginning. Guru Nanak did away with the consciousness of caste-status and obliterated the gap between the rich and the poor in terms of status-consciousness. By repudiating the Brahmanical scriptures, Sikhism and the Sikh Panth cut themselves away from the perennial source of caste ideology. Cutting itself away from Hinduism, Sikhism delinked itself from the daily operation of the Hindu Dharma. The Sikh Gurus had no veneration for the cow and they discarded the notion of ritual purity and pollution. There was no priestly class among the Sikhs, and Brahmans remained insignificant within the Sikh Panth. By eliminating the influence of Brahmans, the Sikh society eliminated the 'kingpin of the caste system' from within its ranks.[22]

The achievement of the Sikh Gurus was not restricted to the ideological plane. By founding the Sikh Panth, Guru Nanak started the process of founding a 'separate society'. His successors worked consistently to establish a separate identity of the Sikh Panth as of the Sikh Church. The creation of the Khalsa by Guru Gobind Singh was the acme of the Sikh movement. The Sikhs were militarized not only to fight religious and political oppression but also to capture political power for an egalitarian cause. The Khalsa made a clean break with the caste society. The *raison d'être* of the Khalsa and the proof of its separate identity was its success in giving an egalitarian socio-political orientation to the Sikh society. The Khalsa had a plebian base. If anything, the spirit of equality, brotherhood and fraternization was reinforced by the Khalsa. The leaders of the Khalsa included members of the erstwhile lower castes and even outcastes. Caste prejudices and caste priorities were abolished in matters of commensality. The Sikh revolution raised the social and political status of a large section of the commoners *en bloc*. The taste of political power made the Sikh Jat feel prouder than the Rajput, and made the Ranghretas feel equals of the Sikh Jats.[23]

Jagjit Singh's exposition of the subject is looked upon by Justice Gurdev Singh as radically different from McLeod's. Therefore, we may go into a little more detail. On the theme of caste ideology, Jagjit Singh quotes Guru Nanak to the effect that the Hindus who looked down upon the Chandals as foul were themselves perverse and vain and their acts produced strife. The Vedas created myths and illusions regarding what is good and what is evil. Guru Nanak identified himself with the lowliest of the low, and denounced the pride of caste as the source of errors. Guru Gobind Singh writes that he does not accept the Vedas, Shastras, Smritis and Puranas. This presumably is the evidence for Jagjit Singh's view that Guru Nanak and his successors discarded caste ideology. He goes on to say that according to Bhai Gurdas, Guru Nanak made the *dharma* perfect by blending the four castes into one; the prince and the pauper were treated on equal footing and even the outcastes were regarded as noble. The grammatical construction of Bhai Gurdas's language indicates that he was not repeating a precept of the Gurus but referring to actual practice. This evidence enables Jagjit Singh to infer that all distinctions of caste stood obliterated within the Sikh Panth. The evidence for the rejection of all notions of purity and impurity is the well-known verse of Guru Nanak to the effect that if the ideas of impurity are admitted there is impurity in everything — cow dung, wood, grain and even water. According to the *Mahima Prakash*, all castes were treated as equal in the congregation and *langar* of Guru Angad; Guru Amar Das made it compulsory for all visitors to eat in the *langar*. According to Koer Singh, Sikhs of all castes, including the Shudras, ate together. According to Ratan Singh

Bhangu, even the Ranghretas were included in inter-dining.[24] This evidence is cited to show that there were no restrictions on commensality in the Sikh Panth.

On the question of Brahmans and their influence within the Sikh Panth, Jagjit Singh refers to their insignificant numbers within the Panth rather than to any statement of a Guru or a Sikh writer. On the question of a separate Sikh society, Jagjit Singh gives quotations from different sources in support of the distinct identity of the Sikhs in religious and social terms. The quotations which have a bearing on caste within the Sikh Panth are to the effect that all four castes were blended in the Khalsa and they ate together. Thus, the discussion of this point does not carry the argument any further. On the question of a new socio-political order, Jagjit Singh emphasizes the presence of lower castes and outcastes in the Khalsa Panth, the spirit of equality among the Khalsa, the spirit of service among the Sikhs, and the emergence of lower caste leaders (including outcaste leaders). Their success in capturing political power raised the status of individuals and groups coming into power.[25] The basic point made here relates to upward social mobility through the medium of the Sikh movement.

Jagjit Singh's assumption of a more or less egalitarian Sikh Panth before the establishment of Sikh rule has interesting implications for his treatment of caste in the Sikh Panth after the establishment of Sikh rule. He thinks in terms of 'aberrations in Sikh society' due to the large influx of proselytes from the caste society who retained some of their caste prejudices and usages. But even so the Brahmans did not become a point of reference with regard to social status or hierarchy, and Sikhs have never owed allegiance to a scripture other than the *Guru Granth Sahib*, or to any *dharma* other than the Sikh Dharma. Therefore, notions and practices regarding connubium and commensality, or the survival of hierarchy in villages, must be seen as a heritage from previous connections with the caste society. Their survival must not be connected with any of the three facets of the caste system, namely the caste ideology, the dominance of Brahmans and the caste society as an institution. The only relevant question, therefore, can be the extent to which some of the prejudices and practices inherited from the caste society have been shed off or modified at various levels of the Sikh society.[26]

Jagjit Singh takes up this point at what he calls 'the Panthic level' first. The large-scale conversions to the Panth during the late eighteenth century, and the continuation of this process in the nineteenth and twentieth centuries, indicates that the Panth remained open to all castes, including in fact the outcastes. This in itself should be seen as a radical departure from the caste ideology which admits 'no change of caste'. The institution of *langar* has been kept alive as an anti-caste heritage. People from all castes, including the Mazhabi Sikhs, take part in preparing the food and in serving it to others. Commensal restrictions did creep into the Sikh society, but it is not clear when. Evidence for the late eighteenth century is contradictory. Even when such restrictions crept in, only the outcaste Sikhs were not allowed to eat with others. The Jat Sikhs, Khatri Sikhs, Arora Sikhs and Ramgarhia Sikhs interdined. In fact, they were not castes in the Brahmanical sense as they did not constitute an hierarchy. There was no question of superiority or inferiority between the Jat Sikhs on the one hand and the Khatri and Arora Sikhs on the other. The Ramgarhias were not a subcaste among the Tarkhans. In any case the Ramgarhias do not accept the Jat Sikhs as superior to them and there was no outside pressure on them to do so. Like the Ramgarhias, the Kalal Sikhs (the Ahluwalias) raised their social status after capturing power during the eighteenth century. The other artisan groups among the Sikhs face no social pressure, except that the Jat, Khatri, Arora and Ramgarhia Sikhs are reluctant to intermarry with them.[27]

At the village level, since hierarchy was a heritage from the remotest past, it would be too much to expect drastic changes in social hierarchy in Sikh villages, or in the social status of the artisans and menials who embraced Sikhism so late as the post-Khalsa period. Nevertheless, Jagjit Singh maintains that they do not have the same degree of social stigma attached to them as their counterparts in the caste society. The Sikh Chhimbas are not treated as outcaste. The Jhiwar and Labana Sikhs have hypergamous relations with their Hindu counterparts. Sikhs of all *jatis*, except the Mazhabis, inter-dine in the villages. The Mazhabis sit with others in *gurdwaras*. On the whole, the position of artisan and menial groups in the Sikh society is better than the position of their counterparts among the Hindus, or even the Muslims. Nonetheless, the Chuhras and Chamars present a really tough problem.[28]

Jagjit Singh insists that the achievement of the Sikh movement should be judged in the context of the Indian caste system and not in comparison with some other societies. No other movement in India enabled the Shudra Jat to regard his status as higher than that of the Rajput; raised Jats, carpenters and Kalals to be the rulers of the land; and made the Khatris, Aroras, Jats, artisans, village menials and outcastes forget their caste biases to merge into a genuine brotherhood on equal terms.[29]

The success of the Sikh movement in matters of marriage on caste lines was negligible even in relative terms. Jagjit Singh's explanation is rather significant. In his view, the role of endogamy in the caste complex has been over-emphasized. Even in those societies which have no castes, individual and group prejudices regarding marriage exist on the basis of various kinds of considerations. Few societies have tended to lay down positive laws governing marriages between different social groups and classes. What makes endogamy obnoxious in the caste society is the caste ideology. The Sikh Gurus did not object to inter-caste marriages, but they did not want to take any steps which might adversely affect the very objectives of their movement. They could not risk the future of the movement by insisting on inter-caste marriage. To fight the religious and political oppression of the rulers of the day was more urgent and more important than the abolition of all caste distinctions. The prejudices of the caste society, which was the recruiting ground of the Sikh movement, coupled with priorities of the Gurus, explain their politic attitude towards caste endogamy within the Sikh Panth. Moreover, they could hope that caste endogamy would disappear with the disappearance of caste-status and the ritualistic barriers between castes.[30]

THE TWO VIEWS IN COMPARISON

McLeod and Jagjit Singh have written on caste in the Sikh Panth independently of each other. Both of them make a clear distinction between *varna* and *jati*. Both of them look upon commensality and connubium as of crucial importance in a discussion of caste. Both subscribe to the view that restrictions on inter-caste marriage and inter-caste dining were there in the Sikh Panth during the nineteenth century and have survived into the present. However, for Jagjit Singh, such restrictions were far smaller in commensality than the caste patterns of marriage. Both McLeod and Jagjit Singh seem to agree that there was no caste system among the Sikhs in the sense of an accepted order of caste status. Jagjit Singh is more emphatic, however, that there was no hierarchy even when the caste prejudices persisted. Both see the relevance of Sikh ideology for caste relations within the Sikh Panth. However, Jagjit Singh gives it far greater importance than McLeod.

Jagjit Singh makes a distinction between empirical inequalities in the Sikh Panth surviving as legacies from the pre-Sikh past and the Sikh ideology as completely egalitarian. There is no approval of inequalities in the *Granth Sahib*. Jagjit Singh attaches importance to ideas, feelings and sentiments in illustrating the operation of the ideal of equality. McLeod appears to insist on the intractability of social realities already in existence. Consequently, McLeod and Jagjit Singh differ in their understanding of the character of the Sikh social order even before the establishment of Sikh rule. Jagjit Singh does not visualize any restrictions on commensality but recognizes the continuance of the traditional patterns of marriage. McLeod does not visualize any change in the patterns of marriage and looks upon commensality as confined virtually to the ritual distribution of sacred food and the institution of *langar*. Jagjit Singh is right in asserting that there was no formal restriction on inter-dining among the 'caste' groups which joined the Sikh Panth, but he appears to go a little too far when he asserts that even the 'outcastes' were included. He cites only Ratan Singh Bhangu in support of his statement that the Ranghretas (the erstwhile Chuhras) used to inter-dine with the other Sikhs. But he fails to notice Bhangu's observation on the same page that his maternal grandfather, who was among the prominent leaders of the Khalsa during the eighteenth century, made a clear distinction between the 'caste' and 'outcaste' members of the Panth in matters of commensality.[31] Nevertheless, the extension of commensality from the Brahman to the clean Shudras of the traditional order was a telling expression of the ideal of equality.

McLeod and Jagjit Singh appear to hold the stick from opposite ends, the former from the end of empirical realities as he sees them and the latter from the end of ideology as he understands it.

There is hardly any doubt that Sikh ideology introduced equalities in the religious, social and political spheres of the Sikh Panth and that the Sikh Panth was more egalitarian than the traditional social order. At the same time, some of the traditional institutions and practices were taken for granted and the ideal of equality left them unaffected. Consequently, inequalities existed side by side with new equalities. It is nonetheless important that Sikh ideology does not support any notions of hierarchy based on birth or occupation. At the same time, differences of wealth were accepted as God given.

RECENT VIEWS OF GENDER RELATIONS

Writing on Guru Nanak forty years ago I took notice of Kapur Singh's categorical statement that Sikhism declares woman to be 'the very essence of social cohesion and progress'. She could not be relegated to 'an inferior status in any manner'. The verse quoted by him from the *Asa di Var* is frequently quoted by other scholars. It poses the rhetorical question, 'why denounce her who gives birth to rajas?' This verse does refer to the woman's indispensability for procreation, and as mother and wife. Guru Nanak appears to defend woman against those who would regard her as inferior on the basis of sex. Guru Nanak Panth was open to women. Thus, women was placed at par with man, just as the Shudra was placed at par with the Brahman.[32]

However, Guru Nanak appeared to have little overt concern for the plight of widows or divorced women. By far the largest number of his metaphors came from the conjugality, presenting the traditional image of the ideal wife. Beautiful, accomplished and well mannered, she was humble and modest before her husband. She was completely devoted to him and obeyed his commands with pleasure. She could not bear separation from her husband. She adorned herself only to please him. She was faithful to him. Fidelity, however, was mutual. Guru Nanak's conception of conjugality clearly kept the woman in the home though it tended to imply monogamy. There was no direct criticism of what would be regarded as 'social evils' in the twentieth century. On the whole, therefore, it seemed necessary to see the general idea of equality in relation to the empirical realities of the Sikh social order.[33]

Writing in 1996, W.H. McLeod states that Sikhs invariably turn to the famous *shalok* in *Asa di Var* which says, 'Why cast aspersions on her who gives birth to rajas'. McLeod goes on to add that this verse is held to summarize the attitude of all Sikhs to the place that women occupy and it would seem to maintain complete equality for women with men. 'Certainly Guru Nanak's words carry us well beyond the conventional view of his time or, for that matter, the present time as well. Without a woman man is nothing, so should she ever be called weak or polluting?' The other Gurus support the stand taken by Guru Nanak, opposing such practices as dowry, seclusion, and female infanticide. Their views were vastly ahead of those of their contemporaries.[34]

McLeod goes on to underline that Sikh history did not support the idea of complete equality between men and women. In the first place, all the Gurus were men. Even the contemporary Sikh institutions are strongly male-dominated. This suggests the possibility that what was understood from the very beginning was that women deserved every respect but it was the duty of men to protect them and, for this, to assume 'the role of leaders in the affairs of the family, locality and nation'. The entire span of Sikh history was almost completely the history of the doings of men. Minor qualifications and a few exceptions would only prove the rule. As a result of the Singh Sabha reform, the situation of women within the Sikh Panth had been improved.[35] But this improvement did not apply to leadership within the Panth. Therefore, the issue of female subordination remains insistent. McLeod's analysis of the issue of gender relations in the Sikh Panth makes the general point that the idea of equality did not make women equal to men in Sikh society, expecially in public life.

In a note to his essay, McLeod refers to the works published by Nikky-Guninder Kaur Singh and Doris R. Jakobsh, both of whom have used the evidence of the *Dasam Granth* in their exposition and discussion of gender relations within the Sikh Panth.[36] The latter, entitled *Relocating Gender in Sikh History*, is far more comprehensive in its scope than the former. In any case, Jakobsh gives an overview of gender formation in the early period of Sikh history, though the 'major focus' of her work is on the nineteenth and the early twentieth century.

Not being a scripture scholar, Jakobsh has relied heavily upon a few secondary works and a few translations. Guru Nanak, in her view, maintained that women, like members of the lower castes, were not barred from attaining enlightenment. However, procreation was central to his vision, especially the procreation of sons, as in the verse about the woman giving birth to *rajan*. Jakobsh thinks that by placing *rajan* at the top of the contemporary hierarchical order, Guru Nanak indicated his support for 'the dominant social and political order of his time'.[37] But there is ample evidence in his compositions to suggest that Guru Nanak denounced the political and social elite of his time in strong and clear terms.[38] Therefore, the inference drawn by Jakobsh from Guru Nanak's verse is not justifiable.

According to Jakobsh, women are often associated with *maya* in the compositions of Guru Nanak, indicating his apprehension of the female as a barrier to the attainment of emancipation.[39] However, the husband is also a lure and the woman is a dupe as well as a part of *maya*. The view taken by Jakobsh is partial and, therefore, misleading. She also thinks that there are negative images of women, compounded by ambivalent messages towards the outcastes: 'Evil-mindedness is a low woman, cruelty a butcher's wife, a slanderous heart is a sweeper woman, wrath which ruineth the world a pariah woman.'[40] However, Guru Nanak is addressing a Brahman and the images of outcaste women are used contextually for the message to regard evilmindedness, cruelty, slander, and wrath as untouchable. If Guru Nanak could identify himself with outcaste men, there could be no problem with outcaste women.[41]

Jakobsh thinks that Guru Nanak grieved over the rape of women during the invasions of Babur but he did not show any concern about the plight of the widow, or the evils like *sati*, and female infanticide. Therefore, he seems to throw the path of liberation open to women without discarding the traditional notion of woman's inferiority.[42] This formulation is self-contradictory. There is ample evidence in the compositions of Guru Nanak that a person who has attained liberation is actually superior to others. Logically, a woman who has attained liberation would be superior to all men who have not.

The first instance of social criticism in Gurbani for Jakobsh is the comment of Guru Amar Das on the practice of *sati*: 'They are not satis who are burnt alive on the pyres; rather satis are they who die of the blow of separation (from their husbands).' The issue is seen as having become more palpable with increase in the number of Sikh men and women, including the Khatris who generally subscribed to the ideal of *sati*.[43] But this would not explain the emergence of a value: why does the Guru tell the Sikhs that there is no merit in the act of becoming a *sati*?

Guru Ram Das is partially quoted to show that men are ridiculed when they are not dominant: 'Men obedient to their womenfolk are impure, filthy, stupid; men lustful, impure, their womenfolk counsel follow.'[44] Elsewhere in the book the verse is translated as: 'Sinful men, licentious and stupid, act as their women command. Lust abounds; thus do impure men take orders from their women and act accordingly.'[45] Actually, the Guru is talking of the *manmukh* in contrast with those who follow his instruction; the sinful and ignorant men are those who listen to their women out of lust as a moral weakness, and ignore the Guru's instruction. Clearly, the reference is not so general as it is made out to be.

Jakobsh thinks that women were given a role in leadership in the time of Guru Amar Das. But the evidence to support this assumption is extremely thin, and much later to the time of Guru Amar Das. Jakobsh accepts McLeod's suggestion that the number of Jats within the Sikh Panth was increasing during the time of Guru Amar Das. The Jat women were as assertive as Jat men. This would explain the increasing assertion by women in the Sikh community.[46] The whole of this construction is conjectural. Jakobsh invokes no contemporary evidence for the time of Guru Arjan either, but suggests that women would be relegated to positions more in line with the traditional roles because of the heightened politicization of the Panth. The masculine ethos is said to be back before Guru Gobind Singh created the Khalsa with its hyper-masculine ethos.[47]

In the *Janamsakhis*, on the whole, there is little criticism of the society in which Guru Nanak lived. In other words, the compilers of the *Janamsakhis* do not appear to have been seriously concerned with gender relations, neither for the time of Guru Nanak nor for their own.[48] However, Jakobsh misses the most relevant message of the *Janamsakhis*: the path of Guru Nanak was open to women in their own right. In the context of the seventeenth century this was also the most important message.

With a clear conception of gender theory, Jakobsh appears to be unclear of the significance of the evidence she has used, and unaware of the importance of the evidence she has not used. She is the only scholar to have tried to interpret the evidence in a socially meaningful way. It is necessary, therefore, to take notice of some of the contemporary evidence that has a close bearing on the issue of gender relations in the early Sikh social order.

CONTEMPORARY EVIDENCE ON GENDER RELATIONS

A number of verses in the compositions of Guru Nanak state the ideal of equality. God is in all living beings. The one who created the 'vessels' placed the same light in all. His light is in every 'heart'. It is God's light that shines in all. God created both 'man and woman'; God's light is in both 'man and woman'. There are both female and male devotees of God.[49] Thus, at one level Guru Nanak upholds woman's equality with man.

God's creation is impermanent in contrast with his eternal existence; it is 'false' in contrast with God's 'truth'. The whole universe is his *maya.* As a part of *maya*, both man and woman belong to the realm of falsehood. There is 'pleasure in women'. The conjugal bed and beautiful women are among the objects of attachment. Female beauty and male desire are closely linked.[50] However, the conjugal bed is enjoyed not only by men but also by women. They are the counterpart of men who suffer a similar fate for the same reason. The woman wishes to have as much sensual pleasure as she can. The son is also an object of attachment for the mother. The woman is as much a dupe of *maya* as man.[51] There are unregenerated women just as there are unregenerated men. The term *manmukh* applies to both men and women.

Guru Nanak is opposed to women's denigration. The verse in which he emphatically defends women relates to the custom of observing *sutak* which is denounced in rather strong terms.[52] He does not approve of discrimination against women. In fact, womanhood *per se* is defended and appreciated.

Guru Nanak expresses great appreciation for the householder. Most of his metaphors come from relationship of conjugality. He talks of the *sohagan*, the *dohagan*, and the woman in separation from her spouse. He talks of the woman with merit and the woman without merit. The metaphors refer simultaneously to two parallel situations: the devotee accepting the will of God and uniting with him through his grace, and the wife dedicating herself to the husband to be enjoyed by him at will. It can be argued that the woman's subordination to her husband is reinforced. However, the metaphor also carries the implication that she can attain liberation.[53] The woman who accepts the Guru's instruction is dear to her spouse and enjoys the peace of *sahaj*: she becomes a *sohagan* by finding God as her spouse; she has discarded all demerit to become a *bairagan* in search of Hari; through God's grace she is now beyond sorrow and separation. The boon of the Truth, the Name and the *Shabad* is obtained only through God's grace. The path offered to the woman is the same as the one offered to the man.[54]

On the whole, the woman in the compositions of Guru Nanak is at par with the man in relation to God. Attached to *maya*, her kith and kin, the pleasures of the senses, and a life of luxury, she is a victim of the 'five adversaries' (*kam*, *krodh*, *lobh*, *moh*, *ahankar*), very much like Guru Nanak's *manmukh*, the self-willed fool of a man. She can appropriate the Truth, the Name and the Word through the mediacy of the Guru, like the Gurmukh of Guru Nanak's conception. No human being can 'achieve' or 'earn' emancipation: in the last analysis it depends on God's grace. The ultimate objective for woman as for man is *sahaj*, the state of eternal bliss in union with God, the mingling of light with light.

Paradoxically, however, Guru Nanak creates spiritual space for women without discarding the inegalitarian partriarchal framework. He takes the institution of family for granted. Built into this social institution was inequality and subordination. The use of metaphors from conjugality results actually in reinforcing the institution. The scholars studying gender relations in the Sikh social order have to grapple with the tension between the normative ideal of equality and the intractable institution of patriarchal family.

The *shaloks* of Guru Angad reinforce Guru Nanak's basic position. The ideal of equality is underscored. The human body, ungendered, is the *khand* which has the nine treasures of the Name. The *shabad* of the Guru is meant for everyone. All have only one Master, and none can be regarded as inferior. There is the same nectar in everyone; it is found through the Guru's grace. They who appropriate the Name may receive grace. Whoever has the desire to meet God may find the reward for good deeds. The ideal of equality among human beings is consistently stated.[55]

Guru Angad talks of conjugal love. There is always spring for the woman who has the spouse in the home. Miserable is the woman whose spouse is in foreign lands. 'Every woman has a support of one kind or another but I have no support other than you. I cry and die if I do not lodge you in my heart'. The way to meet the spouse lies in remembering him in sorrow and comfort, all the time. The *dohagan* remains in misery because she is attached to some one else, and not to her spouse. The *sohagan* is at peace because she loves her spouse.[56] Guru Angad takes the family for granted.

There are only two other images of women in the *shaloks* of Guru Angad. In one, the false woman is in the forefront in the Kaliyuga, just as the mischievous man is the *chaudhari*. By implication, this has to be changed. In another *shalok*, earth is the mother, just as water is the father and air is the Guru. Bracketing the mother with the father and the Guru is not without significance. On the whole, Guru Angad appears to treat men and women alike. It is highly significant in this context that he makes an explicit statement that the *bani* of Guru Nanak, unlike the Vedas, does not uphold the inequality of caste and gender.[57]

Turning now to a Sikh of the Guru, Bhai Gurdas, who was nurtured on Gurbani, we find that he compares a Sikh with a *sohagan* as the woman who was loved by her mother and father as a girl, treated as a beloved sister by the brothers in both the maternal and paternal families; lakhs were spent on her marriage when she was loaded with ornaments and given a large dowry; she is respected in her marital home which is made honourable by her presence; she enjoys the bridal bed with her beloved husband, eating all kinds of delicious foods and always adorned with ornaments; she is rightly regarded as an equal part and the means of liberation.[58]

The Gurmukh for Bhai Gurdas is a householder (*gharbari*); he is devoted to one woman as his wife. Superior to a celibate, he looks upon other women as daughters and sisters. He does not go near another woman. The Sikh of the Guru does not touch a woman other than his wife. The man who sleeps with another woman is a thief:

his nose and ears are cut-off. The husband of two women, like the wife of two men, remains in misery.[59] Bhai Gurdas stands clearly for monogamy and mutual fidelity.

Bhai Gurdas refers to the plight of the abandoned woman; she is welcome nowhere. Worse than her is the prostitute who entertains many men and indulges in sin; herself ruined she ruins others; her son gets no family name; she is outside the norms of the society. The prostitute adorns herself and sings to attract all and sundry; she has no husband and her son has no maternal or paternal name. The man who goes to a prostitute incurs sin and suffers from disease. Bhai Gurdas refers to the practice of *sati* for underscoring the merit of dying to the self. The family of a widow who becomes a *sati* is respected and honoured; the Sikhs are respected and honoured for eradicating their *haumai* in the *sadh-sangat.*[60] If the wife comes to know that her husband is unfaithful to her, she does not start going to other men.[61] Above all, a woman's primary obligation is towards the Guru and God. Without the perfect Guru, a beautiful woman, enjoying her conjugal bed and other pleasures of *maya*, goes to hell. People appreciate and admire the love of Laila and Majnun, Sorath and Bija, Sassi and Punnun, Mahiwal and Sohni, and Ranjha and Heer, but preferable over these is the love of the Sikh for God.[62] Bhai Gurdas takes it for granted that women could be liberated through devotion to God, like Daropati (Draupadi), Gautam's wife Ahilya, and a sinful prostitute.[63] Like the outcaste men, women may receive God's grace. The *sadh-sangat* of Bhai Gurdas was not confined to men.

The *B40 Janamsakhi* makes it unambiguously explicit that the path enunciated by Guru Nanak was open to women. In the *sakhi* of Raja Shivnabh the courtesans are so affected by the *bani* of Guru Nanak that their meeting with him becomes the source of *brahmgian*; they start reciting 'Guru, Guru' and become intoxicated with the love of God; they tell Raja Shivnabh that they have been liberated by a Great Man. In the *sakhi* of Guru Nanak's visit to a country inhabited by women, they use their magical powers to turn Mardana into a ram but they are powerless against Guru Nanak. Impressed by his spiritual power, they wish that their country too should have men. They are blessed by Guru Nanak and they gain peace. They begin to recite the name of God. Another *sakhi* visualizes a *dharmsal* close to the palace of a raja whose wife is the daughter of a Sikh. They visit the *dharmsal* and the *sangat* performs *ardas* for the birth of a son. In another *sakhi*, Guru Nanak praises the women who recite the name of God. In yet another *sakhi*, the father, the mother, and the son are praised as good Sikhs; the term used for the mother is *sikhni*.[64]

The *Chaupa Singh Rahit-Nama* contains injunctions for three categories of Sikhs: the *keshdharis*, the *sahajdharis*, and the Sikh women. They all belong to the Sikh or Khalsa community. They are not supposed to have any association with the Minas, Dhir Mallias, Ram Raiyas, the Masands and their followers. Only the *keshdharis* among the Khalsa are baptized through the rite of the double-edged sword. Thus, women in this work are not alone in not being baptized through this rite. Injunctions with regard to women are scattered in the *Rahitnama*. The Sikh of the Guru is instructed not to have any association with a woman other than his wife. This injunction is repeated several times. He should never kill a girl child and should not associate with those who resort to this practice. This injunction too is repeated several times. A Sikh in the service of the state was exempt from all obligations except three: he should not smoke, should not observe *bhaddan* (which involved shaving of the head), and he should not kill a girl child. A Sikh who goes to a Muslim prostitute and enjoys the dance performance of a prostitute at the time of marriage is a defaulter. A Sikh woman should not read *Granth Sahib* in a *darbar* of Sikhs; she should only listen. But a Sikh woman could read *Granth Sahib* in a gathering of Sikh women. There are also injunctions which reflect male prejudices against women.[65]

Apart from these scattered injunctions with regard to gender, there are injunctions addressed explicitly to Sikh women at one place.[66] A Gursikhni should sustain a docile and dutiful disposition, and regard her husband as her lord. Other male relatives should be treated like a father, a brother, or a son, in accordance with their age and position. A Gursikhni should not prepare or serve food if she is not clean. However, most of the injunctions are what may be called the counterpart of the injunctions meant for men. A Gursikhni should not bathe naked; she should not stand naked in water and cast it towards the sun. Both the water and the sun are like her father.

A Gursikhni should sit in a *satsang* with her head covered. She should learn how to read the *Granth* and she should abandon singing of popular or vulgar songs. A Gursikhni should instruct her husband in the Sikh faith. The men of the Kaliyuga have weakness for women. Therefore, instruction imparted by a Sikhni is more effective. A Gursikhni should serve better food to a Sikh in need than to a member of her own family. A Gursikhni should learn portions of the Guru's scripture by heart. Twice a day she should visit a *dharmsal* and pay homage to the *Granth Sahib*. She should weave cloth with the cotton she has herself spun and, depending upon her resources, offer it either as a wrapping-cloth for the *Guru Granth Sahib* or as a covering for the floor. A Gursikhni should set aside a handful of flour from the family's daily supply and offer it to the Guru by giving it either to a *dharmsal* or to a needy Sikh. She should not pray at tombs and cenotaphs. She should accept only the guidance of the Guru and believe in none but the Guru, her husband, and the true congregation. Finally, the injunctions of the *Rahitnama* are said to be for Gursikhs and Gursikhnis who are equally important components of the Khalsa Panth.

Common injunctions for both men and women is the most of striking feature of the *Prem Sumarag*. A person who follows the prescribed *rahit*, whether a man or a woman, shall enjoy the reward meant for the Panth of Sri Guru Akal Purkh Ji. Whosoever follows what has been written, whether a man or a woman, shall receive the reward in this life. The first two chapters relate to religious beliefs and practices, to *nam*, *dan* and the *sikhkhi* of Akal Purkh Ji. Not only men but also women should be initiated through baptism of the double-edged sword. They should acquire Gurmukhi learning and read and love *shabad-bani*. They should gather together and reflect on the *shabad*. The *sohagan* should serve her husband and respect his wishes, and the husband should not have any association with another woman.[67]

The rites and ceremonies to be performed on the birth of a daughter are the same or similar to those performed on the birth of a son. The female child, like the male, is to be administered baptism of the double-edged sword. The author is keen to emphasize that considerations of caste and status are a temporary compromise. There are no distinctions among the Khalsa of Sri Guru Akal Purkh

Ji: they are deemed to belong to one and the same caste and shall become one in the future. The author talks of 'Khalsa Sikhnis'.[68] There is hardly any doubt that the woman is an equal member of the Khalsa Panth for the author of the *Prem Sumarag*.

There is no prohibition against marrying the girl of another caste, or a slave girl, or even the daughter of a *mlechh* (Muslim). The injunction with regard to sexual intercourse carries the implication that it is meant for procreation. The rites after death for women of all ages are similar to those for men: common to both are *kirtan* and *ardas*.[69] In the Sikh state visualized by the author of the *Prem Sumarag*, no one should remain unmarried. The parties to adultry should be publicly humiliated. Prostitution is bad, but it is better than adultery. The best thing is to avoid both. The ruler of the Sikh state should give greater attention and consideration to the householders.[70]

The author of the *Prem Sumarag* does advocate the necessity of remarriage for a widow who has no son or daughter even if her marriage was consummated. He may appear to take a very dim view of women when he states that they have low intelligence; they do not know what is good or bad for them; their essence is obstinacy which is the source of all good or bad they do. The woman has a much greater sexual urge than the man. Even a mother should not sleep in the same room as her grown up son. However, this traditional or popular view of the woman is used to argue that if a man cannot live without a wife, how can a woman live without a husband? Therefore, a widow should be allowed to get remarried if she cannot control her sexual urge. Not only a widow who is childless but also a widow who does not have any surviving children may get remarried. But the widow who has a daughter or a son should not remarry.[71]

If a man dies without a son, his property should go to his daughter's son or to his daughter. If a man has only a daughter, on his death she should inherit his property. The daughter's daughter should inherit like the daughter's son. It is made absolutely clear that if there is no son or grandson, the property of the deceased should go to his daughter. And if there is no daughter either, it should go to his sister.[72]

The *Prem Sumarag* presents an ideal Sikh social order. The woman is not exactly at par with the man in this social order. But the degree of equality between Khalsa men and Khalsa women makes them almost equal. Gender in Sikhism is conceptualized as a balance between the norm of equality and the demands of a patriarchal family.

NOTES

1. Gurdev Singh (ed.), *Perspectives on the Sikh Tradition*, Patiala: Siddharth Publications, 1986, 'Introduction', p. 9.
2. Ibid., p. 31.
3. W.H. McLeod, *The Evolution of the Sikh Community*, New Delhi: Oxford University Press, 1975, p. 83.
4. Ibid., p. 84.
5. Ibid., pp. 85-6.
6. Ibid., pp. 86-7.
7. Ibid., pp. 87-90.
8. Ibid., p. 91.
9. Ibid., p. 92.
10. Ibid., p. 93.
11. Ibid., p. 94.
12. Ibid., pp. 95-7.
13. Ibid., pp. 98-101.
14. Ibid., pp. 101-3.
15. Ibid., p. 103.
16. Ibid., p. 104.
17. Jagjit Singh, 'Caste System and the Sikhs', in *Perspectives on the Sikh Tradition*, p. 231.
18. Ibid., pp. 232-7.
19. Ibid., pp. 238-6.
20. Ibid., pp. 256-8.
21. Ibid., pp. 258-63.
22. Ibid., pp. 263-72.
23. Ibid., pp. 272-6.
24. Ibid., pp. 263-4, 266-7, 270, 272.
25. Ibid., pp. 271-9.
26. Ibid., pp. 280-90.
27. Ibid., pp. 290-7.
28. Ibid., pp. 297-303.
29. Ibid., pp. 303-5.

30. Jagjit Singh, 'Inter-Caste Marriages', in ibid., pp. 315-20.
31. Ibid., pp. 271, 310 n. 197.
32. J.S. Grewal, *Guru Nanak in History*, Chandigarh: Panjab University, 1998 (rpt.), p. 192. For Kapur Singh's statement, see Kapur Singh, *Parasharprashna: An Enquiry into the Genesis and Unique Character of the Order of the Khalsa with an Exposition of the Sikh Tenets*, ed. Piar Singh and Madanjit Kaur, Amritsar: Guru Nanak Dev University, 1989, p. 252.
33. Grewal, *Guru Nanak in History*, pp. 193-6.
34. W.H. McLeod, *Essays in Sikh History, Tradition and Society*, New Delhi: Oxford University Press, 2007, pp. 190-1.
35. Ibid., pp. 192-6.
36. Ibid., p. 196 n. 1.
37. Doris R. Jakobsh, *Relocating Gender in Sikh History: Transformation, Meaning and Identity*, New Delhi: Oxford University Press, 2003, pp. 24-5.
38. See Grewal, *Guru Nanak in History*, pp. 151-65.
39. Jakobsh, *Relocating Gender in Sikh History*, p. 25.
40. Ibid., pp. 25-6.
41. Grewal, *Guru Nanak in History*, pp. 190-2.
42. Jakobsh, *Relocating Gender in Sikh History*, p. 26.
43. Ibid., p. 29.
44. Ibid., p. 12.
45. Ibid., p. 34.
46. Ibid., pp. 35-6.
47. Ibid., pp. 27-9.
48. Ibid., pp. 44-5.
49. *Adi Granth*, pp. 13, 19, 62, 223, 228, 580, 663, 879.
50. Ibid., pp. 14-15, 72, 142, 222, 229, 351, 416, 468, 728, 1288.
51. Ibid., pp. 417, 596, 1187.
52. Ibid., pp. 472, 1289-90.
53. Ibid., pp. 225, 730, 772, 1329, 1332.
54. Ibid., pp. 54, 557, 843, 1232.
55. Sahib Singh, *Shalok Guru Angad Sahib Steek*, pp. 59, 78, 114, 117, 121, 124.
56. Ibid., pp. 51, 57, 96, 99, 100, 127.
57. Ibid., pp. 62, 122, 130.
58. Bhai Gurdas, *Varan Bhai Gurdas*, ed. Giani Hazara Singh, Amritsar: Khalsa Samachar, 1962 (7th edn.), *Var* 5, *pauri* 16 (5.16).
59. Ibid., 6.8; 6.12; 6.18; 12.4; 33.3; 33.7.
60. Ibid., 3.19; 5.17; 17.10; 19.7; 31.14; 33.9; 34.6; 35.13.
61. Ibid., 5.8; 30.14; 34.14.

62. Ibid., 15.7; 27.7; 35.20.
63. Ibid., 10.8; 10.18; 10.21; 27.1.
64. *Janamsakhi Sri Guru Nanak Dev Ji* (Pbi), ed. Piar Singh, Amritsar: Guru Nanak Dev University, 1974, pp. 57-8, 78-9, 109-10, 132-3.
65. *Chaupa Singh Rahit-Nama*, tr. & ed. W.H. McLeod, Dunedin: University of Otago, 1987, pp. 59-60, 66-7, 69, 75, 77-8, 105, 111, 113, 127.
66. Ibid., pp. 188-90.
67. *Prem Sumarag Granth* (Pbi), ed. Bhai Randhir Singh, Amritsar: Sikh History Society, 1953, pp. 8, 17, 20-1.
68. Ibid., pp. 25, 27, 41, 43-4, 49.
69. Ibid., pp. 56-7, 74-5, 77, 86-90.
70. Ibid., pp. 108-9, 110.
71. Ibid., pp. 46-8, 84-5.
72. Ibid., pp. 126, 131.

PART THREE

INTERPRETING THE SINGH SABHA MOVEMENT

CHAPTER 8

'Ham Hindu Nahin'

CULTURAL RE-FORMATION AND SIKH IDENTITY

W.H. McLeod starts with the perception of the Singh Sabha reformers that everything was not right with the Sikhs and their beliefs and practices. Hinduized ritual was being practised in contemporary *gurdwaras*, and the presence of Hindu idols disfigured the Golden Temple. The observance of caste, especially discrimination against outcastes, was another feature which disfigured the Panth. It infringed the clear intentions of the Guru embodied in the institutions of *sangat* and *langar* and in the common bowl for initiation. In the villages it was often impossible to distinguish a Sikh from a Hindu, and the villagers were not even conscious of differences. They could seek favours at the tombs of Muslim *pirs* and worship Sakhi Sarvar and Gugga. Some Sikhs cut their hair and smoked. How could such men be accepted as Sikhs of the Guru? The solution thought of by the Singh reformers was to purge the Panth of false beliefs and superstitions, whether Hindu or Muslim. 'Sikhs must be summoned to a genuine reaffirmation on their Khalsa loyalty.'[1]

The Amritsar Sabha was an elite organization concerned with issues affecting the Sikh Panth. Conspicuous amongst its founders were titled gentry, affluent landowners, and noted scholars. Particular emphasis was laid on the promotion of periodicals and other appropriate literature. British officers were invited to associate with the Sabha and matters relating to government were excluded from its range of interests. The Singh Sabha movement never lost its elite texture, but the leaders of the Amritsar Sabha were challenged by the Lahore group which proved to be much more aggressive. The Lahore Sabha attracted intellectuals with a more radical approach to the Panth's problems. They insisted on Khalsa exclusiveness and this was eventually accepted as orthodox. The Khalsa tradition came to be regarded as 'standard' and Sahajdharis were accepted as 'slow-adopters'. The reformist section of the Singh Sabha movement came to be known as Tat Khalsa (the 'True' or the 'Pure' Khalsa). They were opposed by the Sanatan Khalsa. Each side had its own interpretation of the nature of Sikh tradition. The Singh Sabha Movement is generally equated with the Tat Khalsa in terms of doctrinal formulation, social policy, and historiography. Prominent among the Tat Khalsa reformers were Bhai Kahn Singh of Nabha and Bhai Vir Singh. To be closely associated with them was M.A. Macauliffe.[2]

McLeod summarizes the Tat Khalsa understanding of the Sikh tradition in general and the role of the Singh Sabha in particular. He also summarizes the opposing viewpoints put forth by those who identified themselves as Sahajdhari Sikhs and by Punjabi Hindus who were not formally associated with the Panth. The debate was conducted in terms of whether or not the Khalsa were Hindu, leaving out the possibility of Sahajdhari identity being treated as 'Sikh'. On both sides the historical past was manipulated to defend contemporary perceptions. Moreover, McLeod finds these interpretations as 'much too simple to be acceptable'. To claim that the twentieth century Khalsa was 'identical' with the early eighteenth-century Khalsa was to ignore 'the never-ending sequence of response which any religious group must necessarily make to changing circumstances' (unless it is 'moribund'). To insist that the Khalsa were Hindu was to ignore the self-identity of the Khalsa, their conviction that they were not Hindu. McLeod tries to clarify the point with reference to *amritdhari* and *keshdhari* Sikhs: they are not identical but no one doubts the Sikh identity of the *keshdhari*. A critical and historical analysis must recognize 'the continuity which extends from the earliest days of the Nanak-panth to the end of the nineteenth century'. However, this would be insufficient by itself. 'The force of intervening circumstances must also be recognized.'[3]

McLeod looks upon the military policy of the British in its bearing on the Sikhs as 'a significant element' in the debate concerning Sikh identity from 1875 to 1925, but he does not accept Richard Fox's hypothesis.[4] He is prepared to concede 'a variety of identities' in the nineteenth-century Sikh Panth, but the claim presented by Fox amounts to a serious exaggeration. McLeod maintains that to imply that no dominant tradition existed was to ignore the clear evidence of earlier periods. Although the Khalsa was not the sole claimant to the title of Sikh, it was by far the strongest and it carried into the British period conventions which enable us to recognize a clear connection between the Khalsa of the eighteenth century and that of the twentieth. Fox's suggestion that the 'Singh identity' was selected by the British and then appropriated by a particular caste for its own class purposes is unacceptable. As a theory it is no more valid than the claim that the Khalsa identity was invented by radical members of the Singh Sabhas. Far more important than economic and military policy was the larger colonial context in which new patterns of administration, a new technology, a fresh approach to education, and entry of Christian missionaries meshed together to produce great impact.[5]

Most of the men who met in Amritsar and Lahore to form the first Sabhas in 1873 and 1879 came from the Sikh elite. They were reacting to a perceived attack on their inherited traditions, and these traditions were to be defended in whatever ways might seem appropriate. The traditions were derived from their pre-British past, reflecting the earlier acceptance of a dominant Khalsa. The chosen method of defence involved educational influence and use of available technology, and this pattern became increasingly evident as the movement progressed. Remaining loyal to the inherited tradition, the Tat Khalsa reformers began to produce definitions and to shape systems in the light of ideals and modes of thinking acquired from education and Western literature. As a result:

> It was Sikh tradition, and specifically a Khalsa tradition, which they developed and glossed. To suggest that they developed a new tradition is false. Equally it is false to claim that their treatment of it can be described as a simple purging of alien excrescence or the restoration of a corrupted original. The Khalsa of the Singh Sabha reformers was both old and new.

The Khalsa ideal now was distinguished by a new consistency and a new clarity of definition. The earlier features which were not acceptable were either rejected or suitably modified. Quest for distinctive rituals was initiated, and attempts were made to produce acceptable statements of the *rahit.* 'An appropriate version of the Panth's history was formulated, a powerful stress was laid on the doctrine of Guru Granth, and Sikhs were exhorted to observe conventions which would proclaim their separate Khalsa identity.' Prominent amongst these conventions was observance of the 5 Ks. A fierce debate developed with the Arya Samaj apologists, with insistent stress on the claim that Sikhs could never be regarded as Hindu. All this time, the pressure of contemporary attitudes operated on the desire to protect traditional loyalties. McLeod illustrates this with reference to Anand Karaj. Whether or not there were any precedents, the Tat Khalsa took it up as their ideal and campaigned for the Anand Marriage Act which was passed in 1909.[6]

McLeod takes notice of the 'Sanatan' opposition to the Tat Khalsa ideology. It was only gradually that the Tat Khalsa views are said to have gained ascendancy amongst the intellectual leaders of the Panth but eventually they did secure dominance within the Singh Sabha. The Amritsar Sabha continued to reflect the Sanatan conservatism of many of its early supporters but the 'philosophical initiative' passed increasingly to the Lahore group. Their strength was 'the strength of ideas and effective communication rather than that of direct political influence'. Though the Chief Khalsa Diwan, founded in 1902 to unite various Singh Sabhas, was dominated by relatively conservative landowners, they were not unwilling to advance 'the progressive cause'. The more conspicuous and influential contribution in terms of debate and publications came from the Tat Khalsa whose ideal was to promote reform through education, journalism and preaching.[7]

Sikh identity appeared to the Tat Khalsa to be the key issue. The debate was greatly intensified when the widow of Dyal Singh Majithia went to the Chief Court after his death in 1898 to contest his will in favour of the 'trust' he had founded. Two pamphlets entitled *Sikh Hindu Hain* were published under the name of Sikh authors. Bhai Kahn Singh presented the opposite viewpoint in his *Ham Hindu Nahin*, first issued in Hindi in 1898. Soon afterwards he also made an attempt to produce a coherent statement of the *rahit* in his *Gurmat Sudhakar*. This was one of several such attempts which culminated in the publication of the *Gurmat Prakash Bhag Sanskar*. Though implicitly Khalsa in contents, this manual did not exclude the Sahajdharis altogether from its scope. Two major claims of the Tat Khalsa can be seen as gaining general acceptance: one, that Sikhs are not Hindu and the other, that a true Sikh will normally be a Khalsa. This interpretation stopped short of any claim to exclusive possession of the entire Panth.[8]

The British administrators who were given the charge of framing laws had to face the question of Sikh identity. In 1891, census enumerators were instructed to return all those persons who kept their hair uncut and abstained from smoking as Sikhs. Thus, the Keshdharis alone were to be treated as Sikhs. The Sahajdharis could return themselves as Nanak-Panthis, or as followers of other Sikh Gurus. In the census of 1901, sects were not included. But in 1911 it was decided to enter every person who claimed to be a Sikh as Sikh. The category of 'Sikh-Hindu' was also permitted. No change was made in 1921.

At the time of the elections for the Shiromani Gurdwara Prabandhak Committee, elected members were required to wear the 5 Ks. In the Sikh Gurdwaras Act of 1925, the Sikh is defined as a person 'who professes the Sikh religion'. At the same time, the following declaration was required if any doubt arose: 'I solemnly affirm that I believe in the Guru Granth Sahib, that I have no other religion.' This does not necessarily exclude the Sahajdharis. In fact, in theory, it places them at par with the Khalsa. The task of redefining the *rahit* devolved on the SGPC after the Act of 1925. In the *Sikh Rahit Maryada*, published by the SGPC in 1950, the Sikh is defined as a person 'who believes in Akal Purakh; in the ten Gurus; in Sri Guru Granth Sahib and other writings of the ten Gurus, and their teachings; in the Khalsa initiation ceremony instituted by the tenth Guru; and who does not believe in any other system of religious doctrine'. This definition implies preference for the one taking *amrit*, includes the Keshdhari, and does not exclude the Sahajdhari. In the Delhi Gurdwara Act of 1971, the Keshdhari Sikh is included but not the Sahajdhari Sikh.[9]

The *Adi Granth* provided the doctrine of the divine Name as the assured means of liberation, authority superior to that of the SGPC and even the doctrine of Guru Panth. The second feature relevant for Sikh identity was the *gurdwara* in which the egalitarian principles of the Panth were most effectively applied through the impartial distribution of *karha prasad*, the convention of the *langar*, and the traditional concept of service in addition to congregational worship. Veneration for the Gurus, as embodied in the Sikh prayer (*ardas*), was added as the third feature of Sikh identity.[10]

In generic terms, McLeod finds no meaning in 'race', but the term 'nation' seeks recognition for the Sikhs as a political community. Speaking pragmatically, McLeod mentions three categories on the ground: the Amritdhari, the Keshdhari, and the Sahajdhari. Of these three, the first two are regarded as almost of equal validity. The third, however, has lost much in comparison with its former recognition. Among the additional features of Sikh identity was preference for the Khalsa *rahit* including the 5 Ks, denial of caste distinctions in spite of the tolerance of caste practices, equality of women with men in theory in spite of the existing differences in practice, and the universality of the message of Sikhism with the implication that the Panth is open to all human beings, irrespective of their caste, creed or nationality.[11] Thus, the Singh Sabha Movement is presented as having rationalized and sharpened the Khalsa Singh identity which was the predominant Sikh identity in the early nineteenth century.

RUPTURE WITH SANATAN SIKHISM

Harjot Oberoi on the other hand looks upon the Singh Sabha Movement as 'a rupture'. His conception of 'Sanatan Sikhism', for which his evidence comes largely from the late nineteenth century, particularly for 'Sanatanist' ideas and attitudes, is relevant for a proper assessment of his position.

Oberoi tells us that in a public lecture at Guru Ka Bagh in Amritsar, Gulab Singh referred to the Sikh faith as 'the true Sanatan religion'. For him, the four Vedas were the religious books of the Sikhs too. Giani Gian Singh backed his statement of Gurmaryada with 'extensive proofs from the Vedas'. Avtar Singh Vahiria debated doctrinal issues with reference to the *Gurbilas*, the Vedas, the Puranas, and the Epics 'in the same breath'. He counted Guru Nanak among a long line of *avtars* born out of Brahma and united with Brahma after their earthly mission. He expected a Sikh to show the same allegiance to the descendant of a Guru as to the ruler. In his view, any person who accepted the teachings of Guru Nanak qualified to be a Sikh. The Sahajdharis are regarded as a part of the Panth in a work sponsored by Sodhi Narain Singh and written mostly by Avtar Singh Vahiria. Oberoi quotes from this manual to the effect that 'the untouchable groups' among the Sikhs were to be regarded as agents of 'pollution' by the Sikhs of all other castes from the Brahman to the Nai or the Jhiwar. It was due to this purity-pollution polarity that the Sikh 'untouchables' were barred entry into the major Sikh shrines. The acceptance of the Brahmanical paradigm of *varna-shrama dharma* gave 'a logical place' to the Udasis within the ambit of Sikh tradition, legitimizing asceticism. Idols were allowed to be worshipped within the precincts of the Golden Temple and the Akal Takht.[12]

About the practices of the Sanatan Sikhs, Oberoi refers to the Sodhis of Anandpur receiving the obeisance of the people and accepting offerings from them at the time of the Holi festival. The *pothi* and *mala* in the possession of the Sodhis of Har Sahai, which were believed to have come down from Guru Nanak, attracted people to the place at the time of the Baisakhi fair every year so that they could pay homage to the sacred relics of the Guru. The *Granth Sahib* in the possession of the Sodhis of Kartarpur was revered in a similar fashion by princes and the common people. Not only the Sodhis but also other representatives of the Guru lineages established *guru-sikh* relationship with a large number of clients. For eminent writers, Oberoi cites a few examples of Nirmalas rather than Udasis, the most notable being Pandit Tara Singh Narotam who wrote on Sikh theology and scriptures. In his *Gurmat Nirnay Sagar*, published in 1878, Pandit Tara Singh Narotam developed an elaborate theological statement of 'Sanatan Sikhism' based on the compositions of the Gurus. Giani Gian Singh received his formal training and instruction from him. Sant Atar Singh was educated at a Nirmala establishment. Atma Singh, a Nirmala scholar of Amritsar, was associated with Ernest Trumpp in his project of translating the *Adi Granth*.[13]

The longest chapter in Oberoi's book is on Sikh participation in 'popular religion'. In his view, the popular form of religious expression 'worked out a comfortable relationship' with Sanatan Sikhism. His evidence comes largely from the critics of these practices, the Tat Khalsa. The objects of worship in popular religion were Sakhi Sarvar, Gugga, the Devi (Goddess) under many different names, especially Sitala, the sainted dead, Khawja Khizr, village godlings, the sun, the earth, and sacred trees. Then there was belief in evil spirits, witchcraft, sorcery and magical healing, involving a number of practices based on that belief. Similarly, belief in astrology and divination was quite common. The festivals like Baisakhi, Diwali and Holi were celebrated by Sikhs as much as by others. There were monthly festivals timed according to the different phases of the moon, like *puranmasi* and *sangrand*. A closely related theme was that of fairs (*melas*) held in honour of persons as well as gods and goddesses. The intermediaries in popular religion, like its objects of worship, were also different, consisting of *pirs, bharais, mirasis, ojhas* and *sianas*.[14]

Oberoi does not attach much importance to disapproval of popular religion by certain Sikh individuals and groups he refers to. The author of the *Gurbilas Chhevin Patshahi*, written in the early nineteenth century, tells his readers that they should not visit non-Sikh places because heaven can be attained by bathing at Sikh religious centres, and that those who were afraid of the messengers of death should seek to breathe their last at the Golden Temple. Readings from the Sikh scriptures as well as pilgrimage to Sikh shrines could lead to fulfilment of wishes for male progeny, cure against fevers, and the like. The idea was to discourage Sikhs from going with such expectations to non-Sikh places or persons. The author of the *Sau-Sakhi* tells the readers not to worship Sitala Devi to seek cure from small pox, not to partake of offerings made to her, and not to participate in the practices associated with the cult of Sakhi Sarvar. The supposed ends of magic and witchcraft can be attained by relying on Sikh sacred scriptures, especially when combined with *hom*. Baba Dayal, the founder of the Nirankari movement, insisted on constant reading of Sikh sacred text and remembrance of the divine name in a manner that carried implicit disapproval of the magical universe of popular religion. The Namdharis or Kukas were aggressively explicit on the point: they started desecrating, demolishing and destroying village shrines and sacred ancestral sites in the countryside. They also destroyed some tombs and places sacred to Hanuman and Lakshman. But even the Kukas betrayed the impact of Sanatan modes of thought in suggesting 'alternatives.'[15]

Oberoi is conscious of the obligation to show the 'relationship' of popular religion with his 'great tradition'. Whereas the Sanatan categories of thought and behaviour were influenced by texts, both Sikh and non-Sikh, popular religion was independent of texts of any kind. The Sanatan tradition was mainly an urban phenomenon; popular religion belonged to the countryside. Despite such differences, however, these two forms of religious expression seem to have worked out a comfortable relationship. The best examples in Oberoi's view come from the area of goddess worship. When Fateh Singh Ahluwalia was afflicted with small pox as a prince, the royal family of Kapurthala arranged for the worship of Sitala, and held a thanksgiving ceremony in her honour when the prince was cured. Raja Fateh Singh and Maharaja Ranjit Singh together undertook pilgrimage to Jwalamukhi, and performed all the religious rites at the shrine of the goddess, 'a sister of Sitala Devi in popular mythology'. Ranjit Singh gifted large amounts of money to the shrine and had its roof gilded. Karam Singh, the ruler of Patiala, built a temple for Mansa Devi at Kalka. These examples do give indication of what Oberoi has in mind when he talks of relationship between popular religion and 'Sanatan Sikhism', but practices of Sikh rulers are equated with Sikhism.[16]

Oberoi argues that Sikhism was not in 'a state of decline' after the British annexation of the Punjab. The decline in Sikh numbers was a myth created by the British and perpetuated by the Tat Khalsa. Actually, 'decline' meant the prevalence of 'Sanatan Sikhism'. Oberoi refers to J.D. Cunningham as a witness to the vigour of the Sikh faith in the mid-nineteenth century.[17] Oberoi fails to see, however, that Cunningham was talking of the vigour of the faith of the Khalsa Singhs.

With reference to the colonial situation, Oberoi states that the traditional intellectuals, holy men, and other religious figures among the Sikhs were hit adversely by the policies of the British administrators of the Punjab who regarded these established representatives of the old order as parasites. Their revenue-free grants were withdrawn and indigenous education was discouraged. The British administrators were keen to introduce social reform. The practice of female infanticide was successfully eliminated by the 1870s. To avoid the impression of direct interference with indigenous customs, the British administrators encouraged the Punjabis to undertake reform. The Anjuman-i Punjab, founded in 1865, had a great impact on Sikh society. It proved to be the training ground for the leaders like Khem Singh Bedi, Attar Singh of Bhadaur, and Professor Gurmukh Singh. The Punjabis founded their own associations, following the example of the Brahmo Samaj in which Dyal Singh Majithia played a very prominent role.[18]

In this general atmosphere of reform, Christian missionaries employed a two-pronged strategy to propagate the gospel effectively: publishing evangelical literature in the vernacular and opening mission schools. The intention of a few Sikh students of a Christian mission school to convert to Christianity became the immediate occasion for the founding of the Singh Sabha at Amritsar. A Sikh aristocrat and a Sikh *giani* convened a meeting of leading public figures and traditional intellectuals among the Sikhs. Prominent among the participants were Baba Khem Singh Bedi, Kanwar Bikrama Singh, and Giani Hazara Singh. They decided to institute the Sri Guru Singh Sabha, Amritsar, with a democratic constitution as a registered body, having elected office-bearers. It remained in the control of Thakur Singh Sandhanwalia, Raja Bikram Singh, Baba Khem Singh Bedi and Kanwar Birkarm Singh. Prominent among the intellectuals of the Sabha were Giani Hazara Singh and Avtar Singh Vahiria. Four decades after the founding of the Singh Sabha, Vahiria liked to believe that its purpose was 'to safeguard the ancient customs, rites and rituals of the Sikh community'. The first publication sponsored by the Sabha, the *Sri Gurpurab Prakash*, published in 1885, narrated the biographies of the Sikh Gurus and listed the day, month and year of birth and death for each of them. In response to Trumpp's *Adi Granth*, Giani Badan Singh prepared an annotated edition of the *Adi Granth* under the patronage of the rulers of Faridkot. It took more than twenty years to appear in print as *Sri Guru Granth Steek* in 1905-6 in three volumes. The fourth volume appeared still later.[19]

The ideas and attitudes of the leaders of the Amritsar Singh Sabha were reflected in its monthly magazine *Sri Gurmat Prakashak*. All those who believed in the Sikh Gurus and the sanctity of the *Adi Granth* were Sikhs. The Sahajdharis were qualified to be Sikhs as much as the Khalsa. The term *mona* was appropriate only for a

Sikh who cut his hair after taking *pahul*. The low caste Sikhs were not to be given the same religious rights as the high caste Sikhs. Sikh men could neither dye their beards nor roll them into a thick bun. The recitation of hymns not found in the *Adi Granth* was to be discontinued. These items of *rahit* indicate that radical change was not on the agenda.[20]

Instead of showing the Amritsar Singh Sabha as representing 'Sanatan Sikhism', Oberoi compliments the Sanatanists for recognizing the existence of several traditions within the Sikh Panth and accepting multiple sources of authority. The Sanantan Sikh tradition could thus accommodate the beliefs of folk Sikhism and diverse elements from popular culture. This inbuilt tolerance enabled the Sanatanists to face dissent, social inversions, and even the total abandonment of community renunciation with great ease and grace. 'By legitimizing "deviation" the Sanatanists not only ensured the vitality of the Panth but also significantly reduced the possibilities of conflicts with other religious communities.' Individual Sikhs enjoyed wide religious freedoms, with a vast terrain from which to choose their rites, rituals and beliefs. 'This is reflected, for instance, in the fact that if a Sikh so desired, he or she could in the same year go to a khanaqah [*sic*] of a Muslim pir like Sakhi Sarvar in western Punjab, undertake a pilgrimage to the Golden Temple in central Punjab, and visit Hardwar to take a dip in the holy Ganges.' This sort of ritual exercise caused no ripples within 'the Sikh sacred hierarchy'. There was a place in the Sanatan tradition for all individuals, types, personalities, categories, groups and traditions. Recreation, fun, amusement and joking were an integral part of the myths, stories, and ritual practices of Sanatan Sikh tradition. This ludic element enlivened religion, encouraged innovation, and enriched religious tradition: 'the ludic provided a rich resource of creativity, and as a result religion was not so much dreary and repetitive but rather lively and invigorating. It was able to constantly renew and change itself.' For Oberoi, the 'carnivalesque Sanatan tradition' exemplifies the strength and richness as well as the actual state of the nineteenth-century Sikh religious tradition. His great appreciation for this tradition comes to the fore despite his professed scholarly neutrality. He sounds almost regretful that the Sanatanists had to yield place eventually to the Tat Khalsa.[21]

The Amritsar Sabha was followed by the Singh Sabha founded at Lahore in 1879. Subsequently, more than a score of other Sabhas were founded in the next five years. By the end of the nineteenth century the number of Singh Sabhas exceeded one hundred. All the cities, most of the towns, and some villages of the province could boast of a Singh Sabha. Khalsa Diwans were founded to coordinate the activities of the Sabhas. With the proliferation of Singh Sabhas emerged a new kind of leadership. Oberoi refers to this leadership as the 'new elites'. They were new in their functions and in the instruments of transmission they appropriated: anglo-vernacular education and print culture. They evolved a 'sub-culture' for wider dissemination: 'they were not just engaged in aping the west, but in exploring and constructing avenues to come to terms with the altered historical situation.'[22]

Gurmukh Singh and Bhai Harsa Singh provided the initial impetus for the Lahore Sabha. They started publishing a weekly in Punjabi, the *Gurmukhi Akhbar.* The Khalsa Press was opened in 1883. An Urdu weekly of the Sabha, the *Khalsa Gazette*, began to appear in 1884. The Punjabi weekly *Khalsa Akhbar* and the monthly *Sudharak* were launched. A Khalsa Diwan was set up at Lahore in 1886 to coordinate the activities of the increasing number of Singh Sabhas. Their success was due largely to the 'immense seduction' their discourse held for 'a restless and upwardly mobile Sikh elite'. The other prominent leaders of the Lahore Sabha were Bhai Jawahar Singh Kapur, Ditt Singh and Attar Singh of Bhadaur.[23]

In the Tat Khalsa view of the world, the *Granth* was the rightful heir of the ten Sikh Gurus, and it took precedence over all other sacred texts: the Vedas, the *Gita*, the Puranas, and even the *Dasam Granth,* the 'great code' of the Sanatanists. It was gradually eased out of rituals and lost its textual hegemony. In the early 1880s the Tat Khalsa began to reconstitute sacred space by initiating three measures: a campaign against certain seasonal fairs held within the precincts of Sikh shrines; the removal of non-Sikh icons from the Sikh sacred centres; and a strident call for the reform of temple management. Oberoi thinks that management of the major temples 'had always been the prerogative of the rulers and not the ruled'. The Tat Khalsa would wage an all-out battle to push out what they saw as a corrupt and irresponsible religious establishment simply because it was Sanatan. In their view, 'all Sikhs had a right over the community's sacred resources'. By directing all sacred resources into Sikh temples the Tat Khalsa made the gurdwaras 'Sikh corporate symbols *par excellence*'.[24]

The Tat Khalsa consolidated the *Rahitnama* tradition by rigidly enforcing external symbols and codifying life-cycle rituals. The sanctity of the *kesh* was brought into high relief in narratives of martyrdom. Repeated emphasis on *khande ki pahul* in Tat Khalsa literature succeeded in turning baptism into the most salient of the Sikh *rites de passage.* All Sikhs were required to perform the same rituals without any reference to their caste or *biradari* tradition. What began as changes introduced by a small minority gradually came to be accepted by the Sikh public at large. The passage of the Anand Marriage Act in 1909 boosted the Tat Khalsa position on *rites de passage.* In Oberoi's view, 1909 can be seen as a watershed in the history of 'modern Sikhism'. To the evolving inventory of 'separatist symbols' were added the Gurmukhi script and the Punjabi language as exclusive emblems of Sikh identity, with perhaps the most far-reaching implications.[25]

The norms of the Tat Khalsa discourse were radically opposed to the prevailing Sanatan tradition and popular religion. The widespread practice of worshipping popular saints like Sakhi Sarvar and Gugga Pir came under attack. In fact, all forms of popular worship became the target of hostile polemic. Village gods, local shrines, ancestral spirits, holy nature-spots, and *devis* like the small pox goddess Sitala were ridiculed and proclaimed to be powerless. Similarly, attendance at seasonal agrarian fairs, listening to folk songs, the singing of bawdy songs by women at the time of wedding – all these invited the censure of the Tat Khalsa. Their intolerance was matched by their disdain for customary forms of family entertainment: song, dance and music. Fasting was viewed with great hostility, particularly by men. Sikh participation in the festivals of Lohri, Holi, Dussehra and Diwali was denounced as mark of Hindu domination over Sikhs.[26]

The Sanatanists waged a long struggle against the increasing influence of the Tat Khalsa. Baba Khem Singh Bedi, as President of the Amritsar Khalsa Diwan, proposed at the annual meeting of the Diwan in 1884 that all Singh Sabhas in future should be called

'Sikh Singh Sabhas'. This could attract the Sahajdharis, the Nirmalas and the Udasis as well as the Khalsa. But he had to drop the motion because of bitter opposition from its radical members. In 1885, they raised objection to the use of a cushion (*gadela*), in the presence of the *Granth Sahib*, and an overwhelming majority of the members supported them. This resulted in a split in the Khalsa Diwan.

Avtar Singh Vahiria publicized his view that Sikhs could worship Durga without inhibition. He was prepared to concede that Brahmans need not negotiate between the families of a couple to be married, but he insisted that the couple must circumambulate a fire, which amounted to rejecting the Anand ceremonial. In his view, Anand marriage was an innovation of the Nirankaris; there was no evidence that the Sikh Gurus ever performed their marriage rituals according to the Anand procedures. He also supported the right of a bereaved family to take unburnt bones for immersion in the Ganges. In his view, the Khalsa initiation rite was not obligatory; each tradition within the ambit of Sikh experience could have its own initiatory rite. In Oberoi's view, Avtar Singh Vahiria spoke for all Sanatan Sikhs. They became the natural allies of personnel working in shrines and other sacred establishments. 'In their turn, the support staff at Sikh gurdwaras was closely aligned to Sanatan ideology.'[27]

In order to broadcast their ideology, the Sanatan Sikhs began to make increasing use of print culture. Avtar Singh Vahiria began to edit and publish the *Sri Gurmat Prakashak* in 1885. It was used to discredit the Lahore Singh Sabha and its leaders: 'For them Sri Guru Granth Sahib is merely a book and they consider the worship of Sikh gurdwaras a form of idol worship. They have no respect for Sikh Takhts and the *hukum-namas* issued from these takhts.' The 'Sanatan' leadership barred radical Sikh activists from the major Sikh shrines. Gurmukh Singh, was prevented from addressing a Sikh congregation at Manji Sahib, close to the Golden Temple, by the steward of the Golden Temple 'accompanied by a police sargeant'. Two decades later, in 1907, Babu Teja Singh, received a similar treatment at Damdama Sahib. Its 'Sanatan' management issued a proclamation against all members of 'the Singh Sabhas' and in favour of Nirmalas and 'the guru lineages'. Authoritative encyclicals in behalf of the 'Sanatan Sikhs' were matched by direct action against the radicals. When the move to expel Gurmukh Singh from the Khalsa Diwan was frustrated in 1885, he was threatened with physical violence and forced into hiding at Jalandhar. He was excommunicated in 1887 by an edict issued by Man Singh, the manager of the Golden Temple, at the instigation of Baba Khem Singh Bedi and Raja Bikram Singh.[28]

The basic strength of Sanatan values came from 'Sikh personnel at the major Sikh shrines and sacred establishments'. Khem Singh Bedi was the first to declare that Sikhs were Hindu, thus entering the Arya-Sikh controversy against the radical Sikhs. He was joined in this by the rulers of Faridkot and Patiala. Avtar Singh Vahiria explained that Sikhism was like a wing within a large inn called Hinduism: 'It shared the same foundation and courtyard but had its own separate rooms and terraces.'[29]

According to Oberoi, the non-elite consisting of the peasantry, agricultural labour and artisans in both rural and urban areas often defied the norms sought to be established by the Tat Khalsa. Their hostility towards the Singh Sabhas was expressed through folk sayings, participation in rituals denounced by the radicals, and in festive cycles like Holi and Diwali. As noted in contemporary sources, this opposition appears to be 'erratic, diffuse and piece-meal'. This is because of the received notions of 'what constitutes resistance'. We should look for it not merely in the field of politics but also in its everyday manifestations to become aware of 'how dominant cultural definitions are breached'.[30]

The situation created by the colonial rule in the Punjab was favourable in some ways to the Tat Khalsa. Oberoi refers to the customary social relationships replaced by market relationships; the *sepidari* system became a victim of this change. The British army authorities appreciated the Khalsa identity and insisted upon its continuance for the Sikhs who joined the army. The British civilians tended to equate the Sikhs with the Khalsa. Furthermore, they thought in terms of monolithic religious communities, obliging the Sikhs to accept the monolithic construct. This identity could be invoked to keep 'others' out of competition for jobs. The expansion of local self-government created another arena for competition. All such factors enabled the Tat Khalsa to muster support from a much larger number of the Sikhs than the Sanatan Sikhs could. In any case, the colonial state and its institutions played a significant role in the emergence of a homogeneous Sikh religion.[31]

The colonial state and its institutions had much greater importance than the Khalsa tradition of the eighteenth century for the emergence of 'modern Sikhism'. The need of a new set of ideas and institutions to meet the challenge posed by political, economic and cultural changes brought about by the operation of colonial rule was even more important. The 'new elites' created a 'sub-culture' through a dialogic process in which new readings of the *Adi Granth*, the *Janamsakhis* and the *Gurbilas* literature were combined with an indigenous understanding of Western philosophy and social thought. Finally, Oberoi suggests that the emergence of a corporate Sikh identity was facilitated through a dialectical process begun by similar 'transformations in imagination, experience and cultural organization' among Hindus and Muslims.[32]

Oberoi underlines the change brought about by the Tat Khalsa in the following words:

> For over three hundred years the chequered history of the Sikh movement had not generated an all-embracing definition of a Sikh. The Tat Khalsa, through a series of innovations, purges and negations, supplied this definition in less than three decades. They endowed Sikhs with their own texts, histories, symbols, festivities, rituals calendar, sacred space, life-cycle rituals, in short a meaningful universe, separate and radically different from other religious traditions. Sikhs could now confidently lay claim to being an exclusive pan-religious community.[33]

'Religious identity' for Oberoi does not imply 'merely the formal beliefs that distinguish a group of people' and which may lead them to conceive of themselves 'as distinct from the rest of the population'. Equally important is the historical process by which 'a cohesive community of believers comes to be produced, consolidated and reproduced through a cultural fusion of texts, myths, symbols and rituals with human bodies and sentiments'. He goes on to add that texts, myths, symbols and rituals have to be considered together, and not just one or another in isolation, to avoid 'questionable conclusions'.[34]

Oberoi's conception of 'rupture' emerged from the concepts of 'episteme' and 'praxis'. Routine and intentional activity are derived from an 'episteme', one cannot exist without the other. Important changes in social, cultural and economic contexts can lead to 'a situation of praxis', that carries with it the possibility of 'a historical rupture'. Such a rupture was brought about by the Tat Khalsa and, according to him, 'modern Sikhism' stands clearly distinguished not only from the Sanatan tradition but also from the earlier Sikh tradition, including the Khalsa.[35]

For Oberoi, the Singh Sabha consisted of two components: the Sanatan and the Tat Khalsa. The former was holding the field when the Tat Khalsa appeared on the scene to triumph despite opposition. In Oberoi's formal discussion of the Sanatan tradition, its representatives turn out to be Sodhis, Bedis and Nirmalas, and a few other individuals associated with them, notably Avtar Singh Vahiria. In their exposition of Sanatan Sikhism, Oberoi mentions their acceptance of the authority of the Vedas and Puranas in addition to the Sikh scriptures, their belief in incarnations, their acceptance of the Sahajdharis as equal members of the Sikh Panth, their acceptance of *varnashrama dharma* which legitimized the Udasis and the idea of pollution, their tolerance of idol-worship and popular religion, and their belief in living *gurus*.

A scholar who appreciates Harjot Oberoi's book observes that his main thesis centres around a Sikh world consciously 'reconstructed' in the modern image of Khalsa ideology from the late nineteenth century onwards. However, it has yet to be proved empirically that the Khalsa identity was such a minor player within Sikhism before this time. Even if the Sikh elites of the late nineteenth century defined the 'boundaries' more clearly or precisely, these boundaries were limited by the sacred text and religious traditions dating from Guru Nanak. In other words, the case for rupture is extremely weak. A more serious objection is that Oberoi presents Sikh ethnicity as the product of 'narratives' which can be constructed variously according to circumstances. Finally, Oberoi is uncritical in accepting the *status quo* of structures against which Sikh ethnicity is defined, contested and determined.[36]

Oberoi ignores the presence of the Namdharis and the Nirankaris who do not strictly fit into his conception of Sanatan Sikhism. The Sahajdharis cover all non-Singhs; their acceptance by the Singhs carries the implication that the latter formed the main component of the Sikh Panth. This is what we find in the census.

If some Singhs looked upon Sikhs as Hindus, a large number of Sahajdharis protested they were not Hindu. Oberoi himself says that discrimination was confined to the untouchable groups and did not extend to Shudras. He appears to assume that this discrimination was not there earlier. Though Oberoi talks of 'Sikhism' in relation to popular religion, he is actually talking of popular religious practices among Sikhs. By its sheer existence, popular religion does not become 'Sikhism'.

Oberoi has argued that Sikhism was not on the decline in the third quarter of the nineteenth century. Much of the evidence on the question of decline refers actually to the decline of the Khalsa tradition and not of Sikhism. According to Oberoi, the religious elites of the time of Ranjit Singh and his successors suffered under the British never to regain their former importance. However, the religious elites among the Sikhs during the colonial period were associated with the central Sikh shrines. Their close association with the colonial state, the native princes and the Sikh aristocracy is noticed by Oberoi himself but without any comment on its significance. Almost literally, they represented 'vested interests'. They were opposed to the Tat Khalsa even on the issue of the Anand Marriage Bill.

Oberoi is not aware of a contradiction in his presentation of Sanatan Sikhs. If the basic tenet of Sanatan Sikhism was belief in the Sikh Gurus and the *Adi Granth*, it would include the Khalsa and the Sahajdharis but not a category like the Udasis. Oberoi's assertion that the Sanatan Sikhs recognized several Sikh identities is belied by the evidence of his so-called Sanatanists: they recognized only two identities, the Khalsa and the Sahajdhari. In the light of all these observations, Oberoi's generalizations about the Sanatan tradition lose their validity. His statement about a Sikh going to the Golden Temple, Hardwar and the shrine of Sakhi Sarvar in the same year is not a factual but a hypothetical statement. It was most unlikely to find such a person on the ground. Incidentally, Oberoi's unreserved appreciation for his Sanatan tradition implies a value judgement which infringes the academic neutrality he professes to espouse.

Education and print culture were the instruments used by both the 'Sanatan Sikhs' and the 'Tat Khalsa'. There could be a difference of degree only. Similarly, the importance given to the *Adi Granth* was not a new thing. If there was anything new, it was the emphasis on exclusiveness. Belief in the ten Gurus was an old belief, and so was the rejection of incarnations and gods and goddesses. Oberoi is wrong in stating that management of the Sikh shrines was always a prerogative of the rulers. The control and management of the Golden Temple, for example, was taken over for the first time by Sikh rulers, and that too on behalf of the Sikh Panth. The Tat Khalsa revived interest in the doctrine of Guru Panth. In theory, whatever belonged to the Gurus earlier belonged now to the Panth. This was the claim put forth in opposition to the control and management of the instruments of the colonial rulers. Oberoi has paid no attention to the control and management of sacred space in the early Sikh history. Therefore, he looks upon the Tat Khalsa attitude as something novel. He is justified in underlining the importance of the rites of passage, but according to his own presentation, only the Anand marriage was an 'innovation'. Even for this, however, there was the precedent of the Nirankaris, and probably a still earlier practice. Gurmukhi script was regarded as sacred by the Sikhs from the sixteenth century onwards. Punjabi was the language of much of their literature. When the question of scripts and languages cropped up in the late nineteenth century, it was quite natural and logical for the Sikhs to espouse the cause of Gurmukhi and Punjabi. On the whole, Oberoi tends to raise differences of degree into differences of kind and ignores the context as well as the background in his use of the label 'innovation'. The concepts of episteme and praxis predispose him to go all out to prove a hypothesis. In search of novelty, he minimizes the importance of the Khalsa tradition in accounting for the success of the Tat Khalsa.

CULTURAL REVIVAL AND SIKH IDENTITY

G.S. Dhillon disagrees with McLeod in regarding the Singh Sabha Movement as a 'reformist movement'. In order to determine its character he suggests four points: (a) ideology of the Sikh movement, (b) the level of its achievement in practice, (c) 'fall' if any, and (d) the changes brought about by the leaders of the Singh Sabha Movement. The first two relate to the ideas, attitudes and institutions of the Sikh Gurus and their followers till the establishment of Sikh rule. The third relates to the period of the Sikh and early British rule in the Punjab. The fourth relates, obviously, to the Singh Sabha Movement itself.

In his interpretation of the early Sikh tradition, Dhillon remains pretty close to the view presented by Daljeet Singh. Briefly stated, Sikh ideology was 'entirely new' and opposed to all contemporary religions. Guru Nanak denounced all those religious traditions which denied the unity of God; he discarded belief in gods and goddesses; and he opposed idolatry, ritualism and asceticism. He challenged the 'fanaticism' and 'hypocrisy' of the Brahmans, and the political oppression of contemporary rulers. He led a crusade against the caste system and stood against political despotism and economic exploitation. He rejected the Brahman's claim to superiority and put an end to his mediacy between man and God. He emphasized the brotherhood of man and stood for equality and fraternity among human beings. His ideal of emancipation recognized no distinctions of caste and creed. He stood for human rights and values. In his view the world was real and the purpose of life was to carry out the creative and attributive will of God. Social responsibility was an integral part of the spiritual life of the ideal man. This is an essential tenet of Sikhism and accounts for 'its distinctive and historic character, role and personality'.[37]

The operation of Sikh ideology can be seen in the history of the Sikhs from Guru Nanak to Guru Gobind Singh. With each succeeding Guru, Sikhism became 'increasingly crystallized and institutionalized' into a distinct faith and society. Guru Arjan presents a major landmark in the history of Sikhism: he compiled the scripture for the new society; he created 'a state within the state'; he sought confrontation with the empire and made the supreme sacrifice of his life. The doctrine of *miri-piri* was a corollary of Guru Nanak's path of love and sacrifice in the service of man, rejection of monasticism and asceticism, acceptance of the householder's life and responsibility, and the ideal of securing justice, equality and freedom for all men. This doctrine justified the use of force to uphold justice and righteousness, and to defend the oppressed. Guru Tegh Bahadur sacrificed his life for justice and emancipation of man. Guru Gobind Singh created the Khalsa to pursue the right path and to resist and undo injustice, tyranny and aggression. Four of the *panj piaras* belonged to the caste of Shudras, a clear indication that the Khalsa were meant to obliterate all distinctions of caste and creed to create a cohesive society. The *panj piaras* initiated the Guru into the Khalsa, which was meant to demonstrate that the Guru was the Khalsa and the Khalsa was the Guru. This made Sikhism 'the most democratic religion of the world'. The institution of *daswand* made the Khalsa a 'self-contained' society. The doctrine of *nash*, which involved 'giving up of those beliefs, prejudices and traditions that stood in the way of the sole worship of the Supreme Being', is said to have made complete break with the past religious systems, traditions and customs. Clearly, thus, the Khalsa was unique both in its 'external form' and 'internal features'. It was meant to, and did, play a vital role in Indian history.[38]

Throughout the eighteenth century the Khalsa were politically active, fighting for survival or political power. Their number remained rather small because their activity involved risks. Dhillon does not recognize the existence of any non-Khalsa Sikhs during the eighteenth century. In the early nineteenth century it became profitable to join the ranks of the Khalsa. In his view, this process had begun with the establishment of the Khalsa Commonwealth which gave opportunity to Muslim and Hindu population of the Punjab to seek conversion to Sikhism for mundane reasons. The ten or eleven lakhs of Sikhs estimated to have been living in the kingdom of Ranjit Singh were not simply the descendants of the Khalsa of the eighteenth century. The new converts, who constituted the bulk, were slow to shed some of their old beliefs and prejudices at personal, familial and social levels, including faith in local gods and goddesses, and in saints, *pirs* and *faqirs*. After the loss of political power, Sikh *gianis* turned to Hindus for the employment of their talents, and started teaching their religious books. Hindu tint was given to Sikh doctrines. While the Hindu converts to Sikhism tended to revert to their old prejudices, some Sikhs felt attracted to other religions, notably Christianity. Dhillon's hunch is that more than 70 per cent of the Sikhs in the 1870s belonged to the segment which had not shed their Hindu prejudices.[39]

Another factor which accounted for this situation was the activity of some of the descendants of the Sikh Gurus who had been lavishly patronized by the Sikh rulers earlier. They started the cult of 'personal worship' and collected offerings. It was in their interest to encourage both Sikhs and Hindus to become their followers. Their protégés started propagating that the Gurus had preached the religious system of the Vedas. Notable among them were Avtar Singh Vahiria and Gulab Singh. Nevertheless, even in this situation there were Sikhs who observed the *rahit* of the Khalsa, and the Nirankaris adhered to the teachings of the *Guru Granth Sahib* as their sole scripture.[40]

The Singh Sabhas made the Sikhs aware of their great spiritual and cultural heritage. By emphasizing the importance of Khalsa practices, social laws, customs and Punjabi language, the Singh Sabha leaders welded the Sikhs, once again, into an independent community, bound together by faith in the teachings of their Gurus. The keynote of the Singh Sabha was 'back to *Guru Granth Sahib*'. Its object was to restore the purity of Sikhism by abolishing those accretions and practices which did not stand the test of Sikh *maryada* or the teachings of the Gurus. The Singh Sabha is said to have made no innovations in Sikh thought and practices. Far from being a rupture or even a reformist movement, the Singh Sabha Movement was a 'revival' of the true Sikh tradition for socio-religious regeneration of the Sikh community. For this purpose it was necessary to devise a suitable strategy and to choose effective means. The new steps taken by the Singh Sabha leaders related to education on modern lines, and publication and propagation of religious literature.[41]

Dhillon, understandably, is critical of both McLeod and Oberoi. His criticism of McLeod is largely misplaced. It is based on a wrong reading of McLeod who, contrary to Dhillon's assertion, nowhere maintains that distinct identity was imparted to the Sikhs for the first time by the Singh Sabha. In fact, Dhillon goes on to attribute to McLeod something far removed from McLeod's actual position: that the British promoted the Khalsa identity out of several Sikh identities prevalent at the beginning of their rule and, therefore, the Singh Sabha can be regarded as a creation of the British.[42]

Dhillon seems to have read Oberoi more carefully. This may be because his own work on the Singh Sabha has been criticized by Oberoi. One objection which Dhillon raises against Oberoi is that he takes a partial view of Sikhism in the late nineteenth century and then projects it backwards in time, presenting a distorted interpretation. Dhillon regards this as a serious lapse in methodology. Oberoi forgets that the Tat Khalsa were by no means the first to denounce belief in gods and goddesses. This had been done by the Gurus from Guru Nanak onwards. The statements of Baba Khem Singh Bedi and his associates, especially Avtar Singh Vahiria, are treated by Oberoi as evidence on the whole of Sikhism whereas they represented only a partisan view. Oberoi equates their understanding of Sikhism with the Sanatan tradition which is further equated with the Sikh tradition during the nineteenth century. In the process, periphery comes to occupy the centre of the stage. Popular religion existed among Sikhs in spite of the norms of Sikhism: its incidence was far less than what Oberoi makes out; and it never became an accepted part of Sikhism. The Sikh Panth, according to Dhillon, consisted of the Khalsa and the Sahajdharis who held many common beliefs and observed many common practices. There is no justification for treating the Tat Khalsa as representing a 'sub-culture'. Oberoi is totally mistaken in seeing a parallel between what happened in 'Hinduism' and what happened in 'Sikhism'.[43]

AN ALTERNATIVE VIEW

Despite their differences with one another on several important points, all the three authors are more or less agreed that the leaders of the Singh Sabha Movement revitalized the Khalsa Singh tradition. In their understanding of the linkages between the Singh Sabha and the earlier Sikh tradition, the difference is the widest between Oberoi and Dhillon. Oberoi's view of the Singh Sabha as a new episteme arising out of praxis precludes the possibility of any meaningful linkages with the past. What is hammered by Oberoi is rupture even in its ordinary connotation. Dhillon argues that the Singh Sabha was a revival of the earlier Sikh tradition. His depiction underlines the close links of the Singh Sabha with the Sikh past. McLeod is emphatic that the Khalsa tradition was systematized and clarified by the Singh Sabha reformers to make it consistent and effective for propagation.

One of the reasons why Oberoi appreciates Sanatan tradition is its tolerance and its adjustment with differences and deviations, obviating tension with others around. By contrast, the Tat Khalsa became the source of tension within the Panth and with outsiders, resulting in the withdrawal of certain groups from the Panth, and in a running debate with the Arya Samajists and others. In fact, the Tat Khalsa came into conflict with the state. Sikh identity for Oberoi becomes the source of tension with the state. For Dhillon, on the other hand, the unwillingness of the state to recognize the Sikhs as a political community is the essential source of crisis.

In the late nineteenth century Sikh identity had begun to acquire a political character. Bhai Kahn Singh Nabha could see the political dimension of the assertion that Sikhs were Hindu. His exposition of Sikh identity was meant to show its distinctiveness as much as its political implication.[44] The equation of the Sikh Panth with the Sikh *qaum* made the Sikhs a political community. Sikh politics came to be based on Sikh identity. The Chief Khalsa Diwan before and after 1920, the Shiromani Akali Dal before and after 1947, and the recent movement for Khalistan invoked Sikh identity as the basis of their politics. Sikh identity has become an issue of vital importance because of its political character. And that makes it 'a sensitive issue'. It is easy to recognize the distinct socio-cultural identity of the Sikhs from the sixteenth to the twentieth century as an academic issue, but the issue was no longer academic in the twentieth century. New to this situation was rational argument for a distinctive Sikh identity with its political implications, and not Sikh identity itself.

NOTES

1. W.H. McLeod, *Who is a Sikh? The Problem of Sikh Identity*, Oxford: The Clarendon Press, 1989, pp. 60-70.
2. Ibid., pp. 70-2.
3. Ibid., pp. 72-7.
4. Ibid., pp. 77-9.
5. Ibid., p. 79.
6. Ibid., pp. 79-81.
7. Ibid., pp. 82-3.
8. Ibid., pp. 84-6.
9. Ibid., pp. 87-98.
10. Ibid., pp. 99-106.
11. Ibid., pp. 106-21.
12. Harjot Oberoi, *The Construction of Religious Boundaries: Culture Identity and Diversity in the Sikh Tradition*, New Delhi: Oxford University, Press, 1994, pp. 102-8.
13. Ibid., pp. 11-13, 126-30.
14. Ibid., pp. 139-93.

15. Ibid., pp. 190-201.
16. Ibid., pp. 201-3.
17. Ibid., pp. 207-16.
18. Ibid., pp. 216-35.
19. Ibid., pp. 235-52.
20. Ibid., pp. 241-2, 253.
21. Ibid., pp. 254-7.
22. Ibid., pp. 260-78.
23. Ibid., pp. 279-303.
24. Ibid., pp. 305-28.
25. Ibid., pp. 328-51.
26. Ibid., pp. 306-16.
27. Ibid., pp. 382-92.
28. Ibid., pp. 387-92.
29. Ibid., pp. 395-6.
30. Ibid., pp. 397-401.
31. Ibid., pp. 351-76.
32. Ibid., pp. 422-4.
33. Ibid., p. 381.
34. Ibid., p. 4.
35. Ibid., pp. 29-30.
36. Gurharpal Singh, 'Sikh Ethnicity and Panjab', *Ethnic Conflict in India: A Case Study of Punjab*, London: Macmillan Press, 2000, pp. 77-8.
37. G.S. Dhillon, 'Singh Sabha Movement: A Revival', in *Advanced Studies in Sikhism*, ed. Jasbir Singh Mann and Harbans Singh Saraon, Irvine, CA: Sikh Community of North America, 1989, pp. 234-6.
38. Ibid., pp. 236-8.
39. Ibid., pp. 339-40.
40. Ibid., pp. 241-2.
41. Ibid., p. 241.
42. G.S. Dhillon, *Insights into Sikh Religion and History*, Chandigarh: Singh & Singh Publishers, 1991, pp. 185-6.
43. Dhillon, 'Singh Sabha Movement: A Revival', in *Advanced Studies in Sikhism*, pp. 243-51, 258. G.S. Dhillon, 'Sikh Identity: A Continuing Feature', in *Recent Researches in Sikhism*, ed. Jasbir Singh Mann and Kharak Singh, Patiala: Punjabi University, 1992, pp. 228-35, 237-8, 240-2. See also Dhillon's essay in the *Abstracts of Sikh Studies* (July 1994), pp. 109-15.
44. J.S. Grewal, 'Nabha's *Ham Hindu Nahin*: A Declaration of Sikh Ethnicity', in *Sikh Identity: Continuity and Change*, ed. Pashaura Singh and N. Gerald Barrier, New Delhi: Manohar, 2001, pp. 231-51.

CHAPTER 9

The Issue of Martyrdom

OPPOSING VIEWS

Harjot Oberoi takes notice of Sikh 'martyrs' in connection with the construction of religious boundaries in Sikhism during the late nineteenth and early twentieth centuries. He thinks that the external symbols recommended in the eighteenth-century *Rahitnama* literature were rigidly enforced by the Tat Khalsa as the most important symbolic expression of corporate Sikhism. The *Rahitnama* tradition was consolidated by arguing that only those individuals who upheld *rahit* injunctions, particularly the rules of external appearance and Khalsa initiation through baptism of the double-edged sword, had the right to call themselves Sikhs. Since this was a new claim, the Tat Khalsa encouraged the re-writing of history of martyrs.[1]

In popular biographies of martyrs, Sikh heroic figures from the eighteenth century were shown to have been punished, tortured and killed for desiring to retain cultural markers. Several Sikh martyrs became household names: Tara Singh, Mani Singh, Bota Singh, Mahtab Singh, Taru Singh, Subeg Singh, Dip Singh and Gurbakhsh Singh. The most salient meaning generated by such tales of martyrdom was martial bravery. Underneath their bloody surface lay a corpus of multivocal *signata* conveying, among other things, the ideal Sikh modes of bodily comportment. Bhai Taru Singh, as portrayed by Bhagat Lakshman Singh in his *Sikh Martyrs,* could not submit to the insult of having his *kesh* being cut; he welcomed the removal of his scalp with his *kesh* intact. Oberoi goes on to underline the message embedded in such narratives: 'If the Sikhs of the eighteenth century could uphold the five K's at a time when they had to lay down their lives in their defence, why should the contemporary Sikhs lack will to follow their illustrious forefathers.' They who failed to live up to the high standards of the past had no right to the membership of the community. Thus, 'the martyr's blood provided the Tat Khalsa with unlimited potential to recast the façade of Sikhism in a form very desirable in the nineteenth century'.[2]

Harjot Oberoi is not talking of 'martyrs' in the Sikh tradition. He is talking actually of the Sikh heroic figures of the eighteenth century and their martial bravery. The point sought to be made is that the Tat Khalsa treated them as 'martyrs' and dwelt on their acts of sacrifice to underline that the external symbols of the Khalsa were an essential feature of Sikh identity.

W.H. McLeod's treatment of martyrdom in the Sikh tradition is a little more elaborate. He introduces the theme in connection with 'the militant aspect' of the Sikh tradition. It can be seen as the heroism of the warrior Khalsa and it can be seen also from the closely related angle of martyrdom. The two perspectives are two ways of viewing the same obligation to be supremely brave and undaunted, never to yield to an enemy under any circumstance. This ideal of militant bravery runs through Sikh history from the early seventeenth century and emerges with particular force from the founding of the Khalsa onwards. The term used for the martyr was *shahid*, an Arabic word brought in by Muslims and originally introduced into Punjabi to express an important feature of Islamic culture. It is said to have served as the source of derivation for the Sikh usage. A significant part in its development was played by Punjabi folklore. The traditional bards (*dhadis*) began to sing of the courage and sacrifices of the Sikh heroes in the eighteenth century, and made them 'martyrs'.[3]

According to McLeod, the ideal of militant bravery became a central theme of the Tat Khalsa during the Singh Sabha period. As a result of their preaching, it remains at the heart of orthodox Sikhism. Since the time of Guru Arjan to the present day, there have been phases of Sikh history marked specially by martyrdom. For the individual they meant pain and death, steadfastly endured. For the Khalsa they brought triumphant glory. The martyr ideal has lived on in the Panth and provided much inspiration to Sikhs. It is not a passive ideal; whenever evil returns weapons are to be used, even though as a last resort. Swords can be brandished or guns fired in the interest of justice, not for the benefit of an individual. 'For justice and Panth, all Sikhs should be prepared to undergo suffering, even to the point of martyrdom'. Though this message was not new to the Panth, it was clearly spelt out by the Tat Khalsa and it received 'a force and a coherence which previously it had not attained'.[4]

For McLeod, Khalsa Sikhism is 'a militant faith'. The Khalsa prayer (*ardas*) refers to 'those loyal members of the Khalsa' who laid down their lives for the Panth. This idea is reinforced by the Sikh museums in Delhi and Amritsar. Together with the collection of weapons, the art work convincingly demonstrates 'the related themes of heroism and martyrdom'. In the popular posters, Baba Dip Singh figures as frequently as Guru Nanak or Guru Gobind Singh. Indeed, there are three dominant themes of popular Sikh art: the doctrine of the Divine Name, the heroism of the Panth in the fight for justice, and martyrdom or the conviction that bravery is not sufficient unless it extends to the ultimate stage of death.[5]

As presented by McLeod, the ideal of martyrdom acquired a new force and coherence from the Tat Khalsa in the late nineteenth and the early twentieth century. The eighteenth century was marked by heroism, and *dhadis* began to sing of the heroic deeds of the Khalsa. The death of a hero made him a martyr for whom the term *shahid* was borrowed from Islamic culture. The Sikh tradition is said to be emphatic about the status of Guru Arjan and Guru Tegh Bahadur as martyrs, but they do not fit into McLeod's understanding of martyrdom as the culmination of militant bravery. Like Harjot Oberoi, McLeod does not see any relevance of Sikh ideology for the ideal of martyrdom in the Sikh tradition.

By contrast, Bhai Jodh Singh has presented Sikh martyrdom as grounded firmly in Sikh ideology: In his view, Guru Gobind Singh's '*jin prem kiyo tin hi prabh payo*' was an echo of Guru Nanak's '*jau tau prem khelan ka chao*'. The Sikh conception of *prem* involved the willing acceptance of God's will (*bhana*). Guru Nanak says: 'If you aspire to play the game of love, come with your head on the palm of your hand to follow my path. Give your head without the slightest hesitation when you set your foot on this path.'

Guru Arjan reiterated that if love could be purchased with gold then Ravan (master of the golden Lanka) would not have given his head (to Shiva). The gift of love does not come without sacrifice. For instituting the Khalsa, Guru Gobind Singh's invoked the principle of sacrifice in love. Standing before the congregation on the Baisakhi day he gave the call: 'is there anyone who loves the Guru so much that he is ready to give his head for the sake of *dharm*?'[6] It can be argued, that the verses of Guru Nanak and Guru Arjan refer to sacrifice 'on the path' and the call of Guru Gobind Singh was to die 'for the path'.

Kharak Singh has argued that the goal of life for Guru Nanak was not a passive state of bliss but a life of action in accordance with the will of God who is All Love. Struggle against oppression was a logical corollary of this commitment. Guru Arjan provided the first landmark in Sikh history with his martyrdom as 'an open act of confrontation with the state'. Guru Tegh Bahadur responded to 'the oppression in Kashmir' by opting for martyrdom. The principle of 'total commitment' and sacrifice for 'the cause' was implied in the selection of volunteers by Guru Gobind Singh. A fundamental feature of the Khalsa tradition was to make sacrifice for 'the cause of righteousness, love and truth'.[7] In other words, maintains Kharak Singh, the ideology of Guru Nanak created a sense of commitment that inspired Guru Arjan and Guru Tegh Bahadur to lay down their lives. Perhaps unconsciously, a distinction is made here between 'on' and 'for' the path.

For J.P.S. Uberoi, Guru Arjan was the first 'modern' martyr of India. His life, work and death perfectly represented all that Guru Nanak had founded and anticipated. Guru Arjan urged 'the claims of pluralism' as a matter of conscience, against imperialism which stood for uniformity. The dimension of 'martyrdom *versus* kingdom' in defence of pluralism inherent in the ideology of Guru Nanak was made manifest by Guru Arjan. The whole pattern exemplifying the 'grammar of conflict' was made manifest then by the voluntary martyrdom of Guru Tegh Bahadur in 1675. At the end of the seventeenth century, Guru Gobind Singh asked every Sikh 'to forfeit life rather than faith'. The free Sikh of the new commonwealth was ever to try not like the soldier and the hero to be stronger than the other 'but like a martyr or a saint to be stronger than oneself'.[8] Oberoi makes it clear that the figure of the martyr is distinct from the figure of the hero, or the victim. Martyrdom consisted not in death but in 'death for a cause'.[9]

A HISTORICAL APPROACH

Louis E. Fenech states at the outset of his *Martyrdom in the Sikh Tradition: Playing the 'Game of Love'* that the concept of martyrdom, though a fundamental feature of the Sikh tradition for many contemporary Sikhs, 'has not always been as fundamental to Sikhism as the Sikh people and popular histories suggest'.[10]

Fenech examines in detail what he regards as the most relevant evidence in detail and comes to the conclusion that the contemporary and near contemporary sources do not substantiate the popular claim that Guru Arjan died the glorious death of a martyr, or that his son enjoined the Sikhs to bear arms in response to this horrific ordeal. This evidence merely shows that Guru Arjan acquired the enmity of the Mughal state by appearing to support the rival claim of Khusrau, that he was imprisoned by the emperor's minions, and that subsequently he died in Mughal custody in Lahore. Fenech argues further that there was no conception of martyrdom at this point in Sikh history and, therefore, there was no link between Sikh ideology and the martyrdom of Guru Arjan.[11]

For Fenech, the well-known passage in the *Bachittar Natak* on Guru Tegh Bahadur's martyrdom is the first to aver that the 'great deed' of stoically sacrificing one's life for the 'purpose of righteousness' ensures 'a spot in paradise'. This is 'something entirely new to the Sikh tradition'. Never before had such courage been absorbed into a conceptual system which treated the heroic sacrifice of one's life for a righteous cause as a source of liberation. A conception of martyrdom appears to be emerging later in Sainapat's *Gursobha* though he does not use the word *shahid* or *shahidi.*[12]

However, there was no contemporary or near contemporary evidence to judge whether or not the 'martyrs' died for any ideal. The Persian accounts of the execution of Banda and his men agree on the stoic composure and cheerful countenances of the Sikhs when they were led to the place of execution. Fenech asserts that this 'extraordinary heroism' was highlighted by the Persian writers in order to underscore the courage and daring of their captors. Surman and Stephenson also refer to the 'remarkable patience' with which the Sikh captives underwent their ordeal: none 'apostatized from his new-formed religion'. Their evidence does seem to indicate that the choice to Islam was offered to at least some of the captives. For Fenech, however, the difference between being offered the choice and 'not apostatizing' is 'a crucial one in this context'. Since the conception of martyrdom had emerged by this time, the contemporary Sikhs could feel that these deaths warranted the status of martyrdom.[13] There was no evidence on their motivation.

Fenech refers to the evidence of George Forster, John Malcolm, and Cunningham to suggest that they were reflecting the lore created by the *dhadhis*. As *dhadhis* wandered from village to village, Sikh heroes and martyrs were brought to life, along with a number of other popular warriors. According to Fenech, Seva Singh's *Shahid-bilas* was the first work to project the *shahid* as a martyr 'who provides testimony to injustice, heroically witnessing to the truth with his blood'. This understanding of the martyr is reflected clearly in Ratan Singh Bhangu's *Guru Panth Prakash* in which the term *shahid* is frequently used. However, Fenech then points out that in Bhangu's text there are instances where the term *shahid* implies far more than the pious witness to the glory of Sikhism. For example, Guru Tegh Bahadur's martyrdom is seen as leading to the decay of the Mughal empire, and Gurbakhsh Singh Nihang reincarnates as Maharaja Ranjit Singh. Such passages suggest that the term *shahid* was far less exclusive than the Singh Sabha construct of the martyr, that is, 'a Sikh who dies heroically in the defence, maintenance, or establishment of dharam'.[14]

Fenech goes on to argue that the earlier Sikh understanding of martyrs was different from that of the Tat Khalsa. In his view, the passage on Guru Tegh Bahadur in the *Bachittar Natak*, the sacred thread and the frontal mark were a part of the Sikh religious culture. But in the Singh Sabha understanding the Guru offers his life for another's right to practise a religion with which he himself personally disagreed. For a composite picture of the *shahid*, Fenech gives great importance to the *Sau Sakhian*, an anonymous work of the mid-nineteenth century. What Guru Gobind Singh tells the Sikhs about the *shahids* clearly indicates that the Sikhs venerated the martyrs of other religious faiths as well as their own.[15]

According to Fenech, Bhai Vir Singh transformed the martyr of Ratan Singh Bhangu into the Singh Sabha martyr while editing his *Guru Panth Prakash*. For Bhangu, the Sikhs were essentially Hindu. Bhai Vir Singh replaced the word 'Hindu' of Bhangu's text with

'Sikh' or 'Singh' wherever he felt that it was used for a Sikh. The original word 'Sikh' was replaced at times with 'Khalsa'. In the narratives of martyrdom, where the extant manuscripts of Bhangu's work show 'Sikhs happily sacrificing their lives for the Devi', the version supplied by Bhai Vir Singh shows the same Sikhs 'sacrificing themselves for their Guru and for the benefit of the Panth'. In the manuscripts, Guru Gobind Singh offers his four sons as a sacrifice to the Goddess but in the printed version of the manuscripts he is presented as sacrificing all he holds dear for the sake of the Panth. In Bhai Vir Singh's text the martyrs become brave Khalsa Sikhs, truly worthy of the Panth's praise and reverence for their singular sacrifice on its behalf, 'not lives given in sacrificial frenzy to the goddess, an act which would make these recently dead deserving of propitiation in "Hindu" understandings'.[16]

Though Fenech argues that the Singh Sabha writers transformed a 'composite' conception of martyrdom into a 'Sikh' concept,[17] he finds one martyr narrative in Bhangu's original where a specific Sikh identity, as opposed to Hindu, may be a question. Bhai Taru Singh chooses death over having the sacred *kesh* shaved from his head. Though an exception, it seems to demonstrate 'the inherent element of identity' which could be exploited by the Tat Khalsa. Fenech adds that Bhangu's Khalsa Sikh is set within the Sanatan Sikh paradigm put forth by Harjot Oberoi. The keen similarity between the original text and Bhai Vir Singh's edition in respect of martyrdom can be explained in terms of their historical situation. Both the texts were meant to inspire and enthuse Sikhs of the times to which Bhangu and Bhai Vir Singh belonged. Fundamental to both were the heroic ideals in a situation of conflict with the British.[18]

The enormous devotion the Sikhs have towards the Tat Khalsa interpretation of Sikh tradition is said to be as much due to the Akalis of 1920-5 as to the nineteenth-century reformers. 'The power of the reformers was that of ideas but the power of the Akalis was putting such ideas into practice. Speaking, writing and touring were replaced by the ideals enunciated therein: 'suffering, standing true to vows, and dying'. The Tat Khalsa message penetrated the very heart of the Punjab due largely to the rhetoric of martyrdom. Thus, according to Fenech the Singh Sabha projection made martyrdom a far more fundamental feature of the Sikh faith than what it really was.[19] His elaborate argument supports the view presented by Harjot Oberoi and McLeod.

Like Harjot Oberoi, Fenech looks at the pre-colonial Sikh tradition in the light of his understanding of a particular phase of Sikh history during the colonial period. In a conscious competition with the Singh Sabha projection of the importance of martyrdom in the early Sikh tradition, he appears to minimize its importance by equating the 'historian's art' with blunt skepticism. It is quite legitimate to ask how martyrdom in the earlier Sikh tradition was interpreted by the protagonists of the Singh Sabha movement. But, in order to do this, it is necessary first to understand martyrdom in the early Sikh tradition in its own terms.

EARLY SIKH IDEOLOGY

We may notice first of all that Guru Nanak was aware of the tradition of *shahid* in the Islamic culture of his time. The word occurs in one of his compositions which shows his familiarity with the categories of religious persons who were believed to hold a recognized status in the Indo-Muslim society. Among them were *shahids.* Ravidas mentions them as being worshipped like *pirs* by Muslims.[20] They were important enough to be taken notice of. But they had no sanctity in the eyes of Guru Nanak. It is absolutely clear that the *shahid* of Islamic culture had no fascination for him. However, the word had already become a part of the popular vocabulary.

In the context of Muslim beliefs and practices, Bhai Gurdas refers to people going to the places of *shahids* for pilgrimage. He has no appreciation for them. At another place in his *Vars,* it is made absolutely clear that no category of devotees is comparable with the Gurmukh who is indifferent to death and selfless in hope (*asa vich niras*). The Islamic categories of religious persons, including *shahid* are mentioned in yet another *pauri* which underlines that none gets liberated without the Guru and none gets rid of *haumai* without joining the *sadh-sangat.* Finally, the term *shahid* is used by Bhai Gurdas to express the Sikh ideal of becoming dead-in-life to serve the Guru.[21] Paradoxically, the word *shahid* is given a Sikh connotation at the same time as the *shahid* of Islamic culture is rejected.

For appreciating the relevance of ideology for the emergence of martyrdom in the Sikh tradition we should study attitudes and values rather than look for a direct statement. The path of *sikhkhi* is underlined by Guru Nanak as a hard path. It is 'sharp like the edge of a double-edged sword (*khandedhar*). It is so narrow that to pass through it is like the sesame passing through the oil-press. Guru Amar Das says that the way of the true devotees is sharper than the edge of a double-edged sword and narrower than the width of a hair. One has to destroy *haumai* to follow the path of total dedication to God.[22]

The path of *sikhkhi* demands sacrifice. In the familiar verse of Guru Nanak, the words used are '*prem khelan ka chao*', '*sir dhar tali*' and '*sir dijae*' which find their echoes in later Sikh literature in empirical contexts: the metaphor becomes a reality. Guru Nanak himself says that they who give their head attain liberation and find honour in God's court.[23] The phrase used here is '*sir de*'. The sacrifice referred to is the sacrifice of self, of *haumai*, and of all that one possesses: the body, the mind, and the riches.

The concept of liberation is central to Sikh ideology. It is not a state of eternal bliss after death but an experience of God in life. Essential for liberation-in-life (*jivan-mukti*) are fear and love of God (*bhau-bhagti*). In contrast with *bhakti* in Vaishnavism, Guru Nanak makes it absolutely clear that only they who cultivate *bhau* (awe) can appropriate *bhav* (love). Without *bhai* there can be no *bhagti*. Guru Amar Das reiterates that there can be no *bhagti* without *bhai*. Awe of the Lord and love of the Name go together. The awe of God lodged in the heart eradicates *haumai*, and the love of God leads to complete dedication. Through awe one finds the Fearless One.[24]

The state of liberation is a state of fearlessness. Guru Nanak says that all fears are removed by the awe of God, and Guru Angad says that they who have awe of God have no other fears. Guru Amar Das says that they who lodge Achinta in their minds, they have no *chinta* whatever. Guru Ram Das says that they who meditate on the Fearless One (*nirbhau*) all their fears are removed. Guru Arjan prays for the boon of *abhaipad,* the state of fearlessness. He advises others to strive for this gift by singing God's praises in association with others. Guru Tegh Bahadur too prays for *abhaidan*, the boon of fearlessness. One who has realized God is afraid of none; nor does he frighten others.[25] Thus, fearlessness is an essential feature of the Sikh conception of the liberated-in-life.

Neither before nor after liberation has one to renounce the world. Guru Nanak refers to the householders who have awakened to God and pursue the life of *nam*, *dan* and *isnan* through the Guru's instruction. Indeed, the householder who prays for *jap*, *tap* and *sanjam* and who practises *punn* and *dan* is pure like the water of Ganga. Guru Arjan says that one attains liberation (*mukti*) while laughing, playing, dressing and eating. For Guru Nanak, true conduct is higher than the realization of truth. Without an honest occupation, even charity brings discredit. Guru Nanak has no respect for those who live on charity: only he recognizes the true path who works hard to earn his living and gives something to others.[26]

The liberated-in-life pursues life's activities in a spirit of detachment. Guru Nanak refers to this state as *asa mahi niras*, a state in which one remains hopeful that God will take care of everything and one has no desire of one's own, a state of selfless hopefulness. Guru Amar Das refers to this state as *ghar hi mahi udas*. There is no attachment (*moh*) or desire (*piyas*) in this state. He who meditates on the *shabad* gets rid of *haumai* and becomes detached in action (*nih karmi*). Service (*seva*) is a supreme criterion of good conduct. The epithet used by Guru Ram Das for the Gurus is *parupkari*.[27] Their followers are expected to be *parupkari*.

Acceptance of God's will and acting in accordance with it is the distinguishing trait of the liberated-in-life. According to Guru Nanak, a true devotee of God is he who recognizes God as his Master, accepts His will and gets rid of his own self or *haumai*. To accept His will is to affirm one's faith in Him. Guru Nanak gives expression to this ideal by saying that he remains happy in whatever condition he is kept by God. Guru Amar Das advises everyone to act in accordance with God's *hukam* and to accept whatever he does. Guru Arjan addresses God: 'Whatever you do tastes sweet'. Finally, action should conform to profession. According to Guru Nanak, a self-oriented person (*manmukh*) has *kathni* but no *rahit*, his talk is tall but his conduct does not correspond to what he says. But a person who has attained *gian* and *dhian* through the Guru has a true *rahit* and a true mind. True happiness lies only in true *rahit*.[28]

On the whole, thus, there are several dimensions of Sikh ideology which have a bearing on the ideal of sacrificing one's life to uphold the tradition promulgated by Guru Nanak: the hardness of the path, its demand for sacrifice, the conception of liberation, the idea of selfless service, active detachment born of social commitment, and the willingness to accept God's will and to act in accordance with it.

Bhai Gurdas talks of the Sikh Panth as a unique development in human history. He underlines the greatness of the Name in the Kaliyuga. There is no other means of liberation. The Nirmal Panth of Guru Nanak is a distinct (*nirala*) Panth. The Gurmukh Panth is distinct from all others and it cannot be confused with any. The True Guru is the True King and he has shown the highway (*gadi rah*) to liberation and life. The Gurmukh *marag* is the path of truth (*sachch*) and they who appropriate it become true (*sachiar*).[29]

According to Bhai Gurdas, the Sikh of the Guru quafs the cup of love and attains liberation. The path of *Gursikhkhi* is hard in the extreme; it is like licking a saltless slab; it is sharper than the edge of a double-edged sword; it is narrower than the width of a hair. The other paths bear little fruit in comparison with *Gursikhkhi*. The Sikhs of the Guru taste the cup of love, like the moth that burns itself on the flame, like the deer that gets killed while absorbed in the sound of the hunter's bell, like the black bee stuck to the flower, and like the fish in water. Absorbed in the *shabad* in association with other Sikhs, they drink the cup of love and bear the unbearable. The cup of love enables them to see the unseeable.[30] The occupation of Bhai Gurdas with 'the cup of love' (which is used for martyrdom in the Sikh tradition) is quite remarkable.

Bhai Gurdas talks of love and awe (*bhau-bhav*) as the means of liberation. The True Guru shows the way to dedicate oneself in love and to tread in awe; the Sikh remains intoxicated and alert at the same time. The True Guru, who is eternally free from awe, removes the awe of death and rebirth. The Gurmukh is born in awe, lives in awe and walks in awe. The Sikhs of the Guru are born in awe, live in awe and die in awe to live for ever. In awe, they become liberated-in-life and accept the *bhana* of God. As instructed by the True Guru, they accept God's will and abandon their own 'self'. Bhai Gurdas uses the term *hukmi banda* for the Sikh of the Guru who follows the Sikh way of life by cherishing the *bhana* of the Master. He lives in accordance with the Divine Order.[31]

The earth is the place of *dharm* for Bhai Gurdas. It is the arena where one attains liberation and helps others to attain liberation.

Bhai Gurdas talks of liberation-in-life at many places in his *Vars*. A Sikh of the Guru should become a dust of his feet, die unto himself and live for God. The Gurmukh dies to his 'self' and becomes liberated-in-life. Bhai Gurdas makes it clear that liberation-in-life is to live in hope without any hope of one's own (*asa vich niras*). The liberated-in-life is a householder who is not affected by attachment. The Gurmukh dies to himself and lives for God. To die unto oneself is to get rid of the *haumai*; to live in accordance with the instruction of the Guru is to discard *haumai* so as to be dead in life.[32]

Bhai Gurdas underscores the importance of honest living. He talks of manual work and *kirt* of *dharm*. There is hardly any doubt that *ghal khana* and *sukirt karna* are linked up with *asa vich niras* in the life of a Gursikh. Bhai Gurdas lays much emphasis on remaining detached in attachment. He uses the familiar phrases: *ghar hi vich udas, asa vich niras, maya vich udas*. These phrases are repeatedly used to emphasize the importance of detachment. The Sikh of the Guru does not laugh in happiness and he does not cry in suffering.[33]

The Gurmukh who discards his 'self' and becomes a *jivanmukta* serves the Sikhs of the Guru and looks upon them as his mother and father, brother and friend. Bhai Gurdas himself wishes that a Sikh of the Guru may wear shoes made from his skin. It is expected of the Sikhs of the Guru to serve the Sikhs. They serve the *sadh-sangat* and reap the fruit of service. The liberated Sikh enables other Sikhs to attain liberation. The Sikhs of the Guru are *parupkari:* while others return good for good, they return good for evil. The identifying mark of the Sikh is that he never forgets the welfare of others (*parupkar*). As *parupkaris*, the Sikhs of the Guru meet everyone with a smile.[34]

Finally, the Gurmukh spreads knowledge in the world. He discards ego and purifies his inner self. He cultivates truth and contentment and he discards lust and anger. Being devoid of enmity (*nirvair*) he entertains enmity towards none. He gives instruction to all the four *varnas* to lead them to liberation (*sahaj*). Praise be to the mother who has given birth to this supreme warrior.[35] The supreme warrior of Bhai Gurdas is primarily a Gurmukh committed to the welfare of humanity.

It is important to know how Bhai Gurdas looks upon Guru Arjan. With the same light and status as Guru Nanak, Guru Angad,

Guru Amar Das and Guru Ram Das, Guru Arjan represented eternal intoxication (*abchal arkheo*). He enabled all the four *varnas* to follow the path of truth. He filled the storehouse of Gurbani and remained absorbed in *kirtan* in the *sadh-sangat.* His court is true, his *nishan* is true, and true is his strength and his honour; his *raj* is to stay for ever. Innumerable Sikhs flock to him from all the four directions; he transforms them into true devotees who, like Janak, live detached amidst the attachments of the world.[36]

In the *pauri* which relates to Guru Arjan's martyrdom, he exhorted the Sikhs till the end that they should never forget the *updes* of the Gurus. The *sadh-sangat* is the source of comfort, love and the blissful state (*sahaj samadhi*). Guru Arjan did not think of anything but God under the severest of physical tortures which ended with his death. The metaphors used are those of the fish that remains alive only in water, a moth that burns itself on the flame, the deer which remains absorbed in the sound of the hunter's bell, the black bee which remains wrapped inside the lotus, and the rain bird that constantly cries for union. All the metaphors relate to love to the point of self-sacrifice.[37] They occur in a composition of Guru Arjan.[38] As taught by Guru Nanak, a warrior-hero accepted God's will in life and in death.[39] This was the game of love.

It is relevant to add that Bhai Gurdas records Guru Hargobind's martial measures and supports his position. Guru Hargobind is the destroyer of hostile armies, a brave warrior, and a great *parupkari.* He teaches his Sikhs how to tread the path that is as sharp as the edge of a double-edged sword. He has put a defensive cordon round the Sikhs, as the *kikar* trees are planted to protect an orchard. The *sadh-sangat* is attached to his feet and the Sikhs bear all hardships by drinking the cup of love. Guru Hargobind is the master of both the spiritual and the temporal realm (*din duni*); he is the king of kings, with the moonlike canopy spread over his head by the Perfect Brahm, the Adi Purkh.[40]

Bhai Gurdas says further that some people criticized that the Guru does not sit in a *dharmsal* at one place; he was sent to the fort (Gwalior) by the emperor instead of paying homage to the Guru; he is not accessible to his followers because he moves fearlessly from place to place; instead of instructing the Sikhs from a seat (*manji*), he goes out hunting with dogs; he does not recite, sing or listen to *bani*; he gives preference to the others than his *sevaks*. In spite of all such criticism, the Sikhs were enamoured of his lotus feet. Bhai Gurdas fully supports the new measures of Guru Hargobind against his critics. Guru Hargobind bears the unbearable. The change in appearance (*sang*) is merely external; Guru Hargobind is essentially one with his predecessors.[41] He is occupying the same throne; he is cherishing and promoting the same heritage. The cup of love includes and justifies politicization, says Bhai Gurdas.

MARTYRDOM OF GURU TEGH BAHADUR

The martyrdom of Guru Tegh Bahadur was more clearly a deliberate act. We have a contemporary comment on the event. The relevant verses in the *Bachittar Natak* may be rendered into English as follows:

> The Master protected their *tilak* and *janju*, performing a great deed in the Kaliyuga. This he did for the sake of *sadhs*, giving his head without a sigh of pain. He performed this great deed for the sake of *dharm*, giving his head but not giving up his resolve. The men of God hesitate to resort to dramatic tricks and ill deeds. Breaking the pot of life on the head of the ruler of Delhi he went to God's abode. What Tegh Bahadur did, none else could do. There was sorrowful mourning everywhere on his departure from the world but in the heaven there were shouts of praise.[42]

These verses indicate that Guru Tegh Bahadur was asked to perform a miracle as a proof of his nearness to God, but in his view miracles did not behove the true devotees of God. It is equally clear that Guru Tegh Bahadur gave his head deliberately in confrontation with the ruler of Delhi for the cause of truth (*dharm*) and for the sake of the pious (*sadhs*). The religious import is obvious enough. The frontal mark and the sacred thread (*tilak, janju*) in this context refer to the symbols of the Brahmanical tradition.

However, Guru Tegh Bahadur did not sacrifice his head for the sake of the Brahmanical tradition alone. Even in the *Bachittar Natak*, *sadhs* and *dharm* are mentioned. In the *Sri Gur Sobha* are mentioned *karm-dharm*, *dharmsala* and *sarb-dharm*, along with *tilak* and *janju* as protected by Guru Tegh Bahadur. We know that Guru Tegh

Bahadur is generally called *Hind di chadar* (the protector of Hind) and the saviour of 'Hinduism'. But Sainapat calls him *jagg chadar* (the protector of the world).[43] 'Hind' is not excluded from 'the world' and 'Hinduism' is not excluded from *sarb-dharm*. But Guru Tegh Bahadur may be seen as defending with his life the principle of the freedom of conscience. This principle was implied in Guru Nanak's denunciation of the discrimination practised by the state which taxed gods and their temples.[44] Aurangzeb was using political power to promote the interests of Sunni Islam at the cost of other religious traditions. The conflict between the principle of freedom and the practice of coercion was inevitable.

The *Sri Gur Sobha* is significant in another way too. At one level the Khalsa represents direct affiliation with Guru Gobind Singh. But this affiliation is affirmed by the baptism of the double-edged sword. The *khandedhar pahul* symbolizes the determination to lay down one's life in a righteous cause. The choice of *khanda* thus carries a great significance. After the first evacuation of Anandpur, when Guru Gobind Singh and his Khalsa were attacked at Nirmoh, Sahib Chand died fighting in the field. The author of the *Sri Gur Sobha* makes the general statement that the 'perfectly fortunate' ones proved themselves to be the *khalsa* by sacrificing their life. When Sahibzada Ajit Singh died fighting in the battle of Chamkaur, Guru Gobind Singh himself remarked: 'Today he has become the Khalsa, in the court of the True Guru (*aj khas bhae khalsa satgur ke darbar*).' The reference to 'the cup of love' in this connection is highly significant. The idea of martyrdom was built into the institution of the Khalsa. The younger Sahibzadas are seen as following the example of their grandfather, Guru Tegh Bahadur, in preferring their faith over their life. They too are regarded as martyrs.[45]

The term *shahidganj* is used in the *Rahit-Nama* of Chaupa Singh for the place 'where Sikhs have given their heads for the sake of their faith' (*jiththae sikhan sis dittae hovan sikhkhi upron*). The Sikhs are asked to look upon such places as sacred. They are told to 'light a lamp there' (*diva balna*).[46] Not only the word *shahid* for the Sikh martyr makes its appearance here, but also the sanctity of the place of martyrdom is highlighted.

The *Rahitnama* of Chaupa Singh is generally placed in the mid-eighteenth century but an earlier date for this work may be more realistic. In any case, this work suggests a close connection between *pahul*, *kesh* and martyrdom. Its author talks of two categories of Sikhs: the *keshdhari* and the *sahajdhari*. The former has taken *pahul*. Even the latter are told not to practise *bhaddan*, that is, the ritual shaving of the head and the Brahmanical rites associated with it. Furthermore, a Sahajdhari should not observe traditional mourning; he should arrange reading of the *Guru Granth*, ending with *kirtan*, *bhog* and *ardas*. To keep the *kesh* without taking *pahul* is to act like a buffoon (*bhand*) and a dancing boy (*bhagtia*). Clearly, thus, *kesh* and *khandedhar pahul* go together. The sanctity of the *kesh* is underlined in a score of ways. The *kesh* are the outward symbol of the inner faith of the Sikh. The *kesh* symbolize *sikhkhi* which should be preserved till the end of life. The *mukta* Sikhs are defined as those who sacrifice their life in battles against the 'Turks'. In this way, they preserve their *sikhkhi*. Thus, the *pahul*, the *kesh* and martyrdom go together. It is not surprising that the removal of hair is equated with incest in this *Rahitnama*.[47]

In the *Rahitnamas* of Chaupa Singh and the *Sakhi Rahit Ki* attributed to Bhai Nand Lal, the *kesh* serve as the marker of a distinct Sikh identity. Just as Guru Arjan prepared a scripture distinct from all others, so did Guru Gobind Singh create a Panth distinct from all others. The Keshdhari Sikhs are like a particle of stone in the eyes of Hindus and Musalmans: it cannot be removed, it does not get dissolved, it remains a source of constant irritation. According to Bhai Nand Lal, the Khalsa have been given such a marker that even a single Sikh stands out in a crowd of lakhs of Hindus and Musalmans. How can he with his *kesh*, turban and flowing beard be concealed?[48] Thus, the *pahul*, the *kesh* and martyrdom not only go together but also serve as the markers of Sikh identity.

MARTYRDOM IN THE LATE EIGHTEENTH-CENTURY SIKH LITERATURE

Some of the Sikh writers of the late eighteenth century introduce the episode of the Goddess in connection with martyrdom which is not without significance. For Kesar Singh Chhibber, Guru Arjan is conscious of his impending martyrdom. Deliberately, therefore, he installs Hargobind as the Guru and tells the Sikhs that the time had come for putting his head on the stake (*sis laggana*). He had to face the Turks but he had no fear; welcome to him was the *bhana* of the Master. The Guru was subjected to tortures. He abandoned his body, throwing dust on the heads of his oppressors. The Turks were unjust in supporting the enemies of Guru Arjan. But Jahangir had no hesitation, later, to pacify Guru Hargobind. The Sahi Khatris of Lahore were delivered to him for punishment. The whole family of Chandu Sahi, except his daughter-in-law who was sympathetic to Guru Arjan, was killed. Furthermore, Guru Hargobind took up the sword and the *khanda* in order to destroy the Turks in accordance with the will of Guru Nanak: to fight and to die without any fear. In a situation of confrontation, Guru Har Krishan refused to see Aurangzeb's face and chose to sacrifice his life.[49]

The confrontation between Guru Tegh Bahadur and Aurangzeb leads Aurangzeb to ask the Guru to show a miracle or accept Islam. Otherwise, he should be prepared to get his head cut-off. Guru Tegh Bahadur says that one should not abandon one's faith for another; to show a miracle is to draw God's wrath upon oneself; the head is not everlasting; its removal depends on God's will. Finally, however, Guru Tegh Bahadur decides to give up his life. He says that he would tie a thread to his neck to make the sword ineffective. When the sword was struck, his head was cut-off. This was a stratagem to give his head. Had he not done so, no Hindu would have been left in the world. He saved his *dharm* and earned the praises of the whole world. Chhibber quotes two lines from the *Bachittar Natak*, carrying the implication that Guru Tegh Bahadur made this sacrifice to save the sacred thread and the sacred mark and for the sake of *sadhs*. Some other lines from the *Bachittar Natak* are quoted a little later. Chhibber goes on to add that only two Sikhs, Mati Das and Sati Das, stayed with the Guru to sacrifice their life. Guru Gobind Singh then decided to give such a marker to the Sikhs that they would never be able to conceal their identity. As Chhibber tells us later, this marker was the uncut hair (*kesh*).[50]

The narrative of the Goddess is more elaborate in Kesar Singh Chhibber's *Bansavalinama* than in any other work of the eighteenth century. It is important, therefore, to see its relevance for the Khalsa. Guru Gobind Singh tells the Brahmans that he has been commissioned by God to establish *dharm* by protecting the pious and destroying the wicked. For this purpose, he has to create a *panth* for sovereign rule. The Sikhs of the Guru were to be made distinct in the world to pursue both Raj and Jog (*Yoga*). After a long discussion with Pandit Kalakdas, the Goddess was invoked through an elaborate ceremony. The eight-armed Mata Devi appeared in all her splendour. Kalakdas received a *khanda* from her. This *khanda* was presumably used for preparing *amrit.* The Goddess exempted the Khalsa from *janju, tikka, bhaddan* and *kirya.* Their place was taken by the *kesh*, arms, and the epithet Singh. The Khalsa adopted the blue dress of Mata Kali. Their objective was to fight the Turks and to remove them for ever. *Hukamnamas* were issued to promulgate the new *rahit.* The Masands, who were opposed to the new programme, were killed or removed. The third *panth* was made distinct from both Hindus and Musalmans for waging a righteous war. *Pahul* was administered to create the *keshdhari panth* to wield the sword in the cause of righteousness. The Sikhs who were prepared to give their head were chosen for rulership. The rule of the Shudras was sanctified through this process. To fight for *dharm* and sovereignty involved death, and whoever died fighting went to heaven. Thus, in spite of the Goddess or rather because of her, *pahul, kesh, kirpan, dharm, raj* and *sis dena* go together. For Kesar Singh Chhibber, the rulers of the land in his own time were the companions of Banda Bahadur who had remained steadfast in their faith and given their heads.[51]

In Sarup Das Bhalla's account of Guru Arjan's death, the enmity of the Sahi Khatri, Chandu, figures prominently. He made much of the hospitality offered by Guru Arjan to Prince Khusrau at Tarn Taran. Guru Arjan could see that the time had come for his light to mingle with the Light. Addressing the Sikhs, he referred to his confrontation with the Turks, and told them to look upon Hargobind as the Guru, saying that 'there is no difference between me and him'. Then Guru Arjan deliberately went to the abode of *dharm* to assume the *nirban* form. The people sent imprications upon Chandu. Even the Badshah felt regret over what Chandu had done. Raj-Jog was made manifest by Guru Hargobind. Jahangir blamed Chandu for the death of Guru Arjan and entrusted Chandu with his family to Guru Hargobind for punishment. People began to call Guru Hargobind *sachcha patshah.* Guru Har Rai agreed to help Dara Shukoh on his request. Aurangzeb called the Guru to Delhi but he refused to go.

The emperor sent an *amir* against him. Eventually, Guru Har Rai sent his elder son Ram Rai to Aurangzeb with the instruction that he should take a dignified stand but should not reveal his supranatural powers. He infringed this injunction, and Guru Har Rai installed Har Krishan as the Guru.

Aurangzeb called Guru Har Krishan to Delhi. On the pretext of having his *darshan*, the emperor offered him the insignia of spirituality and many valuable articles. Guru Har Krishan accepted the former but rejected the latter. When Aurangzeb wanted to see him again, Guru Har Krishan said that there was no possibility now of a meeting with the Turks. This was God's *bhana*. Guru Har Krishan told the messenger to tell the emperor that he was suffering from small pox. Consequently, small pox appeared on his body. After five days he told his mother that he would now go to *dharm-dham* and his light would mingle with the Light. The *sangat* was told that they would find his successor in Bakala.[52]

The *sangat* discovered Guru Tegh Bahadur. Dhir Mal complained to Aurangzeb and he called Guru Tegh Bahadur to Delhi. The emperor was keen to see a miracle but the Guru did not believe in revealing such powers. He told Aurangzeb that by demonstrating supranatural powers one became *mushrik* and this was not to the liking of the *la-sharik* (God). Servanthood behoved men, as justice behoved the ruler. The Hindus and Turks had the same Master and a king should be kind to both. God liked justice and not oppression. Nothing happened without His will. Aurangzeb kept quiet but later on demanded a miracle. Mati Das argued that the 'men of God' did not perform a miracle. He was sawn into two, but his head still recited the *Japu*.[53] This was nothing short of a miracle.

Guru Tegh Bahadur went towards the east to meet the Sikh *sangats*, visting sacred places on the way. The tenth Nanak was born at Patna. The Guru went to Monghyr, Dhaka and Kamrup where he established peace between the local chief and Raja Bishan Singh. Before returning to Delhi with the Raja, Guru Tegh Bahadur installed his son Gobind as the Guru. The time had come for sacrificing his life for the sake of *dharm* and to save the sacred thread and the sacred mark. He demonstrated in the Kaliyuga how to retain faith rather than save the head.[54] Bhalla's borrowing from the *Bachittar Natak* is obvious.

The twentieth *sakhi* in the *sakhis* of Guru Gobind Singh is actually the *Bachittar Natak*, a declaration of his mission. This *sakhi* is preceded by the institution of the Khalsa. The Masands were exposed and removed. In their place, five Sikhs administered *pahul*. The congregation of the Khalsa at Anandpur was not liked by Hindus and Turks. The Guru asked the Sikhs to come with arms. There were armed conflicts, and many Sikhs were killed, sacrificing their life in dedication to the Guru. Not to reveal his own supra-natural powers, Guru Gobind Singh thought of Chandi to establish the *dharm* of *chhatris* (Kshatriyas) in order to destroy the *mlechh*. The ceremony called *khadag-jagg* was performed at the top of the hill. The *hom* was performed for the sake of *dharm*. The Pandit who acted as the priest could call Chandi but he could not face her. When the eight-armed Goddess appeared, the *pandits* lost their senses and Guru Gobind Singh made the offering to her. She left the *khanda* in the fire pit. It was taken out and named 'Sri Sahib'. It was used for preparing *pahul* to be administered to Sikhs. They became Keshdhari Singhs, and the Guru adopted the same form. Both *deg* and *tegh* were bestowed upon them. The Hindus and Turks felt as if a mote had entered their eyes. Without wealth and without any territory yet, the Singhs became sovereign, like rulers.[55]

The younger Sahibzadas were asked by Jhutha Nand (Suchcha Nand) to do *salam* to the Subedar of Sirhind and they replied: 'we have done *salam* to the True King (*sachcha patshah*) and we do *salam* to no one else'. The Subedar ordered the executioner (to slaughter them). At that spot now stood the *dehura* of the two Sahibzadas. The two elder Sahibzadas had died fighting. Thus, all the four sons of Guru Gobind Singh became martyrs (*shahid*). Banda Bahadur is said to have been appointed later on by Guru Gobind Singh for vengeance (upon the Subedar of Sirhind).[56]

In the *sakhis* of Sarup Das Bhalla martyrdom does not come into sharp focus. Nevertheless, there is confrontation between the Gurus and the Mughal emperors leading to deliberate sacrifice for the faith, the distinct identity of the baptized Sikhs, their sovereign status, the righteous war and the sacrifices involved in it. In this general context, the explicit references to martyrdom acquire great importance. The Goddess serves a limited purpose in the righteous war. Her role subserves the commission of Akal Purkh, and to him goes the allegiance of the Sikhs.

Sukha Singh invokes Guru Nanak and Guru Gobind Singh in his *Gurbilas Patshahi 10* in the opening couplet of his work. At the end of the Chaupai that follows he refers to Kalka. Then for getting the gift of the sword for the Khalsa, Guru Gobind Singh decides to invoke Shakti Mata, the destroyer of the wicked. The Brahmans advise him to meditate on Kalka and worship Chandi as Adi Bhavani. Kalka appears after two and a half years and Guru Gobind Singh receives the boon from her. This gift came from the Wielder of the Sword for creating the Khalsa Panth. The Masands were opposed to the idea of creating the Khalsa Panth. They were punished and removed. At Keshgarh then Guru Gobind Singh addressed the Sikhs: 'Is there any Sikh who can offer his head to the Guru?' On the third call, a Sikh volunteered himself. He was taken into a tent, given a sword, and asked to slaughter a goat. Its blood flowed for everyone to see. Nevertheless, other Sikhs responded to the call till the number reached five. The people began to attribute the sacrifice of these five men to the adverse effect of getting a boon from Kali. However, Guru Gobind Singh came out of the tent with all 'the five beloved' (*pancho piaran*). They were dressed afresh and armed with weapons. *Amrit* was prepared and administered to them. In this way 'Sri Khalsa' was made manifest. Guru Gobind Singh made an earnest request to them to administer *amrit* to him.[57]

This was an extraordinary request. Therefore, 'the five beloved' wanted to know how they could presume to do such a thing. The explanation given by Guru Gobind Singh is extremely significant. The eternal and formless creator of the universe intervened in its affairs to redress the imbalance between the *bhagats* and the *dusht.* In the Kaliyuga the *mlechh* Turks had become predominant. The *sants* were oppressed. The whole earth groaned in pain and God sent Guru Gobind Singh to destroy the Turks root and branch. For this purpose the Khalsa Panth was created. They represented the eternal Guru as the form of the eternal Master. After this explanation 'the five beloved' prepared *amrit* and administered it to Guru Gobind Singh. They discarded the false thread and put on the sword to take refuge in God. The others were then initiated into the fold and the entire body of the Khalsa asked for *rahit.* Guru Gobind Singh said many things. Sukha Singh mentions the most important: appropriation of *nam* and *dan*, *seva*, *bhagti* and the *mantar* of the True Name; not to believe in anyone other than the Wielder of the Sword; to remain fully armed; to destroy the *dusht* and to promote the *sants*; to fight battles with the Turks; not to smoke and not to observe *bhaddan*; not to recite anything other than the *shabad*; to associate with *sadh-sangat* all the time. It must be pointed out that the Goddess figures nowhere in the *rahit* of the Khalsa. Strictly speaking, she is out. Her position in relation to God is of no consequence whatever. The insertion of even an elaborate episode in the narrative of the institution of the Khalsa does not make her important in the context as a whole. The episode does not integrate with the narrative. It remains an interpolation.

Sukha Singh is emphatic about the unique identity of the Khalsa and its totally egalitarian character as much as about the unity of the Supreme Being. Having imbibed *amrit*, the Khalsa roared like lions in battle and never stepped back. They died fighting in battle and went to the eternal abode. Their heroism was inspired by *dharm juddh*. By giving up their life for the sake of *dharm* they became immortal. The death of the younger Sahibzadas in their firm commitment to the faith made them immortal and cut at the very roots of the *mlechh*. Even at the time of his departure from the world, Guru Gobind Singh told the Khalsa to fight against the Turks. Without using the term martyr (*shahid*), Sukha Singh talks of sacrifices made for the faith which included the fight for sovereignty. The ideal of martyrdom was built into the institution of the Khalsa.[58] Talking of the same light in all the ten Gurus, Sukha Singh refers to Guru Arjan as the bestower of the gift of fearlessness on the world. Guru Tegh Bahadur gives his head in sacrifice for saving the Bharat Khand. It was relevant for Sukha Singh to note that Guru Tegh Bahadur's father had put on two swords, he had created the Takht Bunga, and he was the scatterer of armies. Guru Tegh Bahadur went to Delhi, destroyed the *mlechh* (through his sacrifice), and went to the eternal abode. He had been asked to accept Islam but he refused with contempt and remained steadfast in his faith. Deliberately, he ordered a Sikh to cut-off his head. Nevertheless, Sukha Singh looks upon Guru Tegh Bahadur as a martyr. The essential commitment and not the mode of death is relevant for him.[59]

AN INTEGRAL PART OF THE SIKH TRADITION

Ratan Singh Bhangu's *Guru Panth Prakash* makes martyrdom central to the Sikh tradition. He expected his work to confirm the reader, the reciter and the listener in his faith. They who listen to it go to the battle never to turn their back; they die on the field of battle and mingle with the *shahids* as water mingles with water.[60] Bhangu talks of the martyrdom of Guru Arjan, Guru Tegh Bahadur, the Sahibzadas, Bhai Tara Singh, Bhai Mani Singh, Bhai Bota Singh, Bhai Mahtab Singh, Bhai Taru Singh, and Nihang Gurbakhsh Singh, among others. In the process, he reveals his own ideology of martyrdom.

Guru Tegh Bahadur gave his head for the sake of others (*parsuarth*): he saved the *dharm-karm* of the Hindus. The Brahmans of Kashmir and other Hindus were being forcibly converted to Islam. Fear spread everywhere and Brahmans from several places came to Guru Tegh Bahadur for help. It was decided that the Turks should be asked to convert the Guru first. He went to the Turks on his own initiative. They asked him to perform a miracle (*karamat*) or to accept Islam. Guru Tegh Bahadur asserted that *karamat* invited God's wrath (*qahr*). Eventually, however, to save his *dharm-karm* he said that he would show a miracle: he would tie a thread to his neck and they will not be able to cut-off his head. They were taken in. He was beheaded. This was how he gave his head for the sake of others. The *pirs* and *paighambars* of the Turks were removed by the True Lord from His True Abode (Sachch Khand): 'from that moment the *patshahi* of Dilli began to decline, from that moment the power of the Turks began to diminish'.[61]

Bhangu presents the Sahibzadas and the other Khalsa who died fighting after the final evacuation of Anandpur as *shahids*. The idea of *parsuarth* is reiterated and martyrdom diminishes the power of the Turks. Where did the status of *shahid* come from? Guru Gobind Singh tested his Sikhs: 'is there any Sikh who can give his head?', he asked the congregation. The Sikhs who thought of Bhai Gurdas's reference to the 'Guru's *sang*' offered themselves. The Guru slaughtered goats instead. For their readiness to lay down their lives, the five volunteers were given the martyr's status (*shahidi pad*).[62] Bhai Tara Singh 'used to carry his head on his palm', standing for justice and defying the Turks. He believed that martyrdom led to *patshahi*. By his deliberate acts he invited attack from the Mughal administrators. With twenty-two other like-minded Singhs he faced the enemy undaunted, refusing to take the chance to escape. He attained martyrdom, living up to the words of the Guru: 'give your head but never give up your resolve'.[63]

Bhai Mani Singh changed the arrangement of the contents of the *Guru Granth* and a Sikh commented that his limbs would be hacked. Believing that this would come true, Bhai Mani Singh approached the *sangat*, which is no different from the Guru, to pray that his body may be cut into pieces but his faith (*sikhkhi*) may remain intact. Years later, Bhai Mani Singh was hacked limb by limb but his head remained one piece with its *kesh*. Thus, his *sikhkhi* was saved. After his martyrdom Bhai Mani Singh becomes the *deodidar* of the Sahibzadas in Sachch Khand. Bhangu quotes a *kabitt* of a contemporary Bhatt which refers to Bhai Mani Singh as the 'foundation of *sikhkhi*'; in utter fidelity to his faith, he allowed his body to be cut into pieces; no one else was his equal for the way in which he lived and died as a Gursikh.[64]

Bota Singh sacrificed his head to honour the prophecy *raj karega khalsa*. When the Singhs were virtually eliminated by the Mughal administrators someone saw him and remarked 'how is this Singh still alive'? Others commented that he could be an imposter, or a coward. 'The Khalsa fights in the van, unafraid of death. The Khalsa defies the state to stake his head.' As if stung by a scorpion, Bota Singh resolved to defy the Mughals openly, to give his head, to prove his Khalsahood, and to justify the Khalsa's claim to *patshahi*. He built a platform on the highway to Lahore and began to collect duty at one *anna* a cart and one *paisa* a donkey. He was joined by a Ranghreta Singh. He sent a taunting message to Zakariya Khan. Troops were sent against them, but the two Singhs refused to submit, fought stubbornly to their last breath, and attained martyrdom. They are said to have joined the *dera* of *shahids* who were holding the *pirs* and *paighambars* (of the Turks) under a siege.[65]

The martyrdom of Bhai Taru Singh underscores the sanctity of the *kesh* even more emphatically than the martyrdom of Bhai Mani Singh. Taru Singh's scalp was removed with his hair intact while he was alive. Bhangu gives some detail to show that as a true Sikh, Bhai Taru Singh supported the Khalsa with his modest means and without giving any offence to the administration. For the sake of the Panth, and to expose the Turks, he bore all kinds of hardships. He tells the Sikhs gathered around him when he was being taken to Lahore that 'the true Guru had given his head for the sake of the Sikhs. As the Sikhs of that Guru, how can we save our heads'? Bhai Taru Singh and Subeg Singh saved the honour of the Panth as true Sikhs by attaining martyrdom. Mahtab Singh did not wish to lag behind in giving his head to weaken the Turks. This was his way of being faithful to *dharm* and to *sikhkhi*. Not to lose faith and not to forget the Guru while giving one's head was his ideal too. How else can a Khalsa attain the status of *shahid?* Offering himself voluntarily to be broken on the wheel, he attained martyrdom.[66]

Bhangu narrates the episode of the *dehura* (memorial or *shahidganj*) raised for the younger Sahibzadas in Sirhind. The Afghan governor of Sirhind was defeated and killed and the fort of Sirhind was occupied by the Khalsa. They decided to build a *dehura* at the spot where the two younger Sahibzadas were slaughtered. The old men of the place were consulted to identify the exact location. The Khalsa resolved to erect a *darbar* there, with standards and a drum (*nagara*). A *diwan* was held and a platform was constructed. Five weapons were placed at this *takht,* regarding them as the form of the Guru (*gur-sarup*). A Singh was appointed as the custodian (*mukhtiyar*) of this place. A *rababi* was appointed for reciting *shabads.* Jagirs were assigned for the maintenance of this *dehura.* Offerings were made there by many who circumambulated the place and recited *bani.* All their wishes were fulfilled.[67]

A *shahidganj* was raised at the spot where Nihang Gurbakhsh Singh was cremated along with other martyrs just behind the Akal Bunga in Amritsar. Prayers made there were believed to find a sure response and many Sikhs distributed *karha parshad* there for their wishes having been fulfilled. Nihang Gurbakhsh Singh had always led the Khalsa in battle. He was leading the Singhs who died fighting against an overwhelming number of Afghans to ensure sovereign rule for the Sikhs. They had resolved not to leave the place and offered the prayer (*ardas*) that they may preserve *sikhkhi* with the *kesh* on their heads. Gurbakhsh Singh was exultant like a bridegroom and observed all the rites of marriage. To wed death was to wed *patshahi.* As members of 'the marriage party' they all resolved to die with him. 'May we attain martyrdom' (*shahidi*) was their constant prayer, and they were determined not to show their back. On their martyrdom they were welcomed by Bhai Mani Singh and Bhai Taru Singh and taken to the presence of the True Guru. Nihang Gurbakhsh Singh was later born as Ranjit Singh with the blessing that his authority would be recognized by the entire Khalsa.[68]

There is hardly any doubt that martyrdom for Ratan Singh Bhangu was the core of the Khalsa tradition which was equated with 'the Sikh tradition'. It was linked with *parsuarth* or selfless sacrifice. In the case of Guru Tegh Bahadur the sacrifice was made for the Hindus; in the case of others it was made for the Panth. Commitment to the Sikh faith and concern for its visible emblem, the *kesh*, was common to all Sikh martyrs. Martyrdom was closely linked with the idea of the sovereignty of the Panth. In this connection Bhangu presents the myth or metaphysics of martyrdom. From this metaphysics flowed the sanctity of the places of martyrdom and the efficacy of the prayers offered there. Logically, monuments were raised to be known as *shahidganj* and maintained as sacred spaces.

Like the Sikh writers of the late eighteenth century who refer to the Goddess, Bhangu refers to Guru Gobind Singh 'awakening' Chandi to aid the Khalsa with the obligation to offer 1,25,000 heads. This could be done in three ways: by slaughtering the enemy, dying fighting on the field of battle, or making deliberate sacrifice of one's life. The cause for all the three modes was the same: to establish sovereign rule. The phrase used for such situations is *chandi-bhet.*[69] Fenech has missed the essential point. He has also missed the point about identity. 'Hindu' identiy in the pre-colonial centuries was interpreted in three ways: (a) the caste status in the social order, (b) membership of the Brahmanical religious orders, and (c) the position of a non-Muslim Indian. For Bhangu, the Khalsa are 'Hindu' in relation to Muslims but they have a distinct identity of their own in relations to 'Hindus' of the first two categories. Bhangu is explicit on the point that the Khalsa (Sikhs) represent the 'third *panth*', the other two being Muslim and 'Hindu'.[70]

In Sikh literature of the pre-colonial centuries, on the whole, martyrdom remains an essential feature of the Sikh tradition. The Sikh who died fighting valiantly for the cause of the Panth was greatly admired, but the martyrs regarded as the most venerable were not warriors. The ultimate source of martyrdom was not the heroic tradition of the Punjab but Sikh ideology. As evident from the sources, the Sikh tradition of martyrdom developed historically in response to the changing environment.

NOTES

1. Harjot Oberoi, *The Construction of Religious Boundaries: Culture, Identity and Diversity in the Sikh Tradition*, New Delhi: Oxford University Press, 1994, pp. 328-30.
2. Ibid., pp. 330-3.
3. Hew [W.H.] McLeod, *Sikhism*, Harmondsworth: Penguin Books, 1997, pp. 128-30.
4. Ibid., p. 129.
5. Ibid., pp. 130-1.
6. Bhai Jodh Singh, 'Jin Prem Kiyo Tin Hi Prabh Payo', in *Ek Murit Anek Darsan* (Pbi), ed. S.S. Amol, Jalandhar: Khalsa College, 1967, pp. 44-5.
7. Kharak Singh, 'Martyrdom in Sikhism', *Abstracts of Sikh Studies* (January 1994), Editorial.
8. J.P.S. Uberoi, *Religion, Civil Society and the State*, New Delhi: Oxford University Press, 1996, pp. 61, 88-9, 93-4, 96-7.
9. Ibid., pp. 114-23, 135, 151.
10. Louis E. Fenech, *Martyrdom in the Sikh Tradition: Playing the 'Game of Love'*, New Delhi: Oxford University Press, 2002 (2nd imp.), pp. 1, 23.
11. Ibid., pp. 63-102, 117-23.
    Fenech takes notice of *pauri* 23 in *Var* 24 of Bhai Gurdas with reference to its use by J.S. Grewal in *The Sikhs of the Punjab*. Fenech bases his translation on the commentary of 'Vir Singh' (actually Giani Hazara Singh), and points out that his interpretation is based on the understanding that *pauri* 23 deals with the martyrdom of Guru Arjan. Fenech appears to argue that this *pauri* does not refer to the martyrdom of Guru Arjan. Ibid., pp. 137-8.
12. Fenech, *Martyrdom in the Sikh Tradition*, pp. 123-9.
13. Ibid., pp. 129-32.
14. Ibid., pp. 11, 132-7, 148, 150.
15. Ibid., pp. 151-70, 172.
16. Ibid., pp. 189-92, 217-18.

17. Ibid., p. 193.
18. Ibid., pp. 193-6.
19. Ibid., pp. 275, 297.
20. *Adi Granth* (*AG*), pp. 53, 1293.
21. *Varan Bhai Gurdas*, ed. Giani Hazara Singh, Amritsar: Khalsa Samachar, 1962 (7th edn.), *Var* 21, *pauri* 13 (21.13), 8.8; 8.24; 40.8. An English translation of the *Vars* is now available in Jodh Singh, *Varan Bhai Gurdas: Text, Transliteration and Translation,* 2 vols., Patiala: Vision and Venture, 1998.
22. *AG*, pp. 918, 1028.
23. *AG*, pp. 421, 1412.
24. *AG*, pp. 465, 722, 831, 788, 1288.
25. *AG*, pp. 11, 151, 464, 587, 701-3, 788, 820, 1427.
26. *AG*, pp. 62, 419, 472, 522, 952, 1245.
27. *AG*, pp. 26, 128, 243, 749, 992.
28. *AG*, pp. 94, 141, 421, 440-1, 831, 1343.
29. *Varan Bhai Gurdas*, *Var* 1, *pauri* 16 (1.16); 1.23; 1.29; 1.31; 1.45; 3.5; 3.7; 5.13; 9.17; 18.20; 23.17.
30. Ibid., 4.18; 6.5; 9.2; 16.21, 20.13; 28.1; 28.17-18.
31. Ibid., 3.13; 11.1; 18.5; 18.17; 20.13; 20.20; 26.19; 28.16-17; 29.13.
32. Ibid., 3.19; 5.2; 6.15; 6.18; 9.19; 12.13; 13.14; 20.3; 28.9.
33. Ibid., 1.3; 3.2; 5.5; 5.13; 6.2; 6.15; 18.14; 18.20; 19.8; 20.3; 28.14, 28.15.
34. Ibid., 1.3; 5.2; 6.14; 9.18; 14.17; 20.10; 28.11; 28.13.
35. Ibid., 19.18.
36. Ibid., 1.47; 11.18-28; 13.25; 24.18-20; 27.34; 38.20.
37. Ibid., 24.23.
38. *AG*, p. 462.
39. *AG*, pp. 579-80.
40. *Varan Bhai Gurdas,* 1.48; 11.29-31; 13.25; 24.21; 24.25; 39.3-4.
41. Ibid., 26.24, 35.20; 35.23.

    On the themes of *abhaidan*, *abhaipad*, *bhau*, *jivan-mukt*, *parupkar*, and *sadachar*, there are useful entries in Rattan Singh Jaggi, *Guru Granth Vishavkosh* (Pbi), 2 vols., Patiala: Punjabi University, 2002, vol. I, pp. 44, 141-3; vol. II, pp. 31-3, 207-8, 313-15.
42. *Sri Dasam Granth Sahib*, ed. Rattan Singh Jaggi and Gursharan Kaur Jaggi, New Delhi: Gobind Sadan, 1999, vol. I, p. 144.
43. Sainapat, *Shri Guru Sobha*, ed. Shamsher Singh Ashok, Amritsar: SGPC, 1967, pp. 10-11, 15.
44. J.S. Grewal, *Guru Nanak in History*, Chandigarh: Panjab University, 1998 (2nd imp.), pp. 157-8.
45. Sainapat, *Shri Guru Sobha*, pp. 29-30, 33, 40-2, 63-4, 90, 94.

46. *The Chaupa Singh Rahit-Nama*, tr. & ed. W.H. McLeod, Dunedin: The University of Otago, 1987, p. 110.
47. Ibid., pp. 63-5, 68, 83, 88-9, 112, 120, 133. The alternative use of the phrase *kesan di pahul* leaves no doubt about the inevitable link.
48. Ibid., pp. 80, 134.
49. Kesar Singh Chhibber, *Bansavalinama Dasan Patshahian Ka* (Pbi), ed. Rattan Singh Jaggi (*Parkh*: Research Bulletin of Panjabi Language and Literature, ed. S.S. Kohli, vol. II), Chandigarh: Panjab University, 1972, pp. 52-5, 65, 69, 78-9.
50. Ibid., pp. 87-97, 126.
51. Ibid., pp. 128-9, 132, 134, 138, 143, 148, 151, 153, 157, 176.
52. Sarup Das Bhalla, *Mahima Prakash* (Pbi), ed. Gobind Singh Lamba, Patiala: Punjab Languages Department, 1971, vol. II, pp. 410-16, 420, 423-5, 435, 590, 598, 601-7, 641-3, 646-7.
53. Ibid., pp. 656, 660-6, 673-79.
54. Ibid., pp. 682, 709, 760-1.
55. Ibid., pp. 797-806, 815-28, 832-70.
56. Ibid., pp. 877-8, 882, 888-9, 892.
57. Sukha Singh, *Gurbilas Patshahi 10* (Pbi), ed. Gursharan Kaur Jaggi, Patiala: Punjab Languages Department, 1989 (rpt.), pp. 1-2, 130, 134, 136, 145, 160, 170-8.
58. Ibid., pp. 77-9.
59. Ibid., pp. 180-1, 185, 198, 207, 319-21, 323, 333, 441.
60. Ibid., pp. 5, 7, 9, 58, 64, 65.
61. Ratan Singh Bhangu, *Prachin Panth Prakash*, New Delhi: Bhai Vir Singh Sahit Sadan, 1993 (rpt.), pp. 470-1.
62. Ibid., pp. 34-9.
63. Ibid., pp. 55-9, 61-4.
64. Ibid., pp. 176-8.
65. Ibid., pp. 187-98.
66. Ibid., pp. 223-8. Some other Sikhs were also reportedly broken on the wheel at the horse market in Lahore.
67. Ibid., pp. 243-6.
68. Ibid., pp. 268-72, 287-92, 301-2, 352-3.
69. Ratan Singh Bhangu, *Sri Guru Panth Prakash*, ed. Balwant Singh Dhillon, Amritsar: Singh Brothers, 2004, pp. 3, 29-30, 38, 147, 160, 253, 258.
70. Ibid., p. 31. Bhangu's frequent use of the term 'Hindu' for non-Muslims is the obvious source of confusion.

PART FOUR

THE SACRED TEXTS

CHAPTER 10

The *Kartarpur Pothi*

The debate about the Sikh scripture started with the issue of the authenticity of the *Kartarpur Pothi*, leading to the issue of its compilation and its relationship with the *Guru Granth Sahib*. These concerns get related to the issue of scriptural Guruship. In this chapter we propose to take up the controversy about the *Kartarpur Pothi* in terms of its authenticity and compilation.

AUTHENTICITY SUSPECTED

W.H. McLeod was not the first scholar to suggest that the authenticity of the *Kartarpur Pothi* was suspect. He was preceded by a considerable number of Sikh scholars and two Western scholars, namely J.C. Archer and C.H. Loehlin. Bhai Jodh Singh had tried to place the authenticity of this *Pothi* beyond any doubt in his *Sri Kartarpuri Bir de Darshan* in 1968. Since the *Kartarpur Pothi* was believed to have provided the base for the *Guru Granth Sahib*, any doubt cast on the former's authenticity could be seen as a doubt cast on the authenticity of the latter. It is understandable, therefore, that Justice Gurdev Singh charged McLeod with doubting the authenticity of 'the current version of *Guru Granth Sahib* which is widely accepted and used by the Sikhs'.[1]

In his essay on the Sikh scriptures in the *Evolution of the Sikh Community*, McLeod gives the maximum space to the *Adi Granth* as by far the most important of the Sikh scriptures. He refers to the traditional explanation of why Guru Arjan decided to compile the *Granth*, with a collection traditionally attributed to Guru Amar Das as his principal source. It consisted of two volumes, generally known as the *Goindval Pothis*, contained the works of the first three Gurus and several Bhagats. The Goindval volumes could thus be regarded as 'a first recension of the *Adi Granth* and Guru Arjan's collection as an enlarged second recension'. The manuscript was written by Bhai Gurdas.[2]

The history of the manuscript, according to McLeod, was surrounded by 'considerable mystery'. It was believed to be in the possession of the Sodhis of Kartarpur and there was 'sound reason for accepting this claim'. The early Sikh tradition carries the implication that it came into the possession of Dhir Mal and remained with his successors at Kartarpur. In 1849, the manuscript was found in the custody of the Lahore court. On an application from Sodhi Sadhu Singh of Kartarpur the volume was restored to him in 1850. A copy of the manuscript was presented to Queen Victoria and it is now in the British Library (India Office Library, MSS Panj. E2).[3]

With the rise of the Singh Sabha Movement, exclusive authority came to be accorded to the *Adi Granth* and the need of a definitive authorized version became increasingly important. The Shiromani Gurdwara Prabandhak Committee prepared blocks for printing in 1953, but the completion of the work was postponed due to a dispute 'concerning the correct order of invocation and *rag* titles'. A decision was reached in 1962, but the actual printing of the approved version was still pending at the time of McLeod's essay on the Sikh scriptures. The veneration in which the Sikhs hold the *Adi Granth* explained this cautious hesitation on the part of their highest religious authority.[4]

The affectionate reverence of the Sikhs for the *Adi Granth* is due to the fact that for them it is the Guru. 'The same spirit which successively inhabited the bodies of ten men is now believed to dwell in this particular Book.' The deep reverence of the Sikhs for the *Guru Granth Sahib* should not be interpreted as worship. The scriptural Guru is not worshipped, just as the human Gurus had not been worshipped by their followers. However, all aspects of Sikh worship relate directly to the *Guru Granth Sahib* and practically 'the entire content of all worship is drawn from it'. The prominence accorded to it in regular Gurdwara worship is extended to all other Sikh ceremonies. 'The centrality of the *Guru Granth Sahib* in Sikh custom, and the manifold uses to which it is put, leave no room for doubt concerning its enormous importance to the Panth.'[5]

McLeod talks about the language and script of the *Adi Granth* and the unusually systematic arrangement of its contents before taking up the scriptures like the *Dasam Granth* and the works of Bhai Gurdas and Bhai Nand Lal.[6]

Finally, McLeod comes to what he regards as the problem. It appears to arise from a comparison of the Kartarpur and Banno versions. He thinks that the version which remained in greater currency until well into the eighteenth century was the Banno version and not the Kartarpur version. The Banno version contains some extra material which is not there in the Kartarpur version and the Damdama version. If the Banno version is a copy of the original, and the Kartarpur version is the original, then this extra material should have been there in the Kartarpur version too. This is where deletions in the Kartarpur version become relevant.[7]

The most important instances of the extra-material cited by McLeod are a hymn by Mira Bai, another by Sur Das, and the third by Guru Arjan. The standard printed edition contains two fragments, a single couplet in *Rag Ramkali*, and a single line in *Rag Sarang*. McLeod draws the inference that the bulk of these two hymns must have been deleted, leaving a small remainder in each case. The *Ramkali* hymn by Guru Arjan in the Banno version describes the puberty rites conducted at the initiation of his son Hargobind, involving the shaving of his head. This obviously goes against the later prohibition of hair-cutting. There was a good reason for its deletion. McLeod was inclined to conclude that the Banno version was the original text and the Kartarpur manuscript was its shortened version. A few portions were deleted 'because they could not be reconciled with beliefs subsequently accepted by the Panth'. The implication of his arguments is: the Kartarpur manuscript is not the original *Granth* prepared by Guru Arjan. The Damdama version could be prepared by omitting the problem passages and adding the works of Guru Tegh Bahadur. The problem passages were 'rather ineptly obliterated' in the Kartarpur manuscript 'to bring the two versions into line'.[8]

McLeod goes on to add and this was his reasoning before Bhai Jodh Singh's *Sri Kartarpuri Bir de Darshan* appeared in 1968. It is not clear why McLeod refers to this apparently irrelevant reasoning. The Mira Bai hymn, according to Bhai Jodh Singh, is not there in the original manuscript. The hymn of Sur Das in *Rag Sarang*, however, is represented in the original manuscript by a single line, followed by blank space of four lines. Similarly, in the case of Guru Arjan's *Ramkali* hymn, there is only a couplet followed by blank space. This couplet is in the same hand but written with a different pen. In other words, the Damdama version corresponds with the Kartarpur version in two out of the three instances of extra-material. McLeod himself says that the hymn of Mira Bai involves an interesting textual problem that is interesting but is of 'no great importance'. What is important for him is whether or not the *Ramkali* hymn was composed by Guru Arjan. If it was, 'the relationship of the later Khalsa discipline to the earlier teachings of the Gurus could be made dramatically clearer'. But a firm conclusion could not be drawn from the evidence before him.[9] In other words, Bhai Jodh Singh's work does not remove McLeod's doubts.

AUTHENTICITY REAFFIRMED

Daljeet Singh refers to 'some oblique but incorrect observations of McLeod which tend to throw doubt on the authenticity of the Kartarpur manuscript as the original *Granth* prepared by Guru Arjan. He wonders why without examining the Banno Bir or reading what others have written about it on the basis of personal inspection, and even after reading what Bhai Jodh Singh had written about the Kartarpur manuscript, McLeod suggested that the Kartarpur manuscript was a copy of the Banno version. This may be due to 'sheer ignorance', or his anxiety 'to suppress known but awkward facts', or his 'conscious or unconscious bias because of his thirteen years of working and association with a Christian Mission in Punjab'. The *Banno Bir* was prepared not earlier than 1642 and the Banno story is a myth. Therefore, 'the very basis of the argument about the Kartarpur Bir being a copy of the Banno Bir is knocked out'. Furthermore, Bhai Jodh Singh has observed that the *Ramkali* hymn attributed to Guru Arjan was never recorded in the Kartarpuri Bir. Therefore, the question of its deletion does not arise. Even in the Banno version it is an interpolation in a different shade of ink and in smaller letters. Moreover, there are manuscripts of 1675 and 1682, examined by Principal Harbhajan Singh, which do not have the additional hymns of the Banno version.[10] Thus, the whole explanation of deletions after the creation of the Khalsa becomes irrelevant and redundant.

Daljeet Singh's primary purpose in his essay is to establish that the Kartarpur manuscript is the original *Granth* prepared by Guru Arjan. That is why he thinks it relevant to emphasize that the claim of being the original *Granth* was never made for any other recension. His main argument, however, is based on internal evidence. Daljeet Singh presents eight features of the Kartarpur recension as conclusive proofs of its 'originality'. It is the only recension which has the *Japu* recorded in the hand of Guru Ram Das. All other known recensions mention that their *Japu* was a copy of a copy. Or, the words 'Japu Nisan' are recorded. The second important feature of the Kartarpur Bir is the date of the demise of Guru Arjan: it is in the hand of the original scribe but with a pen and shade of ink different from the one used for the dates of demise of the first four Gurus. Moreover, the day is also mentioned in the case of Guru Arjan. In Daljeet Singh's view, this entry was made by Bhai Gurdas later. Equally conclusive are the words *sudh* and *sudh keeche*: these are in the hand of Guru Arjan because the writing resembles that of the *mulmantar* inscribed by him as his *nishan*. The date of its completion is given as 'Sammat 1661 *miti* Bhadon *vadi ekam* I *pothi likh pauhnche*'. It is supported by the date of completion mentioned in historical writings and the Sikh tradition. The unused space of 586 pages out of a total of 1948 pages in the Kartarpur recension could never occur in a copy. Similarly, duplication of *shabads* could occur only in the original compilation. Rectification of inadvertent incongruities, which are pointed out by Daljeet Singh, point in the same direction: no other Bir has a particular set of incongruities in the text and the corresponding portions of the table of contents (*tatkara*). Finally, a large number of 'corrected mistakes' could also occur only in the original compilation.[11]

Then there are some 'other important factors' which leave no doubt that 'the Kartarpur Bir is the original *Adi Granth* compiled by the Fifth Guru in AD 1604'. The *nishan* of Guru Arjan on a profusely decorated page as a mark of adoration and its mention in the *tatkara*; the words 'the *shabad* is right' in the margin of a page; two additional *shabads* of Guru Arjan and his *Basant ki Var* included after Bhadon AD 1604; the *nishan* of Guru Hargobind who was associated with the collection of the *bani* and the preparation of the scripture, and who presumably added *dhunis* of some *Vars* at a later date – all these important factors go to prove that the *Kartarpuri Bir* is not a copy but the *Granth* compiled by Guru Arjan.[12]

AUTHENTICITY DENIED

Piar Singh's disagreement with Daljeet Singh is fundamental, though rather incidental. He accepts the tradition that the recension prepared by Guru Arjan and the recension prepared by Guru Gobind Singh were lost. Fortunately, however, copies of both these recensions had come into currency before the loss. Therefore, Piar Singh was in search of the authentic *Adi Granth*. For this purpose he analysed a large number of manuscripts coming down from the sixteenth and seventeenth centuries, paying special attention to features like the *mulmantars*, entries of the dates of death (*chalittar*), the presence or absence of stray numerals (*latakde ank*), whether or not the source of *Japu* is the one written by Guru Ram Das, the presence or absence of additional compositions (*faltu banian*).

In Piar Singh's view, there is not one but four or five hands in the Kartarpur recension, and none of these resembles the handwriting in the *gutka* in the possession of the Sodhis of Kartarpur which is said to be in the hand of Bhai Gurdas. The style of writing and the way in which letters are written appear to have advanced over the known early manuscripts. A large number of blank pages are found in several other manuscripts which are avowedly copies. Therefore, blank pages cannot be regarded as a peculiarity of the Kartarpur recension. Blank space left for a composition of Guru Arjan himself is also very significant. This appears to go against one of Daljeet Singh's arguments in support of the originality of the recension. Piar Singh sees a more intriguing situation in the tables of contents. There are three tables in the recension: *tatkara ragan ka*, *tatkara tatkara ka*, and *tatkara shabdan ka*. As Bhai Jodh Singh has noticed, these tables are in a different hand from those of the text. The *shabads* in the text do not correspond to the *tatkara shabdan ka* in every case. This disjunction is of three kinds: ten *shabads* do not figure in the *tatkara*; eight lines of *shabads* in the *tatkara* have a variant reading in the text; and a few *shabads* are shown in the *tatkara* at places different from their actual places in the text. Piar Singh draws the conclusion that the tables of contents were taken from another recension and added to the Kartarpur manuscript. The recension from which these tables were taken contained a smaller number of *shabads* and variant reading. In the *tatkara shabdan ka*, the entire Bhagat *bani* is indicated with a single entry *bani bhagtan ki*. The *shabads* of the Gurus are indicated with their opening lines but the *shabads* of the Bhagats are not. If the tables of contents were taken from a different source, the date of completion given on the *tatkara* also loses its relevance for dating the Kartarpur recension. This date has been used by Daljeet Singh as an argument in favour of the originality of this recension.[13]

Even more serious is Piar Singh's view of the *nishan* of Guru Arjan. If this *mulmantar* was an integral part of the manuscript, there was no need to repeat it in the *Japu* which has its own *mulmantar* in this recension. Piar Singh is inclined to think that the decorated page carrying the *nishan* of Guru Arjan has been pasted on a page of the Kartarpur recension. Piar Singh finds is rather odd that the *nishan* of Guru Hargobind is mentioned in the 'table of contents' too. If the *Granth* was completed in 1604, it does not appeal to reason that the *nishan* of Guru Hargobind should be there. Piar Singh suggests that the date of the completion of this recension was later than the time of Guru Arjan.

Piar Singh refers to Bhai Kahn Singh Nabha to say that the *Ragmala* was accompanied by several other entries, including the *ratanmala* and the *rah mukam*. It is interesting to note that in the *tatkara ragan ka*, the entry is *ragmala tatha singhaldip ki sibnabh raje ki bidh*. Moreover, the last five words are in a vertical line in continuation of the entry started in a horizontal line. This entry appears to refer to some compositions in addition to the *Ragmala*. Bhai Randhir Singh too thinks that all the 'extraneous compositions' were there in the manuscript at one time, but they were all removed later except the *Ragmala*.[14]

Piar Singh points out that all deletions in the Kartarpur recension are not due to repetition. Kabir's *shalok*, *dhar ambar vich velari*, in *Rag Gauri* is deleted. Guru Arjan's *Chaupada* in *Rag Asa*, starting with *har jan liney prabh chhudaey*, stands deleted. More significantly, it stands deleted in the *tatkara* too. Piar Singh's inference is that this *Chaupada* was there in the manuscript from which Kartarpur manuscript was copied. Variant readings worry Piar Singh even more than deletions or additions. Bhai Manna Singh noticed about two hundred variant readings in the Kartarpur recension when compared with the printed *Granth Sahib.* Sant Gurbachan Singh Khalsa stated that there were about fifteen hundred variants of this kind. Piar Singh has classified these variants into six categories and looks upon the readings in the Kartarpur recension as incorrect (*ashuddh*). He has no hesitation in saying that this recension is not the ideal original with which to correct other recensions. Piar Singh feels convinced that a manuscript written by Bhai Gurdas could not have so many mistakes.[15]

The Kartarpur recension contains stray numerals in *Rag Gauri* and *Rag Asa.* These were meant originally to indicate *juz* numbers for the copyist so as to ensure that nothing was left out. In the original recension these numbers would have been superfluous. The use of the *mulmantar* and *mangals* in the Kartarpur manuscript does not conform to what we find in the printed *Granth Sahib.* In some sections of the manuscript there is no *mangal.* In some cases the *sirlekh* or heading precedes the *mangals.* The words *sudh* and *sudh kichey* at the end of the *Vars,* supposed to be the instructions given by Guru Arjan to Bhai Gurdas, are not there in four *Rags*: *Jaitsri, Suhi, Maru* and *Basant.* The survival of several 'old' elements in the Kartarpur recension suggests that the compiler was making use of some older collections or compilations. There are other features which point to the manuscript being a copy: use of *chhakka* for enumeration at a few places, the presence of undifferentiated *shabads* in some Rags, the use of the letter *ura* without the *aunkar,* and the presence of words coming from the oral tradition. Furthermore, some of the errors of the original sources are retained in the manuscript. For instance, the use of *dakhni* with *Onkar,* of Tall instead of Kall for the Bhatt author, the presence of additional compositions at wrong places, and the presence of unauthentic *bani.*[16]

Piar Singh comes to the conclusion that the Kartarpur recension is a compilation independent of the *Granth* prepared by Guru Arjan. It was completed in the time of Guru Hargobind at the earliest. Far from being the original *Granth* prepared by Guru Arjan, it is not even a good copy. However, Guru Arjan did prepare a *Granth* which was written by Bhai Gurdas, and copies were prepared by some other people in due course. In a recension seen by Bhai Randhir Singh at Patna Sahib it is explicitly stated that it was copied in 1692 from a copy made by Fateh Chand from a copy of a copy made by Puhkar which had been corrected by comparing it with the one got prepared by Guru Arjan in the hand of Bhai Gurdas. The *Ragmala* was not a part of that *Granth.*[17]

Much before the coming of the British, Guruship was bestowed on the *Adi Granth* by Guru Gobind Singh. During the rest of the eighteenth century, attempts were made to 'correct' the existing manuscripts by comparison. Then, with the establishment of Sikh rule, relics of the Gurus began to be rediscovered and venerated. Revenue-free lands were given to the owners of old recensions in the name of the *Granth* in their possession. In this situation, an earlier date was sought to be given to the recensions of Bhai Banno and Bhai Bura Sandhu. The Kartarpur recension was now proclaimed to be the original *Granth Sahib* inscribed by Bhai Gurdas to receive large grants from the Sikh rulers. In Piar Singh's considered view, this recension had been corrected by a comparison with the original *Granth* some time during the seventeenth century, and it could now be used to 'correct' other manuscripts.[18]

Categorically stating in his second book that his interest in the compilation and canonization of Gurbani had sprung from the controversies about the *Ragmala*, the *mangals* and the variants, Piar Singh reinforces his earlier arguments with facsimiles. One of these is meant to show that the *nishan* of Guru Arjan was pasted later. Another is meant to show that all the dates of demise were written 'at one go' after the martyrdom of Guru Arjan. The facsimile of the *suchi-patra*, which carries the date, is meant to show that it was a 'lifted document'. Another facsimile is given to show that the *mulmantar* of the first page of the *Japu* is in the hand of the main scribe and not in the hand of Guru Arjan. It varies from the *nishan.* Therefore, the *nishan* was not there when the scribe wrote the *mulmantar.*[19]

The 'Var Ramkali M3' is not free from mistakes and yet it has the word *sudh* at its end. The reference to Guru Hargobind as 'Mahala 6' in the entry for his *nishan* shows that it was made in the time of Guru Hargobind. A hymn of Kabir, included initially in the compilation but deleted later, is 'so patently out of tune' with Sikh ideology that no Sikh Guru would have countenanced its inclusion in a scripture. Apart from numerous additions, deletions and emendations in the *Kartarpuri Bir*, there are inaccuracies which could never be expected to occur in a *Granth* written by Bhai Gurdas under the supervision of Guru Arjan. Piar Singh reiterates his earlier conclusion that the *Kartarpuri Bir* is an independent compilation prepared not much earlier than 1642.[20]

We may also note that Piar Singh refers to a new spirit of 'repression' that was gaining ground. Sardar Kapur Singh, the National Professor of Sikhism, had categorically stated that 'the Bir which the Sodhis of Kartarpur have, is a fake one', but no 'motives' were attributed to him and no 'ghosts of conspiracy' were seen in his statement. The suggestion that Guru Arjan gave its present form to the *mulmantar* had been made by Giani Mahan Singh in 1968. Significantly, he expressed this view in the *Gurmat Prakash*, a journal of the Shiromani Gurdwara Prabandhak Committee. In those days there was said to be 'no inquisitive body' and 'no people with closed mind' in the Sikh community.[21]

Piar Singh argues at some length that all the constituents of the *mulmantar* of the *Goindval Pothis* are there in *Guru Granth Sahib*. The epithet *saibhang* occurs only in the *mulmantar* and not in the *bani* even of Guru Arjan.[22] Furthermore, the doctrine of the same spirit, or the unity of Guruship, gave Guru Arjan the authority 'to make a change in the Holy Word'. They who infringe this doctrine are 'themselves guilty of blasphemy'.[23] What is more to the point, the changes made in the *mulmantar* do not infringe but elucidate the connotation of the original attributes. These changes are of *sachu* into *sati*, *kartar* into *karta purakhu*, *nirikar* into *nirvair* and *sambhau* into *saibhang*.[24] Piar Singh knows that the whole debate about the *mulmantar* is intimately linked with the idea of the revelatory character of Gurbani. He subscribes to the view that revelation came 'in ideas, concepts or truths' and not as 'linguistic units'. Furthermore, transmission of the *bani*, whether written or oral, involved human agency. Consequently, even the early codices contain colloquial formations, corrupted texts, different sequence of verses, and incomplete hymns. The *Kartarpuri Bir* too bears the imprint of this situation. It is impossible to think that it was prepared from 'the holographs' of Professor Sahib Singh's hypothesis.[25]

REAFFIRMATION ON THE BASIS OF LARGER EVIDENCE

Gurinder Singh Mann was able to examine the *Kartarpur Pothi* on three different occasions. It is a dated document. The statement about the completion of the work in 1604 is clearly made in the handwriting of the scribe who prepared the *Pothis*' table of contents and inscribed most of the text. There is no perceptible evidence of tinkering in this entry.[26]

The presence of the *nishan* of Hargobind as the sixth Guru is explained by Mann with reference to the evolution of the institution of Guruship. It had become 'hereditary' by this time. The succession of Hargobind as the only son of Guru Arjan was almost a certainty in 1604. Therefore, the scribe could request him to inscribe his attestation at the beginning of the second half of the *Pothi*, and recorded it in the table of contents as 'the attestation of the sixth guru'.[27]

About the death dates of the first six Gurus and Baba Gurditta on folio 25, the first five are not only in one hand but also written at one time. Mann is of the view that the list of death dates was added to the *Pothi* after 1606 on folio 25 which had been left blank in the original writing. The reference to this list was naturally added to the table of contents after 1606. That is why it is in a different ink and with a different pen from the rest of the table of contents.[28]

Giani Gurdit Singh and others have rejected the authenticity of the *Kartarpur Pothi* on the grounds that Kesar Singh Chhibber categorically states that the *Granth* was complete in 1601. Mann points out that Giani Mahan Singh had already highlighted inconsistencies in Chhibber's dates and convincingly argued against 1601 as the date of compilation. Mann concludes, therefore, that the invocation in the hand of Guru Hargobind, the listing of the death dates of the first five Gurus, and Chhibber's reference to 1601 as the date of compilation can all be explained without challenging the recorded date of the *Pothi* or the authenticity of the Sikh tradition that the manuscript was compiled under the supervision of Guru Arjan.[29]

Turning to the internal structure and contents of the *Kartarpur Pothi*, Mann notices that the opening folio and the one at the beginning of the section on *Rag Suhi* are extensively illuminated in blue and gold. The blank folios appear most frequently at the ends of the Rag sections or sub-sections within each Rag unit. The binding of the *Pothi* is not the original one and its laminated pages make it impossible to separate the gatherings from each other to understand their sequence. There is problem with the numbering of folios and there are some extra folios without margin lines which differ visibly from the original ones.

G.S. Mann differs from Bhai Jodh Singh and Daljeet Singh on the issue of the *Pothi's* original contents. Writing in 1918, Bhai Kahn Singh Nabha had reported that the *Kartarpur Pothi* contained in its concluding section, after the *Rag Mala*, a brief narrative called the *Hakikat Rah Mukam Raje Shibnabh ki* and a few entries regarding a land grant, a fire in 1777, and a visit by Maharaja Ranjit Singh in 1831. Bhai Jodh Singh was equally categorical in the late 1940s that there was no such matter in the *Kartarpur Pothi* after the *Rag Mala*. Bhai Jodh Singh accused Bhai Kahn Singh Nabha for giving false information but Mann accepts the accuracy of assertions of both. In his view, the matter in question was removed from the *Kartarpur Pothi* in the late 1920s when it was rebound.[30]

According to G.S. Mann, the custodians of the *Kartarpur Pothi* allowed these 'anachronistic alterations' in the structure of the *Pothi* in 'a misconceived attempt' to prove its authenticity. Their idea was to make the *Pothi* conform to the *Adi Granth* which ended at the *Rag Mala*. Mann's explanation clarifies several other issues. The copy of the *Kartarpur Pothi* sent to Queen Victoria in the late 1850s, is actually identical with the text of the *Adi Granth* minus the compositions of Guru Tegh Bahadur. Similarly, the copy of the *Pothi* made at Patiala in the early 1860s has the same text as that of the *Adi Granth*. The table of contents of the *Kartarpur Pothi* still carries the entry *Ragmala tatha Singhladip ki Shivnabh ki Bidhi*. As yet, no copy of the *Kartarpur Pothi* as it stands now (that is, without the excised matter) has come to light.[31]

On the whole, the history of the *Kartarpur Pothi* and the evidence in support of its compilation in 1604 confirm that it was prepared as early as it claims to have been. The *Pothi* is the authentic manuscript associated in Sikh tradition with Guru Arjan and, therefore, a very significant text in the evolution of the Sikh scripture. Though the issue of the contents of the *Pothi* is open to debate, the table of contents appears to reflect its contents faithfully for the closing section. This understanding of the *Kartarpur Pothi* clarifies the history of the Sikh scriptural text during the seventeenth century and, in turn, gets confirmed.

We can see that Mann has challenged the position held by a group of influential scholars like G.B. Singh, Gurdit Singh, Inder Singh Chakarvarti, Piar Singh, Piara Singh Padam, Pritam Singh and Randhir Singh, and he supports the position taken up by Bhai Jodh Singh and Daljeet Singh on the authenticity of the *Kartarpur Pothi*. Mann points out, however, that Bhai Jodh Singh's work was done in an atmosphere of fierce controversy over the continued presence of the *Rag Mala* in the *Adi Granth*. He interpreted any question about the authenticity of the *Kartarpur Pothi* as a challenge to Sikh canon and consequently an attack on the very foundation of the Sikh community. The assumption that those who do not recognize the *Kartarpur Pothi* as a genuine document pose a threat to the text of the *Adi Granth* introduces a religious dimension into a purely academic debate. In Mann's view, traditional Sikh claims regarding the history of the *Kartarpur Pothi* are fully authenticated by the evidence available to us.[32]

Pashaura Singh accepts Mann's view of the authenticity of the *Kartarpur Pothi* but differs with him on some matters of detail. He suggests, for example, that possibly 'a new index was prepared on a new leaf after the death of Guru Arjan when the autograph of the sixth Guru was also included in the volume'.[33] He looks upon Mann's argument that the *Kartarpur Pothi* remained at Kartarpur from the 1630s as 'misleading' in view of certain notes in Ram Rai's recension at Dehra Dun copied in 1659 at Kiratpur.[34] However, according to Mann, the note says that it was 'compared' with the original, which implies that it was not copied from the original. Pashaura Singh states that no textual critic can afford to ignore the arguments of Piar Singh even though 'one might not agree with him on every point'.[35] His agreement with Piar Singh is on matters of detail but not on Piar Singh's basic position that the *Kartarpur Pothi* is a later compilation and, therefore, not authentic.

DEBATE ON THE EARLIER MANUSCRIPTS

Scholars differ equally widely over the process of compilation of the *Kartarpur Pothi* even when they accept its authenticity. One set of scholars look at the *Kartarpur Pothi* as the earliest authentic manuscript. Another set of scholars invoke the evidence of earlier manuscripts to trace, understand and reconstruct the story of the texts culminating in the compilation of the *Kartarpur Pothi.* There are further differences of detail among the same set of scholars.

Professor Sahib Singh examined the *Suraj Prakash, the Gurbilas Chhevin Patshahi,* and *Tawarikh Guru Khalsa* and came to the conclusion that their accounts of how Guru Arjan collected the *bani* of his predecessors did not appeal to reason. Turning to the *sakhis* of Guru Nanak he perceived that he had collected his own *bani.* According to the *Puratan Janamsakhi* this collection was given to Lehna when he was installed as Guru Angad. The *bani* of Guru Angad, especially in comparison with the *bani* of Guru Nanak, also indicated that Guru Angad possessed the corpus of Guru Nanak's *bani.* Similarly, a close comparison of Guru Amar Das's *bani* with that of Guru Nanak showed that Guru Amar Das possessed the corpus of Guru Nanak's *bani.* In short, the *bani* of the first four Gurus came into the possession of Guru Arjan as a legacy. Professor Sahib Singh argued that there was no substance in the story that Guru Arjan sang a particular hymn to Baba Mohan to get the *Goindval Pothis.* The Bhagat Bani too was a part of the legacy coming down from Guru Nanak. Guru Arjan had only his own *bani* to add to compile the *Pothi* which was written by Bhai Gurdas in 1604 and which was in the possession of the Sodhis of Kartarpur.[36]

Balwant Singh Dhillon reinforces the thesis put forward by Professor Sahib Singh in a modified form. Literary activity among the Sikhs can be traced back to the times of Guru Nanak. The Sikh Gurus and the Sikhs commissioned by them took good care of recording and copying Gurbani for circulation among the Sikhs. A tradition of Gurbani in scribal form flourished under the Sikh Gurus. The successors had access to the *bani* of their predecessors and the *bani* of the Bhagats. The process of recording, compilation and canonization took place over and over again for nearly a century, ending with the codification of the *Adi Granth* in 1604. Besides the main tradition, however, four rival traditions also developed, that is, the Udasi, the Bhalla or Mohan, the Mina and the Hindali. In Dhillon's view, all the extant manuscripts earlier than the *Kartarpur Pothi* belonged to one or another of the rival tradition. These manuscripts appear to have played no role in the compilation of the *Kartarpur Pothi.*[37]

Unlike Sahib Singh and Balwant Singh Dhillon, Gurinder Singh Mann and Pashaura Singh attach considerable importance to manuscripts earlier than the *Kartarpur Pothi* to understand its making. Gurinder Singh Mann treats the *Guru Harsahai Pothi* as the original collection made by Guru Nanak in the 1530s or its copy and, therefore, an authentic text. In Mann's view, there is no basis for challenging the claim of the Sodhis of Guru Harsahai that the *Pothi* had remained in their possession ever since Guru Ram Das gave it to his eldest son Prithi Chand who could project it as a symbol of authority. The photographs taken by Giani Gurdit Singh from the opening section of the *Pothi* show that its script is of extremely early origin. The invocation (*mangal*, *mulmantar* or *sirlekh*) on the opening folio is also very simple: *Onkar sachnam kartar*. There is no organization according to *Rags*. Quotations from the *bani* of Guru Nanak in the literature of the successors of Prithi Chand appear to have come from the opening section of the *Guru Harsahai Pothi*. In any case they do not use the music-related category of *ghar* along with the *Rag*. On the whole, early orthography, the text of the invocation, inclusion of the hymns of Guru Nanak also, and lack of any principle of organization all suggest a date that is the earliest in Sikh tradition. To this section were added at later stages the hymns of the successors of Guru Nanak and those of the Bhagats, and the organization of the added corpus was also tightened. The *Anand* of Guru Amar Das in the *Guru Harsahai Pothi* has 39 *pauris* whereas the *Kartarpur Pothi* has 40. The later section of the former can thus be seen as earlier than the Kartarpur recension.[38]

Pashaura Singh has pointed out that the *mulmantar* of the *Guru Harsahai Pothi* contains the signature 'Baba Nanak', which suggests that it was written by a Sikh scribe and not by Guru Nanak. G.S. Mann in his view has taken recourse to traditions for attributing the opening section of the *Pothi* to Guru Nanak. Pashaura Singh believes that 'traditions are notoriously unreliable sources for historical data'. Therefore, for the time being, 'we must suspend our judgement on the issue of its identity with Guru Nanak's pothi'.[39]

Giani Gurdit Singh's observations are the only source of Balwant Singh Dhillon as for others for the *Guru Harsahai Pothi*. Dhillon points out that the information provided by Giani Gurdit Singh is extremely meagre. Therefore, hardly any statement can be made with certainty. There are indications that Miharban's writings also formed a part of the *Pothi*. The index of the *Pothi* suggests organization in terms of *Rag* units. Like Pashaura Singh, Dhillon argues that the so-called *mulmantar* of the *Pothi* could not be attributed to Guru Nanak. A new index of 1625 refers to the *nishan* of Guru Arjan but no *nishan* is there, 'a clear proof that the *Pothi* did not belong to the main Sikh tradition'. The text of its *Bhagat Bani* has not come from the main Sikh scriptural tradition. The internal evidence of the *Pothi* establishes beyond any doubt that it was recorded between 1606 and 1625. Therefore, Dhillon maintains that to regard the *Pothi* as a document of pre-scriptural Sikh tradition originating in the time of Guru Nanak is 'absolutely unwarranted and uncalled for'.[40]

The *Goindval Pothis* have been studied rather thoroughly by Gurinder Singh Mann.[41] Though only two *Pothis* are extant, Mann has argued that their number was four. Both the extant *Pothis* are primarily in a single handwriting. The work indicates excellent professional skills. Thirty hymns of the Bhagats were added by another scribe. This addition appears to have been made soon after the compilation of the *Pothis*. Five hymns in a third hand and some other matter were added later. Blank folios are found only at the end of *Rag* sections and sub-sections of the hymns of the Gurus. The scribe knew that he had all the hyms available to him for inscribing. The writing clearly runs continuously and the scribe left no provision for adding a hymn of Guru Nanak in the text. The text of the *Pothis* was written serially towards the end of Guru Amar Das's life.[42]

Mann argues that the *Goindval Pothis* were the primary source for the *Kartarpur Pothi* in two principal ways: the actual corpus of the sacred hymns, and their arrangement in a particular order. For the variations, Mann offers a few explanations. He underlines that a comparison of the hymns of Guru Nanak and Guru Amar Das in the *Goindval Pothis* and the *Kartarpur Pothi* shows that almost all the hymns of the two Gurus in the latter were available in corresponding *Rag* sections of the former. The *Kartarpur Pothi* thus included the text of the *Goindval Pothis* plus the hymns of Guru Ram Das and Guru Arjan in these compilations. There is no other manuscript comparable to the *Goindval Pothis* that could have served as the source of the *Kartarpur Pothi*. The *Goindval Pothis* show the expansion of the sacred corpus and the evolution of its arrangements. 'On the basis of this information, we can form a clear picture of the development of the Sikh sacred text in the sixteenth century. This is a cause for celebration. No other major religious tradition possesses manuscripts that illustrate the evolution of its scriptural sources so clearly.[43]

Pashaura Singh does not agree with Mann on the issue of the date of the extant *Pothis.* The *Pothi* at Jalandhar (also called the *Ahiyapur Pothi*) gives 1695 as the date. Giani Gurdit Singh has suggested that this date was inserted later. As his evidence for the compilation in the time of Guru Amar Das, Giani Gurdit Singh refers to the marginal note in the *Pothi* at Pinjore which refers to Jeth Chand (the original name of Guru Ram Das), as 'your enraptured slave' (*gulam mast tainda*). Pashaura Singh says that we cannot be sure whether Jeth Chand wrote this note or the Bhalla family inserted it later. A careful examination of the note reveals that it was inserted later in a different hand. It clearly states that the *Pothi* was written at the instance of Guru Amar Das. It refers also to the blessings of three generations, which implies that the note was written after the death of Guru Amar Das. It appears to challenge the Guruship of Guru Ram Das. Nevertheless, concedes Pashaura Singh, the two extant volumes of the *Goindval Pothis* remain 'the oldest manuscripts at our disposal'. The style of their script would place these two in the second half of the sixteenth century. He concludes that 'the two available volumes must be regarded as copies rather than as the original Goindval pothis'.[44]

Pashaura Singh makes an interesting suggestion with regard to the *Goindval Pothis.* The testimony of Baba Sundar's *Sadd* in *Rag Ramkali* indicates that the *Goindval Pothis,* as the Guru's true word (*gur sabadu sachu nisanu*), were given to Guru Ram Das at the time of his succession to Guruship, and they were passed on to Guru Arjan in a similar situation. However, copies of the *Goindval Pothis* were made. One such copy, or a copy of a copy, was in the possession of Baba Mohan, son of Guru Amar Das. According to Pashaura Singh, Gurinder Singh Mann's work provides a generally accurate description of the two available volumes but his identification of the writings by Gulam Sadasewak with those of Guru Ram Das (before he actually became the Guru) is questionable. These writings, subsequently deleted, appear to have been written in competition with Guru Ram Das. They might have been written by Baba Mohan himself. The poetic style of these compositions is flattering and plodding, unlike the authentic *bani* of Guru Ram Das. Another point on which Pashaura Singh disagrees with Mann is that of correspondence in the *Rag* sections of the *Goindval Pothis* and the *Kartarpur Pothi*. In *Rag Maru* there is a difference of 66 hymns, with only ten in the former and seventy-six in the latter. Pashaura Singh sees a vital connection between the *Goindval Pothis* compiled by Guru Amar Das and the *Kartarpur Pothi*, but the extant *Pothis* remained redundant, he maintains. Guru Arjan did not need them because he had in his possession the original *Goindval Pothis*.[45] Incidentally, this would imply that the extant *Pothis* shorn of the additional matter are close to the original *Pothis*!

Gurinder Singh Mann is criticized by Balwant Singh Dhillon also for attributing 14 hymns to Guru Ram Das as Jeth Chand or Gulam Sadasewak. The aspiration of the author of these hymns to establish his own guruship is depicted in one of the hymns. He uses the epithet 'Nanik' for himself, which was another way of putting forth the same claim. Therefore, the author of these hymns was either Baba Mohan or someone commissioned by him. Dhillon also argues that the colophon with the date 7 January 1596 was not inserted later. The presence of the hymns of Guru Ram Das and Guru Arjan in one of the *Pothis* would also confirm a later date of compilation. The Bhagats are sometimes referred to as the Bhagats of Baba Nanak placing them at a pedestal lower than that of Guru Nanak. The *Pothis* also contain some apocryphal writings attributed to the Sikh Gurus, Bhagats, Gulam Sadasewak, and Sharaf. The inclusion of *kachchi bani* in the *Pothis* shows clearly that the *Pothis* owe their origin to 'schismatic trends in Sikhism'. Therefore, the extant *Pothis* are not even copies of the original *Goindval Pothis*. Their role in the codification of the *Kartarpur Pothi* is 'more imaginary than real'.[46]

Even more controversial than the *Guru Harsahai Pothi* and the *Goindval Pothis* is the *MS 1245*, a manuscript without a history acquired by Guru Nanak Dev University in March 1987. The text of the *MS 1245* is structured in three parts. The opening section contains the liturgical texts of the *Japuji* and the *Sodar*. The main body is organized into 30 *Rag* units. The last part includes the *shaloks* and hymns of the Gurus and the panegyrics of the Bhatts. Nearly the whole *bani* of the first four Gurus and the bulk of the *bani* of Guru Arjan are included in the manuscripts. The hymns of the Bhagats are excluded except the *shaloks* of Kabir in the *vars* of Guru Amar Das and Guru Ram Das.

Gurinder Singh Mann argues that the contents and structural features of this manuscript indicate that it was compiled before the *Kartarpur Pothi.* Its *mulmantar* is somewhat different from that of the *Goindval Pothis.* In the *Kartarpur Pothi,* only one further change is made: *satguru prasadi* in the *MS 1245* is replaced by *gurprasadi* in the *Kartarpur Pothi.* Five hymns of the *Sohila* are added to the *Sodar* in the *MS 1245.* The overall *Rag* sequence in the *MS 1245* differs considerably from that of the *Goindval Pothis* and appears in the *Kartarpur Pothi* only with slight alterations. The sequence of *chaupadas, chhants* and *ashtpadis* in the *Goindval Pothis* is changed to *chaupadas, ashtpadis* and *chhants* in the *MS 1245* and this altered sequence appears in the *Kartarpur Pothi* as well. There are other indications to suggest that the text of the *MS 1245* is located in the transitional stage between the *Goindval Pothis* and the *Kartarpur Pothi.* All this internal evidence points towards an earlier origin of the *MS 1245* than that of the *Kartarpur Pothi.* The hymns of Guru Arjan in the *MS 1245* which refer to events related to the life of Guru Hargobind show that this manuscript was compiled after 1695, the year of Guru Hargobind's birth. Mann suggests 1600 as a reasonable date.[47]

The crucial significance of the *MS 1245* for Mann lies not in its origin as an independent effort, as maintained by Balwant Singh Dhillon, nor in its serving as a draft for the *Kartarpur Pothi,* as maintained by Pashaura Singh, but rather in its manifesting a conception of Sikh scripture different from the type represented in the *Goindval Pothis* and the *Kartarpur Pothi.* The *MS 1245* appears to have been compiled at a time when the earlier conception of the Sikh scripture was being reconsidered. Around 1600, Guru Arjan was thinking of dropping the non-Sikh contributions altogether or separating them from the compositions of the Sikhs and appending them as a distinct unit towards the end of the scriptural text. This would also explain the neglect of the *MS 1245.* Reversion to the familiar type in the *Kartarpur Pothi* left the *MS 1245* permanently incomplete, and it was allowed to sink into oblivion to have no history. Its importance for the making of the *Kartarpur Pothi* lies in the fact that it served as a channel between the *Goindval Pothis* and the *Kartarpur Pothi.*[48]

Pashaura Singh suggests that the *MS 1245* was possibly placed in the custody of Bhai Buddha, who is said to have inscribed a particular hymn of Guru Amar Das in the manuscript, and remained with his family (after it was used as a draft for the *Kartarpur Pothi*). The dates of the demise of the first five Gurus (added later than its compilation) are given on folio 1255a. The entire manuscript is in one hand. Its archaic orthography suggests a date prior to the *Kartarpur Pothi.* Pashaura Singh surmises that this manuscript was being compiled towards the end of 1598 when Akbar met Guru Arjan. It was completed in 1599. Apart from variant readings, the *MS 1245* does not have a number of hymns found in the *Kartarpur Pothi.* In all its three parts it has broad similarities with the *Kartarpur Pothi.*[49]

Pashaura Singh comes to the conclusion that the *MS 1245* represents the pre-canonical stage of the Sikh scriptural tradition. It is still in its incomplete form, and illuminates the textual process through which the evolution of the Sikh scripture took place. Its relationship with the *Goindval Pothis* and the *Kartarpur Pothi* is quite obvious. Its value to the textual scholar is equally obvious. It soon became irrelevant to the Sikhs because of its incomplete nature but survived as 'a spiritual relic'. There are other such manuscripts, like the *Bahoval Pothi* and the *Pahinda Sahib Pothi*, which reflect the fluid state from which the various structures of organization and the final form of various hymns emerged in the first canonical text of the *Kartarpur Pothi.*[50] This is called 'draft theory' by Pashaura Singh's in a later work.[51]

Balwant Singh Dhillon presents an elaborate analysis of the *MS 1245* and comes to the conclusion that it was prepared by the Minas. He points to a number of elements in the *MS 1245* which are similar to those of the Mina tradition and ascetical ideals. The dates of the passing away of the first five Gurus, the *nishan* of Guru Tegh Bahadur, orthographic style and textual variants suggest a date after the compilation of the *Kartarpur Pothi.* In Dhillon's view, the *MS 1245* was a deliberate act of editing on the part of its scribe, or his patrons, 'who were weary [*sic*] of some writings that had been made part of the *Adi Granth*', that is, the *Kartarpur Pothi*. Thus, the *MS 1245* was neither an earlier draft nor a source for editing the *Kartarpur Pothi*.[52]

Gurinder Singh Mann is aware of Balwant Singh Dhillon's view that the *MS 1245* was compiled later than the compilation of the *Kartarpur Pothi*, and also that it represents a parallel scriptural text developed by the descendants of Prithi Chand. Mann sees a fundamental problem with Dhillon's argument. The hymns of Guru Arjan figure prominently in the *MS 1245*. How could this support Prithi Chand's family to promote their agenda of creating 'new Gurudom'. A hymn of Guru Arjan refers to the conspiracy between some dissident Sikhs and the Mughals and the divine intervention to protect the Guru. Miharban's family is the subject of the hymn. It does not support Dhillon's argument that Miharban created this document. It does not contain any composition of Miharban. The incomplete nature of the manuscript does not support Dhillon's idea that it was prepared to be sent to some distant congregation. The affinity of the text of the *MS 1245* with the writings of the family can be better explained in terms of both belonging to an early phase of the evolution of the sacred Sikh text.[53]

Pashaura Singh suggests that the *nishan* of Guru Tegh Bahadur was pasted on the fourth decorated page much later than the compilation of the *MS 1245*. It proves moreover that the manuscript belonged to the mainline Sikh tradition. It could not be a work of the Minas because neither Prithi Chand nor Miharban appear in the list of the dates of the demise of the Gurus. The similarity of the text of its *Japuji* with that of Harji's *Japu Parmarth* could be due to the fact that both were copied from a common source.[54]

Balwant Singh Dhillon sticks to his view that the *MS 1245* is a Mina document prepared after the *Kartarpur Pothi*. Gurinder Singh Mann and Pashaura Singh see its link with both the *Goindval Pothis* and the *Kartarpur Pothi* as a manuscript got prepared by Guru Arjan. However, Pashaura Singh's 'draft theory' makes no sense, not only for Dhillon but also for Mann.

The views expressed by these three scholars on the three manuscripts spring from their general approach and outlook. Mann approaches the subject strictly as a historian, paying serious attention to extant manuscripts and comparing their texts for understanding the process of the making of the *Kartarpur Pothi*. The *Guru Harsahai Pothi*, the *Goindval Pothis*, and the *MS 1245* represent three stages in this evolution. Balwant Singh Dhillon is a scholar of religious studies. He believes that certain matters should not be made a subject of analysis. He assumes that Sahib Singh's hypothesis of the making of the *Kartarpur Pothi* is correct. Since the extant manuscripts do not conform to that hypothesis, Dhillon's primary concern is to show that they do not belong to the mainstream Sikhism. For him, the *Kartarpur Pothi* is the earliest extant manuscript of the mainstream scriptural tradition. All others are believed to have been lost. Pashaura Singh suspends his judgement on the *Guru Harsahai Pothi's* authenticity and looks upon the extant *Goindval Pothis* as a copy. He lays great stress on the editorial activity of Guru Arjan and looks upon several manuscripts as 'drafts' got prepared by Guru Arjan to produce the *Kartarpur Pothi* as the Sikh canon. Paradoxically, the mode of analysis adopted by Gurinder Singh Mann remains the most relevant for understanding the evolution of the scriptural tradition culminating in the making of the *Kartarpur Pothi* even if the two earliest manuscripts are seen as copies. The evolution from the simple towards the complex enables us to appreciate the 'transitional' character of the *MS 1245*. The story of the making of the *Kartarpur Pothi* proposed by Mann is the most satisfactory on the whole.

NOTES

1. Gurdev Singh (ed.), *Perspective on the Sikh Tradition*, Patiala: Siddharth Publications, 1986, 'Introduction', p. 10.
2. W.H. McLeod, *The Evolution of the Sikh Community*, New Delhi: Oxford University Press, 1975, pp. 59-61.
3. Ibid., pp. 61-2.
4. Ibid., pp. 62-3.
5. Ibid., pp. 63-9.
6. Ibid., pp. 69-70.
7. Ibid., pp. 81-2.
8. Ibid., pp. 76-8.
9. Ibid., pp. 78-9.

10. Daljeet Singh, 'Authenticity of the Kartarpuri Bir', in *Advanced Studies in Sikhism*, ed. Jasbir Singh Mann and Harbans Singh Saraon, Irvine, CA: Sikh Community of North America, 1989, pp. 138, 152-9.
11. Ibid., pp. 139, 141-50.
12. Ibid., pp. 150-2.
13. Piar Singh, *Gatha Sri Adi Granth* (Pbi), Amritsar: Guru Nanak Dev University, 1992, pp. 175-8, 181-6.
14. Ibid., pp. 187-9.
15. Ibid., pp. 190-200.
16. Ibid., pp. 178-90, 450-4.
17. Ibid., pp. 454-6.
18. Ibid., pp. 472-4.
19. Piar Singh, *Gatha Sri Adi Granth and the Controversy*, Michigan: Anant Education and Rural Development Foundation, 1996, pp. 1-2.
20. Ibid., pp. 81-111.
21. Ibid., pp. 115, 135-6.
22. Ibid., pp. 137-44.
23. Ibid., pp. 153-6.
24. Ibid., pp. 148-51, 157-8.
25. Ibid., p. 152.
26. Gurinder Singh Mann, *The Making of Sikh Scripture*, New Delhi: Oxford University Press, 2001, pp. 62-3.
27. Ibid., pp. 63-4.
28. Ibid., p. 64.
29. Ibid., pp. 64-5.
30. Ibid., pp. 65-7.
31. Ibid., pp. 62, 66-7.
32. Ibid., pp. 67-8.
33. Pashaura Singh, *The Guru Granth Sahib: Canon, Meaning and Authority*, New Delhi: Oxford University Press, 2000, p. 54.
34. Ibid., p. 58.
35. Ibid., p. 59.
36. Sahib Singh, *Adi Bir Bare* (Pbi), Amritsar: Singh Brothers, 1995 (6th imp.).
37. Balwant Singh Dhillon, *Early Sikh Scriptural Tradition: Myth and Reality*, Amritsar: Singh Brothers, 1999, pp. 59-60.
38. Mann, *The Making of Sikh Scripture*, pp. 33-40.
39. Pashaura Singh, *The Guru Granth Sahib*, pp. 32-3.
40. Dhillon, *Early Sikh Scriptural Tradition*, pp. 64-88.
41. Gurinder Singh Mann, *The Goindval Pothis: The Earliest Extant Source of the Sikh Canon*, Cambridge: Harvard Oriental Series, 1996.

42. Mann, *The Making of Sikh Scripture*, pp. 40-7.
43. Ibid., pp. 47-50.
44. Pashaura Singh, *The Guru Granth Sahib*, pp. 34-8, 39.
45. Ibid., pp. 38-41.
46. Dhillon, *Early Sikh Scriptural Tradition*, pp. 89-147.
47. Mann, *The Making of Sikh Scripture*, pp. 51-7.
48. Ibid., pp. 57-9.
49. Pashaura Singh, *The Guru Granth Sahib*, pp. 47-51.
50. Ibid., pp. 52-3.
51. Pashaura Singh talks of 'a more balanced perspective' through which he looks upon the *Kartarpur Pothi* as the result of a 'collaborative approach' based upon the 'theory of working drafts'. See *Life and Work of Guru Arjan*, New Delhi: Oxford University Press, 2007 (2nd imp.), p. 136.
52. Dhillon, *Early Sikh Scriptural Tradition*, pp. 183-241.
53. Mann, *The Making of Sikh Scripture*, pp. 53, 57-8.
54. Pashaura Singh, *The Guru Granth Sahib*, pp. 42-3.

CHAPTER 11

The *Guru Granth Sahib* and the *Dasam Granth*

Only two scholars have continued the story of the making of the *Guru Granth Sahib* with the *Kartarpur Pothi* as the starting point: Gurinder Singh Mann and Pashaura Singh. The former takes the story first up to the *Adi Granth*, that is, the *Granth* which came to be regarded as the Guru. Then he talks of the three centuries of Sikh scriptural history from that point onwards. Pashaura Singh tells this story in a chapter entitled 'The Adi Granth traditions and Canon Formation'. Unlike Gurinder Singh Mann, he equates the *Kartarpur Pothi* with the *Adi Granth*. They agree that the Damdama version was based on the *Kartarpur Pothi* and the *Guru Granth Sahib* represents the Damdama version. However, they differ in their understanding of the process through which this development took place. Mann's story takes into account a much larger number of manuscripts. In contrast with the story of the *Guru Granth Sahib*, the story of the *Dasam Granth* is still vague, conjectural, and controversial.

MAKING OF THE *DAMDAMI BIR*

According to Gurinder Singh Mann, the *Kartarpur Pothi* began to be copied almost immediately after its compilation in 1604. We find references made to the manuscripts of 1605, 1619, 1637, 1640 and 1641, but these manuscripts are no longer extant. From 1642 a good number of manuscripts are available. Mann gives a list of 27 manuscripts compiled from 1642 to 1692. A study of these manuscripts shows that, with the exception of two, they fall into two branches: 11 into what is traditionally called the Lahore branch and 14 into what is traditionally called the Khara Mangat branch. Mann labels these two as branch 1 and branch 2, respectively. The *Kanpur*

Pothi, known as *Banno Bir* and also called the *Khara Mangat Bir*, prepared in 1642, did not originate from the *Kartarpur Pothi*. In fact, no single manuscript is an exact copy of *Kartarpur Pothi*. The common assumption that the *Kartarpur Pothi* was identical with the *Adi Granth* minus the compositions of Guru Tegh Bahadur has to be discarded for appreciating the real significance of the extant manuscripts of the two branches.[1]

A manuscript of branch 1 was present at Gurdwara Dera Sahib, Lahore, at the turn of the twentieth century but there is no evidence that it originated in Lahore. The earliest extant manuscript of branch 1 is the *Amritsar Pothi* prepared in 1654. Its comparison with the *Kartarpur Pothi* shows that within a broad layout there are variations in terms of contents and the order of their arrangement. This is illustrated by Gurinder Singh Mann in some detail, with the basic explanation that, though the inscription of the *Kartarpur Pothi* was completed in 1604, the hymns composed by Guru Arjan between 1604 and 1606 were added to it later, and the original manuscript that generated the *Amristar Pothi* was prepared when the *Kartarpur Pothi* was reaching its finished form. This explanation accounts for the higher frequency of differences in the opening and closing sections of these manuscripts. An entry in the *Amritsar Pothi* is of crucial significance in this connection. It reads:

> In the presence of the Guru [Arjan] the manuscript was completed. It was inscribed by Bhai Bura Sandhu in the presence of the fifth Guru. Bhai Milkhi of Peshawar commissioned its inscription. He who will come to the presence of the manuscript will see the body of Guru Nanak. Forgive flaws and omissions. God! The true guru! [The manuscript] is completed in Sammat 1662 (1605 CE).

This note, according to Mann, clarifies that the original manuscript of this branch was copied from the *Kartarpur Pothi* of 1605. Copies of this manuscript were generated in the Peshawar area and in the seventeenth century one such copy came into the possession of the Bhallas who later received a grant of Rs. 35,000 a year from Maharaja Ranjit Singh in the second decade of the nineteenth century. The manuscripts of this branch disappear after the turn of the eighteenth century, largely due to the fact that the compositions of Guru Tegh Bahadur were added to a manuscript of branch 2.[2]

The *Kanpur Pothi* or *Banno Bir* was inscribed in 1642 but its structure is identical with that of the *Kartarpur Pothi*. They share the same table of contents. Other details too connect the two *Pothis*, including the statement in the *Kanpur Pothi* that the text of the *Japuji* was a copy of the text recorded by Guru Ram Das. This feature of recording the exact number of stages by which a manuscript was removed from the original continued in the later manuscripts of this branch. There can be no doubt that the *Kanpur Pothi* is a direct copy of the *Kartarpur Pothi*. However, the *Kanpur Pothi* contains at least two compositions which are not there in the *Kartarpur Pothi*; the *Ratanmala* and the *Hakikat Rah Mukam Raje Shivnabh Ki*. The traditional claim that the *Kanpur Pothi* generated an independent branch of seventeenth-century manuscripts was based on the misconception that all the manuscripts which included the supposedly extra compositions were its copies. A correct understanding of the original contents of the *Kartarpur Pothi* makes it clear that the manuscripts supposed to have followed the *Kanpur Pothi* were in fact copies of the *Kartarpur Pothi* itself. Thus the manuscripts of branch 2 were post-1606 copies of the *Kartarpur Pothi*, whereas the branch 1 manuscripts were copies of pre-1606 *Kartarpur Pothi*. By the mid-1660s, however, the scribes appear to have become aware of the hymns originally absent from the manuscripts belonging to branch 1, and they began to add them to the copies they prepared. The manuscript at Dehra Dun at the seat of Ram Rai belongs to branch 1. Within the Sikh community no distinction appears to have been made between the two branches in terms of their status. The signatures recorded in the hands of different Gurus appear on the opening folios of the manuscripts of both the branches.[3]

The next step in the history of the scriptural text was taken by Guru Tegh Bahadur. The *MS 1192* in the Library of the Panjab University, Chandigarh, contains the complete corpus of Guru Tegh Bahadur's hymns. Below his *nishan* on its opening folio there is a note that reads: 'This attestation was obtained by presenting [the manuscript] to the ninth master, in the presence of the whole congregation, on Sammat 1731 [AD 1674], the full moon day of Jeth.' This carries the implication that the hymns of Guru Tegh Bahadur were incorporated into the scriptural text in his lifetime. It is important to add that the word used for the *nishan* of Guru Tegh

Bahadur in the note is *darshan*. Its appearance in the manuscript made it symbolic of the Guru's sight. Perhaps, this was the import of the *nishan* rather than confirming the authenticity of a manuscript.

The final stage of this evolution was marked by the compilation of the *Adi Granth* in the 1680s under Guru Gobind Singh. The incorporation of Guru Tegh Bahadur's corpus is affirmed in the manuscripts of 1682, 1688, 1691 and 1692, the phase in which the *Adi Granth* was compiled. Furthermore, a set of compositions available in the earlier manuscripts of branch 2 were probably dropped from the final text. Thus, the larger version was updated to create the *MS 1192* version in the mid-1670s, and the *Adi Granth* compiled in the early 1680s, which is distinct from the *MS 1192*, acquired the status of the canonical text. This carries the implication that the tradition with regard to the Damdama Sahib (Talvandi Sabo) has to be modified.[4]

'POWER HYPOTHESIS' IN SUPPORT OF THE BANNO VERSION

Pashaura Singh presents a different story. In spite of Guru Arjan's remarkable editorial achievement in establishing the first canonical text in 1604, three different recensions emerged in course of time. Pashaura Singh puts forth 'power hypothesis' to account for these three categories of recensions. For him, significant textual variations appear to reflect the diversity of the Sikh Panth due to factional divisions or external interference in the affairs of the Panth. He goes into the issue of external interference by Mughal officials and factional divisions, 'to discover their possible impact on various groups within the Panth that were seeking to promote their versions of the Adi Granth'.[5]

Pashaura Singh talks of the Lahore recension of the *Adi Granth* prepared in Lahore in 1710 when Guru Hargobind was imprisoned in the fort of Gwalior. The Lahore recension does not prescribe heroic tunes for the *Vars* in different *Rag* units of the *Adi Granth*. There are two extra hymns in the concluding section of the text of the Lahore recension: one by Trilochan and the other by Namdev. Pashaura Singh suggests that their followers were responsible for the insertion of these hyms into the scripture. These hymns were originally turned down by Guru Arjan. In a copy of this tradition written in the early nineteenth century there is a solitary couplet of Guru Har Rai added after the *Mundavani* of Guru Arjan.[6]

The first *Banno Bir* was prepared in 1642 when the centre of Sikh activities had already shifted from Amritsar to Kiratpur in the Shivalik hills. Pashaura Singh refers to Sahib Singh's theory that extra-material in the *Banno Bir* was inserted by the Hindalis on the argument that the *Bhai Bala Janamsakhi*, which was popularized by the Hindalis, contained quotations from this extra-material. Pashaura Singh goes on to say that Sahib Singh's theory appeared to be too simplistic. The *Ratanmala* included in the *Banno Bir* is an exposition of *hatha-yoga* techniques, which could not be the work of Guru Nanak. It was definitely an Udasi work. They might have joined forces with the Hindalis and members of the Bhatra community to insert the extra-material in the Banno text. The Banno version came to the fore during the second half of the seventeenth century as a result of political disturbance which promoted Hindali influence. The eighteenth-century situation provided ample opportunity for the Banno group, particularly the Hindalis, to exert their influence with the help of the Mughal officials. Pashaura Singh tabulates 15 manuscripts of the Banno tradition from the mid-seventeenth to the nineteenth century, noticing that all the manuscripts, 'varied from one another to some degree'.[7]

Pashaura Singh refers to Harbhajan Singh's reference to two manuscripts of 1682 and 1691 which contained the compositions of Guru Tegh Bahadur at appropriate places with *Rag Jaijavanti* following the *Rag Prabhati* in the standard way. Harbhajan Singh called them Damdama versions because they were written at a place called Damdama in Anandpur Sahib. These two manuscripts did not contain the extra-material of the Banno Bir. Udasi Harnam Das refers to a manuscript of the Damdama tradition written in 1691, and Pashaura Singh himself has seen another manuscript of this tradition written in 1796.[8]

Pashaura Singh's story of the making of the *Damdami Bir*, the *Adi Granth* of Mann, is not only different from that of Mann but also rather thin. It is based on a far smaller number of manuscripts and even when Pashaura Singh talks of manuscripts he is predisposed to place them in one or another of the three categories postulated in the beginning. He talks of the close bearing of factional interests and external interference on the creation of three types of recensions but he produces little credible evidence in support of his contention. Anxious to put forth a radical 'power hypothesis', Pashaura Singh has come up with a lot of irrelevant evidence in support of a vague, largely conjectural, and a palpably incoherent story.

INCREASING CURRENCY OF THE *DAMDAMI BIR*

Gurinder Singh Mann refers to the two main conclusions drawn by Pashaura Singh in his work on the *Granth Sahib*: one, that during the eighteenth and the early nineteenth century the Sikhs used four different versions of the *Adi Granth*, and two, that Maharaja Ranjit Singh used his political influence in favour of 'a sole authorized canon' at the beginning of the nineteenth century. Along side the *Adi Granth*, which is the fourth tradition for Pashaura Singh, all the three traditions of the seventeenth century continued to flourish. Even Ranjit Singh could not enforce strict uniformity in the Sikh scriptural tradition. For Mann, there is no evidence to support the view that Maharaja Ranjit Singh played a role in the formation of Sikh canon. He gave patronage to the *Kartarpur Pothi* and *Kanpur Pothi* but there is no evidence to suggest that his enterprise was meant to create a 'standard text' of the *Adi Granth*.[9]

The manuscripts examined by Mann appear to fall into two categories and not four, as maintained by Pashaura Singh, nor one, as traditionally believed. One of these is the *Adi Granth* or the *Damdami Bir* of Pashaura Singh. The other is a version of the seventeenth-century manuscripts of branch 2 with the compositions of Guru Tegh Bahadur added. In the central places like Anandpur and Damdama Sahib, the extant manuscripts are almost always the *Adi Granth*. Mann argues that the vesting of Guruship in the *Adi Granth* made it the eternal Guru and its manuscript copies contain no date. The other manuscripts are generally dated. There are substantive variations among them. The *Adi Granth* and the other manuscripts were not competing with each other. Therefore, it is irrelevant to talk of the eventual triumph of the *Adi Granth*. The scribes who produced the other manuscripts were unaware of the textual differences between the *Adi Granth* and the earlier texts from which they were copying. The *Adi Granth* achieved relative harmony in the Sikh scriptural tradition at the beginning of the eighteenth century and this hegemony has remained unchallenged to the present day. In the phase of political struggle during the eighteenth century, when the Khalsa horsemen remained mostly on the march, the size of the *Adi Granth* became smaller. With the establishment of the rule of the Khalsa in the late eighteenth century and its expansion under Maharaja Ranjit Singh, the size of the *Adi Granth* became larger and larger.[10]

The first lithographed edition of the *Adi Granth* was published in 1864-5. Eleven different editions and reprints had appeared by 1893. The centre shifted from Lahore to Amritsar in the early years of the twentieth century, and the publishing house of Chatar Singh Jivan Singh became the major producer of the *Adi Granth.* The Shiromani Gurdwara Prabandhak Committee resolved to produce a standard edition. Its *Adi Sri Guru Granth Sahib Ji* was published in 1952, with the standard pagination of 1430. The scholars who participated in the production of this text used the *Kartarpur Pothi* and an undated manuscript at Damdama Sahib. Playing on the Sikh religious susceptibility, the publishing lobby challenged the SGPC's right to make even positional changes in the text of the *Adi Granth.* The SGPC brought out a revised edition in the mid-1960s. In this debate it was argued that the *Damdami Bir* and not the *Kartarpur Pothi* should be the model. There was a similar controversy later about whether or not the words of the *Adi Granth* should be separated as the SGPC had done in the 1970s. In 1996, the SGPC resolved to create a committee to look into the issue of variants in the published editions of the *Adi Granth* by the SGPC. Along with this increasing standardization, the text of the *Adi Granth* became available in a digital format in the 1990s, a mode that demands uniformity in spellings and format.[11]

AN ALTERNATIVE BUT POOR HYPOTHESIS

Pashaura Singh states that no single version of the *Adi Granth* was acceptable to all the Sikhs in the eighteenth century. By the beginning of the nineteenth century the Sikhs were using 'more than four different versions' of the *Adi Granth.* Maharaja Ranjit Singh changed this situation by promoting the Damdami version. 'It is quite possible that Maharaja Ranjit Singh appointed a council of prominent scholars to prepare an authorized version of the *Adi Granth*.' Having suggested this possibility Pashaura Singh goes on to add that there is no historical evidence on the details of this operation.[12] In other words, there is no evidence that any such council was appointed. In fact, there was no need to appoint a council if the Damdama version was generally taken to be the authorized version.

Pashaura Singh talks of 'the manuscripts of the period' and of 'canonical texts' but refers only to the manuscript presented by Sodhi Sadhu Singh to Queen Victoria in 1859. This manuscript is a copy of the Damdama version. The most significant point about this manuscript, according to Pashaura Singh, is that at its end the total number of its letters is given in another hand as 9,91,032 'all of which are the limbs (*ang*) of the *Guru Granth Sahib Ji*'. This note reflects the self-understanding of the contemporary Sikh community, and how it perceived the *Guru Granth Sahib* as the 'living embodiment of the Guru'. What is even more significant is that Pashaura Singh goes on to add that 'the new version was, in fact, revival of the earlier Damdama version, compiled during the period of Guru Gobind Singh in the late seventeenth century'. Pashaura Singh simply assumes that the Damdama version had gone out of circulation during the eighteenth century. On this assumption, he refers to some other manuscripts to show that Maharaja Ranjit Singh promoted the copying and distribution of the Damdama version. Pashaura Singh suggests that the authors of the *Gurbilas Chhevin Patshahi* and the *Suraj Prakash* were possibly 'members of the Sikh council responsible for the project undertaken with the specific approval of Maharaja Ranjit Singh' because they do not include Mira Bai among the *bhagats* whose compositions are incorporated in the *Guru Granth Sahib*. Despite the standardization of the text of the *Adi Granth*, the Banno version remained in use in some sections of the Sikh community, especially in the area of Gujrat district.[13]

It is interesting to note that the manuscripts referred to by Pashaura Singh are mostly of the Damdama tradition. He argues, rather unconvincingly, that this was a new development of the early nineteenth century sponsored by Maharaja Ranjit Singh. In matters religious, Ranjit Singh was very particular about continuing the practices of the late eighteenth century which had been developed by the Khalsa since the time of Guru Gobind Singh. Pashaura Singh himself says that the coming of the printing press provided another impetus for the Damdama version to be universally accepted by the Sikh community.[14] This was happening decades after Ranjit Singh's death, but Pashaura Singh does not pause to think why. His concluding statement is even more significant. Apart from a small number of disputed passages 'there has always been complete agreement on the contents of the *bani* in all three versions of the *Adi Granth* even in the seventeenth-century manuscripts'.[15] Pashaura Singh does not realize that with this confessional his radical 'power hypothesis' goes down the drain. In any case, he never tries to relate texual variations to his hypothesis which remains hanging in the mid-air.

THE CASE OF THE *DASAM GRANTH*

The history of the *Dasam Granth* is still not so well known as the history of the *Adi Granth* in recent scholarship. The authorship of the *Dasam Granth* has been the subject of controversy for over a century by now. A number of Sikh scholars in the early twentieth century attributed its authorship to Guru Gobind Singh. D.P. Ashta in *The Poetry of the Dasam Granth* was following this tradition, interpretating it in his own way. In the late eighteenth and the early nineteenth century, however, Sikh writers like Sarup Das Bhalla and Bhai Santokh Singh attributed some of the works included in the *Dasam Granth* to the court poets of Guru Gobind Singh. J.D. Cunningham reflected this understanding when he wrote his *History of the Sikhs* in 1849. Since the late nineteenth century, a number of Sikh and Western scholars have contested the view that the entire *Dasam Granth* is the work of Guru Gobind Singh. If anything, the subject has become extremely sensitive and the SGPC does not approve of its public discussion. The *Dasam Granth* calls for a scholarly attention.[16]

Writing after D.P. Ashta, C.H. Loehlin points out that the compositions usually considered the Guru's own were the *Jap*, *Akal Ustat*, *Bachittar Natak*, *Chandi Charitar I* and *II*, *Var Bhagauti Ki*, *Gian Prabodh*, *Hazare Shabad*, *Savayye*, and the *Zafarnama*. The others were 'probably the work of the bards'. The Guru's authentic compositions cover only about 168 pages out of the 1428 in the

Dasam Granth. When Guru Gobind Singh proclaimed the *Granth Sahib* as the only Guru of the Sikhs, there was no *Dasam Granth.* It was compiled by Bhai Mani Singh in 1734. But it proved to be influential. Whereas the *Adi Granth* aims at developing the mystical and contemplative side, the *Granth* of the tenth Guru promotes the martial side. 'These two *Granths* helped form the Sikh ideal of man, the soldier-saint.'[17]

Loehlin gives a brief description of the books of the *Dasam Granth.* The *Jap,* written by Guru Gobind Singh, gives a thousand names of God on which to meditate. He is without a body, has no name, and he cannot become incarnate. The *Akal Ustat* is a jumble of subjects. Apart from the negative description of the immortal, there is a pantheistic section which could not be written by the Guru himself. Durga too appears in the *Akal Ustat.* The *Bachittar Natak,* generally regarded as an authentic composition of Guru Gobind Singh, is autobiographical. The picture of an ideal warrior-saint emerges from it with the twofold nature of his mission: to destroy the evil-doers by force, and to extend the true faith of loving devotion by peaceful proclamation.[18]

Three versions of the story of Chandi or Durga are presented in succession. It seems plausible that bards translated the first two in Braj and Guru Gobind Singh himself wrote *Var Sri Bhagauti Ji* in Punjabi. All the three versions represent possibly an allegory of the struggle between good and evil. At the end of *Chandi Charitar* I occur the well-known lines which state the purpose of the warrior-saint's life: never to avoid good deeds, ever to fight the enemy, and to die fighting. At the beginning of the *Var Sri Bhagauti Ji* are the lines which are now recited at the beginning of the Sikh prayer (*ardas*). The *Gian Prabodh* contains much that 'seems contrary to the Guru's authentic teaching'. It is hard to think of Guru Gobind Singh as the translator of the *Chaubis Avtar* either. All its contributors had imbibed the culture and mythology of Hinduism. Guru Gobind Singh says at the end of the *Ram Avtar* that he does not accept the opinions of the *Qur'an* and the Puranas, nor the doctrines of the Smritis, Shastras and Vedas.[19]

The *Hazare Shabad,* written by Guru Gobind Singh, could be part of a much larger collection. The famous stanza addressed to the Beloved Friend is included in the *Hazare Shabad.* The thirty-three *Savayye*, written by Guru Gobind Singh, include the well-known lines on 'a pure member of the Khalsa'; the *savayyas* in praise of the Khalsa show his rapport with them: 'From top to toe, whatever I call my own, all I possess or carry, I dedicate to these people.'[20]

The *Shastar Nam Mala* contains fanciful names for weapons and riddles. One cannot imagine the Guru himself taking the time for so much laborious and often trivial compilation. The *Charitaro Pakhian* covers two-fifths of the *Dasam Granth*. Of these 404 tales, 78 relate to the bravery, devotion or intelligence of women; 269 stories relate to their deceit and lack of scruples; 26 relate to the deceit of men. The rest are moral or folk tales. At the end comes the prayer (*Benati Chaupai*) for the protection of Sikhs and the destruction of their enemies. The *Hikayat*, for the most part, are Persian versions of the *Charitaro Pakhian*.[21]

In the *Zafarnama*, the Guru upbraids Aurangzeb for breaking his oath on the *Qur'an*. This refers to the treachery of his generals in the battle of Anandpur when they promised safe conduct but attacked and plundered the Guru's baggage train. The emperor responded by ordering the Mughal functionaries to make arrangements for the Guru's meeting with the emperor. Guru Gobind Singh was on his way to the South when Aurangzeb died. The *Zafarnama* left to the Khalsa an unshaken faith in their destiny and a legacy of hope in final victory.[22]

W.H. McLeod has taken notice of the *Dasam Granth* as a supplementary scripture. In his view, it embodies a considerable diversity of material, owing a particular debt to the Puranas and to anecdotes from current oral tradition. The contents of the *Dasam Granth* fall into four groups: the autobiographical, like the *Bachittar Natak* and the *Zafarnama*; the works expressing militant piety, like the *Jap*, the *Akal Ustat*, the *Gian Prabodh* and the *Shabad Hazare*; the miscellaneous works, like the *Savayye* and the *Shastar Nam Mala*; legends and anecdotes, like the *Chandi Charitar*, *Chandi di Var*, the *Chaubis Avtar*, and the *Tria Charitar* or *Charitaro Pakhian*. The first three groups, together, cover less than 250 pages, whereas the *Krishan Avtar* alone covers more than 300, and the *Tria Charitar* covers 580 pages. The first two groups are said to be the works of Guru Gobind Singh, and also perhaps the *Chandi di Var*. The remainder was substantially, and probably entirely, the work of others present at the court of Guru Gobind Singh. The various works were collected after his death, perhaps by Bhai Mani Singh. McLeod underlines the importance of the *Dasam Granth* as a historical source of critical importance for the evolution of the Sikh Panth, especially as an expression of the impact of the Shakti cult of the hills upon the Jat culture of the Punjab plains. During the eighteenth century, the *Dasam Granth* was given as much respect as the *Adi Granth*: 'It too was regarded as the visibly present Guru and thus received the same veneration.'[23]

Gurtej Singh has refuted D.P. Ashta's view that the *Dasam Granth* provides 'excellent evidence of influence exercised by Hindu theology, mythology, philosophy, history and literature on the life and activities of Guru Gobind Singh'. Ashta's assumption that all the works contained in the *Dasam Granth* were composed by Guru Gobind Singh is wrong. He insinuates that the Sikh Gurus borrowed the views of Hindu *bhagats* like Ramanand and Kabir, the Upanishads and the *Bhagvadgita*. He was out to prove that Sikhism was closely aligned with Hinduism. But this is contradicted by his own quotations from the genuine works of Guru Gobind Singh. Ashta ignores the fact that Guru Gobind Singh did not use 'Nanak' for himself in his compositions. That his own writings were not to be made a part of *Guru Granth Sahib* is explicitly stated by Kesar Singh Chhibber. Ashta does not take into account the differences within 'Hinduism'. In the seventeenth century there were Vaishnavas, Shaivas and Shaktas, with their own systems of religious beliefs and practices. All these are represented as different systems in the *Dasam Granth*. Brahma's incarnations are also included, and even the Muslim Mir Mahdi is a part of this literature.[24]

According to Gurtej Singh, Jaggi has carefully considered the opposing arguments in the controversy about the authorship of the works included in the *Dasam Granth* and come to some logical conclusions. He rejects the evidence of the letter attributed to Bhai Mani Singh about the collection of the Guru's works because it was a later forgery. The four manuscripts of the *Dasam Granth* examined by Jaggi reveal material differences. They were not compiled in the time of Guru Gobind Singh and the material put together represents diverse and scattered writings, lacking a common theme. The compilers did not attach any sanctity to the compilation. The pages supposed to have been inscribed by Guru Gobind Singh are often materially inaccurate. According to Giani Gian Singh, these pages were forged by Charhat Singh, son of Sukha Singh. Several contributors to the *Dasam Ganth* regarded gods, goddesses and incarnations as objects of worship. Jaggi has convincingly demonstrated that the ideology of the authentic compositions of Guru Gobind Singh is totally different from that of the rest of the volume.[25]

Daljeet Singh points out that the early Sikh writers do not make any reference to the *Dasam Granth.* The first reference to some of the writings of Guru Gobind Singh is in the *Bansavalinama* of Kesar Singh Chhibber who talks of two *Granths* prepared by Guru Gobind Singh: *Samunder Sagar* and *Avtar Lila.* The first was thrown into the Sutlej by the Guru himself and the second was lost after the evacuation of Anandpur. This part of Chhibber's story does not add anything to our knowledge about the 'Dasam Granth writings'. Chhibber also states that Bhai Mani Singh compiled a *granth* in 1725, combining the *Adi Granth* with the writings that subsequently came to be known as the *Dasam Granth.* But, according to Chhibber himself, Guru Gobind Singh had rejected the request of the Sikhs to combine the *Adi Granth* with his own writings. Sarup Das Bhalla mentions 'Vidya Sagar' as the *granth* prepared by Guru Gobind Singh, containing translations of Sanskrit works. Thus, Daljeet Singh maintains that Chhibber's story that Bhai Mani Singh compiled the *Dasam Granth* is not reliable.[26]

Daljeet Singh goes on to add that Bhai Santokh Singh, who mentions of the *Dasam Granth*, repeats the story of Bhai Mani Singh. However, the letter of Bhai Mani Singh about the collection of *Charitaro Pakhian* has been found to be fake. None of the four manuscripts of the *Dasam Granth* examined by Jaggi appears to have been compiled in the eighteenth century. There is no uniformity between any two manuscripts. The numerous errors in the manuscripts suggest a non-Sikh origin. Except for about 70 pages which cover the *Jap*, the *Akal Ustat* (excluding the hymns in praise of Durga), the *Savayye*, the 'Asphotak Chhands' and the *Zafarnama*, the contents of the *Dasam Granth* involve worship of *avtars, devis* and Mahakal, all rooted in Puranic literature. These writings are opposed to the doctrines of *Guru Granth Sahib.*[27]

Originally, most parts of the *granth* were called 'Bachittar Natak Granth'. The various writings were deliberately mixed up with the works of Guru Gobind Singh. The name *Dasam Granth* was given much later. Daljeet Singh suggests that the authenticity of the works included in the *Dasam Granth* can be judged from their consonance with or opposition to the *Guru Granth Sahib* as the sole Guru and guide of the Sikhs. Many outside scholars accept the *Dasam Granth* as the work of Guru Gobind Singh and argue that he brought the Panth into the Hindu fold, and drew inspiration from the Puranic past and the Shakti cult to confront the Mughals. They ignore the fact that those who actually believed in the Puranic incarnations and Shakti were not inspired to confront the Mughals.[28]

Jagjit Singh too goes into the history of the origin of the earliest known manuscripts on the basis of the same sources as Daljeet Singh and comes to the conclusion that there is no historical basis for linking the *Dasam Granth* in its present form, either with Guru Gobind Singh, or with the literature thrown into the river or lost, or with any known or tangible material existing for over a century before its appearance.[29]

That the *Dasam Granth* was not compiled by Guru Gobind Singh in its present form is clear enough, and also that the writings of Guru Gobind Singh were not meant to be a part of the Sikh canon known as the *Adi Granth.* The assertion of some scholars that the *Dasam Granth* came to be bracketed with the *Adi Granth* in all respects, including the status of Guruship, appears to be totally unjustified. In the entire range of Sikh literature before the advent of colonial rule in the Punjab, the *Adi Granth* alone is referred to as 'Guru'. Kesar Singh Chhibber advocates respect and veneration for 'The Book of the Tenth Master' (*Dasven Patshah ka Granth*) as 'a younger brother' of the *Adi Granth*, with the implication that the Sikhs in general were not treating it as 'Guru'. John Malcolm, whose authority on this point is quoted, nowhere refers to *Dasama Padshah ka Granth* as 'Guru'.[30]

Like some other scholars, McLeod talks of the great influence of the *Dasam Granth* on the religious life of the Sikhs, especially of the goddess, but several Sikh scholars have questioned this. Actually, this aspect of the Sikh tradition has not yet been seriously studied. Even when the goddess is introduced by Chhibber

Brahmans in connection with the creation of the Khalsa, she is not the Supreme Deity and her role is clearly subordinate and extremely limited. The Sikh writers who introduce the goddess do so rather mechanically. She does not become an integral part of the whole work in which the exclusive supremacy of Akal Purkh and the doctrines of Guru Panth and Guru Granth are highlighted or taken for granted. What may appear to be simple is actually a complex matter and calls for a much more sophisticated conceptualization.

The evidence presented by Gurinder Singh Mann throws some light on the history of the *Dasam Granth*. Neither the title nor all its contents can be traced to any compilation of the time of Guru Gobind Singh. However, there was three separate compilations: *Charitaro Pakhian Granth* (1696), *Bachittar Natak Granth* (1698), *Sri Sarab Loh Granth* (1698). None of these works could be attributed to Guru Gobind Singh. These compilations began to be combined at a later stage. In two early manuscripts in which the *Bachittar Natak Granth* and the *Charitaro Pakhian Granth* are combined, the tables of contents are recorded along with their respective texts. In some later manuscripts, however, the master table of contents is placed at the head of the combined text named *Dasvin Patshahi ka Granth*. This title turned into *Dasam Granth* in the late nineteenth and the twentieth century. In the gurdwaras of Nihangs, the title given now is *Dasam Sri Guru Granth Sahib Ji*.[31] Mann's account misses one crucial stage in the history of the *Dasam Granth*: incorporation of the genuine works of Guru Gobind Singh in the compilation.

A new dimension of the *Dasam Granth* has come to the fore in recent scholarship. Some of the works in the *Dasam Granth* have been studied from the viewpoint of gender relations. Nikki-Guninder Kaur Singh talks of Durga becoming Guru Gobind Singh's favourite literary subject out of the myriads of gods and goddesses of the Hindu pantheon. Aware of the controversial character of the texts included in the *Dasam Granth*, Nikki Singh states that Durga is 'recalled' by the Guru as a figure of myth and not 'invoked' as a goddess. Nowhere does Guru Gobind Singh profess himself to be a devotee of the goddess.[32]

Nikki Singh argues that the controversial Durga compositions are Guru Gobind Singh's very own. The *Chandi Charitar* is mentioned in the *Bachittar Natak*. Bhai Desa Singh in his *Rahitnama* attributes it to Guru Gobind Singh. The first verse of the *Chandi di Var* forms the beginning of the prayers recited by the Sikhs to this day. The most telling argument of all, however, lies in the very content of the poems themselves. There is an utter absence of worship of the goddess in Guru Gobind Singh's versions, a worship that is central to the *Markandeya Purana* and to her overall image in Hinduism. In the *Chandi di Var*, Guru Gobind Singh states clearly that Brahma, Vishnu and Shiva are the creation of God. He goes on to say that it is from God that Ram received his prowess in piercing with his arrows the ten-headed Ravana; it is from the One that Krishna received the power to catch Kansa by the hair and tear him apart. 'You are the One', says the Guru, 'who created Durga and caused the demons to be destroyed'. The original account is considerably condensed. The martial exploits of Durga are celebrated but she is not deified as against the original Sanskrit text. Her invocation by the gods in the Puranic account is absent from Guru Gobind Singh's versions.[33]

According to Nikki Singh, the choice of Durga by Guru Gobind Singh means unequivocal acknowledgement of woman's power in society. The Guru singled her out as a model of moral force and martial prowess for both men and women. By reading, hearing and reciting the myth of Durga, the inert society could be invigorated, and ethical principles could be upheld. Durga is the one goddess in the Puranas without husband, consort, or lover. She is independent and powerful. She is the central figure in the story of the battle against the demons. The affirmation of female power by Guru Gobind Singh illustrates the overall positive attitude towards women in Sikh speculation. Durga's qualities could inspire men and women to positive action; they could overcome their weakness and cowardice, overthrow the unjust political authorities, abolish social inequalities, and ultimately forge a new structure based on more just and egalitarian values.[34]

The mythical Durga is exalted and, through her, all women. The treatment of Durga is totally exempt from any kind of detraction. The Puranic goddess and her heroic exploits are handsomely magnified. She appears in all her legendary glory. In this recalling she loses nothing of her dynamism and fire. The heroic or the martial mood dominates, though the romantic is gently woven into it. The similes are never conventional or hackneyed. New words are frequently coined. The metre chosen is Sirkhandi Chhand, with rhyme in the middle of the verse, which produces a stair like momentum. Guru Gobind Singh adopted such a dynamic art form with the object of inspiring bravery, dispelling cowardice, and infusing the hearts of his people with confidence and courage, for the creation of an inspired and invigorated community of Sikh men and women.[35]

Through Guru Gobind Singh recalling Durga by the term *bhagauti*, the sword achieves a feminine indentity: the metaphor of the sword leads us towards a recognition of the female principle. Whether goddess or sword, *bhagauti* is the annihilation of negative forces, and a symbol for crusade against evil. The glorification of the sword was meant to secure the fulfilment of divine justice. Thus, *bhagauti*, whether as Durga riding her lion or as the sword carried by a Sikh citizen, is an assertion of the right to freedom. The supplication at the end of *Chandi Charitar* is to stand for the right cause and to die for it fighting till the end.[36]

With reference to Nikky Singh's hypothesis, Doris R. Jakobsh comments that it is difficult to draw a line between literary license and veneration. Moreover, to draw 'an unrealistically rigid line between the recognition of Durga's literary merit and actual homage to the goddess is to miss an opportunity to explore how and why a system did away with the feminine which was so obviously and critically integrated into early Sikh society'. In her attempt to suggest the emancipatory implications of the Durga myth for women, Nikky Singh has not fully explored the implications of the Durga mythology for the Sikh tradition at large.[37] From this critique, one would expect some observations from Jakobsh on the literary works related to Durga from the viewpoint of gender, but she chooses to ignore this literature altogether.

Jakobsh points out that in the injunctions about *rahit* there was a harsh prohibition of the killing of female babies. This carried the implication that the practice had gone on largely unchecked since the time of Guru Amar Das who had proscribed female infanticide. A cultural and social gender hierarchy had already been established and a stage was now definitely set for a 'theology of difference', both ritual and symbolic. She suggests that a novel construct of gender difference in the development of Sikhism completed the transformation from masculine to hyper masculine ethos.[38]

Jakobsh supports this hypothesis with evidence from the *Charitaro Pakhian.* The occasion for the collection of these 404 tales in the first place was provided by a wily woman. The collection contains stories in which women play no part, and there are tales of heroic and honourable women too. Woman is portrayed both as victim and inherently powerful over man. But most of the tales relate to love, sexual intrigue and violence, and women are often the seducers. It is explicitly stated in a verse that there is no end to their intrigues. Even God repented after having created them. Jakobsh is inclined to think that the tendency to attribute the *Charitaro Pakhian* to someone other than Guru Gobind Singh developed in the early twentieth century. She endorses the view that in the eighteenth and nineteenth centuries the *Dasam Granth* was held at par with the *Adi Granth.*[39] In other words, the *Charitaro Pakhian* was taken seriously by Sikh men.

Jakobsh suggests that the wiles-of-women narratives are essential for configuring the construction of gender during the time of Guru Gobind Singh, particulary in the light of the specific male construct initiated by him through the Khalsa order. Women in the *Charitaro Pakhian* symbolize the ultimate antithesis of the warrior-saint norm the Guru was attempting to construct. They had the power to turn the warrior-saint away from his true calling. Thus, whether or not Guru Gobind Singh was its author, the *Charitaro Pakhian* was of considerable importance in understanding gender construction in the immediate post-Guru period.[40]

Jakobsh thinks that her interpretation of the *Charitaro Pakhian* gets support from *The Chaupa Singh Rahit-Nama* which she believes as the earliest of all the extant *rahitnamas.* Its evidence shows that women were not included in the 'regular' discipline outlined for the Khalsa. Anyone who administers baptism of the double-edged sword to a woman becomes liable to penance. She should never read the *Granth Sahib* in a general assembly of the Sikhs. Notions of impurity which the earlier Gurus had strictly censured came to be associated with women now. The men who take orders from their women are dubbed as sinful, licentious and stupid.

A Gursikhni should regard her husband as her lord. A Gursikh was expected never to trust a woman. A kind of polarization of sexes was thus brought about by the institution of the Khalsa. The widening of gulf between male and female Sikhs is reflected in the injunction that a true Sikh should not wear red, a colour associated with women's clothing. The aim was to construct divisions along lines of gender. Jakobsh comes to the conclusion that polarization of gender accompanied the emergence of the militarized Khalsa and attention came to be given increasingly to 'true' manliness of the warrior-saint. Women became the opposite of that identity. One gender was predominantly fostered to the detriment of the other.[41]

There is hardly any doubt that Durga figures in the *Dasam Granth*, like Ram and Krishan, as God's creation and not as the Supreme Deity. Her role is similar to that of Ram and Krishan: to fight with great courage and prowess in support of good against evil. Her parity with the male figures in this context is beyond any doubt. Nikky Singh lays emphasis on the emancipatory implications of the myth for both men and women. The question of its implications for gender relations remains rather open. Nor has Jakobsh taken it up, though she is critical of Nikky Singh's exposition.

Jakobsh is much impressed by the 'theology of difference' as a hypothesis. She tends to oversimplify the issue of gender in the Order of the Khalsa. If *The Chaupa Singh Rahit-Nama* recommends penance for a Sikh who administers baptism of the double-edged sword to a woman, the *Prem Sumarag* recommends the administration of baptism of the double-edged sword to a woman. The statement about men who take orders from their women being dubbed as sinful, licentious and stupid (by Guru Ram Das, quoted in the *Rahitnama*) is actually a mistaken interpretation. The reference is to those men who, out of moral weakness, listen to women rather than heed the advice of the Guru. It is not a general statement. The comparative position of Sikh women in relation to Sikh men before and after the institution of the Khalsa is an unexplored area. But even in the *Rahitnama* literature as a whole there is enough evidence to suggest that the 'theology of difference' does not find the kind of support invoked by Jakobsh.

Gurinder Singh Mann takes notice of Nikky-Guninder Kaur Singh presenting the goddess compositions in the *Bachittar Natak*

Granth as a marker of Guru Gobind Singh's 'acknowledgement of the female power in society'. He also takes notice of Doris R. Jakobsh asserting that the *Charitaro Pakhian* condemns what is understood to be implicit in womanhood, and that the wiles-of-women literature must be viewed as essential in configuring the construction of gender during the time of the tenth Guru, particularly in the light of the specific male construct initiated by scholars. Mann, however, does not attribute the texts in question to Guru Gobind Singh. He points out that both the scholars are highly selective in what they cull from the *Dasam Granth*. Their arguments would have faced difficulties if other parts of these texts had been brought into their discussions. Unless properly contextualized, this literature 'cannot help in making sense of either Sikh beliefs and practices or the overall history of the community at that point in time'.[42]

NOTES

1. Gurinder Singh Mann, *The Making of Sikh Scripture*, New Delhi: Oxford University Press, 2001, pp. 69-74.
2. Ibid., pp. 74-9.
3. Ibid., pp. 79-82.
4. Ibid., pp. 82-5.
5. Pashaura Singh, *The Guru Granth Sahib: Canon, Meaning and Authority*, New Delhi: Oxford University Press, 2000, pp. 203-6.
6. Ibid., pp. 206-12.
7. Ibid., pp. 212-20.
8. Ibid., pp. 222-4.
9. Mann, *The Making of Sikh Scripture*, p. 122.
10. Ibid., pp. 122-5.
11. Ibid., pp. 125-8.
12. Pashaura Singh, *The Guru Granth Sahib*, pp. 224-7.
13. Ibid., pp. 227-30.
14. Ibid., p. 230.
15. Ibid., p. 235.
16. For a brief statement on this controversy, see Rattan Singh Jaggi's foreword (*do shabad*) to Shamsher Singh Ashok, *Sri Dasam Granth Te Hor Rachnavan: Ik Adhyain* (Pbi), Amritsar: Bhai Fakir Singh and Sons, 1966, pp. 1-6. See also Rattan Singh Jaggi, 'Dasam Granth', *Guru Granth Vishavkosh*, Patiala: Punjabi University, 2002, vol. II, pp. 100-2.

17. C.H. Loehlin, *The Granth of Guru Gobind Singh and The Khalsa Brotherhood,* Lucknow: Lucknow Publishing House, 1971, pp. 7, 9-10, 18, 57.
18. Ibid., pp. 20-32.
19. Ibid., pp. 33-44.
20. Ibid., pp. 44-7.
21. Ibid., pp. 47-53.
22. Ibid., pp. 54-6.
23. W.H. McLeod, *The Evolution of the Sikh Community,* New Delhi: Oxford University Press, 1975, pp. 79-81.
24. Gurtej Singh, 'Two Views on Dasam Granth', in *Fundamental Issues in Sikh Studies,* ed. Kharak Singh, Gobind Singh Mansukhani and Jasbir Singh Mann, Chandigarh: Institute of Sikh Studies, 1992, pp. 179-83.
25. Ibid., pp. 183-4. For a more recent and more trenchant statement by Gurtej Singh, see 'The Mystique of the Dasam Granth', *Sikh Studies Quarterly,* Chandigarh: Institute of Sikh Studies, January-March 2001, pp. 64-70.
26. Daljeet Singh, 'Dasam Granth : Its History', *Abstracts of Sikh Studies,* Chandigarh: Institute of Sikh Studies (July 1994), pp. 81-4.
27. Ibid., pp. 84-92.
28. Ibid., pp. 92-3.
29. Jagjit Singh 'The Historical Identity of Dasam Granth', *Abstracts of Sikh Studies* (July 1994), pp. 95-9.
30. Malcolm states that *Dasama Padshah ka Granth* was 'composed by Guru Gobind Singh' and completed in 1694. It was 'at least as much revered' among the Sikhs as the *Adi Granth.* These were 'the two most sacred books of the Sikhs'. Both these *Granths* were placed before the chiefs and principal leaders of the Sikhs when general resolutions (*gurmatas*) were passed by them. For initiation, the first chapters of both the *Granths* were read. However, Malcolm had only heard all this from his contemporaries. Significantly, during the proceedings of a *gurmata,* as stated by an upper caste Sikh priest, it was stated: 'The sacred Granth is betwixt us, let us swear by our Scripture to forget all internal disputes, and to be united'. In this statement the Sikh scripture in the singular is most likely to be the *Adi Granth.* Lt. Col. Malcolm, *Sketch of the Sikhs,* New Delhi: Asian Educational Service, 1986 (rpt.), pp. 2n., 31n., 120-2 & n., 182, 186n.
31. Gurinder Singh Mann, 'Sources for the Study of Guru Gobind Singh's Life and Times', *Journal of Punjab Studies,* 15: 1-2 (Spring-Fall 2008), pp. 248-9, 275 n. 131.

32. Nikki-Guninder Kaur Singh, *The Feminine Principle in the Sikh Vision of the Transcendent*, Cambridge: Cambridge University Press, 1993, pp. 121-2.
33. Ibid., pp. 123-6.
34. Ibid., pp. 126-31.
35. Ibid., pp. 132-4.
36. Ibid., pp. 142-8.
37. Doris R. Jakobsh, *Relocating Gender in Sikh History: Transformation, Meaning and Identity*, New Delhi: Oxford University Press, 2003, pp. 15-16.
38. Ibid., pp. 37-44.
39. Ibid., pp. 44-5.
40. Ibid., p. 45.
41. Ibid., pp. 46-8.
42. Gurinder Singh Mann, 'Sources for the Study of Guru Gobind Singh's Life and Times', pp. 250, 276 n. 136.

PART FIVE

METHODOLOGY FOR RELIGIOUS STUDIES

CHAPTER 12

The Historical Method and Sikh Studies

In the course of this controversy, questions have been raised about the application of methods evolved in the study of Christianity to the study of Sikhism, and the validity of the historical method in relation to religious studies. We propose to discuss the issues raised with regard to methodology.

A CRITIQUE OF THE CRITICAL APPROACH

Noel Q. King outlines significant developments in the study of Judaism and Christianity, both from within and outside the Church, and comes to the conclusion that critical study and Christianity 'have come to a *modus vivendi*'. Critical scholarship has been 'a native growth in Judaism and Christianity'. The critical methods developed in the study of religion in the West cannot be turned to the study of another religion without the risk of doing violence to the study. Furthermore, a scholar's own status in terms of belief or non-belief affects his attitude towards other people's religion. One who is critical of Christianity, or cherishes anti-religious ideas and feelings, would be critical of other religions too.[1] King has been frequently quoted on the point of personal bias:

> In a Natural Science like Chemistry it may not be necessary to know anything about the human being who is writing. In any subject which entails human subject, the work must be put into a personal context. Accordingly, one feels every work of critical scholarship should have a government statutory warning that its consumption may be deleterious to the soul's health. If it is to do with religion it should also have a statement of ingredients, including the religious standing of the writer. If he or she is a believer it is necessary to know this, so that the critical reader can allow

for bias. If he or she is not a believer, we should have some indication of that too, lest the disillusionment or enligh-tenment of a post-Christian, a post-Jew or a post-whatever should give the critic rosy-coloured spectacles or a jaundiced outlook.[2]

Furthermore, a scholar's motives do not necessarily come from 'rational intellectuality'. To go into 'personal context' need not be regarded as hitting below the belt.[3]

King observes that 'not many Western critically trained scholars' have turned their attention to Sikhism. Among the fully equipped foreign scholars of Sikhism, King mentions Ernest Trumpp whose 'general bitterness and disappointment is expressed in his vicious remarks about Sikhism in his Preface'. He also apparently suffered from 'some racist views', despised his local informants, and offended them by smoking a cigar while reading the Sikh scripture. Macauliffe did much to 'set right the balance' by the felicity of his work and by showing respect for Sikhism. King's third scholar is Loehlin who had deep respect for the Sikh people and revealed to the world the importance of Sikh religion. He never discussed anything which might be derogatory to the Sikhs in any way.[4]

King has great appreciation for McLeod who is 'easily in the lead among foreign scholars, past or present'. His linguistic competence was unlikely to be surpassed. His work was based on a careful use of 'text-critical, form-critical and other-critical methods' developed in the West during the last two centuries. The issues raised by McLeod could be answered by qualified local scholars. King's concern was to relate them to 'a wider world and human context'.[5]

An educated person in the English-speaking world wanting to learn about Sikhism turns to McLeod's books which have been published by the Oxford University Press, commanding a world market and world publicity. To an uninitiated reader his books convey the impression that 'a great amount of Sikh belief' is based on 'uncritical religiosity'. McLeod's books disappoint the reader by not tapping 'the well-springs' of Sikhism: what made Guru Nanak 'tick' is 'the heart of Sikhism'. Instead, what we find in McLeod's books is 'meticulously and exhaustively carried out drills in certain methods of Western criticism'. For example, his search for the historical Nanak seen in the background of the quest for the historical Jesus enunciates a basic tenet of critical scholarship.

McLeod's readers want to know something different and they get 'the wrong answers'. His purpose and their expectations differ widely. It is a known principle of historical or critical methodology that if you get a non-sense reply from your source then you must re-think your question. For King, a *Janamsakhi* is neither biography nor hagiology, but a genre *sui generis*, a unique literary form. King believes that on the point of what was said and done by Guru Gobind Singh there was 'a living unbroken reliable tradition of the sayings and doings of 1699 quite apart from writing, still alive in the Punjab'.[6]

McLeod appeared not to have tried to collect oral evidence on Panja Sahib which was available with Sikhs, and he did not visit Panja Sahib to see things for himself. His evidence on Guru Nanak's visit to this place comes from European writers of the nineteenth century. Consequently, McLeod treats it as 'etiological legend', that is, a story which tries to account for a thing in existence. It is treated as a tradition by 'invention'. This example is meant to suggest that there could be other cases of wrong inferences drawn by McLeod.[7]

King goes on to add that McLeod's attitude is by no means confined to Sikhs; it embraces 'religion and religious phenomena as a whole'. He has absolute faith in 'the intellectual critical method' as he understands it. Reason is not necessarily opposed to religion. In fact, they 'go hand in hand'. In the final analysis, however, it has to be realized that 'the intellect and its methods', as they are known at present, are not perfect or absolute; they are not infallible; and they do not comprehend the whole to see things in 'focus'. King wishes to underline 'the need to be humble, considerate and courteous'. He advocates that due place be given to 'the *deshi* homegrown production of critical scholarship'. There was not enough of indigenous critical scholarship at present. Like other great religions, Sikhism needs critical scholarship to meet the intellectual need of its educated followers. Sikh scholars in the Punjab, who wished to remain 'in the good books of the Establishment', studiously avoided 'sticking their necks out'. McLeod stands out precisely because there are no critical scholars among the Sikhs.[8]

In King's well considered view expressed elsewhere, the fire of critical method can burn away whatever is gross in a religious tradition, and enable the believers to retrieve the pure metal.[9] King appears to suggest that the critical method can bring out the intrinsic merit of a religious tradition. He holds the view that if sympathetically understood and fairly presented, the Sikh scripture and the Sikh tradition had nothing to fear from 'any true criticism properly used'. Sikhism is a world religion, different from all others. Its study should be of interest to all those scholars who are interested in the study of religion. Though Sikhs have nothing to fear, they should not 'sit around and be overtaken by the outside world and by misunderstanding'. They have to keep their own people and their well-wishers well informed. The ignorant are not necessarily 'enemies' and the Sikhs must tell others 'the truth about their religion'.[10]

The general observations made by King do not undermine the critical scholarship. He observes that 'critical' methodology was developed in the West for the study of Judaism and Christianity. It was assumed that it possessed universal validity, and it was applied by many scholars to the study of religions other than Judaism and Christianity. Both the assumption and the application can be questioned. King suggests further that the critical method should not be allowed to hold undisputed sway in the study of religion. The critical scholar is not free from biases arising out of his or her personal context, nor is the believer. On the whole, thus, critical scholarship is not dispensable even in the study of religion.

King observes that McLeod's intentions differ widely from the expectations of his readers. They want to know something positive to account for the charisma of Guru Nanak and the achievement of his followers. But what they get is discussion of issues raised in Western scholarship. This issue appears to be more relevant for approach than methodology. It is interesting to note in this connection that McLeod's *Early Sikh Tradition* and his *Sikhs of the Khalsa* have been virtually ignored by Sikh scholars.

King observes that McLeod's attitude towards religion in general is completely rational in the sense that he treats it as a historical phenomenon. However, King does not refer to any implication of this attitude for McLeod's study of Sikhism. McLeod is mistaken in regarding *Janamsakhis* as hagiology. But so are they who regard them as biographies. *Janamsakhis* constitute a unique literary form. We may agree with King. But his reference to

European evidence on Panja Sahib as a 'Sirdarji joke' does not clarify the issue. About the sayings and doings of Guru Gobind Singh, King mentions unbroken oral evidence but he does not tell us where it is. On the whole, thus, King's criticism of McLeod relates to his methodology and rational attitude in general. He has a lot of praise for McLeod's work. What is more, he subscribes to the view that critical scholarship is much needed in Sikh studies.

James R. Lewis talks of 'misrepresentation' of the Sikh tradition in the textbooks on world religions written in the West. He refers to the colonial framework in which Europeans held a position of dominance. They carried on a kind of monologue among themselves on the basis of their presuppositions in a conscious or unconscious effort to justify their attributes and to legitimize their dominance. Lewis points out many errors of fact in the work of those who have used the works produced by the colonial writers. Because of their superficial acquaintance with the subject and their sloppy scholarship they compound errors of fact with errors of judgement. This is true even of some recent publications. This is true also of publications which contain extended treatment of the Sikh tradition. Nevertheless, there are some exceptions, made possible either by an author's reliance on good secondary work or by his own familiarity with original sources. Among the exceptions mentioned by Lewis is W.H. McLeod.[11]

Lewis states that every emergent religion relies on prior religious traditions as points of reference for a new vision of spiritual reality. This is true of Sikhism too. However, many a European writer has looked upon Sikhism as a syncretism, a mixture of Islamic and Hindu features. The Hindu and Muslim influences are assumed to be so dominant that there appears to be little new in Sikhism as a religion. Lewis thinks that the notion of syncretism originated with Christian missionaries, or some other group of colonial officials. Their idea carried the implication that Sikhism was something 'spurious'. This view was meant to demonstrate the superiority of Christianity. Lewis rightly points out that McLeod has deliberately and consciously discarded the concept of syncretism and he has emphasized the 'originality' of Guru Nanak. It may be added that by emphasizing originality Lewis is evading the issue raised by McLeod's critics about his placing Guru Nanak within the Sant Tradition.

Another problem of the Western writers on Sikhism relates to the contrast which they see in Guru Nanak's 'pacifism' and Guru Gobind Singh's 'militancy'. Lewis points out that Christianity has its own history of militancy. But the Christian writers who criticize Sikhism remain silent about Christianity. Their view of the Sikh tradition is a projection 'of their own (un-expressed or repressed) condemnation of the Christian tradition'.[12] It is interesting to note that Lewis makes no comment on McLeod's view of 'militarization' of the Sikh Movement.

AN ARGUMENT AGAINST THE HISTORICAL METHOD

Daljeet Singh welcomes the growing interest in India and abroad in the study of Sikh religion, its institutions and its history. However, partly because of the differences in the cultural background of the scholars drawn to Sikh studies and partly because of the methodology they follow, there are a few problems which have to be faced and solved. With regard to the problem of methodology, Daljeet Singh asserts that 'ontology' or 'the spiritual base of a religion' is all important. It is basic to almost every religion that there is a Spiritual Reality which is different from and more real or true than the sensually perceived empirical reality. Its description and definition becomes the basis of the study of a religion. The structure of a religion is determined by answers to the question whether or not that Reality is creative and attributive, and they serve as clues to its character and therefore to its study. No student of *Guru Granth Sahib* can fail to see that 'God is not only creative and Attributive but he is immanent, reveals himself to man, and operates in history with His Will'. Similarly in other religions there are certain conceptions of Reality, or God, which are essential to their proper understanding.[13]

This in Daljeet Singh's view, raises a basic problem. Since the advent of modern science, materialistic philosophies have gained great importance, and materialistic interpretations are accepted by and large as valid in the fields of sociology, economics, political science, psychology and history. All these studies relate to the phenomena of the empirical world, and they take little or no account of the transcendent world. The world-views of these disciplines are said to be partial and lop-sided. Their methods and assumptions can be regarded as valid within their own domains. But the problem arises when they are regarded as valid for the study of religion as well. Religion relates primarily to the transcendent world which is of little concern to the social sciences. Consequently, the methods of social sciences are of little use for the study of religion. Therefore, religion has developed its own methodology and principles of study leading to a world-view which is holistic and comprehensive instead of being limited and narrow. The *raison d'être* of the study of religion is 'the spiritual element'. Deny it, and there is no need of religious studies. Ontology is too central to be ignored.[14]

According to Daljeet Singh, the highest level in human progress is God-consciousness resulting in truthful living. Thus, 'real knowledge' comes from the area of the transcendent. It is noetic, or super sensual. It was not his social milieu but his noetic knowledge of Spiritual Reality that gave Guru Nanak his world-view and his ideology. But in social sciences, the mystic world and its experience are 'just unexplored areas of darkness'. Furthermore, there is no trace of the ethical in the reflective thought of man. That is why for social sciences morality is 'just a defence mechanism' or reaction formation 'in response to environmental impacts'. Religion is treated as a 'behavioural phenomenon'. From the viewpoint of the man of religion the study of religion by an anthropologist is limited, partial and inadequate because of his methodology. Daljeet Singh quotes Noel King with approval on the personal biases of scholars.[15]

There is one peculiar problem related to Sikh studies. In Indian religions there is dichotomy between the spiritual life and the empirical life of man. Guru Nanak was the first man to break this dichotomy, leading logically to the doctrine of Miri and Piri. This doctrine looks odd to 'the votaries of pacifist religions'. The militancy of Guru Gobind Singh is not appreciated by Mahatma Gandhi and Rabindranath Tagore, just as the socio-political activities of Prophet Muhammad are not appreciated by Arnold Toynbee. McLeod fails to appreciate the great stature of Guru Nanak because he fails to see the *miri* aspect of his concerns.[16] Daljeet Singh may be right in identifying McLeod's lack of appreciation on this score but his explanation is not convincing because a 'Christian' like J.D. Cunningham did appreciate this aspect of Guru Nanak's ideology.

Another related problem arises from the increasing secularization of life, so much so that the modern state has also been secularized. In the Indian context, this development has a peculiar bearing on Sikhism with its doctrine of Miri and Piri, or the integral combination of the spiritual and the empirical life of man. To some this appears to be the cause of the recent crisis in the Punjab. Some people look at distinct Sikh identity as 'downright unpatriotic'. There are others who believe that Sikhism in its social reform has been taken over by the state. According to Daljeet Singh, the men of religion feel that 'in view of the growing secularization of modern life', and its tendency 'to encroach on the religious field', it is necessary to study religion with the tools of its own discipline. It is also necessary that the funding and functioning of religious studies 'should be kept free from the influences of modern state and its secular life'.[17] Daljeet Singh has argued at some length that the principles and methods followed in religious studies are different but he does not tell us what those principles and methods are. He does not refer to any other writer in this connection. If these methods and principles are something different from what he has said about the general approach to religion, it is difficult to know what they are. It is possible for a historian to study the conception of God in a religious system and to see its implications for praxis. Ideas and experiences expressed in words and actions remain amenable to historical analysis.

Daljeet Singh himself underlines that the study of religion does not leave the empirical world out. On the contrary, the relationship of religious ideologies with the empirical world is so important that he can look upon history as an expression of ideology. He finds it amply demonstrated in Sikhism. Even in general terms he insists that historical developments should not be studied in isolation from ideas. It becomes difficult to understand the real nature of Daljeet Singh's objection to the historical approach. If his idea is to underline that a historian must give due importance to ideology, it would be acceptable to many historians. The historian subscribes in a way to the idea that God enters history in the sense that faith in God can be a motivating force for action. But whereas Daljeet Singh would look upon the ideas and attitudes springing from religious faith as all important, the historian would look for other factors too in his explanation. We noticed earlier that McLeod objects to Jagjit Singh's explanation precisely because he attaches too much importance to ideology. McLeod, in turn, can be seen as attaching too much importance to environment. But to suggest that only Sikhs can appreciate Sikh ideology is to imply that non-Sikhs cannot understand Guru Nanak's conception of God, which is not really convincing. Nearly all the critics of McLeod admire Cunningham who was a believing Christian and who attached great importance to ideology in Sikh history.

PLEA FOR AN ALTERNATIVE METHOD

Gobind Singh Mansukhani has written briefly on the 'origin and development' of Sikh studies. But he talks neither of origin nor of development. He says nothing about the first century of modern Sikh studies. For him, Trumpp's *Adi Granth* 'dates the origin of Sikh studies'. For the past century he merely catalogues the works produced and that too rather randomly. There is nothing new in the elementary information he provides and there is no coherence in his presentation. Mansukhani is totally unaware that a number of scholars have already written about historical writing on the Sikhs, and on the development of Sikh studies. He has little to say about the personal or social biases of authors, their presuppositions, purposes, motives or methodology. With this kind of simple approach he could hardly be expected to make any meaningful contribution to 'research methodology'.[18]

Elsewhere, Mansukhani says that Sikhism has now been accepted as one of the major religions of the world, and constitutes a new area for religious studies. Western scholars in the area of Sikh studies have been using techniques and criteria of disciplines like history, sociology, anthropology, philosophy and linguistics. Their methodology, though valid in their own disciplines, is not useful for in-depth study of Sikhism as a 'revelatory' and 'sovereign' religion. Mansukhani pleads for 'a balanced, homogeneous and impartial examination of the sources' to pursue 'integrated methodology'.[19]

Mansukhani looks upon the *Guru Granth Sahib*, the accepted *gurbani* in the *Dasam Granth*, and the approved compositions of Bhai Gurdas and Bhai Nand Lal as 'primary' sources for Sikh studies. The word 'primary' carries a different connotation here than what is understood by the professional historian. The *Janamsakhis*, *Gurbilas* literature, *Hukamnamas*, *Rahitnamas* and other books from the eighteenth century to the present day are said to be 'secondary' sources. The works specifically placed in this category are *Gurbilas Patshahi Chhevin*, which in his view was written by Sohan Kavi in 1718, Ratan Singh Bhangu's *Prachin Panth Prakash*, Giani Gian Singh's *Tawarikh Guru Khalsa* and Kavi Santokh Singh's *Gurpartap Suraj*. Muslim writers have generally supplied biased or wrong information in their chronicles, which misled European writers except J.D. Cunningham. To these is added later in the essay another source: *Bhatt Vahis*, which can supply 'missing links' in our present knowledge of Sikh history. Both the primary and secondary sources can be used in the 'new methodology' proposed by Mansukhani, but the primacy of the primary sources must be recognized. Only that part of the secondary sources can be accepted which does not go against the primary evidence.[20] However, this principle may be applicable to the doctrinal and ethical norms but it cannot be a principle of the historical method in which even a forged document presents a form of historical evidence, depending upon what the historian wants to know.

Mansukhani points out that the Western scholars of Sikhism suffer from three main handicaps. One of these is their notion that Sikhism is a part of Hinduism. Second, they are preconditioned by their acquaintance with Semitic religions; they call Sikhism 'a tradition' as if it is something less than a religion; they use the word syncretism for Sikhism to imply that it is not a 'revealed' religion and give 'differential treatment' to Sikhism by using different sets of criteria for Sikhism and their own faith. Their third handicap is their analytical methodology. Mansukhani believes that rational standards and scientific techniques applied to revelation are useless, in fact counter-productive. 'Intellectual knowledge' is not enough in dealing with matters religious.[21] The points made by Mansukhani are not new. He may be right in pointing to Eurocentrism in the works of many Western writers, but he himself equates Sikh history simply with Sikh religion and its ethics.

Mansukhani goes on to mention the 'drawbacks' of analytical methodology. It is not suited to comprehend spiritual phenomenon. The laws of logical proof cannot be applied to the experiential aspects of man and his feelings of love, beauty, truth, peace and happiness. The vision of God cannot be analysed, and revelation cannot be dissected. Secondly, the 'external' approach in itself excludes sympathy with the religion under study. Thirdly, the analytical critic of religion tends to neglect the spiritual nature of man, who is not merely the body but also the mind and the soul. Spiritual experience cannot be quantified. 'Religion is an inner experience, beyond the prism-pendulum-chronograph methods of the scientist'. Familiar examples are given from the works of McLeod with their familiar criticism. Mansukhani draws the conclusion that scholars, whether Western or Eastern, would go on making mistakes so long as they do not understand 'the Gurbani, the Sikh thesis and its doctrines'.[22] Again, Mansukhani is talking of spiritual experience and theology and not of history.

For Mansukhani, 'Sikh traditions' are a part of the oral history, and belong to the category of 'secondary' sources. In secondary sources whatever is not in conformity with Gurmat has to be rejected. If the author of a *Gurbilas* says that Guru Gobind Singh invoked the Goddess, it has to be rejected because it infringes Gurmat. However, the fact that a Sikh historian includes the episode in his narrative is not without significance and it remains a concern of the historian to seek further explanation. Mansukhani says that controversies also can be settled with reference to Gurmat, like the one about whether or not 'outcaste' Sikhs were to be allowed to enter the Golden Temple and offer *karha parshad.* This surely illuminates the operation of the Sikh belief in the doctrine of Guru Granth, but does not relate to methodology.

Mansukhani comes to the conclusion that in the study of religion, there are two distinct areas. One of these relates to the 'historical authenticity of the record' and the other, to the 'internal consistency of the religious doctrines and practices'. Separate techniques are required for each of these two areas. The lack of evidence for an event cannot be taken as a proof of its non-occurrence. So far as the Sikh way of life is concerned, what is enunciated in 'primary' sources does not become invalid in the absence of corroborative evidence in 'secondary' sources. This relates to norms.

Mansukhani assures us that his 'integrated methodology' will be usesful and 'richly improve the quality of Sikh studies'.[23] He is proposing a project for the future. Whatever the merit of his proposal, it is not reflected in his own writings.

Mansukhani appears to paraphrase King and Daljeet Singh on critical methodology. Like Daljeet Singh, he states that critical approach and critical methodology are unsuitable or inapplicable to the study of religion. He points out that Western scholars have generally treated Sikhism as a part of Hinduism or as a syncretic formation. Their critical methodology is also a handicap. There can be no logical proofs in the realm of ethics and aesthetics; the inner experience cannot be dissected or quantified. Critical approach is said to make a scholar unsympathetic to the subject of his study.

As mentioned before, Mansukhani divides evidence on Sikhism and Sikh history into primary and secondary sources. The former consists of scriptures and the works of Bhai Gurdas and Bhai Nand Lal. The rest of the evidence is secondary. It is placed in the category of oral history, presumably on the assumption that the *Janamsakhi* and *Gurbilas* literature was written on the basis of oral evidence, or on the basis of works originally based on oral evidence. Primary evidence gets precedence over secondary evidence for the study of Sikh history as well as the study of Sikhism. Consequently, the secondary sources can only be corroborative or supplementary. They have no intrinsic value. Mansukhani is interested in 'who has said what' and not in the question 'what does it mean?'. His suggestion that the authenticity of a source should be established has been the standing practice in historical studies. His idea that lack of evidence does not mean that a certain event did not occur is even more revealing. He appears to believe that 'historical facts' exist without being established on the basis of empirical evidence. If they do, they are accepted on faith, and not as historical knowledge. There is nothing new in his suggestions regarding internal consistency.

Mansukhani leaves the impression that he has not seen any literature on the philosophy and methods or techniques of history. By now there is a wide range of literature on this subject, and historians often base their understanding of 'history' on this kind of literature. The 'second-order history', or the history of historical thought and writing, goes into the question of unconscious assumptions, attitudes, personal biases and social prejudices of historians. If too much scepticism can be detrimental to a proper understanding of religion, mere good will for the faith can be detrimental to scholarship.

THE HISTORICAL METHOD IN PRACTICE

W.H. McLeod and Harjot Oberoi are the two historians who have been criticized the most for their methodology. Their approach and method may be illustrated with a few concrete instances. McLeod's treatment of the *Rahitnamas* shows that the idea belatedly enunciated by Mansukhani with regard to the 'historical authenticity' of a source and its 'internal consistency' was not unknown to McLeod. In fact, it is his working principle. According to McLeod, part of our problem with the *Rahitnamas* arises from lack of 'early manuscripts'. To search for the earliest possible manuscripts is a well-known principle of historical research. It is equally important to identify manuscripts 'in terms of author, place and time'. In the absence of early manuscripts we have to fall back on 'analysis of language and content', and we are obliged to examine putative authorship rather carefully. Furthermore, we have to make a clear distinction between 'tradition' and 'history'. The former is virtually what is believed about the past and the latter is a form of knowledge based on verifiable evidence. Applied to the *Rahitnamas*, this would mean that what is generally believed or said about them should find support from the *Rahitnamas* as we know them.[24]

McLeod has seen nine *Rahitnamas* produced in the pre-colonial period. Some of these are very brief, concentrating on particular features of the *rahit*. Relatively comprehensive *Rahitnamas* cover all aspects of the *rahit*: fundamental doctrines, personal behaviour, the Khalsa ceremonies, and offences against the *rahit*. It is generally assumed that the substance of the *rahit* was determined by Guru Gobind Singh, a large portion on the occasion of the founding of the Khalsa in 1699 and the remainder shortly before his death. During his lifetime, thus, Guru Gobind Singh is believed to have effectively promulgated a definitive version. This traditional scheme does not find support in the *Rahitnamas* themselves. The traditional account demands consistency and a regular unambiguous form. This is not the pattern which we find in the *Rahitnamas*. The claim that the authors of the *Rahitnamas* were associated with Guru Gobind Singh cannot be accepted on its face value. One *Rahitnama* states that its author had heard Guru Gobind Singh speaking at Abchalnagar (Nander), but the date given is 1695 (when Guru Gobind Singh was actually at Anandpur). In all cases, the language indicates a significant remove from the time of Guru Gobind Singh and his environment. To detach the *Rahitnamas* from the time of Guru Gobind Singh does not oblige us to advance their date far into the eighteenth or to the early nineteenth century: there are features which indicate a relatively early date. *The Chaupa Singh Rahit-Nama*, edited and translated by McLeod, can be safely placed around 1750. Till today, this is said to be the 'earliest of the datable *rahitnamas*'. Furthermore, the composite character of this *Rahit-Nama* points clearly to earlier sources, and it is conceivable that 'portions of it may indeed go back to Chaupa Singh Chhibber of the tenth Guru's entourage'. But these portions are extremely difficult to identify. Then there are other elements which can certainly be identified as later. Therefore, McLeod is inclined to look upon the *rahit* as evolving in time. In any case, the principle on which McLeod is working is rather simple: the evidence of a literary work gains importance and value if we know the date of its composition or compilation. At present, therefore, *The Chaupa Singh Rahit-Nama* provides the most valuable evidence on the *rahit* of the Khalsa in the middle decades of the eighteenth century.[25] It is difficult to find fault with McLeod's method. It does not mean, however, that this by itelf ensures accuracy.

McLeod gives the essential features of the Khalsa *rahit* as it emerges from *The Chaupa Singh Rahit-Nama* and then draws the conclusion that a version of the *rahit* was certainly current during the lifetime of Guru Gobind Singh but that version must be regarded as a nucleus and not as a full-fledged *rahit*. A process of growth took place during the middle decades of the eighteenth century which produced the essential lineaments of the modern *rahit* by the end of the eighteenth century. The developed *rahit* may thus be ascribed to an extended period 'rather than limited to explicit pronouncements' by Guru Gobind Singh. This does not mean that Guru Gobind Singh made no pronouncement at all. Indeed, the first important source of the *Rahitnamas* was the intention of the Guru during the formative years of the Panth's growth, and it was 'codified by Guru Gobind Singh as a nucleus of the later Rahit'.[26]

McLeod has been criticized for suggesting that the 5 Ks were not introduced by Guru Gobind Singh on the Baisakhi day of 1699 when the Khalsa was instituted. The evidence he has examined does not mention the cluster of 5 Ks till we come to the nineteenth century. Therefore, McLeod's suggestion is not baseless, and it is not irresponsible.[27] But, of course, he may be wrong. The only way to correct his mistakes would be to argue on the basis of known evidence, following the accepted principles of source-criticism in historical studies, or to produce fresh evidence which may clearly establish that Guru Gobind Singh introduced the 5 Ks in 1699. A distinction can be made between the present formulation of the 5 Ks and their earlier prototypes. The probability of the prototypes of the 5 Ks having been introduced in 1699 can be visualized. By now it is clear indeed that McLeod's understanding of the *rahit* is seriously inadequate. But this awareness comes through historical methodology itself.[28]

Harjot Oberoi's approach is explicitly stated in the 'Introduction' to his *Construction of Religious Boundaries.* The first point he makes is about the scope of the study of religion. In his view, religious traditions are rarely placed at the centre of social analysis in histories of modern India. In the historical treatment of the socio-religious movements of the nineteenth century the religious factor is brought in to explain other social developments, particularly as 'a handy smokescreen for power-hungry elites'. Consequently, too many questions concerning religion are left unanswered. People appear to play no role in the making of their own history: they are seen as 'betrayed' or 'hoodwinked' by the religious elites. Attention remains concentrated on the urban sections of the populations, leaving the rural people virtually out. It is of paramount importance to separate the practice of religion from its manipulation: the two may be related but they are not the same. Furthermore, religious movements generate division as well as solidarity. Even religious texts like the *Adi Granth* can be interpreted in favour of divergent identities. Also, there is always a significant difference between the religion of the elite and popular religion. Finally, we have to look at religion 'as a social and cultural process; not something given but an activity embedded in everyday life, a part of human agency'. Therefore, a historian of religion has to examine 'the range of people's relations with the sacred and the supernatural'; he or she has to consider how these relations order the world of individuals and groups; 'what feelings, moods and motives they encourage or try to repress'; and he or she has to see 'what means are offered to move people through the stages of their lives, to prepare for their future, and to cope with suffering and catastrophe'. Equally, if not more, important for the historian is 'the context of popular religious life' and 'religious change'.[29] The scope of the study of religion for Oberoi, thus, is very wide, embracing ideas in their relationship with the day-to-day practices in the lives of all the people, and embracing changes in ideas and their relationship.

That Oberoi takes the problem of historical change seriously is evident from his understanding and use of the concepts of episteme and praxis. The concept of episteme is taken from Michel Foucault who defines it as 'the total set of relations'. It is not a form of knowledge or type of rationality. It is 'the totality of relations that can be discovered for a given period' to be analysed 'at the level of discursive regularities'. Furthermore, in any given culture and at any given moment, only one episteme 'defines the conditions of possibility of all knowledge, whether expressed in a theory or silently invested in a practice'. Foucault explores and defines the epistemes of the Renaissance, 'the classical age', and 'the modern age' in Europe. However, he deploys his concept 'to document the intellectual production of a given historical period', and he does not go into the problem of change from one episteme to another. Human societies are not merely episteme governed; they are also subject to 'an unceasing intervention of human practices'. It is on account of such practices that 'much historical change occurs'.[30]

At this stage of the argument, Sherry Ortner's concept of praxis becomes relevant for Oberoi. Praxis is one of the three modes of action postulated by Ortner, the other two being routine activity and intentional action. Routine activity is the stuff of everyday life and it prevents our personal and social life from collapsing. Through intentional action people enact their interests, desires, and intentions, pursuing their goals, plans and projects. What is important here is to determine what kinds of cultural, political or economic forces shape intentional action. Praxis is radically different from intentional action as well as routine activity. It has the potential of transforming existing social and cultural relationship. Oberoi does not say what praxis is. More important for his purpose is the synthesis of the concepts of episteme and praxis. There is a dialectical relationship between an episteme and human practice, whether routine or intentional: 'one cannot exist without the other'. Therefore, changed social, cultural and economic contexts 'can lead to a situation of praxis, potentially carrying the possibility of a historical rupture'. This can account for the dissolution of one episteme and the eventual rise of another. Oberoi's aim is to understand 'the entire process underlying the rise and dissolution of an episteme' with the help of materials from the Sikh past.[31]

Taking the reader into confidence about his view of the scope of the study of religion and his approach to the study of change, Oberoi discusses the state of Sikh studies. In his view two principles have been at work in historical writing on the Sikhs, as in other areas of historiography. One of these is the principle of silence, silence about diversity within the Sikh Panth and the prevalence of popular religion among the Sikhs. The second principle is that of negation. According to this principle, when diversity or popular religion is brought in, it is treated as relapse into Hinduism or deviation or superstition. This approach ultimately goes on to establish that Sikhs were 'delivered from the bondage of un-Sikh beliefs' by the intervention of the late nineteenth-century Singh Sabha Movement. The scholars who favour this view look upon the Singh Sabha reformers as the upholders and propagators of traditional Sikh doctrines. Oberoi's explanation of the general acceptance of the principles of silence and negation is that European observers of the Sikhs were far more concerned with what Sikhism ought to be like rather than what it was; they had far greater interest in recording the ideals of the faith rather than the actual behaviour of its practitioners. Their preoccupation with texts led to 'essentialist formulations' of Sikh tradition. The practices which did not conform to such formulations were treated with disdain and regarded as corrupt accretions, explicable in terms of 'the moral lassitude of the Khalsa, the decline in the political fortunes of the Sikhs, and the boa-like advances of Hinduism'. European assumptions and attitudes were picked up by the Sikh literati which emerged under the shadow of the Raj to reinforce the European discourse. So powerful is this discourse that 'contemporary scholarship either tends to ignore vast terrains of Sikh life in the nineteenth century or views it as superfluous addition which has to be negated'.[32]

Oberoi makes one more point with a bearing on the problem of interpretation. There is a basic difference between the ideology of a period and its explanation. Instead of accepting and repeating the value judgements and categories of the Singh Sabha reformers, a historian of the Singh Sabha Movement should try to explain why at a particular juncture certain forms of behaviour came to be viewed with suspicion and invited censure. 'A firm distinction ought to be made between the way certain beliefs and rituals came to be represented in the rhetoric of socio-religious movements like the Singh Sabha, and their actual place and function in the everyday life of people.' Many a scholar of Sikhism has failed to make this distinction. Oberoi cites the example of G.S. Dhillon who had written a doctoral thesis on the Singh Sabha Movement, largely based on contemporary sources and simultaneously covering the intellectual, educational, religious and reformative facets of the movement. Dhillon accepts the Singh Sabha records at their face value. Consequently, the ideology of the movement is distinctly imprinted on his work. No clear line is drawn between the 'first-order interpretation' or the statements of the leaders of the movement and the 'second order interpretation' or the conclusions drawn by Dhillon. His work, from Oberoi's standpoint remains rooted in the principle of negation. The implication of this interpretation is 'to negate differences and applaud unities'. It becomes a 'political effort' to generate homogeneity and to represent the Sikhs as 'a collectivity which shared the same values and movements'. Instead of recognizing ambiguity, interpretation, and reinterpretation in the process of Sikh history, historians like Dhillon postulate an 'unproblematic corporate identity'. Such historical literature prevents us from seeing the Sikhs 'in a world constantly constructed and reconstructed by them'. Sikh studies can become respectable only if they 'fully open up to the gaze of history'. In other words, no area of Sikh life should be regarded as too sacrosanct or too contemptible to be the subject of rational investigation.[33]

Oberoi raises three issues pertaining to historiography: the scope of historical studies, the concern of the historian with change, and the problem of interpretation involving the historian's attitude towards sources. All these are basic issues of historical thought and method. Oberoi's rationale is intimately linked with a whole range of reflection on these issues by a number of philosophers and historians. Oberoi's use of concepts derived from other disciplines, including social anthropology, is not a novelty.

However, a clear distinction can be made between Oberoi's conception of the scope and methods of historical studies and the application of his theory to his actual interpretation of the Sikh tradition. Even if we accept his rationale we may differ with its application and, therefore, with his findings. In fact, it is possible to argue that the concepts of episteme and praxis, which induce him to look for ruptures, make him prone to over-emphasize change and to underestimate the strength of continuities. Like McLeod, Oberoi is well aware of what is involved in historical methodology. But it is possible to refute Oberoi in detail by using the techniques of historical methodology itself, and to reject or modify his findings by interpreting the same evidence or by invoking evidence which he has not used. To perform this function, one has to have a firm hold on historical methodology, and not to discard it.

SOME OTHER VOICES

We may listen to some other voices with a direct bearing on methodology. Juergensmeyer appreciates the main thrust of Daljeet Singh's *Sikhism: A Comparative Study of its Theology and Mysticism.* He agrees with Daljeet Singh that the Sikh perspective is quite 'dissimilar to the Brahmanical and Vedantic point of view'. The kind of 'worldly asceticism' that Weber sees in Protestantism is discernible in Sikhism too. It 'might have forced Weber to amend his conclusions' on Indian religions 'at least with regard to the Punjab'. However, the sources used by Daljeet Singh for the religious traditions other than Sikhism are not only secondary but also hopelessly inadequate. His conception of mysticism is too simplistic to account for the great variety in the phenomenon of mysticism in the history of religion. Daljeet Singh is at his best when he deals with Sikhism, but his sampling of Sikhism is restrictive:

'Both the teachings of the Gurus and the heritage of the tradition are richer than that.' Nevertheless, Daljeet Singh raises important questions for comparative study of religion. This in itself is a valuable contribution.[34]

For another scholar, Daljeet Singh's approach to the study of comparative religion does not do justice to religious traditions other than Sikhism. Daljeet Singh assumes that different religions of the world can be studied through the uniform standard he has evolved for the study of Sikhism. He ignores the fact that every religious tradition has to be viewed as 'a complete, closed and unique world in itself'. Therefore, no uniform theological framework can be used for studying different religions 'without a danger of misunderstanding them and having a distorted representation of those religions'. A framework based on Sikh theological categories of thought can hardly be said 'to do justice to those dimensions of other religions which are different from Sikhism'.[35] In other words, Sikh-centrism would be as much open to objcction as Euro-centrism for a comparative study of religion.

Barrier sees an increasing divergence in scholarship on Sikhism between 'Indian' and 'Western' academics as clearly reflected in 'polemic' over Harjot Oberoi's *Construction of Religious Boundaries.* Barrier admires Oberoi's book, but for another scholar Oberoi does not realize the limitations of the Western academia and omits to mention the relationship between the Western academy today and similar institutions during the colonial era in their role as the arbiter of 'cultural representation'. Barrier tends to dismiss 'the harsh, and often overtly personal onslaught' against Oberoi as 'communal rhetoric or internal partisan politics'. This dismissal reflects 'a fundamental failure' to acknowledge the existence of a problem concerning the nature of South Asian studies generally, and Sikh studies in particular. Oberoi's own methodology appears to be an 'updated successor of the earlier colonialist epistemology'. Thus, both the Singh Sabha tradition and the academic tradition within which Oberoi writes 'are historically linked'. Oberoi talks of 'repressive hypothesis' in the historiography of the Singh Sabha. This hypothesis is equally operative 'within his own adopted methodology'. Barrier suggests that the kind of debate that his work has generated may lead to 'a new agenda in Sikh studies'.[36]

Another scholar looks upon the *Recent Researches in Sikh Studies* as 'a continuing polemic against recent Western interpretation of Sikhism'. Many of the papers in this volume are intended to be rebuttals of 'the more contentious issues' raised by the work of McLeod and Oberoi. Several other papers merely 'fill up space' rather than tackle 'any specific issues'. The main protest is rather poorly articulated. It is conceded, however, that the book does raise a very important question concerning Western methodology as applied to Eastern religions. Significantly, the procedural methods of the authors of these papers are based upon the same 'episteme' as that of their opponents. Therefore, the problem degenerates into a question of the subjective status of the contestants: 'insider *versus* outsider' or 'believer *versus* non-believer'. The critics of McLeod and Oberoi have failed to develop 'a rigorous hermeneutic that properly confronts reductionist methodology'. Nevertheless, the students of religion, history and anthropology should read books like the *Recent Reseaches* to have 'a more balanced picture of the current state of Sikh studies'.[37]

A WEAK CASE AGAINST THE HISTORICAL METHOD

On the whole, no serious case is made against historical methodology *per se.* But the assumption that methodology in itself ensures veracity is false. It is hard to maintain that religious movements cannot be or should not be studied by social scientists. Ideology becomes relevant for the historian when it finds expression in words or actions, and words and actions are the subject matter of history. A valid objection can be raised to neglect of ideas, assumptions and sentiments or 'mentalities'. Divorced from cosmology, anthropology becomes poorer.

NOTES

1. Noel Q. King, 'Orientalism, Critical Scholarship and the Sikh Religion', in *Perspective on the Sikh Tradition*, ed. Gurdev Singh, Patiala: Siddharth Publications, 1986, pp. 41-4.
2. Ibid., pp. 46-7.
3. Ibid., p. 47.
4. Ibid., pp. 47-8.
5. Ibid., pp. 48-9.

6. Ibid., pp. 49-50.
7. Ibid., pp. 50-1.
8. Ibid., pp. 51-2.
9. Noel Q. King, '*CAPAX IMPERII*? Scripture, Tradition and "European Style" Critical Method', in *Advanced Studies in Sikhism,* ed. Jasbir Singh Mann and Harbans Singh Saraon, Irvine, CA: Sikh Community of North America, 1989, pp. 1-11, 13.
10. Ibid., pp. 11-13.
11. Avtar Singh, 'Sikh Identity and Continuity: A Perspectives from Ethics', in ibid., pp. 165-9.
12. James R. Lewis, 'Misrepresentations of the Sikh Tradition in World Religions Textbooks', in ibid., pp. 271-4.
13. Daljeet Singh, 'Issues of Sikh Studies', in ibid., pp. 16-17.
14. Ibid., pp. 17-18.
15. Ibid., pp. 18-23.
16. Ibid., pp. 24-6.
17. Ibid., pp. 27-8.
18. Gobind Singh Mansukhani, 'The Origin and Development of Sikh Studies', in *Fundamental Issues in Sikh Studies*, ed. Kharak Singh, Gobind Singh Mansukhani and Jasbir Singh Mann, Chandigarh: Institute of Sikh Studies, 1992, pp. 127-35.
19. Gobind Singh Mansukhani, 'An Integrated Methodology for Appraisal of Sources for Sikh Studies', in *Recent Researches in Sikhism*, ed. Jasbir Singh Mann and Kharak Singh, Patiala: Punjabi University, 1992, p. 109.
20. Ibid., pp. 109-10, 117.
21. Ibid., pp. 110-21.
22. Ibid., pp. 112-16.
23. Ibid., pp. 110, 117-20.
24. W.H. McLeod, *Who is a Sikh? The Problem of Sikh Identity*, Oxford: The Clarendon Press, 1989, pp. 28, 36-7.
25. Ibid., pp. 30-4.
26. Ibid., pp. 34-5.
27. Ibid., pp. 39-41.
28. Gurinder Singh Mann places several *Rahitnamas* in the time of Guru Gobind Singh on the basis of dated manuscripts in his 'Sources for the Study of Guru Gobind Singh's Life and Times', *Journal of Punjab Studies*, vol. 15, nos. 1-2 (Spring-Fall 2008), pp. 229-84. It has been argued by another scholar that the *Tankhahnama* attributed to Bhai Nand Lal, could be placed in the time of Guru Gobind Singh. It contains the couplet on the *raj karega khalsa* which, according to McLeod, came into currency later. Karamjit K. Malhotra, 'The Earliest Manual on the Sikh Way of Life', in *Five Centuries of Sikh Tradition: Ideology,*

Society, Politics and Culture, ed. Reeta Grewal and Sheena Pall, New Delhi: Manohar, 2005, pp. 55-81.

29. Harjot Oberoi, *The Construction of Religious Boundaries: Culture Identity and Diversity in the Sikh Tradition*, New Delhi: Oxford University Press, 1994, pp. 19-23.
30. Ibid., pp. 26-8.
31. Ibid., pp. 28-30.
32. Ibid., pp. 30-2.
33. Ibid., pp. 32-5.
34. *International Journal of Punjab Studies*, vol. II, no. 1, pp. 103-12.
35. Ibid., vol. I, no. 1, pp. 144-6.
36. Ibid., vol. II, no. 1, pp. 217-36.
37. Ibid., vol. I, no. 1, pp. 140-3.

Reflections in Retrospect

In a sense, the two most important antagonists in the debate are Daljeet Singh and W.H. McLeod, with their different understanding of Sikhism and the Sikh movement. Daljeet Singh's basic position is supported not only by Jagjit Singh, Kharak Singh, Gurtej Singh, Mansukhani and a large number of Sikh intelligentsia but also by a number of professional academics like S.S. Kohli, Avtar Singh, Madanjit Kaur, Gurdarshan Singh Dhillon, Gurnam Kaur, and Balwant Singh Dhillon. Two Western scholars, Noel Q. King and James R. Lewis, who do not exactly support their ideological position, are nonetheless critical of Eurocentric approach. McLeod's work has been appreciated generally by the academia. Closely associated with him in the controversy are his research students, Pashaura Singh and Louis Fenech, who admire his work and profess to follow the 'critical approach'. Informally associated with McLeod is Harjot Oberoi and his research student, Doris R. Jakobsh. A considerable number of serious scholars are, thus, involved on both sides. The controversy may not exactly be a debate, and far less a dialogue, but it is comprehensive enough to cover what are called the 'fundamental issues in Sikh Studies'.

Indeed, a large volume of Sikh studies produced in the past four decades relates to this controversy, directly or indirectly. One side presents it in terms of Enlightenment *versus* religious faith, or 'critical historians' *versus* 'traditional historians'; the other side presents it in terms of deliberate misrepresentation of the Sikh tradition, lack of empathy and linguistic competence, and inappropriate methodology. There is little mutual appreciation. Consequently, what we hear largely are two sets of monologues. An understanding of their contentions may result in a kind of dialogue.

W.H. McLeod was not the first historian to treat the *Janamsakhis* critically. But he was the first to adopt a peculiar approach to the life of Guru Nanak. Out of the known sources for his life, McLeod looks upon the *Janamsakhis* as by far the most important. But the *Janamsakhis* are concerned more with the religious ideas and ethics of Guru Nanak than with his secular life. Divorced from these concerns there is only a broad chronology of his life. McLeod conducted an elaborate analysis of each *sakhi* to establish facts with regard to the events of Guru Nanak's secular life. He found the *Janamsakhis* wanting and abandoned the project. Thus, starting with the idea of reconstructing the life of Guru Nanak he ends up with the conclusion that *Janamsakhis* give us only a broad outline. He appears to imply that no historical biography of Guru Nanak can be written.

McLeod has been criticized primarily for rejecting a large number of *sakhis*. But even if all the *sakhis* were to be accepted in terms of incidents and events of Guru Nanak's life, the total information would not yield a historical biography of Guru Nanak, particularly if his teachings are excluded. Guru Nanak's life is important precisely because he was a religious figure. If his biographer is not interested in his ideology he or she cannot go far with a biography. Another point made against McLeod is that he has ignored the real import of the *sakhis* in his search for factuality. McLeod himself argues that the *Janamsakhis* present the 'myth' of Guru Nanak, which is briefly stated. But he does not realize that the 'myth' of Guru Nanak is an interpretation of his life and mission and, therefore, the core of the *Janamsakhis*.

McLeod lost interest in the life of Guru Nanak but not in the *Janamsakhis*. His later works, especially the *Early Sikh Tradition*, deal with several aspects of the *Janamsakhis*. This work has been simply ignored by his critics. He wonders why the *Early Sikh Tradition* 'sank like a stone'. At least a part of the answer lies in the fact that he has ignored the heart of the matter, the 'myth' of Guru Nanak. Furthermore, he is aware of the existence of sectarian groups within the Sikh Panth and their *Janamsakhi* traditions, but he does not relate the two. Consequently, he remains unaware that there are 'myths', and not 'the myth' of Guru Nanak, created or projected by different sections of Sikhs. A study of this 'stuff of Sikh history' can be fascinating and rewarding and it can also become alive. McLeod has not done this. Possibly, that is the reason why his scholarship on the *Janamsakhis* appears to run in 'neutral gear'.

More important than the issue of Guru Nanak's 'life' is the 'faith' of Guru Nanak, the starting point of the Sikh movement, and of Sikh Studies. On this issue, the understanding of Daljeet Singh is radically different from that of McLeod. Whereas the message of Guru Nanak for McLeod is liberation through *nam simran* as the supreme purpose of human life, for Daljeet Singh liberation-in-life results in altruistic social action. Consequently, whereas institutionalization of the Sikh movement for McLeod was due to later historical developments, for Daljeet Singh it was built into Guru Nanak's conception of the purpose of life. Whereas Guru Nanak's originality for McLeod lies in giving coherence to the 'Sant synthesis', for Daljeet Singh Guru Nanak's dispensation was something new in which spiritual and temporal concerns are two sides of the same coin of faith. The use of common concepts by Guru Nanak and the Sants does not mean that they occupy the same position. No institutionalization can be attributed to any Sant before we come upon the Sikh movement. For the Sants, liberation-in-life was a personal project; for Guru Nanak it was a social project for the redemption of others. The foundation of the Sikh faith and Sikh Panth can thus be attributed to Guru Nanak. The later Sikh history was intimately linked with this foundation.

McLeod tends to assume that there was no institutionalization in the time of Guru Nanak and Guru Angad. 'Innovations' started with Guru Amar Das with the *langar*, pilgrimage, compilation of *Pothis*, and intermediaries, under pressure from the changing circumstances. McLeod does point out that the place of pilgrimage was Goindval (and not Hardwar or Kashi) yet he refers to 'Hindu' influence as if only Hindus used to have places of pilgrimage. The pull of the environment is of crucial importance for McLeod. His Jat theory of militarization and his 'hypothesis of the Devi cult' appear to spring from this assumption rather than the empirical evidence at his command.

McLeod's impression that the *Sri Gur Sobha* and the *Rahitnamas* were composed several decades later than the time of Guru

Gobind Singh reinforces his general assumption about environment to determine his treatment of the Khalsa *rahit* and doctrines. By now, however, it is clear that this impression is wrong and all the arguments put forth by McLeod about the evolving character of the Khalsa *rahit*, the doctrines of Guru Panth and Guru Granth, and even the ideal of *raj karega khalsa*, have no validity. The most important features of the *rahit* were in place during the time of Guru Gobind Singh or soon afterwards, including the five symbols which later constituted the formulation of the 5 Ks. On the whole, McLeod's hypotheses about the evolution and transformation of the Sikh Panth are the weakest in his treatment of Sikh history. His flawed hypotheses are linked to his partial understanding of Guru Nanak.

In his exposition of the early Sikh identity, McLeod assumes that the Sikhs were distinct from Muslims but their distinct identity in relation to Hindus was not 'uniform'. For Oberoi, it was not 'fixed'. For Daljeet Singh, the early Sikh identity was clearly distinct from that of Hindus and Muslims just as the Sikh faith was distinct from 'Hinduism' and Islam. None of the three scholars have gone into the issue of 'Hindu' identity in the pre-colonial times; they assume it to be known. They are agreed upon the objective differences of the Sikhs from the others around and they talk of the Sikh subjective awareness or consciousness of distinct identity. The Sikh faith and the Sikh Panth in the compositions of the Gurus, Bhai Gurdas and the *Janamsakhis* are seen as essentially distinct from all the religious and social entities around. This self-image is supported by the evidence of the *Dabistan-i Mazahib*. Significantly, though there is an awareness of opposition, neither Hindus nor Muslims are seen as the 'other' in the sense of an opponent or an enemy.

McLeod, Oberoi and Daljeet Singh subscribe to the distinct identity of the Khalsa of Guru Gobind Singh based on a unique form of initiation, outward appearance, doctrines and rites, martial ideals and egalitarian ethos. The Khalsa identity became the dominant Sikh identity during the course of the eighteenth century. For McLeod and Daljeet Singh, this was the dominant identity of the Sikhs during the time of Sikh rule as well. For Oberoi, however, it was replaced by 'Sanatan Sikhism' in the late eighteenth and the early nineteenth century. By now, even McLeod appears to have adopted this view. It is clear from the contemporary evidence, however, that Singh identity was the dominant identity among the Sikhs throughout the period of Sikh rule. Oberoi is not clear about the *sahajdharis* and even McLeod is unaware of the presence of the non-Singh Khalsa in the early eighteenth century. The relationship of the Singhs with the non-Singhs, therefore, is misconceived. The situation calls for a better conceptualization of the dominant Singh identity with its operative limitations.

Both McLeod and Jagjit Singh agree in theory about the egalitarian ideal of the Gurus. Jagjit Singh emphasizes it more than McLeod. Both agree on the relevance and importance of commensality and connubium in a discussion of equality and caste. They agree that the old patterns of matrimony in terms of endogamous *jatis* and exogamous *gotras* continued among the Sikhs. McLeod emphasizes the intractability of the custom for connubium but Jagjit Singh refers to the absence of any felt need for change, particularly when there was no 'caste system' among the Sikhs on the basis of hierarchy. McLeod talks in terms of high and low castes among the Sikhs but no hierarchy was upheld in principle. Hierarchy was not the accepted norm in the Sikh Panth. On commensality, McLeod underlines the sharing of food by all in the sacred space. Jagjit Singh makes the practice more universal during the eighteenth century. Thus, there is a certain measure of agreement between McLeod and Jagjit Singh but there are important differences as well. For the pre-colonial Sikh Panth, the evidence used by McLeod and Jagjit Singh is rather limited. It appears that a distinction can be made between the pre-Khalsa Sikhs and the Khalsa Singhs for a study of equality and caste. But the whole issue calls for a thorough analysis of the whole range of Sikh literature and other contemporary evidence.

This is equally true of the issue of equality and gender. Kapur Singh emphasizes the importance of the principle of equality, McLeod underlines the importance of empirical continuities. Jakobsh tries to suggest two phases in the pre-Khalsa period: one, from Guru Nanak to Guru Amar Das, when women gained some ground in terms of gender relations; and two, from Guru Ram Das to Guru Gobind Singh when the ground gained was lost to the rising ethos of masculinity. This tuned into 'hyper-masculinity' after the institution of the Khalsa with its martial ideals. Though interesting, this hypothesis is flawed due to the use of limited evidence partially interpreted and the importance given to a theoretical assumption. Jakobsh appears to prove a preconceived notion. The evidence available for analysis suggests a far more complex situation in which there is a constant tension between the ideal of equality and the inegalitarian institution of the family which is taken for granted. If anything, the issue of gender relations in the Sikh social order calls for a thorough research.

The Singh Sabha Movement is seen by McLeod as a re-formation of the Khalsa tradition, by Oberoi as a rupture with the Sanatan tradition, and by G.S. Dhillon as a revival of the early Sikh tradition. They all agree that the Khalsa tradition was re-vitalized and Singh identity was successfully espoused. The environment created by the colonial rule was certainly relevant for the success of the Singh Sabha Movement but so was the earlier Sikh tradition from which the leaders of the movement derived all their important doctrines and most of their concerns. Their interpretation of the earlier Sikh literature has not yet been seriously studied, nor the literature which they produced. Instead of a selective use, a close study of this literature can lead to a better understanding. What was new to the situation was not Sikh identity but the conscious argument that a distinct identity turned the Sikhs into a political entity. No attention had been paid to the changing conception and consciousness of Hindu identity in the nineteenth century.

The view that the Singh Sabha Movement produced a radical re-interpretation of the earlier Sikh tradition amounting almost to a kind of 'invention' is reflected in the treatment of the conception and tradition of martyrdom by Oberoi, McLeod, and Louis Fenech. They do no see any relevance of Sikh ideology for the tradition of martyrdom. Several other scholars on the other hand look upon Sikh ideology as the basis of martyrdom. Both sides look for a direct statement on martyrdom in the Sikh scripture, some finding it there and others not finding it anywhere before the nineteenth century. In a historical approach to martyrdom, it is relevant to see the implications of Sikh ideology. The theory of 'heroic tradition' does not explain the martyrdom of Guru Arjan and Guru Tegh Bahadur before the institution of the Khalsa, and of Bhai Mani Singh and Bhai Taru Singh afterwards. The evidence of Sikh literature of the pre-colonial period does not support the view that the Singh Sabha

Movement 'created' the tradition of martyrdom or re-defined it radically for their own religious or political purposes.

Textual criticism entered an important phase with doubts about the authenticity of the *Kartarpur Pothi*, which meant doubts about the authenticity of the *Guru Granth Sahib*. Understandably, much of the literature on this subject relates to the issue of *Kartarpur Pothi*. By now the issue seems to have been settled in favour of its authenticity on the basis of detailed analysis not only of the *Kartarpur Pothi* itself but also of a large number of manuscripts produced before and after. The *Guru Harsahai Pothi*, the *Goindval Pothis* and the *MS 1245* are still controversial but their evidence has provided a historical view of the process that led to the compilation of the *Kartarpur Pothi*. The study of the late seventeenth-century manuscripts shows clearly that the *Damdami Bir*, based on the *Kartarpur Pothi*, had come into existence in the time of Guru Tegh Bahadur and Guru Gobind Singh before the end of the seventeenth century. Guruship was vested in the *Damdami Bir*. Thus, the historical lines of development from the *Kartarpur Pothi* to the *Damdami Bir* and from the *Damdami Bir* to the *Guru Granth Sahib* are clear. Pashaura Singh's 'draft theory' and 'power hypotheses', and his view that Maharaja Ranjit Singh made the *Damdami Bir* the authorized version, are more conjectural than empirical, and therefore misleading. The view made current by McLeod and Oberoi that the *Dasam Granth* had come to be regarded as the Guru before the advent of colonial rule in the Punjab has no empirical basis. The influence of the *Dasam Granth* among the Sikhs during the eighteenth and nineteenth centuries is an area yet to be seriously explored. For this, it would also be necessary to go into the history of the *Dasam Granth* and its authorship much more thoroughly than what has been done so far.

A good deal of importance is given to methodology both by the academia and the intelligentsia involved in the controversies. No one has denied the importance of empirical evidence, or the need of verification of generalizations. Therefore, the distinction between the 'critical historians' and 'traditional historians' may be a difference of degree but not a difference of kind. What is relevant for our purpose is not the world-views themselves but their bearing on one's approach and method. It is quite evident that methodology by itself does not ensure veracity or validity. The historical method in itself is not culturally rooted. It is not Western simply because it was initially developed in the West. Generally, the assumptions and purposes of the contestants have not been separated from their method. A historian would be poorer to the extent he or she ignores ideas or 'mentalities'. A dialectical relationship between ideas and environment, between cosmology and anthropology, may ensure a better historical understanding. No serious case is made against the use of the historical method in religious studies.

Glossary

abhaidan: the gift of fearlessness as the result of liberation through God's grace.

Adi Granth: the Sikh scripture, compiled by Guru Arjan in 1604 (containing the compositions of the first five Gurus and a number of *bhagats, sants* and *sufis*) and authenticated by Guru Gobind Singh with the compositions of Guru Tegh Bahadur. Now known as *Guru Granth Sahib.*

ahankar: pride of possessions or power.

ahimsa: non-injury; the principle of inflicting no physical injury on a living being.

Akali*:* a staunch follower of Guru Gobind Singh; equated with the Nihang in the early nineteenth century; in the twentieth century, initially a volunteer to take over Sikh Gurdwaras and afterwards a member of the Shiromani Akali Dal.

amir: a noble; a rich person.

amrit: the drink that imparts immortality or everlasting life, nectar; used as a metaphor.

amritdhari: one who has taken *amrit*; a staunch Khalsa Singh.

amritsar: literally the pool of the water of immortality; the term originally used for the tank constructed by Guru Ram Das; the usage was extended to the town of Ramdaspur (Amritsar) by the early nineteenth century.

ardas: supplication, prayer; generally made by a Sikh *sangat*, standing with hands folded in the presence of the Formless God; an essential part of worship in the Sikh tradition.

avtar: descent; incarnation of a deity, usually Vishnu.

asa vich niras: literally, hopeless in hope; detached in spirit, working with faith in God's will and grace.

azadi: freedom.

bada bhagat: a great devotee of God.

bani: utterance; used for divine self-revelation through creation and the utterance or the word of the Guru; generally equated with Gurbani.

baoli: a well with steps for easy accessibility to water simultaneously for several persons; the well constructed by Guru Amar Das at Goindval, which came to be regarded as sacred.

baran (*varna*)*:* literally colour, used for each of the four-tier social order.

bhaddan: the rite of removing one's hair in token of mourning, especially on the death of one's father.

Bhai (*bhai*)*:* 'brother'; a Sikh formally connected with religious affairs; an epithet of respect.

bhagat: one who is devoted to God; used generally for Vaishnava *bhaktas*, but the term is used for the Sikh too in Gurbani.

bhagti (*bhakti*)*:* loving devotion and dedication to God.

bhaichara: a caste or clan brotherhood.

bhala faqir: a good devotee of God.

bhana: pleasure, wish; the divine pleasure, everything that occurs due to God's will.

bharai: a drummer by profession; he used to beat the drum (*dhol*) on various occasions.

bharamnash: destruction of illusion.

bhatakshri: a script used by the Bhatts.

Bhatt Vahi (*bhatt vahi*)*:* the record kept by a Bhatt.

bhau: fear; fear of God, awe.

bhav: love, loving devotion directed towards God.

bhog: conclusion of the reading of *Adi Granth*, followed generally by singing of hymns and an *ardas.*

Bir: a recension of the Sikh sacred scripture.

biradari: community; brotherhood.

brahama: used in Persian for Brahmans.

charan pahul: initiation through baptism of the foot, involving drinking of water in which a foot or the feet have been washed.

chaudhari: the hereditary headman of a group of villages for collecting revenues on behalf of the government.

darbar: royal court; used for the Harmandar, and the *Guru Granth Sahib* installed in the Harmandar.

darshan: the sight of a venerable person or place; used in the context of the Sikhs visiting the Guru as an act of merit.

darvesh: a pious Muslim, generally a Sufi; a pious person.

Dasam Granth: the term used for the compilation earlier called the Book of the Tenth King (*dasven patshah ka granth*); its compilation is attributed to Bhai Mani Singh; the authorship of its contents (a number of independent compositions) and the date of its compilation have been the subject of debate.

dehura: a structure raised on a spot of cremation.

dhadi: a singer who generally used a miniature drum (*dhad*) while singing of love or war for the entertainment of his patrons; used as a metaphor for the Guru as the singer of God's praises and also for his Sikh.

dharamnash: the idea that by taking *pahul* the earlier faith of the novitiate is destroyed.

dharam-dham: the place where justice is done; God's abode, God's court.

dharamsal (*dharamsala*)*:* the place for earning merit; Sikh sacred space or the Sikh place of worship in early Sikh history; synonymous with Gurdwara.

dharam juddh: war for the sake of faith, struggle in a righteous cause.

din duni: the faith and the world; spiritual and temporal concerns.

dohagan: a woman who is unhappy because she is not loved by her spouse; a metaphor for the person who has not turned to God through the Guru.

faqir: one who practises *faqr* or renunciation and austerities; a *darvesh*; a pious person; a devotee of God; used generally for a Muslim mendicant.

firqa: a sect, a body.

Five (5) *Ks:* the five items of the Khalsa *rahit*, each starting with the letter k (*kesh, kirpan, kachh, kangha* and *kara*).

fuqara: plural of *faqir.*

gadela: a cushion.

gadi rah: the highway.

ghal khana: to earn through hard work.

ghar hi mahi udas: detached in the home.

gian: knowledge, knowledge of God; enlightenment.

Giani (*giani*)*:* one who possesses knowledge (*gian*); a person well versed in the Sikh scripture.

gharbari (*girhi*)*:* a householder.

got (*gotra*): subcaste; subdivision of a caste; an exogamous group.

Granth: a book; the Sikh scripture.

Granthi (*granthi*): a professional reader of the *Granth*; the functionary in-charge of a Gurdwara.

Gugga Pir*:* a legendary hero, associated with snake, who was an object of worship for Hindus and Muslims.

Gurbani: an utterance of the Guru; the compositions of the Sikh Gurus in the *Granth Sahib.*

Gurdwara (*gurdwara*)*:* 'the door of the Guru'; the Sikh sacred space where *kirtan, katha* and *ardas* are performed, and community meal is cooked and eaten by all; generally the centre of social activity too.

gurmata: decision of a general body of Sikhs, generally taken in the presence of the *Guru Granth Sahib.*

Gurmukh (*gurmukh*)*:* one who turns to the Guru; a good Sikh.

guroh: a group, a set of people, a class.

Gursikh: the Guru's instruction; the Guru's follower; the Sikh of the Guru; the Sikh.

Gursikhni: a Sikh woman.

Guru (*guru*)*:* a preceptor; a religious teacher; an epithet used for the founder of Sikhism and each of his nine successors, and also for the *Granth Sahib* and the Panth.

Guru Granth*:* the doctrine that the *shabad* or the Sikh scripture is the Guru.

Guru Panth*:* the doctrine that collectively of the Khalsa is the Guru.

halemi raj: literally, rule of moderation in which there is no oppression or coercion; an expression used by Guru Arjan for the entire dispensation of Guru Nanak and his successors.

haumai: a kind of self-centredness in which everything is attributed to oneself to the exclusion of God's will.

halal: the traditional Muslim mode of slaughtering animals for meat; anything lawful, as opposed to *haram* (prohibited).

Hindu*:* an Indian; a member of any of the Brahmanical orders; a person who professes to follow the Hindu religion.

hom: a sacrificial act; the ceremony of chanting Vedic hymns around a fire kept burning with oblations of wood, ghee, incense and other such materials, regarded as a way of pleasing gods, or God, through the god of fire.

hukam: order, divine order; the principle that the power of God remains operative all the time in the physical and the moral world.

hukka: a device for smoking tobacco through water, called hubble bubble.

huma: an imaginary bird regarded auspicious.

jagir: an assignment of land revenue in lieu of salary for performing service for the state.

jama'at: an association, an assembly, a faction, a class.

janamnash: the idea that the caste by birth is destroyed by joining the Khalsa through baptism of the double-edged sword.

Janamsakhis: a collection of episodes associated with the life of Guru Nanak, meant primarily to depict his doctrines, ethics and his spiritual status; several traditions of this genre developed in the seventeenth and eighteenth centuries.

jap, tap, sanjam: recitation of *nam* and practice of austerity, and restraint.

jat: an endogamous group, constituted by a number of septs, following generally the same occupation and placed in one of the four *varnas* as a mark of its social position in relation to others, popularly called caste in English.

jat-baran: an endogamous group placed in the fourfold hierarchical order in relation to other such groups.

jatha: a group, a band; used particularly for the fighting unit of the Khalsa in the eighteenth century.

Jati: an occupational group within a larger category of caste indicating the ritual status in the *varna* order.

Jatt: an important agricultural *jati* in the Punjab; used by the Persian writers for the cultivators in general.

jhatka: the mode of slaughtering an animal for meat with one stroke of the sword or some other weapon; the traditional non-Muslim mode of slaughtering animals in India. Unlike *halal*, it did not carry any religious significance.

jivan-mukti: liberation-in-life.

jogi: from *yogi*, or one who practices *yoga*; a person belonging to any of the twelve orders of the followers of Gorakh Nath.

juz: a part; a unit; a certain number of leaves of paper put together for binding a book.

Kabitt: a verse of four rhyming lines.

kachchi bani: compositions of the rival claimants to Guruship in the Sikh movement.

kachcha: raw, unripe, unbaked; temporary.

kachh: drawers.

kam: desire, sexual desire; sexual indulgence.

kangha: the comb kept by a baptized Sikh as one of the 5 Ks.

kara: the iron bracelet worn by a baptized Sikh as one of the 5 Ks.

karamnash: destruction of previous deeds by joining the Khalsa through baptism of the double-edged sword.

karha prasad: sacramental food distributed in Gurdwaras to all persons present, generally prepared with equal quantities of wheat flour, sugar and ghee.

Kaur*:* the counterpart of 'Singh' in the name of a Sikh woman.

kes (*kesh*)*:* the hair of the head.

Keshdhari (*keshdhari*)*:* a baptized Sikh who keeps long unshorn hair.

kirpan: a sword; carried by a baptized Sikh as one of the 5 Ks.

kirt: praise; to sing God's praises; singing of God's praises through the *shabads* of the Guru, generally called *kirtan.*

kirtan: the singing of hymns from the sacred scripture of the Sikhs; hence *kirtan darbar* for an elaborate performance.

khande ki pahul: baptism of the double-edged sword, introduced by Guru Gobind Singh for initiating Sikhs and others into the Order of the Khalsa.

kirya: performance of Brahmanical rites and rituals.

krodh: anger as one of the five adversaries of human beings.

kul: a family extending over several generations, lineage.

labbaik: 'yes, sir'.

lande: a script used by shopkeepers in the Punjab; also called *mahajani.*

langar: community kitchen; the open kitchen in a Sikh *dharamsal.*

la-sharik: one who has no associate or partner, God.

lobh: greed, avarice.

Mahajani: a script used by traders in the Punjab; also called *lande.*

mahal: a place; a palace; a unit area for revenue collection in the Mughal times; used for Guru Nanak and his successors to denote their order as 1, 2 or 3 up to 10; an alternative usage is *patshahi.*

mahapurkh: a great person.

mangal: song of praise; heading; sub-heading.

manji system*:* organization of the early Sikh community through the representatives of the Guru to manage the affairs of the local *sangats.*

manmukh: one who goes by his own inclinations as opposed to the Gurmukh who follows the Guru's instruction and cares for others as well.

Masand*:* a representative appointed by the Guru to look after the affairs of a local congregation of Sikhs, or a number of such congregations.

maya: all creation, all earthly things; seen as the source of entanglement in the cycle of death and rebirth; treated in the Sikh tradition as 'false' in contrast with the eternal truth of God.

maya vich udas: detached while pursuing earthly affairs.

Mazhabi Sikh*:* a term used for a category of Sikhs with the outcaste background.

mela: a fair.

militarization*:* a term commonly used for the politicization of the Sikh movement, with reference to the martial activities of Guru Hargobind.

mirasi: a category of service performers in a village known for their wit and sarcasm, who served as messengers and genealogists; also associated with singing as *dhadis.*

Miri-Piri (*miri-piri*)*:* leadership in both the spiritual and temporal realms associated with Guru Hargobind and his successors.

misl: a combination of Sikh leaders for the purpose of defence and occupation of territories in the eighteenth century.

mlechh: impure; a derogatory term used for an outcaste or a foreigner, both were regarded as outside the four-tier *varna* order.

moh: affection, love, attachment to kith and kin.

modi: a storekeeper.

modikhana: a storehouse.

mona: one who cuts the hair of the head.

mukti: release, emancipation, liberation.

mulmantar: The opening statement on the unity of God and his attributes in the *Guru Granth Sahib.*

nadar: from the Persian *nazr*, 'sight'; grace.

nagara: a drum, a symbol of authority or power.

nam: the name; the Name of God; the transcendent-and-immanent God; the totality of the message of Guru Nanak as *nam-dharam.*

nam, dan, insan: the phrase used by Guru Nanak for the essential features of the Sikh way of life, that is, meditation on God, charity, and both physical and moral purity.

nam marga: the path of the Name as distinct from others.

nam simran: repetition of God's name; remembrance of God.

Nanak-Panthi*:* the general term used by Persian writers for all categories of Sikhs.

naukri: employment.

nih karmi: a person whose actions are altruistic.

nirala: different, distinct, unique.

nirgun bhakti: devotion addressed to attributeless God.

nirguna sampradaya: the collectivity of the devotees of *nirgun* God.

Nirmala*:* a category of baptized Sikhs who devoted themselves to learning and propagation of the faith.

nishan: a sign, a symbol, a flag; used for the *mulmantar* written by any one of the Gurus.

ojha: a folk-therapist who uses magical formulae for cure of psycho-physical ailments.

pancho piaran: a variant of *panj-piare.*

pandit: a Brahman; a learned Brahman; a learned person.

panj-piare: the five beloved Sikhs who offered their heads on a call from Guru Gobind Singh, and who were baptized through the rite of the double-edged sword.

Panth (*panth*)*:* literally a path; the people following a particular path; collectively the followers of the Gurus; the Sikh community.

pap: an evil deed, a sin.

paramesar: the supreme lord.

parsuarh: something done for another, and not in self-interest.

parupkari: one who does something for others; an epithet for God; also used for the Guru and his Sikh.

Patshahi: from *badshahi,* rulership; a metaphor for the tenure of the Guru in the early Sikh tradition.

pir: a *shaikh* or guide among the Muslim mystics who leads on the path to union with God; believed to be a bestower of blessings after his death.

piyas: thrist; the yearning for liberation through dedication to God.

Pothi: a book, a recension of Sikh scripture.

Pujari (*pujari*): the attandant of a shrine; a Brahman priest.
pun: an act of merit, specially religious.
puranmasi: the night of the full moon.
qanungo: a hereditary keeper of the revenue records at the *pargana* or the *ta'alluqa* level.
Rababi: one who plays on the *rabab,* a kind of violin with three strings.
Ragi: a singer, particularly of the hymns of the Sikh scriptures.
rahit: way of life, used especially for the Sikh way of life in accordance with the philosophic and ethical principles advanced by the Gurus.
rahit maryada: the Sikh code of belief and conduct.
Rahitnama: a written code of belief and conduct; norms laid down for the Sikh way of life in accordance with the principles of Sikhism, and also 'corrective punishment' for infringing those principles.
raj karega khalsa: 'the Khalsa shall rule', an idea that became current in the time of Guru Gobind Singh.
Ramdasia Sikh*:* a follower of Ram Das; also used for a Singh whose background was that of an untouchable, generally Chamar.
Ranghreta*:* a Singh whose background was that of an untouchable *chuhra.*
sabda: the word, used for divine revelation as well as a religious composition.
sabha: a society or an association.
sachch: truth, the truth of God who alone is true in the sense of being eternal.
Sachch Khand*:* the realm of truth, the state in which truth is realized and one can see the divine ordinance (*hukam*) operative everywhere in the physical and the moral world.
sachcha patshah: the true ruler, God; used metaphorically for the Sikh Gurus too.
sadh: a person devoted to religious pursuits; a mendicant; a recluse.
Sadhukkari*:* the language used by the *sadhus* and *sants* of northern India in their discourses.
saguna bhakti: devotion addressed to God in human form.
sahaj: a state in which there is no hurry and no tension; the state of liberation as a state of bliss.
Sahajdhari (*sahajdhari*): a Sikh who is not baptized as a Singh and does not observe the Khalsa code of discipline.
sakhi: an eyewitness; testimony; an episode bearing witness to the

spiritual status of a religious guide; a statement bearing witness to the truth of God; a teaching.

Sakhi Sarvar*:* a legendary martyr and an object of popular religion in the Punjab whose followers were mostly from lower and outcastes.

salam: salutation; a bow to a superior.

Sanatan*:* pristine, ancient, old, traditional; a term used by both Hindus and Sikhs in the Punjab during the colonial period to claim that they represented the traditional faith.

sang: impersonation; a character in a theatrical performance.

sangat: assembly, religious congregation; a congregation of Sikhs; the collective body of Sikhs at one place.

sangrand: the first day of the lunar month.

Sant (*sant*)*:* a saint; generally a follower of the figures like Namdev, Kabir, Ravidas and Dadu; equated with the Sikh in the *Guru Granth Sahib*, and now with an eminent Sikh known to be pious.

sant-sipahi: a term used for the baptized Khalsa of Guru Gobind to denote his spiritual and temporal concerns of life.

Sant synthesis*:* the idea that the figures like Namdev, Kabir and Ravi Das combined elements from Vaishnava bhakti, Yoga, and Sufism to evolve a synthesis of their own.

sati: the practice in which the widow burnt herself on the funeral pyre of her dead husband as a mark of her devotion and fidelity to him.

satsang: true association; singing hymns in praise of God in congregation.

savayya: a poetical stanza in a particular metre with a particular rhyme scheme.

seva: service; service of the Guru, a deity, a person; voluntary service of others.

shabad: the word; a hymn; a verse from the *Guru Granth Sahib.*

shabad-bani: used generally for hymns of the Gurus in the *Guru Granth Sahib.*

shahid: a martyr, both in the Islamic and the Sikh tradition; the place of his burial or cremation was regarded as sacred; a Muslim *shahid* was often worshipped by common people.

shahidganj: a structure raised in commemoration of a martyr.

shahidi: the act of becoming a martyr.

shalok: a unit of verse, generally rather short, like a *doha* or a couplet, but could have several lines.

shara'-i Hinduan: the law of the Hindus, their customs.

sharamnash: the idea that the baptized Khalsa of Guru Gobind Singh did not have to follow the hereditary profession.

shiqdar: a person appointed by the king under Afghan rule to look after the civil and military administration of a territory called *shiq*.

Shudra: placed fourth in the ideal *varna* order.

siana: a wise person; the person who used magic foumulae for therauptic purposes.

siddh: a person who has attained to a high spiritual state so as to command supernatural powers.

sifat-salah: praises of God.

sikhkhi: the Sikh faith and its principles.

sirlekh: heading.

Sitala Devi: the goddess of small pox.

sohagan: a woman whose husband is alive, a devoted wife.

sohila: a song of joy; a particular composition of Guru Nanak.

sudh: awareness, undertaking, consciousness.

sudh keeche: the words written by Guru Arjan to indicate that the composition inscribed for the *Granth* needed correction.

Sufi: a mystic of Islam.

tabqa: a class or order of men; race, generation.

ta'ifa: a people, nation, tribe, family.

tark-i duniya: renouncing the world.

tatkara: table of contents.

Tat Khalsa: the staunch Khalsa; used for the Khalsa of Guru Gobind Singh who opposed Banda Bahadur and his followers in the early eighteenth century, and also for the radical Sikh reformers of the early twentieth century.

tirath: a sacred place; a place of pilgrimage; notionally, sixty-eight places in India

udas: detachment.

Udasi: a renunciate belonging to an order tracing its origin to Guru Nanak through his son Sri Chand and not through Guru Angad and his successors.

varnashrama dharama: the fourfold division of society into *varnas* and of human life into *ashramas* or stages.

vismad: the sense of ecstatic wonder on realization of God's greatness.

Vaheguruji ka Khalsa, Vaheguruji ki fateh: the form of salutation introduced by Guru Gobind Singh for the Khalsa.

yagya: a sacrifice; a ritual worship.

zamindar: literally the holder of land; applied alike to the intermediary who collected revenue on behalf of the state, to a vassal chief and a peasant proprietor.

Works Cited*

Advanced Studies in Sikhism, ed. Jasbir Singh Mann and Harbans Singh Saraon, Irvine, CA: Sikh Community of North America, 1989.

Archer, J.C., *The Sikhs in relation to Hindus, Moslems, Christians, and Ahmadiyyas: A Study in Comparative Religion*, Princeton: Princeton University Press, 1946.

Ashta, Dharam Pal, *The Poetry of the Dasam Granth*, New Delhi: Arun Prakashan, 1959.

Avtar Singh, *Ethics of the Sikhs*, Patiala: Punjabi University, 1983.

———,'The Role of Moral Philosophy in Sikhism', in *Fundamental Issues in Sikh Studies*, ed. Kharak Singh, Gobind Singh Mansukhani and Jasbir Singh Mann, Chandigarh: Institute of Sikh Studies, 1992, pp. 23-5.

Barrier, N. Gerald, *The Sikhs and Their Literature*, New Delhi: Manohar, 1970.

———,'The Evolution of Punjab Studies in North America', *The Panjab Past and Present*, vol. XVI, pt. 2 (October 1982), pp. 398-406.

———,'The Role of Ideology and Institution-Building in Modern Sikhism', in *Sikh Studies: Comparative Perspectives on a Changing Tradition*, ed. Mark Juergensmeyer and N. Gerald Barrier, Berkeley: Graduate Theological Union, 1979, pp. 41-51.

———,'Sikh Studies and the Study of History', in *Studying the Sikhs: Issues for North America*, ed. John Stratton Hawley and Gurinder Singh Mann, Albany: State University of New York Press, 1993, pp. 25-33.

Bhalla, Sarup Das, *Mahima Prakash* (Pbi), 2 vols., ed. Gobind Singh Lamba, Patiala: Punjab Languages Department, 1971.

Bhangu, Ratan Singh, *Prachin Panth Prakash* (Pbi), New Delhi: Bhai Vir Singh Sahit Sadan, 1993 (rpt.).

———, *Sri Guru Panth Prakash*, ed. Balwant Singh Dhillon, Amritsar: Singh Brothers, 2004.

Bryant, Kenneth E., 'Sant and Vaishnava Poetry: Some Observations on Method', in *Sikh Studies: Comparative Perspectives on a Changing Tradition*, pp. 65-74.

* Anthologies or collections of papers have been placed by their titles rather than the surname of the editors. However, full reference is given at the first appearance of an individual contribution from a collection.

Chhibber, Kesar Singh, *Bansavalinama Dasan Patshahian Ka* (Pbi), ed. Rattan Singh Jaggi (*Parkh: Research Bulletin of Panjabi Language and Literature*, ed. S.S. Kohli, vol. II), Chandigarh: Panjab University, 1972.

Cunningham, J.D., *A History of the Sikhs*, Delhi: S. Chand & Co., 1955 (rpt. of the 2nd edn. published in 1853, first published in 1849).

Daljeet Singh, *Sikhism: A Comparative Study of its Theology and Mysticism*, New Delhi: Sterling, 1979.

———, *The Sikh Ideology*, New Delhi: Guru Nanak Foundation, 1984.

———, 'Origin of Sikh Faith', in *Perspectives on the Sikh Tradition*, ed. Gurdev Singh, Patiala: Siddharth Publications, 1986, pp. 55-8.

———, 'Nathism', in ibid., pp. 59-75.

———, 'Vaishnavism', in ibid., pp. 76-99.

———, 'Sikhism', in ibid., pp. 100-30.

———, 'Comparison of Nathism, Vaishnavism and Sikhism', in ibid., pp. 131-46.

———, *Essays on the Authenticity of Kartarpuri Bir and the Integrated Logic and Unity of Sikhism*, Patiala: Punjabi University, 1987.

———, 'Issues of Sikh Studies', *Advanced Studies in Sikhism*, pp. 16-29.

———, 'Sikhism, Vaishnavism, Vedanta and Nathism: A Comparison', in ibid., pp. 33-55.

———, 'Sikhism: A Miri Piri System', in *Recent Researches in Sikhism*, ed. Jasbir Singh Mann and Kharak Singh, Patiala: Punjabi University, 1992, pp. 42-60.

———, 'Authenticity of the Kartarpuri Bir', in *Advanced Studies in Sikhism*, pp. 138-60.

———, 'Dasam Granth: Its History', *Abstracts of Sikh Studies*, Chandigarh: Institute of Sikh Studies (July 1994).

———, *Essentials of Sikhism*, Amritsar: Singh Brothers, 1994.

———, 'The Sikh Identity', in *Fundamental Issues in Sikh Studies*, pp. 105-15.

———, 'Punjab River-Waters Dispute', in ibid., pp. 196-228.

———, 'Guru Nanak: The Prophet of a Unique Ideology', in ibid., pp. 3-22.

Dhillon, Gurdarshan Singh, 'Singh Sabha Movement: A Revival', in *Advanced Studies in Sikhism*, pp. 234-62.

———, 'The Sikhs, and the British, 1849-1920', in *Recent Researches in Sikhism*, pp. 173-225.

———, 'The Sikh Rule and Ranjit Singh', in ibid., pp. 347-72.

———, *Insights into Sikh Religion and History*, Chandigarh: Singh & Singh Publishers, 1991.

———, 'Sikh Identity: A Continuing Feature', in *Recent Researches in Sikhism*, pp. 226-46.

———, *Researches in Sikh Religion and History*, Chandigarh: Sumeet Publications, 1989.

———, *India Commits Suicide*, Chandigarh: Singh & Singh Publishers, 1992.

Dhillon, Balwant Singh, *Early Sikh Scriptural Tradition: Myth and Reality*, Amritsar: Singh Brothers, 1999.

Embree, Ainslie T., 'Locating Sikhism in Time and Place: A Problem For Historical Surveys', in *Sikh Studies: Comparative Perspectives on a Changing Tradition*, pp. 55-62.

Fenech, Louis E., *Martyrdom in the Sikh Tradition: Playing the 'Game of Love'*, New Delhi: Oxford University Press, 2002 (2nd imp.).

Fundamental Issues in Sikh Studies, ed. Kharak Singh, Gobind Singh Mansukhani and Jasbir Singh Mann, Chandigarh: Institute of Sikh Studies, 1992.

Ganda Singh, *Early European Accounts of the Sikhs*, Calcutta: Firma K.L. Mukhopadhyaya, 1962.

———, 'Guru Gobind Singh Designates Guru Granth Sahib to be the Guru', in *Perspectives on the Sikh Tradition*, pp. 183-210.

———, (ed.), *Hukamname: Guru Sahiban, Mata Sahiban, Banda Singh Ate Khalsa Ji De* (Pbi), Patiala: Punjabi University, 1967.

Grewal, J.S., *Guru Nanak in History*, Chandigarh: Panjab University, 1998 (2nd imp., 1st pub. 1969).

———, 'The Sikh Panth: 1500-1850', in *Religious Change and Cultural Domination*, ed. David N. Lorenzen, Mexico City: El Colegio de Mexico, 1981, pp. 193-8.

———, 'A Perspective on Early Sikh History', in *Sikh Studies: Comparative Perspective on a Changing Tradition*, pp. 33-9.

———, 'Legacies of the Sikh Past for the Twentieth Century, in *Sikh History and Religion in the Twentieth Century*, ed. Joseph T. O'Connell et al., Toronto: Centre for South Asian Studies, University of Toronto, 1988, pp. 18-31.

———, 'A Brief History of Sikh Studies in English', in *Studying the Sikhs: Issues for the North America*, pp. 161-73.

———, *The Sikhs of the Punjab* (The New Cambridge History of India, II, 3), Cambridge: Cambridge University Press, 1998 (2nd edn., 1st pub. 1990).

———, *Guru Nanak and Patriarchy*. Shimla: Indian Institute of Advanced Study, 1993.

———, *Historical Perspectives on Sikh Identity*, Patiala: Punjabi University, 1997.

———, *Contesting Interpretations of the Sikh Tradition*, New Delhi: Manohar, 1998.

———, 'Nabha's *Ham Hindu Nahin*: A Declaration of Sikh Ethnicity', in *Sikh Identity: Continuity and Change*, ed. Pashaura Singh and N. Gerald Barrier, New Delhi: Manohar, 2001, pp. 231-5.

———, 'Celebrating Liberation: The Var of "Gurdas"', *Journal of Regional History*, vol. VIII (New Series), 2002, pp. 15-24.

———, *Sikh Ideology, Polity and Social Order*, New Delhi: Manohar, 2007 (rev. and enlarged edn.).

———, 'Sikhism from the Late Eighteenth to the Early Twentieth Century', *Journal of Regional History*, vols. XI-XII (New Series), 2005-6, pp. 9-25.

———, 'The *B40 Janamsakhi*', *Lectures on History, Society and Culture of the Punjab*, Patiala: Punjabi University, 2007, pp. 167-217.

———, 'The *Janamsakhi* Traditions', in ibid., pp. 141-66.

———, 'The Bani of Guru Nanak', in ibid., pp. 101-29.

———, 'Guru Nanak and his Panth', in *The Sikhs: Ideology, Institutions and Identity*, New Delhi: Oxford University Press, 2009, pp. 3-21.

———, *A Study of Guru Granth Sahib: Doctrine, Social Content, History, Structure and Status*, Amritsar: Singh Brothers, 2009.

Grewal, J.S. and S.S. Bal, *Guru Gobind Singh: A Historical Biography*, Chandigarh: Panjab University, 1967.

Grewal, J.S. and Irfan Habib (eds.), *Sikh History from Persian Sources*, Delhi: Tulika/Indian History Congress, 2001.

Gupta, Hari Ram, 'Guru Gobind Singh's Creation of the Khalsa in 1699', in *Perspectives on the Sikh Tradition*, pp. 149-79.

Gurbakhsh Singh, 'From Ritual to Counter Ritual: A Critical Analysis', in *Recent Researches in Sikhism*, pp. 273-85.

Gurharpal Singh, 'Sikh Ethnicity and Panjab', *Ethnic Conflict in India: A Case Study of Punjab*, London: Macmillian Press, 2000.

Gurnam Kaur, 'Revelation and Reason in *Sri Guru Granth Sahib*', in *Fundamental Issues in Sikh Studies*, pp. 60-77.

Gurtej Singh, 'Two Views on Dasam Granth', in ibid., pp. 179-83.

———, *Tandav of the Centaur*, Chandigarh: Institute of Sikh Studies, 1996.

———, 'The Mystique of the Dasam Granth', *Sikh Studies Quarterly*, Chandigarh: Institute of Sikh Studies (January-March 2001).

———, 'Political Ideas of Guru Nanak, the Originator of the Sikh Faith', in *Recent Researches in Sikhism*, pp. 61-71.

Habib, Irfan, *The Agrarian System of Mughal India 1556-1707*, New Delhi: Oxford University Press, 2002 (2nd edn., rpt.).

Harbans Singh, *The Heritage of the Sikhs*, New Delhi: Manohar, 1984.

———, 'The Guru Granth Sahib: Guru Eternal for the Sikhs', in *Perspectives on the Sikh Tradition*, pp. 211-27.

Hazara Singh, Giani (ed.), *Varan Bhai Gurdas*, Amritsar: Khalsa Samachar, 1962 (7th edn.).

Invasion of Religious Boundaries: A Critique of Harjot Oberoi's Work, ed. Jasbir Singh Mann, Surinder Singh Sodhi and Gurbakhsh Singh Gill, Vancouver: Canadian Sikh Study and Teaching Society, 1995.

Irschick, Eugene F., 'Sikhism as a Category of Study', *Sikh Studies: Comparative Perspectives on a Changing Tradition,* pp. 53-4.

Jaggi, Rattan Singh and Gursharan Kaur (eds.), *Sri Dasam Granth Sahib,* New Delhi: Gobind Sadan, 1999.

———, 'Dasam Granth', *Guru Granth Vishavkosh,* Patiala: Punjabi University, 2002, vol. II, pp. 100-2.

Jagjit Singh, *Sikh Revolution: A Perspective,* New Delhi: Kendri Singh Sabha, 1981.

———, *Perspectives on Sikh Studies,* New Delhi: Guru Nanak Foundation, 1985.

———, 'Caste System and the Sikhs', in *Perspectives on the Sikh Tradition,* pp. 231-314.

———, 'Inter-caste Marriages', in ibid., pp. 315-21.

———, The Militarization of the Sikh Movement', in ibid., pp. 325-85.

———, 'The Caste System and the Sikhs', in *Advanced Studies in Sikhism,* pp. 278-300.

———, 'The Doctrine of "Meeri-Peeri"', in *Recent Researches in Sikhism,* pp. 136-49.

———, 'The Historical Identity of Dasam Granth', *Abstracts of Sikh Studies,* Chandigarh: Institute of Sikh Studies (July 1994).

Jakobsh, Doris R., *Relocating Gender in Sikh History: Transformation, Meaning and Identity,* New Delhi: Oxford University Press, 2003.

Jodh Singh, *Varan Bhai Gurdas: Text, Transliteration and Translation,* 2 vols., Patiala: Vision and Venture, 1998.

Jodh Singh, Bhai, *Sri Kartarpuri Bir de Darshan,* Patiala: Punjabi University, 1968.

———, *Bani Bhagat Kabir Ji Steek,* Patiala: Punjabi University, 1993 (3rd rpt.).

———, 'Jin Prem Kiyo Tin Hi Prabh Payo', in *Ek Murit Anek Darsan* (Pbi), ed. S.S. Amol, Jalandhar: Khalsa College, 1967.

Juergensmeyer, Mark, 'The Forgotten Tradition: Sikhism in the Study of World Religions', in *Sikh Studies: Comparative Perspectives on a Changing Tradition.*

———, 'Sikhism and Religious Studies', in *Studying the Sikhs: Issues for North America,* pp. 9-14.

Kanwaljit Kaur, 'Sikh Women', in *Fundamental Issues in Sikh Studies,* pp. 96-104.

Kapur Singh, *Parasharprashna: An Enquiry into the Genesis and Unique Character of the Order of the Khalsa with an Exposition of the Sikh Tenets,* ed. Piar Singh and Madanjit Kaur, Amritsar: Guru Nanak Dev University, 1989.

———, *Sikhism: An Ecumenical Religion,* ed. Gurtej Singh, Chandigarh: Institute of Sikh Studies, 1993.

Kharak Singh, 'Sikh Ideology Fundamentalism and Punjab Problem', in *Fundamental Issues in Sikh Studies*, pp. 136-59.

———, 'Need for World Institute of Sikhism', in ibid., pp. 238-54.

———, 'Khalsa: The Saint Soldier', in ibid., pp. 116-26.

——— and Gurdarshan Singh Dhillon, 'Raj Karega Khalsa', in ibid., pp. 187-95.

——— (ed.), *Current Thoughts on Sikhism,* Chandigarh: Institute of Sikh Studies, 1996.

King, Noel Q., 'Orientalism, Critical Scholarship and the Sikh Religion', in *Perspectives on the Sikh Tradition*, pp. 41-52.

———, '*CAPEX IMPERII*? Scripture, Tradition and "European-Style" Critical Method', in *Advanced Studies in Sikhism*, pp. 3-15.

Koer Singh, *Gurbilas Patshahi 10* (Pbi), ed. Shamsher Singh Ashok, Patiala: Punjabi University, 1968.

Kohli, Surinder Singh, 'Constant Unity of Sikh Thought', in *Advanced Studies in Sikhism*, pp. 98-108.

———, 'Janamsakhis: Their Value and Importance', in ibid., pp. 301-16.

———, 'Guru Tegh Bahadur : The Ninth Nanak (1621-1675)', in *Fundamental Issues in Sikh Studies*, pp. 160-9.

Lewis, James R., 'Misrepresentations of the Sikh Tradition in World Religions Textbooks', in *Advanced Studies in Sikhism*, pp. 265-77.

———, 'Some Unexamined Assumptions in Western Studies of Sikhism', in *Recent Researches in Sikhism*, pp. 286-98.

Loehlin, C.H., 'Textual Criticism of the Kartarpur Granth', in *Sikh Studies: Comparative Perspectives on a Changing Tradition*, pp. 113-18.

———, *The Sikhs and Their Scriptures*, Lucknow: Lucknow Publishing House, 1958.

———, *The Granth of Guru Gobind Singh and the Khalsa Brotherhood*, Lucknow: Lucknow Publishing House, 1971.

Macauliffe, Max Arthur, *The Sikh Religion: Its Gurus, Sacred Writings and Authors*, 3 vols., Delhi: Low Price Publications, 1995 (first published in six volumes in 1909 by the Clarendon Press, Oxford).

Madanjit Kaur, 'The Guruship and Succession of Guru Granth Sahib', in *Advanced Studies in Sikhism*, pp. 121-37.

———, 'The Creation of the Khalsa and Prescribing of the Sikh Symbols', in ibid., pp. 195-213.

———, 'Devi Worship Story: A Critique', in *Fundamental Issues in Sikh Studies*, pp. 170-8.

Malcolm, Lt. Col. John, *Sketch of the Sikhs*, New Delhi: Asian Educational Services, 1986 (rpt., 1st pub. 1812).

Malhotra, Karamjit K., 'The Earliest Manual on the Sikh Way of Life', in *Five Centuries of Sikh Tradition: Ideology, Society, Politics and Culture*

(*Essays for Indu Banga*), ed. Reeta Grewal and Sheena Pall, New Delhi: Manohar, 2005, pp. 55-81.

Mann, Gurinder Singh, *The Goindval Pothis: The Earliest Extant Source of the Sikh Canon*, Cambridge (Massachusetts): Harvard University Press, 1996.

———, *The Making of Sikh Scripture*, New Delhi: Oxford University Press, 2001.

———, 'Sources for the Study of Guru Gobind Singh's Life and Times', *Journal of Punjab Studies*, vol. 15, nos. 1-2 (Spring-Fall 2008), pp. 229-84.

Mansukhani, Gobind Singh, 'Sikh-Rahat-Maryada and Sikh Symbols', in *Advanced Studies in Sikhism*, pp. 174-91.

———, 'An Integrated Methodology for Appraisal of Sources of Sikh Studies', in *Recent Researches in Sikhism*, pp. 109-21.

———, 'The Origin and Development of Sikh Studies', in *Fundamental Issues in Sikh Studies*, pp. 127-35.

McLeod, W.H., *Guru Nanak and the Sikh Religion*, Oxford: The Clarendon Press, 1968.

———, *The Evolution of the Sikh Community*, New Delhi: Oxford University Press, 1975.

———, *Early Sikh Tradition*, Oxford: The Clarendon Press, 1980.

———, *Textual Sources for the Study of Sikhism*, Manchester: Manchester University Press, 1984.

———, tr. & ed., *The Chaupa Singh Rahit-Nama*, Dunedin: University of Otago Press, 1987.

———, 'The Sikh Scriptures: Some Issues', in *Sikh Studies: Comparative Perspectives on a Changing Tradition*, pp. 97-111.

———, 'A Sikh Theology for Modern Times', in *Sikh History and Religion in the Twentieth Century*, pp. 32-43.

———, 'The Study of Sikh Literature', in *Studying the Sikhs: Issues for North America*, pp. 55-9.

———, *The Sikhs: History, Religion and Society*, New York: Columbia University Press, 1989.

———, *Who is a Sikh? The Problem of Sikh Identity*, Oxford: The Clarendon Press, 1989.

———, *Sikhism*, Harmondsworth: Penguin Books, 1997.

———, *Exploring Sikhism: Aspects of Sikh Identity, Culture and Thought*, New Delhi: Oxford University Press, 2000.

———, *Discovering the Sikhs: Autobiography of a Historian*, Delhi: Permanent Black, 2004.

———, *Prem Sumarag: The Testimony of a Sanatan Sikh*, New Delhi: Oxford University Press, 2006.

———, *Essays in Sikh History, Tradition and Society*, New Delhi: Oxford University Press, 2007.

Nikki-Guninder Kaur Singh, *The Feminine Principle in the Sikh Vision of the Transcendent*, Cambridge: Cambridge University Press, 1993.

Oberoi, Harjot S., 'From Ritual to Counter-Ritual: Rethinking the Hindu-Sikh Question, 1884-1915', in *Sikh History and Religion in the Twentieth Century*, pp. 136-58.

———, *The Construction of Religious Boundaries: Culture, Identity and Diversity in the Sikh Tradition*, New Delhi: Oxford University Press, 1994.

O'Connell, Joseph T., 'Sikh Studies in North America: A Field Guide', in *Studying the Sikhs: Issues for North America*, pp. 123-7.

Pashaura Singh, *The Guru Granth Sahib: Canon, Meaning and Authority*, New Delhi: Oxford University Press, 2000.

Perspectives on the Sikh Tradition, ed. Gurdev Singh, Patiala: Siddharth Publications (for Academy of Sikh Religion and Culture), 1986.

Piar Singh, *Gatha Sri Adi Granth* (Pbi), Amritsar: Guru Nanak Dev University, 1992.

———, *Gatha Sri Adi Granth and the Controversy*, Michigan: Anant Education and Rural Development Foundation, 1996.

——— (ed.), *Janamsakhi Sri Guru Nanak Dev Ji* (Pbi), Amritsar: Guru Nanak Dev University, 1974.

Planned Attack on Aad Sri Guru Granth Sahib: Academics or Blasphemy, ed. Giani Bachittar Singh, Chandigarh: International Centre of Sikh Studies, 1994.

Pritam Singh, *Bhai Kahn Singh Nabha: Pichhokar, Rachna te Mulankan* (Pbi), Amritsar: Guru Nanak Dev University, 1989.

Randhir Singh, Bhai (ed.), *Prem Sumarag Granth* (Pbi), Jalandhar: New Book Company, 1965 (2nd edn.).

Recent Researches in Sikhism, ed. Jasbir Singh Mann and Kharak Singh, Patiala: Punjabi University, 1992.

Religious Change and Cultural Domination, ed. David N. Lorenzen, Mexico City: El Colegio de Mexico, 1989.

Sahib Singh, *Adi Bir Bare* (Pbi), Amritsar: Singh Brothers, 1995 (6th imp.).

———, *Gurbani Viakaran* (Pbi), Amritsar: Singh Brothers, 1996 (6th imp.).

Sainapat, *Shri Guru Sobha*, ed. Shamsher Singh Ashok, Amritsar: SGPC, 1967.

Schomer, Karine, 'Kabir in the *Guru Granth Sahib:* An Exploratory Essay', in *Sikh Studies: Comparative Perspectives on a Changing Tradition*, pp. 75-89.

Sewa Ram Singh, *The Divine Master: Life and Teachings of Guru Nanak*, ed. Prithipal Singh Kapur, Jalandhar: ABS Publications, 1988 (rpt.).

Shan, Harnam Singh, 'Sikhism, An Original Distinct, Revealed and Complete Religion', in *Fundamental Issues in Sikh Studies*, pp. 41-52.

Sikh History and Religion in the Twentieth Century, ed. Joseph T. O'Connell, Milton Israel, Willard G. Oxtoby, W.H. McLeod and J.S. Grewal, Toronto: Centre for South Asian Studies, University of Toronto, 1988.

Sikh Studies: Comparative Perspectives on a Changing Tradition, ed. Mark Juergensmeyer and N. Gerald Barrier, Berkeley: Graduate Theological Union, 1979.

Studying the Sikhs: Issues for North America, ed. John Stratton Hawley and Gurinder Singh Mann, Albany: State University of New York Press, 1993.

Sukha Singh, *Gurbilas Patshahi 10* (Pbi), ed. Gursharan Kaur Jaggi, Patiala: Punjab Languages Department, 1989 (rpt.).

Surjit Singh, 'A Study of W. Hew McLeod's Methodology as Employed in his Work "The Evolution of Sikh Community" : The Janamsakhis' [*sic*], in *Advanced Studies in Sikhism*, pp. 317-25.

Teja Singh and Ganda Singh, *A Short History of the Sikhs*, Patiala: Punjabi University, 1989 (rpt., 1st pub. 1950).

Trilochan Singh, *Ernest Trumpp and W.H. McLeod As Scholars of Sikh History, Religion and Culture*, Chandigarh: International Centre of Sikh Studies, 1994.

Trumpp, Ernest, *The Adi Granth*, New Delhi: Munshiram Manoharlal, 1989 (rpt.).

Uberoi, J.P.S., *Religion, Civil Society and the State*, New Delhi: Oxford University Press, 1996.

Webster, John C.B., *The Christian Community and Change in Nineteenth Century North India*, New Delhi: Macmillan, 1976.

———, *The Nirankari Sikhs*, New Delhi: Macmillan, 1979.

———, 'Sikh Studies in the Punjab', in *Sikh Studies: Comparative Perspectives on a Changing Tradition*, pp. 26-32.

Index